Working Together in Child Protection

Report of Phase Two, a survey of the experience and perceptions of the six key professions

ELIZABETH BIRCHALL WITH CHRISTINE HALLETT

University of Stirling

STUDIES IN CHILD PROTECTION

LONDON: HMSO

Acknowledgements

We acknowledge with sincere thanks the many people and organisations who have helped us in this research, particularly the many busy professionals who gave their time generously to the questionnaire and those whose participation in the pilot stages helped in the refinement of the research design. The goodwill and interest of the Area Child Protection Committees and agencies in City, County and Metborough were also much appreciated. The initial endorsement of the research proposal by the various professional associations is gratefully acknowledged.

The research has been funded by the Department of Health and staff in the Department and members of the Project Advisory Group have sustained us with their interest, comments and support throughout. Stimulus has also come from many colleagues in the academic and professional fields. Dr Pat McLaughlin and Professor Duncan Timms of the Department of Applied Social Science in the University of Stirling have given most generously of their time and experience regarding questions of computer usage and statistics.

Mrs Pat Young has given willing and efficient secretarial help at all stages of the project and we acknowledge the support and assistance of other administrative and secretarial staff in the University of Stirling.

Contents

List of tables

List of figures

General Introduction

This report presents phase two of a larger research programme investigating coordination in child protection in the UK, funded by the Department of Health. This study addresses professionals' experience and perceptions of the child protection system as regards work with children and families at the individual case level. The service exists to protect children and help families experiencing difficulties in their child-rearing. Their vital perceptions and the outcomes of intervention are, however, not a part of this project but are the subject of several other concurrent research programmes.

The focal questions for phase two of the present study are:

What experience of child protection work do the respondents have?

How convergent or otherwise are respondents' perceptions of cases?

What are their perceptions and evaluations of the local child protection system?

Can the local network be mapped?

What appear to be the most important factors influencing the above?

What interpretations can be offered for the relationships discovered?

What are the implications of the findings for policy and practice?

The first phase comprised an extensive literature review, published separately under the title *Coordination and Child Protection: a review of the literature* (Hallett and Birchall 1992), which explores the complex issues and arguments underpinning the topic of coordination in child protection. The third phase, conducted by Hallett, is an in-depth case study of coordination in child protection in two local areas in the north of England, based principally on an analysis of a sample of case records and subsequent interviews with the varied professionals involved.

Phase two, reported here, is primarily an exploratory study seeking to identify factors that may impede or enhance coordination and collaboration in the management of child abuse cases, by means of an extensive postal survey of a large randomly selected sample of practitioners in six professions. The survey took place in several different locations in the north of England in 1991. The professions involved were: general practitioners, health visitors, paediatricians, specialist police, social workers and teachers. The questionaire covered four main topics:

personal and professional data relevant to respondents' experience of child protection;

a severity rating exercise with a selection of brief case vignettes, replicating on a small scale an earlier US study (Giovannoni and Becerra 1979). (This had previously been set as an important research objective in the UK – Graham et al 1985);

an exploration of perceptions and proposed interventions in a three-stage long vignette of children in questionable situations;

an enquiry into people's expeience and evaluations of the child protection procedures and interprofessional network in their area.

Background to the study

Coordination in child protection is deemed a priority topic for research for several reasons. Some of the issues underpinning the research design are outlined below but reference will be made, as appropriate, throughout the report to the more detailed discussion in the literature review. Coordination is widely perceived both as an important objective and an important problem. It has been a central plank of government policy and an important part of professional rhetoric in this field for many years, since before the cataclysmic impact on the social work world of the Maria Colwell Inquiry which reported in 1974. The predecessors of the present social services departments had a rudimentary or episodic system of case conferences and inter-agency coordination in relation to families with multiple problems. The professional literature, originally emanating mainly from the United States, was also already insisting on the importance of interprofessional collaboration in the management of abused children (eg Kempe and Helfer 1972, BPA 1966). Such collaboration is not only portrayed as necessary for the appropriate delivery of services to the children concerned but sometimes also as a source of strength and security for practitioners in their dealings with very stressful work. For instance, in an empirical study, Bennett et al reported that professional fatigue and interagency conflict were reduced and

> *in most cases sharing the decision-making . . . decreases the anxiety of all professionals and . . . leads to marked improvement in skills and judgement (1982, p. 84)*

There are, therefore, several powerful motivators towards cooperation deriving from official policy and professional precept. Pushing or pulling in the same direction are the fear of public opprobrium or of agency disciplinary sanctions if such policies and precepts are defied.

Nevertheless, while such cooperation is seen as mandatory, it has been simultaneously seen as failing to happen. Failures of interprofessional coordination have frequently been emphasised as important factors in a sequence of official inquiries into child abuse tragedies but there seems to be a continuing inability to eliminate this source of scandal. Organisation theory and the sociology of the professions suggest that coordination might be more problematic than the policy-makers and professional high priests have allowed. Various studies of professional practice have touched on the topic (see Hallett and Birchall 1992) but there has been no large scale empirical study focused on the reality, the feasibility or the value of interprofessional coordination in this matter.

The literature review explored many areas of ambiguity and uncertainty which might be expected to make practical cooperation problematic. It established that concepts of coordination and collaboration in general are ill-defined and uncosted. A wide range of issues from organisational and occupational sociology are pertinent, as well as a variety of legal, administrative, financial and technical opportunities and constraints. In addition, the literature shows the particular field of child abuse to be deeply contentious, beset not only by definitional ambiguities as to what types and severity of behaviours should be categorised as abusive and warranting official attention but also by limited empirical knowledge regarding the fruitfulness of many aspects of intervention. There are many diagnostic dilemmas and the social construction of a case of child abuse is a complex process involving many practitioners. Different services and professions also have competing and widely divergent priorities, techniques and goals – to some extent in their own selection of means to pursue the specific objective of an individual child's welfare and to a larger extent in the differing functions and preoccupations of their agencies in relation to their overall workloads. Nevertheless, at least at the rhetorical level the notions of cooperation and teamwork are highly valued.

Much has been written about conflict and failure in particular cases and over the last 20 years official guidelines have been developed and revised, locally and nationally, to remedy the apparently serious and persistent breakdowns. However, policy documents are written for organisations while actions are performed by people and we actually know little about workers' normal practice (Hallett 1989). Tibbitt (1983) has argued the need to 'put people back into organisation theory'. Cooperation may appear relatively easy when written about at a high level of generality in official guidelines, whether at central government, local interagency or departmental levels, although in practice there can be immense problems in achieving even interdepartmental policy statements, as the Cleveland Report (1988) clearly illustrates. But what does cooperation entail in concrete terms for the changing constellations of individuals who work with each particular child and family, the 'street level bureaucrats' who make judgments about the meaning of what they see and hear and about what responses to make? Cooperation may be more difficult for them than the policy-makers perceive, when they cannot get hold of their counterparts at the moment they are needed or when both want their own task to take precedence, and these frustrations are replicated a myriad times across the network and the workloads of all concerned.

We have not known to what extent practitioners in the various agencies do perceive problems in coordination. We have known little of how they balance the rewards and constraints derived from cooperative behaviour, for instance whether it requires time and effort that they would prefer to invest elsewhere or whether it gives them emotional reassurance or economies of effort in direct work with the child or family. We do not know how important is the role of committed and diplomatically skilled individuals in developing interprofessional collaboration in this field but it has been shown to be important in kindred fields in this country (eg Audit Commission 1986, Griffiths Report 1988) and in the child protection field in other countries (eg Brill 1976, Urzi 1977, Marneffe et al 1985).

The children who become the subject of Inquiries are not typical cases; mercifully, the extremity of their suffering is not representative of children on the child protection register and the breakdowns in service they spotlight may be no more representative. Over 45 000 children were on registers in 1991 and about 20 000 turn over each year (DH 1991c). However, we cannot know how many other children in difficulty escape notice and we do not know how many more may be noticed by frontline identifiers who feel that referral to the child protection system might do more harm than good. As noted above, inter-agency coordination for families in difficulty is not new but over the last two decades the emphasis on child protection has developed concurrently with a period of acute pressure on poor families and resource constraint for the services.

There may well be tensions between professionals' desire to help children, their anxiety that referral to the Social Services Department in the current climate will be ineffectual or even stigmatising and punitive in its effect and, on the other had, their fear of being out of line if they fail to refer. We do not know how robust the generality of cases are when confronted by refusals to refer or by failures or conflicts in the system. We know little about the meaning or efficacy of coordinated services to the families concerned. Nevertheless, much humdrum coordination apparently goes on and much time and money is certainly invested in child protection conferences.

Aims of the study

In designing this phase of the whole study, it was essential to balance the need for a broad view of a field which has received little empirical investigation against the need for a feasible and adequately focused pro-gramme of research (Devons and Gluckman 1982). It was decided that the study would be restricted to matters covered by the child protection system in England, excluding concepts of 'societal abuse' of children (Gil 1975). In the interests of further simplification of a still unwieldy subject, the hypothetical case material was limited to suspicions of intra-familial abuse. This phase of the study also considers issues only from the perspective of practitioners of various ranks as they intervene in individual cases; it does not directly investigate questions of policy development or service design. Nor can it address the effectiveness of coordination in terms of case outcomes or the child's or family's view of the child protection career.

Even so, the complexity of the subject is evident from Figure 1.1 below, which sketches out a range of alternative arguments that might be applicable. It would be impossible to test them all rigorously within a single research programme and it would be impracticable and ethically unacceptable to set up an experimental comparison of case outcomes following coordinated and deliberately uncoordinated professional activity. Yet it would be inadequate to focus on too small a segment and ignore other issues which might be, or be perceived by the participants and readers to be, more important than the aspect chosen. In practice, box (a) in the figure is the starting point of the research and the study focuses on practitioners' views of judgments and activities which might constitute coordination. The impact of coordination on case outcomes would require a totally different study, so box (b) is assumed and the fundamental null hypothesis (v) – that coordination is irrelevant – is ignored.

Conclusions are drawn that distinguish the path (c – d) from the paths through (c – m), (l – m) and (l – n), although the specific causes of frictions and breakdowns, as opposed to their frequency and severity, may be common to both boxes and multiple in either case. The study reveals plenty of evidence of multiple and sometimes serious frictions in the system, arising from factors in all the boxes (e–f) but no evidence of catastrophic breakdowns. While the literature review discusses the poor and generalised conceptualisation of coordination as an obstacle to effective implementation of the policy, the field study has been able to locate many nuts and bolts factors, made connections with theory and made specific proposals for improvement of cooperation in practice.

An earlier version of this figure informed the selection of reading for the literature review. The assumptions on which it was based were as follows. There are incongruities between practitioners in their perceptions of chil-

Figure 1.1. **A sketch of potential research issues regarding coordination and cooperation in case interventions in child protection**

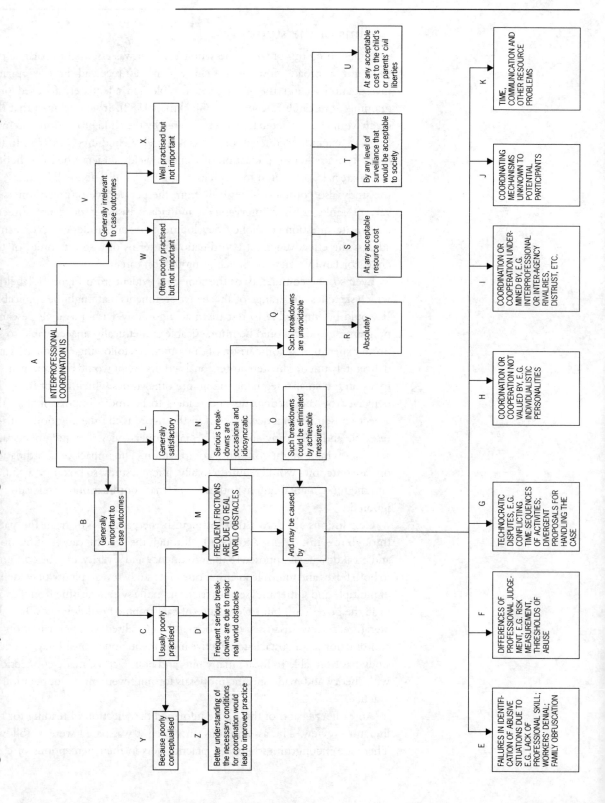

dren's need for protective interventions and in their views of what action would be appropriate but there may also be large areas of sufficient consensus. Both consensus and dissensus arise from practitioners' varied personalities and backgrounds, their professional experience, and their current roles and priorities including those moulded by agency cultures and local policy factors. Their knowledge of one another's roles and the degree of mutual trust between individuals will also vary. Coalitions of interest and common viewpoints will shift among the parties according to the issues. Agreements and disagreements will relate to perceptions of the case, to decisions about interventions and to mutual expectations. They will vary in importance, both because of their intrinsic substance in relation to the conduct of the case at the time and because of the salience of the contending parties. That salience in itself may derive from the needs of the case at the time or from the political and professional status of the individuals or their agencies.

The translation of these issues into a research design, which also seeks to cover different phases in the 'case career' of identified children, is outlined in the next chapter, followed by a chapter which gives details of access arrangements and sampling.

Finally, an important point should be reiterated in the introduction. This research study explores the experiences and views of professional staff actually or potentially involved in the child protection services. The research data are therefore professionally dominated and reflect the perspectives of service providers. The views of children and families in receipt or in need of help from these services have not been explored. This is partly because of the need to focus on the topic of coordination to produce a feasible research design. The decision was, however, taken in the knowledge that this piece of research forms only a small part of a much larger programme, funded by the Department of Health, exploring many facets of child abuse and child protection. Several studies in the larger programme focus specifically on users' views and experiences, (eg Thoburn et al, Cleaver and Freeman, Aldgate et al). The emphasis in this report on the perceptions and actions of professionals should not therefore be taken to imply a lack of concern with those whom the system is designed to serve: namely, vulnerable children and their families.

Chapter 2

Research Methods

Introduction

Chapter One outlines the underlying reasons for the total research programme and also spells out the three separate phases which constitute the
whole. The literature review located the research interests in a very broad and
complex field and helped to refine and focus them. It also provides a context
within which the particular findings of the present study can be examined
and appraised. The results from the relatively large survey of the population of
professionals potentially involved in collaboration in child protection
presented here as Phase Two are, in their turn, compared and contrasted in
the analysis of the qualitative data derived from a study of cases and actual
participants in Phase Three. Given the breadth of the topic, a fundamental
problem was to achieve a defensible level of validity and reliability within a
feasible research design. It would be relatively easy to describe and quantify
many aspects of professional activity in the child protection network and one
objective of the study is in fact to describe and compare different groups'
experience. However, if the enquiry is to have a valuable impact on future
practices, it is necessary to attempt to understand and explain the differences.
The topic requires the exploration of fact, opinion and action choices. In an
ideal world one might seek to subject a series of different but comparable
samples to a range of narrowly-focused but cumulative studies in order to
understand such a multi-faceted topic as interprofessional coordination in
child protection. However, such a programme was not practicable.

Therefore the problem was to devise a study which would at the same time
avoid narrowness and superficiality in its approach. It seemed that it would be
all too easy for critical readers to say 'Ah but if you had asked about a different
aspect or had posed a different set of case material, the responses would have
been entirely different.' It is hoped that the several parts of the research design
and the different aspects within each meet the objective and preclude the
criticism.

Zelditch (1962) criticises the unnecessary opposition of quantitative and
qualitative approaches to field work and says that it is more fruitful to
recognise that any field study is not a single method gathering a single kind of
information. He offers the schema of different methods, shown in Table 2.1,
from which to select as appropriate in order to achieve the whole required by
the topic in question. Not only are different approaches deemed more and
less appropriate for different aspects of a study. Triangulation of varied
approaches is also regarded as an important method of improving the validity
of social scientific work (Bulmer 1977). Deutscher (1973) argues that one

may have a reasonable belief that the use of two or three approaches to the same topic will reduce rather than reinforce the error intrinsic to each.

In addition to the range of methods in the overall programme, a mixture is therefore used within the Phase Two questionnaire as well – closed questions, scaled questions and open-ended opportunities in response both to direct questions and to vignettes (see Appendix 1). This variety serves two purposes. The first is the collection of quantitative data on many aspects of people's experience of and engagement in the child protection system, for which a sample survey is the prototype and best method (Zelditch 1962). The second is to obtain a preliminary understanding as well as an enumeration of practitioners' choices about actions they would take in relation to specific situations. In practice, the system is an interacting one, in which one person's initiative stimulates some reaction from others in the network, but this cannot be replicated in a survey. However, it is possible and valuable to compare people's perceptions and expectations of the system and to locate the likely points of consensus and conflict. Triangulation of methods within the survey assists in the interpretation of responses to the more qualitative issues covered.

Table 2.1 **Schema of research methods for different types of information**

	Methods of obtaining information		
Information types	**Enumerations and samples**	**Participant observation**	**Interviewing informants**
Frequency distributions	Prototype and best form	Usually inadequate and inefficient	Often but not always inadequate; if adequate it is efficient
Incidents, histories	Not adequate by itself: not efficient	Prototype and best form	Adequate with precautions, and efficient
Institutionalised norms and statuses	Adequate but inefficient	Adequate but inefficient, except for unverbalised norms	Most efficient and hence best form

Zelditch 1962, copied from Bynner and Stribley 1978, p. 134

It is important to recognise and explore the evident gap between the exhortatory quality of much of the professional literature about cooperation in child protection and the effect of such themes as domain and status. The latter are potent in the literature of organisational sociology and empirical enquiry and, indeed, appear frequently but fragmentarily in the accounts of interactions in the everyday professional journals (Hallett and Birchall 1992). Some of these areas probe sensitive subjects; whether and how people would act in a given situation may be interpreted as testing their conscientiousness or diagnostic acuity; how well they think the system functions involves value judgments about colleagues as well as mechanical procedures; many aspects may reveal uncertainties or limitations of experience. The introductory letter sent to those intended to participate in the research (see Appendix 2) was intended to assure respondents of confidentiality, acknowledge that there are diverse opinions about ways of managing cases of child abuse and about the logistics of cooperation and stress the importance of understanding the real possibilities and problems of coordination. It is hoped that these emphases encouraged people to reply frankly but, to this end, it was also considered important to use varied approaches within the questionnaire.

Some aspects of respondents' experience of the child protection system and of the interprofessional network can be directly interrogated but the convergence or conflict between them is also explored through their evaluations of the vignettes, long and short. Their views of the system and its relevance and efficacy emerge through their proposals regarding the long vignettes as well as through their responses to direct questions. Thus, it is hoped that the survey reports some of the more hidden attitudes, motivators and constraints that affect people's intentions and not just their 'proper' professional postures.

However, there are important limitations in exploring qualitative matters by questionnaire alone. Firstly, the subtleties of people's experience, understanding and motivations are unlikely to be conveyed even in open-ended responses in the course of an extended questionnaire. Secondly, the situations are necessarily abstracted from concrete action and it cannot be assumed that expressed intentions predict behaviour (eg Dean and Whyte 1958, Wicker 1969, Finch 1987). However, Deutscher (1973) points out that observed actions can also be ambiguous or influenced by the actor's assumptions about others' expectations in particular circumstances. He concludes that we simply do not know the circumstances in which people either say or do what they actually value. Such a nihilistic conclusion must call every form of enquiry into doubt but his assumption that a combination of different approaches reduces the overall level of error suggests that he believes the contingencies would tend to cancel one another out. Before discussing the Phase Two instrument in detail, the general strengths and weaknesses of its main components will be considered.

General observations on postal questionnaires

Sample surveys can cover a large population and provide reliable results capable of generalisation to other similar populations. It is important that policy research undertaken for the national government should have wider reference than the specific territories in which it took place. This objective underlay the selection of the research territories and the sampling method used to obtain the individual respondents (see Chapter Three). However, there are important difficulties intrinsic to postal surveys, over and above the fundamental limitations of questionnaires already mentioned. It is increasingly difficult to obtain high response rates to sample surveys (Bryman and Cramer 1990); there is no obvious or immediate reward or sanction for the respondent and individuals' commitment to completion may vary for a range of reasons. Hoinville, Jowell et al (1977) say a 60% response rate from a specialist population is reasonable while lower response rates would be expected from a general population. However, such figures leave many missing respondents and those who answer may not present a typical profile of the population. An examination of what is known of the non-respondents may limit the areas of uncertainty or possible distortion in the results but not all their characteristics or their reasons for non-response can be reliably deduced. In contrast, once access has been obtained, interviews or observational studies have a much more captive sample.

Secondly, it is difficult to devise a questionnaire which is clear and precise for every respondent at every point. The wording of questions and construction of questionnaires is a major topic in itself (Moser and Kalton 1971, Belson 1986). While questionnaires give standardised cues to every respondent and may be assumed to minimise subjective interactions between researcher and respondents, one cannot eliminate all the latter's different preconceptions as they interpret the question. It may be difficult to identify confounding variables. In interviews, there is an opportunity for clarification and expansion of the meaning as well as the response, so that both are less ambiguous. On the other hand, such further clarifications and probes may introduce subjective bias. Debate continues between those who search for objectivity in social science (eg Belson 1986), those who consider the interaction between the researcher and respondent or subject to be an inescapable element in all science (eg Burgess 1982) and those who see it as crucial data in its own right (eg Duelli Klein 1980).

Thirdly, there is the problem of structuring the whole questionnaire. This involves balancing tolerable length against adequate specificity, particularly if the research task is as wide-ranging or complex as the present one. Hoinville, Jowell et al (1977) say it is a mistake to oversimplify a complex topic with a specialist population, as the respondents would then deem the research trivial and unworthy of their attention. Berger and Patchner (1988b) advise that crucial questions should be placed early in the questionnaire while respondents' interest remains fresh. They also recommend that questions should be grouped either by topic or structure, eg a theme should be pursued or a collection of scaled questions should be grouped, but the two characteristics may conflict. It is also commonly recommended that there should be some lead into 'sensitive' questions. Moser and Kalton remark that the literature on question construction is 'bewildering' and that it is 'exceedingly difficult' to build any general principles.

General observations on vignettes

Relatively small numbers of researchers have used vignettes but several claims are made for the technique. Both West (1982) and Finch (1987) acknowledge that little has been done to validate vignette techniques but the users have a presumption about their intrinsic logic. Vignettes are said to engage respondents better and to elicit more meaningful and considered answers than the usual questionnaire and thus to have a particular value in exploring attitudes (Alexander and Becker 1978, West 1982, Finch 1987). Some argue that the attitudinal answers to concrete stories may be more predictive of real behaviour than those adduced by other survey methods but the validity of this has not been tested. Alexander and Becker argue from the premise that straight questionnaires and interviews are unreliable for such topics either because responses are biased in the direction of impression-management or because the judgments required are often too abstract. They say that 'why' questions are better explored by a 'stimulus . . . as concrete and detailed as possible' (p. 93). Finch agrees that normative issues can thus be explored in a way which approximates to the complexities of reality but also contends that vignettes offer a valuable way of distancing the issues from personal experience. She argues that the answers then more validly reveal contemporary social views than would a more subjective approach.

A range of detailed techniques have been employed by different researchers, involving the permutation of different elements of a vignette to sub-sets of their research populations, in order to control for all the salient variables (Finkelhor and Redfield 1984, Alexander and Becker 1978, West 1982, Finch 1987, Clark and Samphier 1984). Vignettes have also been used in a variety of forms, ranging from two lines devoid of context (eg Giovannoni and Becerra 1979) to several paragraphs of a story unfolding through time (eg Clark and Samphier 1984) or through a sequence of decisions imposed by the researcher (Finch 1987). West argues that these designs reveal a continuum from the minimal which leaves all contextualis-ation to the respondent through to the experimental which seeks to give precisely controlled stimuli.

The notion of a continuum and a valid middle ground would seem problematic, given that the two ends of the spectrum have different rationales, one being based on an interest in the respondent's subjective construction and meanings and the other on a standardisation of cues. Nevertheless, West points out that neither of the extremes is problem-free. If one gives very brief vignettes one may assume but cannot know that the respondent is relating to his/her general images of a category (person or situation) but at the other extreme, if one gives some context, the respondent will need yet more: 'It all depends on whether . . .' West also doubts the positivist stance that one can be clear that the meanings ascribed by the researcher and the respondent are the same. While Finch does think that the particular trigger in a vignette can be located, she appears to share West's doubt that the researcher can thereby claim to have grasped its particular import to the respondent.

The number of vignettes that can be accommodated obviously depends on their format, short or long, single- or multi-stage, and on whether the replies sought are closed or extended in form. Different studies have used a tremendous range, from one to thousands. For instance, West quotes an opinion that 10 vignettes were the limit when investigating more complex responses in an investigation of social status, but he claims four was the realistic limit in his own research on attitudes to dependent people's needs.

The number and content of answers sought have also varied from project to project. Giovannoni and Becerra (1979), whose work is partly replicated in this study, simply asked for a numerical severity rating to be given to a long series of brief vignettes of possible child abuse. Finkelhor and Redfield's study, noted above, used a similar structure but with many more cases. In contrast to these studies and Alexander and Becker, both West and Finch stress the importance of specifically asking 'why'.

Reliability is a problem according to West, particularly when different raters are coding the qualitative data derived from the interpretive end of the spectrum. Since there is a single coder in the present study, this difficulty is minimised. Both West and Finch in their reviews of the vignette technique stress that the fundamental question is to know whether one is seeking a causal relationship between particulars in the vignette and the response, or whether one is exploring subjective interpretations. In practice, both have pursued the interpretive approach but with significantly different designs. They are seeking the meanings people impute to their circumstances and choices. In contrast, Alves and Rossi, and Clark and Samphier have used very different methods to seek responses to fixed stimuli.

The above summary indicates that there has been much variety in the use of vignettes, and the lack of replication seems to justify caution in assuming any authoritative methodologies. The present study uses both short and long vignettes, the short ones being subjective and confined to a single issue of ascribing a severity rating to incidents of possible abuse and the longer ones cuing a series of questions. The latter invite some subjective, free form answers and some fixed choice responses. They lend themselves to varying levels of descriptive and interpretive analysis.

Operationalising the research question and developing the questionnaire

The global and ill-defined concepts of cooperation or coordination in child protection had to be converted into a series of perceptible and measurable variables. Chapter One indicates the broad boundaries within which the questions were framed, ie about practitioners' handling of cases of intrafamilial child abuse. Within those limits, what visible markers of cooperative values and cooperative action can be established? Essential questions relate to the volume of cases which different workers handle and the logistics of the system, but the perceptions of cases which trigger activity in the network and the attitudes and values of the practitioners which encourage or inhibit it are equally important.

Counting the number of times people have communicated with professionals in other disciplines about cases or attended child protection conferences is one very limited measure. In itself, it tells nothing about the value of the interchange. Moreover, people are unlikely to have accurate recall or a readily available log of such data. A case file study might be a preferred method for this particular item, although case records are frequently incomplete and do not necessarily cast light on the actors' values. (A small-scale case study was completed in Phase Three). A diary-keeping study would also be appropriate but would be unlikely to obtain practitioners' compliance. Moreover, both would leave the many other important questions unanswered. A number of questions were therefore designed to triangulate various dimensions of exposure to child protection cases, as reported by respondents.

Other direct measures include asking them to rate the importance of mechanisms such as case conferences or the salience of different professions in the network. The possibility that respondents would give inaccurate answers to attitudinal questions has already been acknowledged. Therefore, a variety of direct questions overlap and the answers are also interplayed with others arising from the vignettes.

A large part of the questionnaire depends upon people's responses to vignettes in two forms, designed to achieve two different purposes. First, brief vignettes were used to test one relatively simple dimension. Do respondents ascribe the same severity ratings to the same incidents of potential or actual abuse? The assumption behind this is that discrepancies between people's ratings are likely to indicate divergent views about how child abuse cases should be handled. It was postulated that people's beliefs, perceptions and thresholds of identification would impact on their engagement in collaboration, both in rating the priority of the problem and in choosing particular case management options. The Cleveland affair illustrated this, inter alia (Cleveland 1988).

Longer and developing vignettes have also been employed to investigate the way people perceive cases in some detail and to find out their proposed patterns of cooperative action. The objectives are to provide a basic description of the network and its activities, to identify its most important points and, if possible, any particular areas of conflict or tension. Respondents were asked a series of specific questions about what they would do and when, eg to check the child protection register, to seek a child protection conference, to talk to whom.

The possible gap between expressed intentions in hypothetical situations and actions in the real world, discussed above, is recognised. It is known that defining a case as child abuse is an emergent process involving a complex construction of the circumstances and background of the case – sometimes called 'moral characterisation' and sometimes a 'denunciation' – which distinguishes 'the battering Walshes' from the many families which possess relevant risk factors or who do injure their children without being officially noticed (Dingwall et al 1983). However, it is likely that any case situation included in a questionnaire explicitly concerned with child protection will be more frequently or strongly identified as child abuse than would the same circumstances in everyday life.

Finch (1987) argues that 'general images' of people's values are best obtained by deliberately eschewing any sense that the questions might apply to their personal choices. If one is asking the public to indicate attitudes to family and State obligations, as West and Finch were, that may be the most effective way to obtain worthwhile knowledge about the moral/political backcloth to public policy-makers' choices. However, the present research is addressed to practical decision makers themselves; it seemed not only probable that they would but desirable that they should consider each sketch in terms of their direct action responsibilities. The 'What would you do?' format was therefore chosen in preference to Finch's 'What do you think he/ she should do?'.

Sometimes the questions were supplemented by an exploration of why the action was chosen but this was limited by the scope and nature of the instrument. While recognising the limitations of a questionnaire and of hypothetical situations for this purpose, it is probable that much of the data is unpoblematic and reliable. Furthermore, people's hypothetical responses are compared with their general observations on the local network and are available for comparison with the findings in Phase Three.

It is probable that respondents have given an optimal account of their intentions rather than their routine practice. Nevertheless, it is assumed that there is valid information about people's views of which others constitute potentially relevant members of the network at different stages of the case and also about their normative expectations of themselves. As already stressed, the various findings from Phase Two are one part of an interlocking design.

A number of personal variables – age, gender, experience of child-rearing – and occupational factors – agency location, profession, rank, length of service overall, length of service in the present rank and locality, degree of specialisation and amount of post-qualifying training in child protection – were collected. They serve as descriptors of the sample but also, when relevant, as independent variables in the analysis of much of the other data.

The instrument was therefore in four parts:

1   Descriptive data about the respondents;

2   The brief vignettes;

3   The long vignettes;

4   General questions about the functioning of the local network and local policy.

Choice of vignettes

The brief vignette exercise derives from Giovannoni and Becerra (1979), using 20 of the originals and three items reduced from long vignettes written for the present study in either its pilot or main phases. For their rating exercise, Giovannoni and Becerra set out a spectrum of 156 vignettes and actually asked every respondent to deal with a random selection of 60. Snyder and Newberger (1986) used half the original series in their replication and Fox and Dingwall (1985) used only 20 in their partial replication in the UK. Chapter Eight lists the vignettes used here and reports the results.

Giovannoni and Becerra modelled their original vignettes on an earlier study which investigated opinions on the seriousness of a range of crimes (Sellin and Wolfgang 1964) but drew their descriptions from case files and legal definitions of child abuse. There was no pre-existing scale of seriousness, but they arbitrarily set a nine-point rating scale. They prepiloted their spectrum of incidents on social work and sociology students and then, from an original pool of 185, weeded out 16% which obtained uniformly extreme responses as to seriousness or triviality. In their main study, virtually the full range of scores was employed by their respondents. Their validation of the vignettes was accepted for this study, as it had been in the other small replications mentioned above. However, in the present study, the acceptability and credibility of the vignettes were tested on several groups during the preliminary design of the total instrument and during the pilot stage. The methods employed are discussed in more detail in Chapter Eight.

The long vignettes were specially created for the present study. It seems desirable to test a topic like the functioning of the child protection network on more than one case example but it is clear that several complex and multi-staged vignettes could not be absorbed into a questionnaire which also encompasses other content. At an early stage in the design and pilot work, it had been hoped to include both a postal questionnaire and an interview with a sub-sample of respondents in Phase Two. This would have split the ground between two instruments, making them both shorter but allowing for other vignettes to be included in the total design. This proved too time-consuming a project. Therefore, it was decided to enlarge the postal sample and split it into different sectors, two halves receiving totally different vignettes and one half being further sub-divided between black and unspecified ethnic variants of the same story. Thus, a wider range of responses and uses of the child protection network has been explored and can be compared.

Prepiloting

All parts of the instrument were tested at various stages of drafting on a range of academic and professional colleagues. These discussions confirmed its content validity. Concepts became more focused and more closed-choice questions were developed. However, a mixture of open and closed questions was retained, because of both the diversity of the topics and a desire to retain respondents' interest throughout a demanding schedule.

The pilot stage

There was considerable delay and difficulty in obtaining the staff lists and drawing the sample and this delayed the start of the pilot stage. Fifty respondents were drawn from the staff lists available, from all professions and the three main areas. This stage revealed two problems that led to significant changes in the programme. The first was the difficulty of obtaining an adequate response rate from all the professions, and this led to modifications in the sample which are discussed in Chapter Three. The second was the realisation that the total project timetable would not allow for the interviews originally planned, especially given the problems experienced in obtaining the staff lists. It was therefore decided that the Phase Two programme would have to be limited to more quantitative methods.

This necessitated redesign of the instrument in order to incorporate the most important aspects of both the questionnaire and the interview schedule. Several questions regarding emotional reactions and stress on the workers were abandoned; although thought likely to affect people's readiness to cooperate, the questions were considered suitable only for an interview. However, in order to retain some diversity of vignettes in the programme, the sample was doubled in size and questionnaires with different vignettes were distributed alternately to main phase respondents. Four schedules of scaled questions about general perceptions of others in the network were included to compensate for the qualitative data which could have been sought in an interview. The coding frame was refined in the light of the pilot responses.

Delivery and chasing

This is discussed in Chapter Three.

Coding, data entry and cleaning

Responses were coded on the original questionnaires and entered into a PC using SPSS-DE. The Data Entry programme builds a strict framework for each variable which limits the range of acceptable entries and provides algorithmic paths so that consequential processes may be precoded and automatically entered. Both these facilities minimise the possibility of literal errors in the computerised data set. The important process of data cleaning (Babbie 1989) is thus made simpler and more accurate. The last step in data cleaning was to check every fifteenth response set against the original questionnaire, revealing an accuracy rate of 99.8%. This was further improved before analysis began.

Analysis

The data were analysed by SPSS-PC. Results are reported at a < .05 probability level or less, unless otherwise noted. Chi-square was used whenever appropriate and possible, with 80% of expected frequencies not less than five (Clegg 1982, Bryman and Cramer 1990). Frequency counts and simple cross-tabulations by profession were routinely done. Agency location was also used as a fundamental variable, based on the assumption that local policies and inter-agency cultures might vary significantly. Analyses by area were restricted to the three core research areas – County, City and Met-Borough; inclusion of the several additional localities selected solely to increase the representation of paediatric staff and the police would have distorted the interprofessional balance.

Other independent variables were selected in the light of Rosenberg's (1968) advice that logic and knowledge should be used to eliminate redundant variables. Those used fell into two categories, relating to respondents' personal and professional identity. Besides occupation, the number of cases encountered and child protection conferences experienced were assumed to be fundamental independent variables, as was exposure to interdisciplinary training. Many of the experiential factors overlapped considerably and when it appeared that further analyses by some of the variables that had been created primarily for descriptive purposes might clarify possible confounding influences, these were also brought into play; they were 'all post-qualifying training' as distinct from 'interdisciplinary' training, degree of child protection specialisation in the work unit, number of days spent in the preceding month on child protection work. Where the literature review, the researcher's professional experience or common sense assumptions suggested that age, gender, or personal experience of child-rearing might affect them, people's responses were crosstabulated by these variables.

Where it seemed important and possible to use third variables, for instance isolating the amount of child protection training or gender from professional identity to test an attitude, this was done. However, small cell sizes constrained the scope of such secondary analysis.

When non-substantive responses are numerous, they are analysed against professional identity in order to distinguish their meaning as closely as possible; teachers gave the most numerous non-substantive responses, followed by general practitioners, and both groups had revealed their slender experience in the field of child protection. When inexperienced respondents expressed substantive views they have of course been analysed and reported as valid aspects of the functioning of the child protection network.

General evaluation of the questionnaire

It had proved difficult to devise a questionnaire that was equally suitable to such a spread of professions but it seemed to work quite well on that score. Some people answered relatively little because they had little or no relevant experience or responsibility. The long vignette sequence in the questionnaire presented more difficulty to a few of those in senior ranks (a small minority of social services principal officers and nurse managers) who had no direct responsibility for cases, despite the rubric instructing them to answer as appropriate either regarding their own imputs or their expectations of their subordinates.

The questionnaire appeared to sustain respondents' interest well. Despite its length, 95% completed it and most of those who failed to finish or gave no reply to specific questions were people with little or no engagement in or knowledge of child protection. Responses appeared thoughtful, discrete and variously appreciative or critical of the network. At the end of the questionnaire, respondents were invited to make any further observations or to raise topics that they felt had been omitted from the schedule and several volunteered additional comments, sometimes both critical and complimentary comments. Eight of the 339 respondents said the questionaire was a valuable exploration of an important topic. Social workers gave the highest compliments – 'extremely well though out paper; good to excellent', 'splendid questionnaire, on the ball' but commendations also came from members of other professions. On the other hand, there were 10 complaints that it was too long for busy people and one respondent said it was tedious.

Chapter 3

Access and Sampling

Introduction

The first and second parts of this chapter describe the selection of the professions and areas in the sample. The third part discusses access to the agencies and workers invited to participate in the study. The last part summarises available staffing details from the agencies involved in the project and compares sampling and response rates against available data about profession, rank, gender and ethnicity in the source populations.

Designing the sample

The two main aspects of sample design – identifying the relevant professions or agencies and identifying appropriate localities – are discussed in turn.

Selecting the appropriate occupational groups

Several occupations were identified as probable key members of the child protection network and included in the research design; these were general practitioners, health visitors, local authority lawyers, paediatricians, police, social workers and teachers. The social services department is designated as the lead agency for child protection, the police have an investigative duty and the necessity for medical assessments is stressed in official guidance. The importance of solicitors' advice and support in consideration of legal proceedings has been highlighted in a number of inquiry reports (eg Jasmine Beckford 1983, Cleveland 1987). Health visitors' and teachers' contact with the majority of children in the community gives them an important role in the child protection network. Broadly, all were selected because they actually have responsibilities for children, although the extent of their engagement in coordinated activity in child abuse cases is precisely the focus of this research programme. It is presumed that an understanding of the values and processes of coordination through the eyes of this group will illuminate the bulk of 'real world' concerns.

In the case of agencies with specialist departments or substructures – social services departments, police, paediatrics – only those staff with some responsibility for child abuse cases have been identified. One area included an NSPCC unit and this was included in the research, as were hospital social workers concerned with children; however, their numbers were too few to analyse separately and they have been combined with the main body of social workers. In some social services departments a number of staff have highly specialised responsibilities for child protection alongside other staff with a wider child care remit which includes some child protection functions. Sometimes, staff have generic roles but possibly a degree of informal specialisation in children's work and yet others have primary responsibilities for adult groups but an occasional involvement in child protection cases. The structure is also complex in the large teaching hospitals where some paediatricians have special responsibility for child abuse cases, others may have a degree of special interest and others specialise in some totally different field of child health but are 'on take' for all new cases on particular days. Some schools have 'named persons' with special responsibility for child protection matters. The teachers were drawn entirely from the primary school sector, not because abuse does not occur to secondary age children but in order to eliminate one complexity from an already complex research design. Thus, the brief vignettes in particular focus on children of an age where both health visitors and teachers might overlap.

Efforts were made to draw the sample more heavily from the specialist staff in the agencies with complex sub-structures, while not exluding the generalists. A few police officers on general duties were initially included in order to investigate whether they perceived any role for themselves in child protection. Their few and incomplete responses and others' refusals to participate due to their lack of involvement led to the decision to delete them from the data set and include only the child protection specialist police.

Given the focus of this phase of the research, many other occupational groups could have been studied. These included:

Accident and emergency medical staff	Nursery teachers, nurses, playgroup staff
Accident and emergency nursing staff	Paediatric nursing staff
Clergy	Probation and divorce court welfare officers
Community psychiatric nurses	Psychiatrists (adult and children's services)
Community workers	
Education welfare officers	Psychologists (educational and clinical)
Foster parents	School nurses
'Helpline' staff	Social security staff
Housing officers	Social workers (residential)
Midwives	Solicitors (private)

Women's refuge staff	Other voluntary sector family and child welfare agencies, eg Family
Youth leaders.	Welfare Association, etc.

These personnel all impinge at times on the lives and welfare of children and may occasionally be actively involved in managing a case of suspected child abuse or contributing information or opinions to a case conference (Jones et al 1987, DH 1991). At the research design stage, some of those consulted argued variously that midwives, psychiatrists, psychologists, paediatric nurses, probation officers or nursery and playgroup staff should have been encompassed. However, such a broad coverage was not feasible within the resources available.

Selecting the areas

The initial decision to locate the study in the north of England reflected a view that relatively little such research was undertaken in the region and access to agencies might be less difficult and the research more warmly welcomed than in more heavily researched areas. It was also practically convenient to the research team which was on the point of moving from Leicester to Stirling University as the project started. It was desirable within budgetary limits to obtain areas with diverse sociodemographic and administrative characteristics, in order to test the possibility that patterns of coordination are significantly affected by local factors.

Several broad characteristics were sought: a socioeconomically deprived urban area, a median urban area and a median rural/small town area; at least one area with a significant ethnic minority population; at least one area with a prominent NSPCC involvement and one without, and, on the advice of the Social Services Inspectorate, a choice of areas in more than one region. The catchment zone is very heavily urbanised with a generally old and declining industrial base and, between the empty moors and the factory yards, it was not possible to select an archetypal country town with a rural hinterland.

Reference was made to 1981 Census data, OPCS Population Trends and Key Population and Vital Statistics, the Department of the Environment's Z Scores, SSI Key Indicators of Local Authority Social Services, Department of Health Survey of Child Protection Registers 1988 and NSPCC Child Abuse Trends in England and Wales 1983–87. The Social Services Inspectorate, both nationally and regionally, also gave advice on the final selection of possible research territories. Three significantly different places were chosen as core areas; a large and very deprived inner city authority and regional centre, with sizeable ethnic minorities of mainly Pakistani and Afro-Caribbean origin; a mixed urban and rural division of relatively high prosperity with a small ethnic minority population in a large, impoverished and very urbanised county; a medium-sized metropolitan borough in the middle range of Z scores with a sizeable ethnic minority population. Their child protection registration rates varied from 1.5 to 4.9 per 1000 children and, although such statistics are recognised to be complex artefacts (Kitsuse and Cicourel 1963, Birchall 1989), they signify a range of child protection activity in the different networks. All three areas agreed to participate and are referred to hereafter as City, County and Metborough respectively. In addition, several adjacent health authorities and police divisions were recruited to increase the available pool of paediatric staff and specialist police.

Negotiating access

The project was funded by the Department of Health and has had support from the research division and the Social Services Inspectorate. Her Majesty's Inspectorate at the Department of Education and Science also expressed support and suggested useful contacts in the education service. A letter was sent to relevant professional associations to introduce the project and seek their support. Most gave encouraging responses and many agreed to put supportive notes in their journals or newsletters to members. A similar letter was addressed to Area Child Protection Committees in the proposed areas and followed up by letters to the heads of the relevant agencies in each area. This letter outlined the project, sought their consent to the research within their agency and requested staff lists.

Responses were generally supportive. Some agencies wished to consult staff or seek union clearance before releasing staff lists. Others delegated even 'in principle' decisions about participation to the level of local units, eg individual schools or area managers of social services. In the case of general practitioners, local lists were obtained diretly from Family Practitioner Committees (now called Family Health Service Authorities). Regional Health Authorities provided details of paediatric consultants and the latter were approached in their turn for lists of junior doctors.

There were personal discussions with a number of senior staff at central office and area level in all Social Services Departments; considerable difficulties arose in locating the relevant hierarchy in the health visiting service due to changes of personnel, shifting structures and changing nomenclature; Education Departments also proved elusive and slow; the police were generally very helpful but one authority was particularly concerned about the possible time demands on staff; local authority solicitors were exceptionally hard to engage; paediatricians had to be approached individually regarding their own participation and for access to their juniors, and their response was very varied. General practitioners were also approached individually, with mixed results. Many months elapsed before sufficient staff lists were in hand to draw the sample effectively and a few agencies which had initially expressed goodwill had eventually to be dropped from the project.

The final stage of the access negotiations was a covering letter introducing the project to the workers concerned, stressing its importance and confidential nature and inviting each individual drawn in the sample to participate. This accompanied the questionnaire, which also included a letter thanking those who agreed for their cooperation. (See Appendix 2 for samples of the introductory letters)

Drawing the sample

It was decided that a stratified random sample from the chosen agencies and their specific sub-units was appropriate (Burgess 1982, Bryman and Cramer 1990), the stratifications being for rank and sex wherever the latter could be established clearly from the staff lists supplied. A pilot sample of 50 was drawn from all lists available in early July 1990; this included most areas and professions but one education authority and two health visiting agencies were not available for inclusion at that stage. As details became available, it was apparent that staff numbers in the different agencies and locations varied more than anticipated. Particularly in County, staff numbers were limited in many agencies and some cooperated in accepting a very high sampling fraction. It proved necessary to add a second division to the catchment zone for County social workers before a sufficient pool was obtained and, had there been time, it would have been desirable to enlarge the County pool of general practitioners similarly. One health authority failed to provide the promised lists of health visiting staff and had to be abandoned; an additional health authority had to be recruited to bolster their numbers. The full lists of primary schools were obtained from local education authorities and head teachers sampled; a further number of the heads were then approached for their own staff lists, from which the teacher samples were drawn. In both County and City, 30% of the schools drawn refused to participate but only 10% refused in Metborough. In the case of the highly specialised and scarce groups – police specialists and paediatricians – it was realised at the initial design stage that several areas should be added to the core areas in an effort to obtain adequate populations. The same approach was taken regarding local authority solicitors but, as the response rate from them did not approach an adequate level for analysis, they have been excluded from the data set and report.

The sampling fraction varied from profession to profession and area to area with the objective of obtaining viable cell sizes for analysis by the main sub-categories of area and profession and two main variant forms of the questionnaire. It ranged from an estimated 3.5% of school teachers to nearly 60% of specialist police. Further details are given in Statistical Appendix 1. Poor response rates from schools and general practitioners in the pilot phase led to an extensive sampling of those groups in order to secure adequate numbers of responses. In other respects, the sample was stratified by gender, rank and apparent ethnicity as far as such data was available. Following the exclusion of general police and lawyers, the original gross sample was 643. These different sampling fractions necessarily give some bias towards individuals and occupations with a greater involvement than others in child protection and it is inevitable that the varied response rates from the different groups accentuate that tendency. However, it is thought that the responses thus obtained give a valuable picture of a broad body of opinion with a more active interest and therefore possibly more influential role in the child protection network.

The professions have widely different organisational structures which affect, inter alia, levels of delegation and decision-making in child protection case work. These differences may themselves cause diverse perceptions of the efficacy, importance and feasibility of coordination (see, for instance, Cleveland 1987, Wightman 1987, Hallett and Birchall 1992). It was important, therefore, to sample from different levels. Nomenclature also varies markedly between agencies and between areas. For the purposes of data analysis only, staff were placed in three ranks:

principal: area officers, assistant area officers and principal social workers; senior nurse managers; head teachers; police inspectors or above; consultant paediatricians;

senior: senior social workers or team leaders; nurse managers; deputy head teachers; police sergeants; registrars;

main grade: field social workers; health visitors; class teachers; police constables; general practitioners; senior house officers.

Table 3.1 **A summary of the rank distribution of staff in the participating agencies**

Rank Area	Principal		Senior		Maingrade		Total	
	N	%	N	%	N	%	N	%
Social Workers	45	12.7	40	11.3	268	75.9	353	100.0
Health Visitors	7	3.0	16	6.8	214	90.2	237	100.0
Teachers	98	8.1	98	8.1	669	85.2	865	100.0
Police	3	5.4	10	17.9	43	76.8	56	100.0
General Practitioners					518	100.0	518	100.0
Paediatricians	47	30.7	41	26.8	65	42.5	153	100.0
Total	200	9.2	205	9.4	1777	81.4	2182	100.0

This ranking is not intended to impute equivalence of professional status but approximately to match the hierarchical functions and roles of diverse organisations. General practitioners are obviously the most difficult to accommodate within the schema because of their personal autonomy alongside varying degrees of seniority. It is also evident that there is not a symmetrical pyramidal structure across all organisations. The rank distribution of staff in the participating agencies is summarised in Table 3.1 and further details are given in the statistical appendix.

Description of the participating agencies

As already indicated, the agencies varied greatly in size and organisation. Many of these differences were anticipated; others led to adjustments of the sampling frame as they became apparent from the staff lists and during the access negotiations. The rate of social workers per 1000 population was twice as high in City as in County. The total teacher population is unknown but there are 446 primary schools in the research areas. The schools about which data is available have a modal size of 10–15 staff, with a range from two in County and Metborough only to 20+ in all areas. County has the fewest big schools and an even spread from two to 15 staff. City has a large majority in the mid-range and Metborough has schools fairly evenly divided about the 10 staff mark. General practices varied from single-handed to nine partners. Paediatric departments in the district general hospitals were very small but in the teaching hospitals there were many more staff.

Agencies also varied widely in degree of specialisation. The staff in units with any degree of specialisation in child protection work comprised 19% of the total sample and just 6% worked in units specialising exclusively in child protection cases. In the three core areas, most of these specialists were found in City. Including those in the NSPCC, just under half the total sample of social workers specialised to some extent in child protection. The structure of the City social services department was very complex with many functionally divided sub-teams in numerous area offices. In contrast, adult services specialists were called in to handle child protection cases at times of pressure in Metborough. One or two health visitors specialised in work which presented an above average number of vulnerable families. Few schools appeared to have officially identified any staff member as the designated liaison for child protection although many signified this would 'of course' be the head or occasionally the deputy; a few heads said they 'supposed' it was themselves. One education office said the schools in half its area were more attuned to the topic than the other half. Child protection proved to be exclusively the province of small specialist police units in these areas; the attempt to enrol generalist police officers quickly made their lack of knowledge and involvement evident. No general practices indicated any specialisation between partners in this matter. Paediatric departments in the district general hospitals were staffed by general paediatricians but in the teaching hospital areas many staff had highly specialised functions, with only a few taking a particular interest in or responsibility for child abuse matters; all were characterised by rapid rotation of junior staff. Some areas indicated that child abuse cases were to be immediately referred to the consultant but others also used clinical medical officers quite extensively.

The sample thus covered a wide range of organisational variables which enrich the data but have not been randomly sampled and are too idiosyncratic to be used as independent variables. Numerous organisational contingencies have been documented, eg the varying liaisons between social services and paediatricians (DH SSI 1987), the variety of roles of child protection consultants in social services and health visiting (Helm 1988), different functions of NSPCC teams in different places (Community Care 1988). A much larger number of areas would have been needed if one sought to compare responses on the basis of specific organisational variables.

As expected, the proportions of men and women in the different agencies varied widely, and women were under-represented in the senior and principal ranks. Even among 237 health visitors, the only two men were in principal ranks. The gender distribution of staff in the police child protection units is markedly different from that elsewhere in the police service. The full list available from one police authority revealed that women comprised 10% of the non-child protection staff and that only one of 43 sergeants was a woman, whereas the one sergeant in the specialist child protection section was a woman and so were two thirds of the constables.

Table 3.2 **A summary of the gender distribution of staff in the participating agencies**

Area	Male N	Male %	Female N	Female %	Not Known N	Not Known %	Total N	Total %
Social Workers	113	32.0	199	56.4	41	11.6	353	100.0
Health Visitors	2	0.8	235	99.2			237	100.0
Teachers*	349	30.2	767	66.5	38	3.3	1154	100.0
Police	19	33.9	37	66.1			56	100.0
General Practitioners	394	76.1	121	23.4	3	0.6	518	100.0
Paediatricians	82	53.6	53	34.6	18	11.8	153	100.0
Total	959	38.8	1412	57.1	100	4.0	2471	100.0

* These figures include all primary school heads in two education authorities and in one division of County but the subordinate staff in only the schools directly sampled.

The Metborough list of general practitioners did not always clearly distinguish gender and the researcher here estimated and perhaps under-estimated the proportion of women. The assumption that the subject was a woman was made where the same names were coupled in a partnership or people had, to the best of her knowledge, female names. In relatively few agencies or cases, however, the staff lists left the person's gender unknown. The gender distribution of the participating agencies is summarised in Table 3.2 but fuller details are given in the statistical appendix.

Responses and non-respondents

The relevant net sample was 562 and there were 339 respondents, giving a response rate of 60.3%. Although the original gross sample was larger, a number were subsequently excluded for various reasons. As reported above, solicitors were excluded from the study because the poor response rate from a small professional group meant their information could not be usefully analysed. General police were excluded when a handful of responses reinforced the impression from the pilot phase that they were not involved in child protection work and instantly referred such few cases as they perceived to the specialist unit. From the remainder, another 4% declined to complete the questionnaire because they had no responsibility or engagement in child protection matters. These were mainly class teachers. Another 62 (9%) were classified as 'deadwood' (Hoinville, Jowell et al 1977) – people who had moved or died, were long-term sick or on maternity leave – general practitioners comprised over half this category but teachers were the next most prevalent. The remainder were small numbers evenly spread across the professions. The exclusions were evenly balanced across the areas.

The overall response rate reached an acceptable level, particularly in a postal survey with a large inner city catchment (Hoinville, Jowell et al 1977). Responses varied across the professions despite at least four efforts to level these up. Two follow-up letters (Appendix 2) were sent and at least two telephone contacts were attempted with persistent non-respondents. These efforts met with a diminishing rate of return, with 131 positive responses to the first letter and only 12 to the final telephone contacts. Repeated efforts involving over 400 calls were made to maximise response rates and obtain explanations for non-response, particularly regarding general practitioners whose response rate remained low and social workers whose central place in the network made their responses seem particularly important. Repeat questionnaires were sent out in 63 cases, ranging from 2.5% of health visitors to 20% of paediatric staff.

In the time lapses between obtaining the earliest staff lists and the eventual mailing of questionnaires to the main sample, and then a further five months up to the last telephone roundup, there were significant changes in staff and agency data. At least one element of identity changed for 17% of the total sample: name, address, telephone number or role; over 2% changed at least two elements. Not surprisingly, this turbulence was lower among those who agreed to participate as respondents, standing at 9%. The degree of mobility and frequent, recurring difficulty experienced by the researcher in contacting people by telephone may offer a sidelight on some of the logistical problems for practitioners, particularly those only occasionally involved, in maintaining liaison in day-to-day case management.

Comparisons of sampling and response rates

Rates of response could be compared with the original sample on four dimensions, those of area, profession, rank and gender. See Tables 3.5 to 3.8 in the statistical appendix. Figure 3.1 shows that response rates from the different areas accorded closely with the rates sampled. Figure 3.2 below compares the ditribution of the professions in the net sample and among respondents. As can be seen, the response rates range from acceptable to very good for all professions except general practitioners. The response rate from general practitioners was worse than in other studies which were perhaps seen as more immediately important to them (Cartwright 1967, Butler 1973). The proportions of each profession in the study roughly mirror those achieved in the pilot phase, except that more police (100%) and fewer paediatricians (33%) responded then. This led to an overoptimistic expectation of police response rate in the main phase but to reasonably successful compensatory efforts to increase the main trawl of paediatricians. However, the actual numbers achieved from these scarce professions, particularly of specialist police, remain fewer than desired for some analyses.

Figure 3.1: **A comparison of the final sample and responses by area**

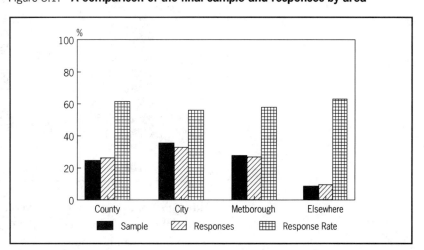

Figure 3.2: **A comparison of the final sample and responses by profession**

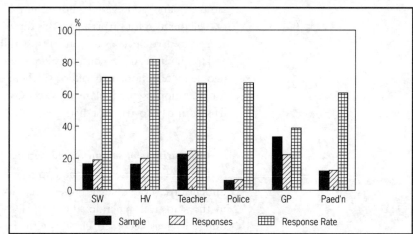

Some unevenness in different professions' responses from area to area was evident. The response rate from all but the city health visitors was extremely high; with small numbers there were marked differences between police and paediatric returns in the different areas. Such discrepant rates make it difficult to infer the local representatives of the poorly responding groups. As Figure 3.3 shows, there was a better response from senior ranks than from main grade staff; this was partly due to the poor response rate from general practitioners who were all classified for this purpose as main grade.

Figure 3.3: **A comparison of the final sample and response by rank**

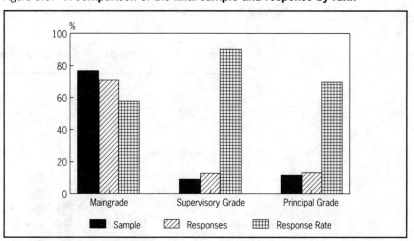

Although ethnicity was not detailed on staff lists, a tentative identification made on the basis of names alone suggested that 78% of the agency populations are mainly white and 22% are probably of Asian origin. The initial classification of respondents' ethnic origins followed the census classifications. Compared with other personal data, a higher number (4%) refused to answer this question. The largest identified group in the sample were male, Indian and in the medical profession; none were health visitors or police officers. Only one respondent in the County was of ethnic minority origin; the rest were fairly evenly spread among the other areas. These results were as expected.

The number of respondents of minority ethnic origin was too few to consider any further analyses by this variable, despite the potential interest of the topic. In the United States Giovannoni and Becerra (1979) did not find ethnicity to be a significant variable in workers' attitudes to child abuse; moreover, the different ethnic groups were differentially distributed between the professions and any impact was confounded with the occupational variable. However, in their study of the lay population, they found Hispanic and black Americans to rate child abuse rather more severely than the white majority. In the UK, the bearing of race and culture on workers' or lay attitudes to child abuse and appropriate interventions is a matter of concern (eg Channer and Parton 1990, Dutt undated) but has so far been the subject of little empirical research. It is an important topic for future study.

Figure 3.4: **A comparison of the final sample and responses by gender**

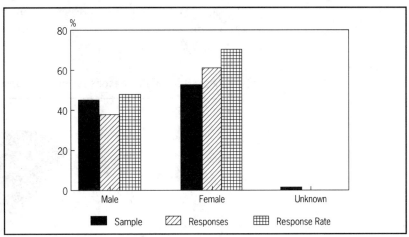

As far as data could be ascertained (Table 3.2 above), 60% of the professional population in the research areas were women. As shown in Figure 3.4, there were more women than men in the sample but not in quite the same proportions as the estimated population, and a small number whose gender was unidentified. However, rather more of the women responded and much if not all of this shift is due to the poor response rate from general practitioners, a large majority of whom are male. No reason is evident but women responded at a slightly lower rate than men in the principal grade. The final result is a gender ratio of respondents which closely matches the source population rather than the stratified groupings.

Reasons for non-response

Where reasons for non-response could be elicited, the commonest was 'too busy'. The results are shown in Figure 3.5. General practitioners and teachers were particularly prone to specify that recent organisational changes emanating from government had streched their time or their goodwill beyond the limit. As already discussed, 9% of the sample had moved, etc., and just under 5% declined due to lack of relevant experience. Although the latter were mainly teachers or generalist police, there was also a tendency for general practitioners and paediatric junior doctors to plead the same reason.

Eleven general practitioners said they never responded to research requests and ten questionnaires were reported lost in the post. Six explicitly stated that the questionnaire was too long or difficult, but that could also have been a covert factor with some of those who asserted they were too busy. The groups most frequently involved in cases, with the exception of local authority lawyers, gave a better rate of response than some others. There was no significant correlation between reasons for non-participation and location, gender or rank.

Figure 3.5:   **Main reasons for non-response**

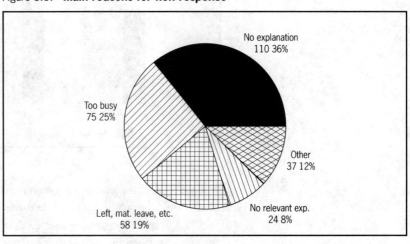

Summary and Conclusions

A stratified random sample of six professions was drawn mainly from three areas in the north of England, supplemented by paediatricians and specialist police from elsewhere. There were 339 respondents, as follows:

62 social workers (18.3%)   22 police (6.5%)

68 health visitors (20.1%)   66 general practitioners (19.5%)

81 teachers (23.9%)   40 paediatric doctors (11.8%)

A response rate of 60% was achieved, varying from 81% among health visitors to 38% among general practitioners.

Overall response rates were satisfactory and the sample yielded cell sizes sufficient for most of the professions and for other basic variables. Different sampling fractions were used for different agencies and ranks to mitigate the effect of varied professional populations and expected discrepancies in response rates. Despite strenuous efforts to draw a large enough sample and achieve a high response rate from all groups, it proved impossible to recruit an adequate number of specialist police and paediatric staff for all desired analyses and, due to their response rate, the general practitioners cannot be seen as representative of their profession but seem likely to be those with more involvement and interest in matters of child protection or interprofessional cooperation than their peers. The varying response rates from the different groups inevitably accentuate the tendency for the data to over-represent the views of workers with a greater involvement in child protection. However, it is thought that the responses thus obtained give a valuable picture of a broad body of opinion with a more active interest and therefore possiby more influential role in the child protection network. In view of the deliberate sampling bias towards the more involved groups and the different response rates, where respondents nevertheless indicate very slight engagement with the network, it seems reasonable to assume that their non-respondent peers would have even less involvement.

Chapter 4

Description of respondents

Introduction

The reasons for selecting the participating professions and the sampling criteria were described in Chapter Three. It seems probable that a number of factors may influence workers' perceptions of incidents of suspected child abuse or their judgements about appropriate interventions. These include not only the particular functions of the different agencies and professionals but also the amount of training and experience the worker has had in the field of child protection. Local policies and practices within or between agencies may differ, and local cultures and patterns of child-rearing may vary from area to area. It is possible that, in a sphere of work where there has been rapid policy development, there will be implementation lags which may vary among respondents of different ages. Some empirical reports suggest that men and women react differently to some forms of child abuse, and gender has been found to be a salient variable in several studies of interprofessional and interorganisational dynamics. Direct experience of child-rearing is sometimes held to affect workers' evaluations of family difficulties. For all these reasons, the 339 respondents are described in greater detail in this chapter and these factors have been used as independent variables in subsequent analyses wherever they have seemed potentially relevant.

Professional and agency data

Respondents were originally classified in 10 different groups, separately identifying hospital and NSPCC social workers, police surgeons and teachers with designated responsibility for child protection. All these sub-groups were represented among the respondents but numbers were too few to use for analytic purposes and they have been included within the relevant professional category. Table 4.1 below shows the distribution of respondents on the separate axes of profession and area, with profession as the dominant break. For comparison, Table 4.7 in the statistical appendix gives the same data with locality as the dominant break.

There are no statistically significant differences between the samples from the three core areas although, as discussed in the previous chapter, the majority of paediatricians and a significant number of police officers were recruited from other areas. Analyses based on the area dimension exclude these other areas. The findings on the professional dimension are therefore indicative for the whole sample and those on the area dimension refer to the three core areas.

Table 4.1   **Number of respondents in each area as a percentage of the sample by profession**

Profession	County N	County %	City N	City %	Metborough N	Metborough %	Other N	Other %	Total N	Total %
Social Workers	19	20.7	25	21.0	18	19.1			62	18.3
Health Visitors	26	28.3	18	15.1	24	25.5			68	20.1
Teachers	23	25.0	28	23.5	30	31.9			81	23.9
Police	4	4.3	8	6.7	2	2.1	8	3.5	22	6.5
General Practitioners	17	18.5	35	29.4	14	14.9			66	19.5
Paediatricians	3	3.3	5	4.2	6	6.4	26	6.5	40	11.8
Total	92	100.0	119	100.0	94	100.0	34	100.0	339	100.0

Personal data

Figure 4.1 shows that most respondents are in mid-career, with less than 10% under 30 years old and only two (teachers) under 25. The age structure of the population does not vary by area but there are significant interprofessional differences. Between 50 and 68% of most professions are aged 30–44 but 59% of health visitors are over 45 compared with only two police officers. Paediatric staff are the most symmetrically distributed but age and rank correlate more closely for them than for other groups.

Figure 4.1:   **Age bands of respondents**

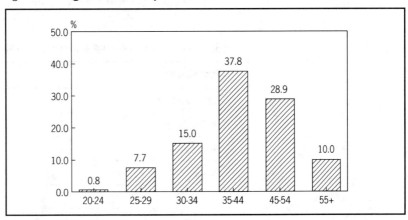

(N = 339)

All subsequent analyses by age have used a three point scale dividing the relatively inexperienced from the well-established and those with many years behind them. The distribution of respondents on the shortenend scale is shown in Table 4.2 below.

Table 4.2 **Age distribution of respondents on a three point scale**

Age band of respondents	N	%
20–29	28	8.3
30–44	179	52.8
45+	132	38.9
Total	339	100.0

Tables 4.3 and 4.4 summarise the child-rearing experience and gender distribution of respondents, both of which, it has been suggested, might alter people's perceptions of acceptable child-rearing behaviour. It is sometimes argued by parents that if professionals have experience of bringing up their own children they would have greater toleration of parents' difficulties. A large majority of respondents have experience of bringing up children but there was some variation between the professions which was independent of their different age profiles. Social workers, paediatricians and teachers are around the mean but the police markedly under, and a rather higher proportion of the men than of the women have child-rearing experience. These data are presented in Table 4.3 and are simply descriptive; wherever tested in this study, parenting experience shows no significant effect on respondents' views of how to handle the case situations.

Table 4.3 **Child-rearing experience among the respondent groups**

Profession	Have reared children
Social workers	77.4%
Health visitors	88.2%
Teachers	80.8%
Police	22.7%
General Practitioners	86.4%
Paediatricians	75.0%
Total	78.1%

p = < .0001; CC .32718;

In some studies, men have been found to show less concern about some forms of child abuse and intra-familial violence but others have argued that professional identity is the dominant factor with which gender may often be confounded. These issues are discussed in the literature review (Hallett and Birchall 1992, chapter 6). Many writers have noted that gender relations are also a powerful dynamic in interprofessional relationships, entangling issues of occupational status and power with more general issues of women's subordinate role in society (Hallett and Birchall 1992, chapter 8). That there are marked gender imbalances between the professions and different seniority levels is well-known (Beechey and Whitelegg 1986, Dex 1985, Hallett 1989).

Gender correlates with several choices regarding case matters and with some perceptions of the network in this study but the factor is frequently confounded with professional identity and could only be distinguished by drawing a much larger sample of those professions in which women are a small minority. In the case of health visiting, the profession is so overwhelmingly composed of women that there is almost no possibility of separating the factors. However, a few results suggest that the factors are operating independently in certain situations. As expected, there was an overwhelming preponderance of women among health visitors while the large majority of paediatricians and general practitioners are men. In contrast to the bulk of the police force, three quarters of these specialist police are women. Social workers' gender distribution lies nearest to the mean for the whole sample. Full details are given in Table 4.8 in the statistical appendix but Table 4.4 presents a summary.

Table 4.4 **Gender distribution among the respondent groups**

Profession	Male	Female
Social workers	38.7%	61.3%
Health visitors	2.9%	97.1%
Teachers	27.2%	72.8%
Police	27.3%	72.7%
General Practitioners	65.2%	34.8%
Paediatricians	67.5%	32.5%
Total	36.6%	63.4%

$p = < .0001$; CC .34801.

Experience and training

Career patterns and mobility

A factor which may affect coordination in practice is the degree of stability in the network. It is notable that 70% of the sample have over 10 years experience in their jobs and less than 8% have worked under three years in their profession. The population falls into approximate thirds as to whether they have been in their current rank less than three years, 3–10 years or more. 40% are deeply rooted, having served over 10 years in the locality, and only about a quarter have been working in the area for under three years. Such stability may not be typical of the national picture, which is itself likely to vary considerably from one locality to another and from time to time; London has presented particular problems in recent times. The finding is an important corrective to notions of perpetual movement and very inexperienced staff. Nevertheless, the failure to reach 9% of the original sample because of movements in the time lapse between agencies' publication of staff lists and the mailing of the questionnaires does indicate that mobility is still a significant factor in these areas. This pattern also varies to some extent between professions within the sample. Many maingrade staff (45%) have worked in that rank for over ten years whereas staff in senior ranks have more mobile patterns. Middle grade staff are scattered across the timespans but 45% of principals have been in post less than three years, approximately a quarter five to nine years and another quarter over ten years. However, it appears that promotion often does not entail moving out of the locality as 57% of the principals have been in the area over ten years.

The professions vary on these different dimensions in complicated and sometimes unexpected ways. In particular contrast to teachers, social services staff tend to be newer in all three factors of profession, rank and locality. The police tend to be newer in the area; general practitioners tend to be the longest-serving 'maingrade' workers in the area; health visitors have little turnover of rank but cluster around the 5–9 year band in the locality. Paediatric staff split predictably into mobile juniors and long-established consultants. Some discrepancies between age bands, rank and length of experience also suggest that social workers and health visitors tend to be recruited at a more mature age than the other professions. Clearly, some of these findings fit in with existing knowledge of generally different patterns of mobility in these groups but others may be less obvious, for instance the number of relatively new principals or the clustering of health visitors' local experience. Many of these discrepancies may affect the way the local network articulates. For instance, the stability of paediatric consultants and head teachers in particular, as compared with the cumulative effects of the turnover factors among social workers, may give the former more power in the local culture and informal politics despite the social services department's formal lead responsibility and generally greater experience of child protection.

It is well-recognised that the professions have different hierarchical structures and it is possible that the tensions may arise because of different authority structures. An attempt was made to obtain a sample which represented all ranks but concentrated on those with most functional responsibility for child protection. There is thus a deliberate over-sampling of senior ranks, particularly in the case of head teachers and paediatric consultants. As reported in Chapter Three, the ranks responded differently so Table 4.5 is descriptive of respondents and not an exact replication of their agency structure.

Table 4.5 **Rank distribution among the respondent groups**

Profession	Maingrade		Supervisory		Principal		Total	
	N	%	N	%	N	%	N	%
Social Workers*	40	65.6	12	19.7	9	14.8	61	100.0
Health Visitors	51	75.0	15	22.1	2	2.9	68	100.0
Teachers	49	60.5	11	13.6	21	25.9	81	100.0
Police	18	81.8	3	14.3	1	4.5	22	100.0
General Practitioners	66	100.0					66	100.0
Paediatricians	11	27.5	11	27.5	18	45.0	40	100.0
Total	235	69.5	52	15.4	51	15.1	338	100.0

*One rank not reported.

Chapter Three noted that the gender distributions at different ranks in the agencies are, as expected, also markedly different. The gender distribution by profession and rank of the sample is shown in Table 4.7 in the statistical appendix. With the exception of general practice, women disproportionately outnumber men in the main grade and men become the majority in the principal rank. The only two male health visitors in the sample are in managerial grades but only 12% of class teachers are male while two thirds of the heads are men. Social workers have a gender profile throughout the ranks which most nearly matches the overall ratio but men still marginally outnumber women in the principal rank. In the main and intermediate ranks, the ethnic breakdown followed the expected ratio but numbers in the principal grade were too few to test for significance. Such discrepant structures may make comparisons of attitude and behaviour by rank difficult to distinguish from those deriving from professional identity or gender, at least in some professions, eg teaching.

Education and training

It has been suggested that attitudes to cases or to interprofessional cooperation might vary according to educational levels (eg Giovannoni and Becerra 1979, Breci 1987; see also Hallett and Birchall 1992, chapter 8). However, if this is so, it is impossible to differentiate in the present study from issues of professional identity. 48% of respondents have non-graduate training while 17% have a first degree and over a third a post-graduate qualification. Despite the increase in graduate recruitment to the police, none in this sample report any qualification other than in-service training. Inevitably, all the doctors are graduates and over two thirds have higher degrees or diplomas; less than half the teachers are graduates; social workers divide equally between non-graduate and post-graduate status whereas all but three of the health visitors are non-graduates. The fewest staff with first degrees are in the middle rank but principals most frequently have post-graduate qualifications.

Many commentators stress the importance of specialised training in the management of child abuse cases, often with an emphasis on interdisciplinary sharing. As discussed in the literature review (Hallett and Birchall 1992, chapter 14), this is believed to be important for two different reasons. First, to increase the different professions' knowledge and skills and their awareness of their colleagues' particular contributions but, secondly, it is also often stressed as a vehicle for improving communications and mutual trust, thus enhancing the processes of collaboration. The most striking finding is how limited the experience is. Only half the sample have any such training and there are marked variations between the professions. Further descriptive detail and the respondents' evaluations of their training are reported in Chapter Five.

Experience of child protection cases

Respondents' professional experience and local knowledge in the field of child protection were studied in a variety of ways. It did not seem realistic to ask people to report exactly the number of cases and child protection conferences, etc, in which they had been involved as many professionals would be unlikely to have such statistical records to hand. However, it was assumed that many would have some sense of their engagement with child protection issues and how that compares with their peers' involvement, although this comparative picture may not be so accessible to all general practitioners. People were asked to report any involvement in any child protection case over a recent four week period. The question asked people to include 'any action or judgement, however small (regarding) new referrals

and ongoing cases, suspected or confirmed'. The following Figure 4.2 shows
that, even with such a liberal definition of involvement, child protection is
peripheral to most people's experience. Over a quarter of respondents had no
contact and 20% had under half a day during the four week period; at the
other extreme, 15% spent over 3 days per week on child protection.

Some respondents volunteered information on longer timescales than
those provided in the questionnaire; in that the information was unstructured
it can only be read impressionistically but it accentuates rather than conflicts
with the scaled answers. The only respondents who said they had never been
involved with any child deemed at risk of abuse were teachers; another eight
teachers and 13 general practitioners had encountered less than five in their
whole careers. On the other hand, some principal grade social workers and a
highly specialised paediatrician report handling several hundred cases in a year
while a police coordinator has some dealings with over 2000 per annum.

Figure 4.2: **Respondents' time expenditure on child protection cases in a
recent 4 week period**

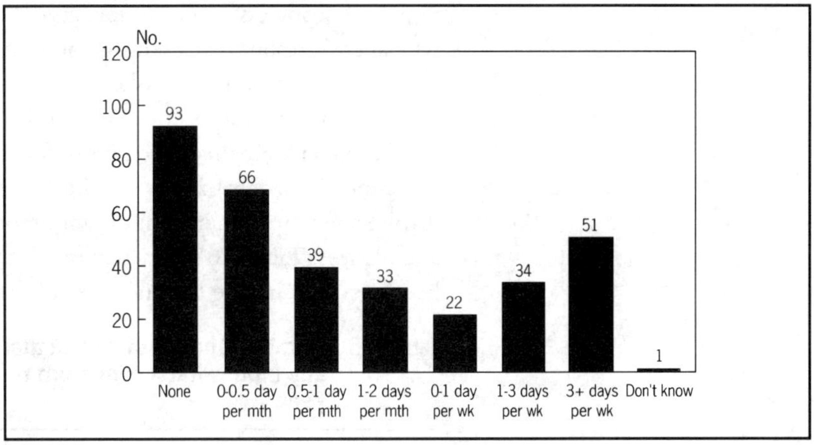

(N = 338)

The above data reveal the huge differences in people's experience and
exposure to the issue. As expected, the heaviest involvement (over 3 days per
week) is concentrated among staff in highly specialised units, mainly the
police units and social services or NSPCC specialist child protection teams.
No doubt, many of these are full-time commitments to child protection and
in these units all ranks give the same amount of time to this work. Two
paediatricians and four health visitors also report spending over three days per
week on child protection but most paediatric staff cluster around either half a
day or two days per month and health visitors range widely from around a day
a month to around two days per week. Over half the teachers and 49% of
general practitioners report no contact in the period. Most of the social

workers do not work in exclusively child protection units and, as described in Chapter Three, some have functions even broader than general child care but, across their ranks, social workers comprise nearly half the total of those working over one day per week on child protection. Thus, the data give clear evidence of Social Services' Departments' onerous commitment to this particular responsibility among their many functions. Even outside the specialist child protection units, senior staff are more heavily involved in child protection than their subordinates, being disproportionately represented among those spending over one day per month on this aspect of their job.

Almost 78% of the sample feel the above time distribution to be normal for themselves. A minority (11%) who feel they had done less than usual outweigh the few who had done more and this tendency is confirmed by the greater number who assert a drop rather than a spate in referrals. The commonest reason for experiencing a lull in referrals is personal, the workers' change of post rather than any fall-off in demand. Half the respondents also feel this work pattern is typical of their peers but significant fractions feel they do either less or more than their peers; 15% did not know. Overall, the responses from every profession give a fair measure of confidence in the typicality of respondents' engagement in child protection work.

Respondents were also asked to report the number of cases they had any dealings with over a recent two month period and in the past year. Only a small number were unable to give definite answers. The 'two month' answers are generally consonant with the 'year' answers and, as expected, case involvements are generally more numerous than child protection conference attendances. Table 4.6 shows that much the largest block of respondents have been involved in one to nine cases in the year.

Table 4.6   **Number of potential or actual child protection cases receiving any input whatsoever from respondents during the preceding year**

Number of cases	Respondents	
	N	%
None	60	17.9
1–9	148	44.2
10–39	59	17.6
40+	59	17.6
Don't know	9	2.7
Total	335	100.0

However, the range across the professions is wide, with two social work managers, one police constable and a paediatrician recording over 60 cases in two months; only 22 (6%) respondents were involved in over 60 cases in the year and these are all police constables or senior ranks from the other professions. Only 3% of social workers, 9% of health visitors, one police officer and one paediatric junior doctor had no cases. By contrast, teachers in particular (44%) and general practitioners (23%) are markedly more likely to report no involvement in the whole year. Figure 4.3 compares the involvement of the four most heavily involved professions (social workers, health visitors, police and paediatricians) with one another and with the mean. It confirms the very heavy involvement of the police and social workers, the former no doubt having generally shorter episodes than the latter.

Figure 4.3: **Percentages of potential or actual child protection cases receiving any input whatsoever from respondents during the preceding year, comparing the total sample with the four most heavily involved professions**

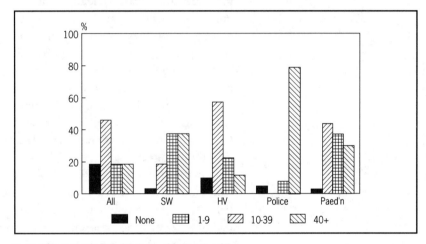

N: All 326; SWs 59; HVs 67; Police 20; Paed'ns 37.

As implied above, the number of involvements in cases was significantly affected by rank. Main grade staff are the most likely to report no involvement but this group is heavily weighted by the presence of the infrequently involved general practitioners and teachers. When they are excluded, only 10 main grade workers are uninvolved. In percentage terms, supervisory ranks strongly outweigh maingrade staff once 10 cases per annum are reached. However, very few head teachers report that many encounters and 10% have had no involvement. There was no statistically significant difference between the three core areas, although there was a tendency for Metborough staff to record no cases more often City.

Summary and conclusions

The personal variables of age, gender, child-rearing experience and educational level show no significant variations across the three main research localities; neither are there inter-area differences in respondents' exposure to child protection work.

There are, however, some interprofessional differences on both the personal and experiential factors, the latter being more expected than the former. Health visitors are significantly older than the other professions and paediatric staff show the clearest differentiation of rank by age. The relationship between age and length of service suggests that health visitors and social workers tend to be recruited at a more mature age than any of the other professions but thereafter there is more rapid overall movement between agencies and through the ranks among the social workers. However, the data suggests that this is not a marked feature of the social services departments in the three study areas. Some of the mobility patterns, for instance among the police and general practitioners and the various paediatric ranks, are as expected but others are less obvious. The gender structure of the professions is as expected, with a clear majority of male doctors and almost all health visitors being women. Men are disproportionately represented in the senior ranks. Educational levels vary markedly between the professions.

As expected, there are great differences between the professions in their experience of child protection work and their exposure to specific training. On average, staff in senior ranks spend more of their time on child protection than do maingrade staff.

This description of respondents indicates that locality will not be a confounding variable in subsequent analyses by either personal or experiential factors. However, both gender and educational level are thoroughly confounded with occupation. It may also prove difficult to distinguish the experiential factors from professional identity.

Social workers, the police and paediatricians clearly emerge as the core professions in the child protection network, most heavily involved on all measures. The police have an exceptionally heavy throughput of cases. Health visitors occupy an intermediate position but general practitioners and teachers are rarely involved. While the data belies the stereotype of social workers as younger than other professionals their more rapid turnover in post may encourage that impression. Moreover, their role as key workers in the child protection system means that they are frequently negotiating with senior staff in other agencies whose subordinates remain less involved. It is well recognised that a number of status factors – professional prestige, rank, educational level, frequently male gender – combine in the person of the consultant paediatrician. If these also coincide with greater age and local experience, power imbalances are likely in the network.

Chapter 5

Professionals' experience & perceptions of interdisciplinary post-qualifying training in child protection & their philosophical approach to cases

Introduction

Specialised training is generally deemed important to skilled assessment and intervention in child abuse cases, and to the appropriate use of colleagues in other professions and agencies. The limitations of knowledge and skill in many aspects of child protection have been a recurring concern in official inquiries into child abuse tragedies as well as in the professional literature. Yet the previous chapter noted that only half the sample had even a minimal amount of such training since qualification. Several questions explored this issue more fully. They covered the quantity of any such training, whether any of it was interdisciplinary and if so with which professions it was shared, and lastly how respondents evaluated it. Another series of questions explored respondents' orientation towards families, whether initially based on an accepting and supportive approach or a more direct focus on parental responsibility for their child's situation.

Training

Amount of relevant post-qualifying training

This training is very limited and unevenly spread across the professions. The basic questions posited a minimal definition of post-qualifying training, encompassing 'any formal training apart from supervised experience' and including attendance at any courses, seminars or training conferences relating to child protection. Respondents' experience of preliminary vocational courses was not investigated. No doubt, the curriculum of the different professions would give varied attention to the topic but no others would be likely to feature it more strongly that social work courses. Since the majority of the sample (70%) entered service before 1980 and another 18% before 1985 and Pietroni (1991) recently reported that it is not a major factor in basic social work training, it is unlikely that child abuse and particularly its later manifestations (eg sexual abuse) would have featured prominently in the basic training of this sample.

Over 40% of the sample have no in-service training in any aspect of child protection or child abuse and only a fifth have received over two weeks in total. It appears from this data that, despite the apparently endless round of training events and professional conferences, there is massive ground still to cover. There is no indication that people who qualified longer ago and might have had least about child protection in their original training have been specifically targeted for in-service training on the topic. The Department of Health's introduction of the Training Support Grant in 1989 is a welcome step, partly used for in-service training of social workers and partly for interdisciplinary training at a local level. However, the most striking finding is the shortfall that remains.

Figure 5.1: **Respondents' experience of any post-qualifying training in child protection**

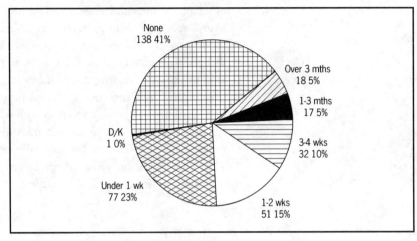

(N = 334).

As figure 5.2 displays, different professions have widely varied exposure to such training. Around 90% of social workers and health visitors of all ranks have had some such experience but four fifths of the class teachers have had

Figure 5.2: **An interprofessional comparison of respondents' experience of post-qualifying training in child protection**

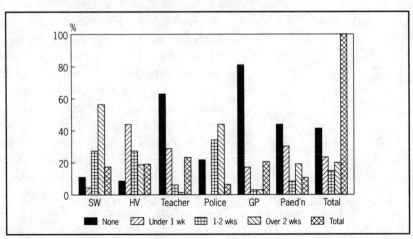

(N = 333).

none. Less than two thirds of the senior and head teachers and only a fifth of general practitioners have had any. Over three quarters of the police constables and paediatric consultants have had some but fewer of the senior police ranks and few of the paediatric junior doctors have attended any such training event.

The core professions of social work, police and paediatric consultants are the most likely to have received over two weeks training but more of this has been on a single-disciplinary basis for the paediatricians. Social workers most frequently (57%) have received more than two weeks and also comprise 11 of the 18 (5%) people with over three months specialised training. Further details, including the distribution of training by profession and rank, can be found in Tables 5.6 and 5.7 in the statistical appendix. The spread across the areas is even and there is no statistically significant difference between the age groups, though there is a slight tendency for more of those in mid-career to have some training.

Experience of interdisciplinary training in child protection

Just over half the sample (51%), the large majority of those with any specific training and all of those with more than a week, have shared some on an interdisciplinary basis. Only 26 (8.5%) have received such training exclusively on a single-disciplinary basis, teachers and general practitioners being the most numerous in this small cohort. However, as Figure 5.3 shows, this interdisciplinary training was less than a week in aggregate for nearly all of them. Further details of the amount of training by profession and rank can be found in Tables 5.8 and 5.9 in the statistical appendix.

Figure 5.3: **Respondents' experience of interdisciplinary post-qualifying training in child protection**

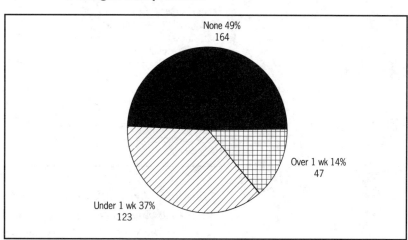

(N = 334).

The spectrum of professions involved varies widely. A few (19) have shared training with only one other group but the majority in steadily diminishing numbers have trained with additional groups, 10% of respondents having shared with at least seven other disciplines and two respondents with 14 disciplines. Table 5.1 shows the range identified by the whole sample as co-trainees at any time. Four professional groups dominate the list and these were all involved in the research programme. Almost one third of respondents have trained alongside social workers and the police, and nearly a quarter with health visitors and teachers. Contrary to impressions gained from the literature review about the salience of different professions, it is notable that school nurses and education welfare officers are more frequently encountered in interdisciplinary training than paediatricians or general practitioners. Very few respondents have trained with solicitors, accident and emergency staff, psychologists or psychiatrists. The low rate of encounter with some professions may simply reflect their scarcity, despite the critically important roles that, for instance, paediatricians and solicitors play in certain cases. However, specialist police are also very scarce but their duties are heavily concentrated on child protection and there are many more reports of training shared with them. It seems that different professions invest interdisciplinary training on this topic with varying degrees of priority.

Table 5.1   **Number of respondents who have trained with specific other professions in post-qualifying training in child protection**

Professions trained with:	Respondents: N (N = 339)	Percent
Police	110	32.4
Social Workers	106	31.3
Health Visitors	84	24.8
Teachers	78	23.0
School Nurses	64	18.9
Educational Welfare Officers	62	18.3
Paediatricians	44	13.0
General Practitioners	40	11.8
Solicitors	36	10.6
Psychologists	36	10.6
Accident & Emergency Doctors	15	4.4
Psychiatrists	13	3.8
Police Surgeons	2	0.6
Miscellaneous	28	8.3

Interprofessional differences in experience of interdisciplinary training

The following data compare in more detail the very different experiences of those with any interdisciplinary training. As noted above, most people who have had any relevant training have had at least part of it on an interdisciplinary basis. It is therefore not surprising that the interdisciplinary experience also varies across the professions in a broadly similar way to the overall pattern of post-qualifying training. Like the vast majority of general practitioners, three quarters of teachers have no interdisciplinary training and only one of either profession has had over a week. In contrast, 82% of the social workers have attended some interdisciplinary event and almost half have shared more than one week. Nearly two thirds of the health visitors have some such experience and nearly a fifth have over a week. Among the police, equal numbers have no such training, less than and more than a week. Over half the paediatric respondents have had none and only three, that is one sixth of the consultants, have had over a week. Besides the varying numbers from each profession, the interdisciplinary breadth also varies markedly; on average the paediatricians have trained with 5.1 other professions but the police with only 2.8 others.

Table 5.2 summarises the interdisciplinary pattern, including only those respondents with relevant experience. The commonest co-trainees are social workers, health visitors and police. However, sub-sets of fellow trainees become more evident thereafter, broadly differentiating the doctors from the others, except that almost all the paediatricians concerned have trained with social workers and the police and most of them also with health visitors. General practitioners name paediatricians as their most frequent colleagues and other doctors relatively more often than most other respondents. School nurses and education welfare officers are rarely named by the doctors or the police but are mid-range to all other groups.

Other variables

The amount of interdisciplinary training varies by rank, with senior ranks generally having had more. All nurse managers have attended and, in marked contrast to class teachers, nearly half the school heads. 80% of paediatric house officers have no such experience and only three consultants (17%) have over a week. Not surprisingly, working in specialised settings and more case experience correlate with one another and both correlate with more training. It had seemed possible that the youngest respondents would have had least opportunity for interprofessional training and that the oldest might have been professionally established before interdisciplinary training in this field became an issue. In fact, neither age nor length of service shows any relationship across the whole population. In age terms, it would seem that the greater involvement of the relatively young main grade social workers and police officers balances the conspicuous absence of class teachers and junior paediatric staff. On the whole, the mix of co-trainees is very similar across the

Table 5.2 **Patterns of interdisciplinary post-qualifying training in child protection**

Respondent / Co-Trainee	SW (N = 51)		HV (N = 57)		Teachers (N = 21)		Police (N = 15)		GP (N = 8)		Paed'n (N = 18)		Total (N = 170)	
	N	%	N	%	N	%	N	%	N	%	N	%	N	%
Police	43	84.3	43	75.4	5	23.8	–	–	2	25.0	17	94.4	110	64.7
Social Workers	–	–	55	96.5	14	17.3	15	100.0	5	62.5	17	94.4	106	62.4
Health Visitors	46	90.2	–	–	12	57.1	7	46.7	5	62.5	14	77.8	84	49.4
Teachers	23	45.1	39	68.4	–	–	4	26.7	1	12.5	11	61.1	78	45.9
School Nurses	16	31.4	32	56.1	9	42.9	3	20.0	0	0.0	4	22.2	64	37.6
Educ Welfare Officers	23	45.1	21	36.8	10	47.6	4	26.7	0	0.0	4	22.2	62	36.5
General Practitioners*	10	19.6	16	28.1	4	19.0	2	13.3	–	–	10	55.6	42	24.7
Paediatricians	13	25.5	18	31.6	2	9.5	3	20.0	8	100.0	–	–	44	25.9
Solicitors	11	21.6	12	21.1	2	9.5	2	13.3	1	12.5	8	44.4	36	21.2
Psychologists	7	13.7	9	5.7	8	38.0	3	20.0	4	20.0	7	38.9	36	21.2
A&E doctors	3	5.9	6	10.5	1	4.8	0	–	4	50.0	1	5.6	15	8.8
Psychiatrists	1	2.0	3	5.3	2	9.5	2	13.3	0	0.0	5	27.7	13	7.6
Total														
% of trained population	30.0		33.5		12.4		8.8		4.7		10.6		100.0	
% of professional pop'n	82.3		83.8		25.9		68.2		12.1		45.0		50.1	

Note: *GPs here include 2 police surgeons

areas although a markedly smaller proportion of City staff have shared training with paediatric staff or general practitioners.

Respondents' perceptions of the value of interdisciplinary training

Respondents with any such experience were invited to evaluate it. Almost everyone gives a generally favourable judgment; 40% found it 'very helpful' and only 4% reported unfavourably. As so few people give a negative view, it is only possible to explore any differences between those who find it very rather than merely helpful. Profession, rank and degree of specialisation are all statistically significant but in no apparently consistent way. Those teachers who have attended appear most appreciative and social workers least so; the latter make most of the few positively critical comments. The very small number of general practitioners also make a relatively guarded response. Maingrade staff are least likely to rate the experience very helpful but so are those in specialist units. One might suppose that the teachers are particularly appreciative because they have so little experience of the child protection system and are grateful for any opportunity to learn more about it, whereas the more heavily involved social workers and specialist staff find the available training too basic. But general practitioners also have a low involvement in the system and a different mechanism has to be postulated for their relative lack of appreciation, maybe one where very limited involvement in cases combines with low interest in the functioning of the network.

An unstructured question sought respondents' views of the particular value the training had for them and the chief purposes that emerged are presented in Table 5.3. These values, except 'other positive' which were too varied to analyse, were cross-tabulated by a range of personal and occupational factors. Most results were not statistically significant but the following appear noteworthy. Health visitors and the police most frequently value learning others' roles and skills whereas paediatricians score this less; teachers very rarely mention this factor but value new knowledge most. Social workers least often claim to have gained new knowledge. The newest arrivals in the area also value learning their colleagues' roles and skills more than better-established colleagues or principal grade staff, and so do those working in partly specialised settings. It seems reasonable to hypothesise that new arrivals would need to learn the contributions of their colleagues but one would also have expected them to rate the opportunity for personal contacts highly. That the most and least specialised workers have less interest in this factor than the partial specialists may reflect, on the one hand, a thoroughly established knowledge of colleagues' contributions and, on the other, no particular need to mesh their own work closely with others'. Women are significantly more likely than men to assert that understanding others' roles and skills and acquiring new knowledge are valuable, but it is probable that

Table 5.3 **The main values ascribed to interdisciplinary post-qualifying training expressed by 170 respondents with such experience**

Ascribed values	Respondents (N = 170)	
	N	%
Understanding diverse roles/skills	65	38.2
Personal contacts	45	26.5
New knowledge about child protection/child abuse	39	22.9
Understanding processes of cooperation	33	19.4
Other positive values	26	15.3
Miscellaneous negative values	20	11.8

gender is here confounded with profession.

Social workers appear more likely than others to value such training to improve their understanding of the processes of cooperation. Appreciation of this factor peaks among respondents handling a medium number of cases and in the supervisory grade. Health visitors stand out as valuing the opportunity for developing more personal contacts, as do those handling a moderate number of cases. One might speculate that the newest entrants would have particularly grasped this opportunity to create links but it is the oldest group who value this most highly; given the predominance of health visitors among the latter, this may simply reflect a confounding of age and profession.

Two remarks under 'other positive values' were eye-catching; one health visitor made the guarded comment that 'It's all I've had up to now' while a teacher gave the heartfelt cry that their own input reminds 'people used to dealing with child abuse that it's TERRIBLE'.

While only a small number asserted any negative values at all, there were occasional complaints about too basic a content or that it was too diffuse in its effort to meet disparate needs. A few complained of poor organisation. Comments arise in the literature on child protection training suggesting that the style can sometimes be more experiential than all the participants are prepared to accept or unwantedly self-revealing but only one person complained along such lines. Proportionately, social workers give most critical responses; other factors did not vary perceptibly. A few social workers and a health visitor complained that other professionals failed to turn up. One social worker made the delicious comment that 'in principle' the interdisciplinary training 'was workable but the participants spoiled things'.

Respondents' orientation to cases

Debate has continued through the years in diverse professional literatures about the most fruitful way to engage families suspected of maltreatment in the helping process. In essence, the question is whether it is more productve to start in a supportive and basically non-challenging relationship with the parents that begins with the shared proposition than 'something is wrong' but does not threaten their fragile self-esteem by an immediate and direct focus on the alleged abusive event or situation, or whether such an immediate focus on the situation and the question of their responsibility for it is an essential reality base for subsequent therapeutic work with them, or whether it is possible to combine the two elements in one person's role. Some writers argue that the dichotomy is false but others emphasise the difficulty of seeking to combine the two elements, particularly in the early stages of work with families. The more clarificatory and psychologically confrontational approach appears to be the dominant ideology in the practice literature on child protection in recent years, although its proponents emphasise that it is honest, therapeutic and productive rather than punitive or antagonistic to parents. It has not been clear how far this ideology is accepted by social work practitioners but it is evident that a number resist it for various reasons, ranging from the pragmatic fact that they are charged with attempting to work with many clients who deny problems in their child rearing behaviour to the belief that many such problems derive from socioeconomic disadvantage and are better ameliorated by relieving the material stresses than by pathologising and further stressing the parents. The ideologies of the different professions in the network and their roles may be expected to lead them towards one or other basic stance.

Another reason for not confronting parents that is from time to time attributed to all the professions is the workers' own denial of the abuse, either psychological avoidance of an intolerable recognition about family life and/ or avoidance of the unwelcome tasks that will ensue. All these issues are more fully discussed in Hallett and Birchall (1992, chapter 10) and a new and sceptical contribution regarding the feasibility of combining the roles has just been published by a judge with a social work background (Hall 1992).

It seems probable that differences in this basic orientation might lead practitioners to disagree about practical interventions. Several questions therefore explored aspects of professionals' general theoretical approach to cases of alleged child abuse, as to whether children are better protected and families most effectively helped to overcome such problems by any approach which is initially accepting or one that is more confrontational from the outset. After noting that professional opinions differ, a key question was worded as follows:

a   Some argue the necessity of 'accepting' and 'supporting' a family in the early stages, without undermining them by making them face that they are personally responsible for their child's distressed condition.

b   Others argue that the parents' acknowledgement of responsibility for their child's distressed condition is essential before therapy can be successfully started.

Which viewpoint do you generally support?
Please tick (a) or (b).

Although the possibility of mixed views was recognised and further explored in subsequent questions and the researcher was prepared to code 'Both' or 'Don't know' answers, such easy ambiguity was discouraged by first presenting the simple dichotomy. It was satisfying that most people answered such a difficult question but, as Figure 5.4 below shows, opinions proved to be divided and uncertain. Less than half the sample supported (b) but they were a majority of those with clear views. Another 30% firmly favoured (a) and another 10%, predominantly social workers, teachers and health visitors, replied 'Both'. Another 10% replied 'Don't know' or failed to respond, mainly the inexperienced teachers and general practitioners.

Figure 5.4:   **Respondents' orientation to the start of therapy: professional acceptance or parental responsibility first?**

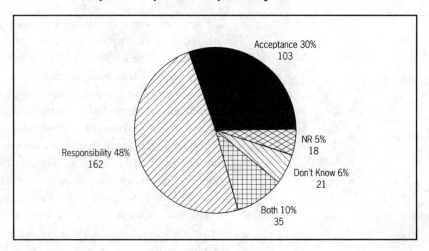

A clear majority (61%) of the substantive opinions favour starting with parental recognition of responsibility. Social workers have the clearest views on this question, with nearly three quarters favouring 'responsibility first' and only 8% taking the other stance but a larger proportion than any other profession (16%) asserting that both approaches could be combined. When the ambiguous minority of responses are excluded, 90% of social workers and a smaller majority of police (65%) and general practitioners (61%) choose 'responsibility first'. Paediatricians, health visitors and teachers held either view in almost equal numbers. Full details are available in the statistical appendix, Table 5.10. There are no perceptible differences of attitude between different areas; neither do rank or experience, whether of cases or of case conferences, show any significant correlations. Personal variables of age, gender and the experience of bringing up children also appear irrelevant. However, those with over two weeks' relevant post-qualifying training are least likely to choose 'acceptance first', but this factor is probably confounded with profession. Oddly, the amount of interdisciplinary training shows no correlation. It is difficult to interpret this pattern of responses.

Recent influential social work writings (eg Dale et al 1986, DH 1988) may have established an orthodoxy within the social work profession in favour of the more direct approach and this position may be prominent in the curriculum of extended child protection training, which has already been shown to be concentrated among social workers. It is not surprising that the same basic stance prevails among police officers, given their role as custodians of law and order and personal responsibility. Why general practitioners and paediatricians should show significantly different orientations from one another and in the directions indicated is far from obvious. Given divided medical opinions, one might expect that paediatricians' greater experience of child protection and greater interaction with social workers and the police would lead them to have attitudes more akin to the latter while general practitioners might retain a more sickness-oriented and determinist attitude to parental failures (which might lead them to the 'accepting' approach).

People were then asked to explore in more detail a number of possible reasons for holding mixed views. While 218 respondents were sufficiently committed to one or other approach not to answer the question, a quarter of the sample did explore these. Of these 87, over 60% reason that all cases are different and require diverse approaches; while eight of the 10 paediatricians replying to this question say this, only just over half the social workers and general practitioners take this view. Another quarter, more frequently health visitors, say parental recognition of responsibility is often a developing process rather than a starting point. Six percent of the sample answered 'Don't know' or gave responses that were classified as 'too difficult to know which view is better'.

However, ambivalence and ambiguity become more evident among larger numbers in subsequent responses. Whether the case falls into the category of physical, sexual or emotional abuse, neglect or grave concern (categories as used in *Working Together 1988* and adopted in most local guidelines) influences the choice between confrontation and support in the opinion of 43% of respondents. Although many others express ambivalence only 17% deem the case category irrelevant. Those who had previously defined themselves as 'accepters' are much more likely than the others to consider case category pertinent. The attempt to investigate differential attitudes to different categories was only partially successful due to some problems with the question sequence, which had originally been intended for use in interview and proved difficult to simplify sufficiently for the questionnaire, but it does suggest some convergence between the two groups in favour of the direct approach in cases of physical and sexual abuse. There is certainly a greater diversity of responses both within and between the two attitudinal groups regarding their preferred approach to other categories. This finding is not surprising, given the greater professional uncertainty about what degree of poor parenting constitutes emotional abuse or neglect and whether the parents should be held responsible in any case.

Over half the sample think the severity of the case determines the approach although a third deem this irrelevant. As Table 5.4 shows, inter-professional differences are particularly marked on this point. The most involved professions are least likely to consider this pertinent, but significant numbers of them (a third of social workers and half the paediatricians and police) would take it into account. On the other hand, large majorities of the teachers and general practitioners who gave a clear opinion consider case severity to be an important factor. Two thirds of health visitors agreed. 58% of the total sample also thought the approach would depend on an assessment of the 'total situation' but 19% disagreed. The same divisions of opinion, although less marked, apply to this topic as to the relevance of case severity. When the 'Don't knows' are excluded, accepters are four and three times respectively more likely than confronters to consider both points relevant. Whereas the more training people have, the less do they deem case category or the severity factor relevant, training bears no relationship to the relevance of the assessment factor in determining people's approach, except insofar as no training is prevalent among the 'don't knows'.

These patterns of response are not the same as those to the initial question about basic approaches. While social workers' attitudes remain consistently 'harder' than others' and paediatric staff remain consistently divided, a proportion of general practitioners appear to have switched from a preference for a direct approach to one determined by the severity of the case or by the total assessment. It may be that the further probing questions led some respondents to more differentiated images of the possible cases. However, the evident preference of the less involved professions for a more discriminating approach contrasts significantly with the more routinely (but not universally) direct approaches of the core professions.

It may be that the divergence of attitudes arises as much from the generally different points of entry of the front line and the core investigative pro-fessions. In answering the questions, the two groups may have visualised a different spectrum or staging of cases or some may also have manifested

Table 5.4 **An interprofessional comparison of positive responses to the relevance of case severity or of the total family situation in determining an initial approach of professional acceptance or parental responsibility first**

Profession	SW		HV		Teacher		Police		GP		Paed'n		Row Total	
	N	%	N	%	N	%	N	%	N	%	N	%	N	%
Severity (N = 271)	21	36.2	38	65.5	45	80.4	10	52.6	38	79.2	16	50.0	168	62.0
Assessment (N = 246)	35	61.4	44	80.0	40	87.0	12	75.0	33	80.5	20	64.5	184	74.8

Note: Percentages do not sum to 100. Each line represents a different question.

conflicting attitudes regarding similar cases. The long vignette findings reported in Chapter Nine reveal, inter alia, that the professions vary in complex ways on a number of their intervention choices. One particularly clear difference is teachers' greater hesitancy in labelling Jane as 'suspected abuse' and their preference for handling the situation themselves at stage one.

Approximately two thirds of those who think the total situation affects the choice between accepting and confrontational approaches answered a question relating to the factors they deeemed relevant. Among these 115 respondents, social workers and health visitors responded most frequently and put forward the largest number of considerations; general practitioners and the police gave fewest responses. The factors could be broadly classified into:

Overall assessment;

Specific risk factors in the family's past and present;

Protective factors around the family;

Vulnerability factors around the family;

Intervention factors.

In addition, only two respondents (social workers) noted the need to consider ethnic or cultural factors.

Such headings give little impression of the particular ideas people put forward. They are varied and too scattered to subject the data to statistical testing but they are summarised in Table 5.5 below. Interpretations must therefore be tentative but the following may be worthy of comment. Particular clusters may be suggestive of the different preoccupations and emphases that different groups will bring to bear in the child protection conference. Many people comment on the importance of a supportive marriage or wider family and friendship network. As befits their role, social workers and paediatricians seem more likely than other professionals to identify a careful appraisal of the abusive event(s) as an essential part of risk assessment. In line with their earlier responses, social workers most often identify the need for parental acknowledgement that there is a problem. Along with health visitors, they note the need for parental cooperation in any intervention. Social workers and health visitors are also most likely to identify various health factors and socioeconomic stresses. The possibly damaging outcomes of intervention are most often mentioned by general practitioners but some police respondents are also alert to the problems of delivering a helpful service to the child.

Table 5.5 **Factors deemed relevant to choosing between professional acceptance or parental responsibility first approaches to families, crosstabulated by profession**

Factor	SW (N = 26)	HV (N = 26)	Teacher (N = 29)	Police (N = 5)	GP (N = 16)	Paed'n (N = 14)	Total (N = 15)
Assessment:							
Unspecified	2		4		1	1	6
Professionally skilled						1	3
Of parents' capacity to change	3	2	1			1	7
Risks:							
Family history	2	4	4	1	3	3	17
Abuse details	9	5	4	1	2	4	25
Safety		1	5		1		7
Protective factors:							
Parents acknowledge problem	7	2	1		4	2	16
Parent willing to protect					1		2
Family supports	8	5	7	1	5	6	34
Bonds with child	1	2	1	3	3	1	8
Vulnerability factors:							
General	4		2	1	1	2	10
Health	1	5			1		7
Emotional/Mental health	4	5	1		3	1	14
Intelligence	3	6			2	2	13
Socio-economic	6	10	2	2	5	2	27
Intervention factors:							
Skills/resources	2	6	3	4		1	16
Iatrogenic risks	2	2	2	1	4		9
Legal grounds	4						6
Parents' cooperation:	11	8	2		2	3	26
'Start at client's pace'		2	2			1	5
Total	69	65	41	14	38	31	258

Summary and conclusions

This chapter has explored respondents' experience of in-service training in child protection and their basic approach to child protection cases. Only around half the sample have any such training and very few have more than a fortnight. The large majority of social workers and health visitors have some but very few teachers or general practitioners. Most of the police and the paediatric consultants have but few junior doctors. For most respondents, some of this training has been on an interdisciplinary basis but the breadth of the interprofessional mix varies widely across the respondent professions and the experience is very narrow for most. Most of the participants find such training a positive experience but there is some evidence that different professions seek and value different aspects of it, with teachers most appreciative of new knowledge, health visitors and the police highlighting the importance of discovering others' roles and skills and social workers most concerned about developing cooperative processes.

The limited scope and spread of relevant training and the evidently varying commitment of the different professions to interdisciplinary training is a matter for concern. Given the extensive literature and other findings in this research regarding difficulties in collaboration between doctors and others and given the crucial role of paediatricians in the network, the omission of interdisciplinary training for junior doctors seems particularly regrettable.

There is controversy in the literature about whether it is more effective to start interventions with parents on the basis of supportive acceptance or an approach which stresses parental acceptance of responsibility or whether it is possible to combine them. It seems possible that such a philosophical rift would cause conflict between workers. A number of questions explored this topic and produced complex results. The initial answer from the majority favoured the more direct approach, particularly among social workers and the police. General practitioners intially appeared more aligned with this view but paediatricians shared more mixed attitudes with the other professions. Apparently, neither experience in child protection nor interdisciplinary training affected the attitude but extended training did correlate with the more confrontational approach.

Further exploration of the topic suggested that many people in all professions had complex and probably confused attitudes, admitting a variety of contingent factors which would affect their choice of approach. However, this probing then showed that paediatricians were rather more akin to the other core professions in tending to dismiss the relevance of contingent factors. On the other hand, like the other front line professions, general practitioners showed more inclination to let situational factors affect their choice. This attitudinal difference between the core and front line professions is far from clear cut. More child protection training was correlated with less attention to contingent factors but is probably confounded with the variable of professional identity.

There is greater homogeneity between and within the professions in advocating a confrontational approach to cases of sexual abuse but overall there were marked variations which appeared to derive from individual as well as professional values. These widespread differences of opinion are only partly influenced by professional orientation or role. They must remain powerful dynamics, whether hidden or openly-debated, in the activities of any group of workers within one agency or across different disciplines.

Chapter 6

Perceptions of local coordination

Introduction

Two separate aspects of coordination of child protection work are considered in this chapter, the first being broadly about procedural matters and the second investigating respondents' perceptions of other factors they might deem conducive or inimical to cooperation over individual cases in this field.

The three long-established mechanisms of coordination at the level of day-to-day case practice are:

local procedural guidelines;

use of the child protection register;

use of child protection conferences.

Since *Working Together* (1988), there has also been formal recognition of the core group as a distinct entity and more widespread use of core group meetings. However, these have been subsumed under the general heading of case conferences in this report; they were only occasionally separately identified by respondents, probably because of the relative novelty of the term at the time of data collection. There is also the prosaic but, according to many Inquiry reports, frequently neglected machinery of recording oral communications on case files and confirming them in writing, whether they be face-to-face or telephone conversations and whether exchanges of information or action proposals. The procedural guidelines issued by the Area Child Protection Committees in the three main research areas all draw attention to the importance of careful recording of information gathered and confirmation of oral exchanges.

Professional perceptions of these mechanisms were investigated in this research programme. The use of written communications and of the local guidelines is discussed in this chapter. Respondents' perceptions and use of child protection registers are explored in the context of the long vignettes (Chapter Ten) and material about child protection conferences follows in the next chapter. Respondents' views of the effectiveness of local coordination of case interventions are reported in the second half of this chapter; these cover general ratings and also views regarding particular behaviours, attitudes and logistical facilitators and obstacles to success in the initial investigative phase of intervention and in ongoing work with the case.

Recording practices

In view of the recurring concerns referred to above regarding missing or ambiguous records of communications between workers, four similar questions were asked about this topic. The basic question was broadly worded and covered internal and inter-agency communications:

> *Messages are frequently passed between workers face-to-face or by phone.*
> *They can cover exchanges of information, requests or referrals. They may*
> *or may not be recorded, either by an entry in the case notes or a letter or*
> *memo.*

> *When you . . . make any oral exchange regarding a child protection case,*
> *do you write it down?*
> *Does the (other) confirm . . . in writing?*

Answers were sought on a four-point scale: 'almost always', 'often', 'sometimes', 'almost never'. (It seemed redundant to include 'always' and 'never' on this scale or any other in this research programme). The topics were applicable to 315–320 (93–95%) respondents, the remainder being excluded because of noninvolvement, and the effective response rate from these subjects was over 95% for each subquestion. It may be speculated that the few who failed to reply or did not know how to answer would not have given more positive responses. Given that the question encompassed something as basic as a note in one's own case record, the responses seem disturbing. Only 60% almost always note their internal messages and nearly a quarter scored 'sometimes' or less. Moreover, exchanges with external

Figure 6.1: **Recording behaviour regarding internal and external communications in child protection cases**

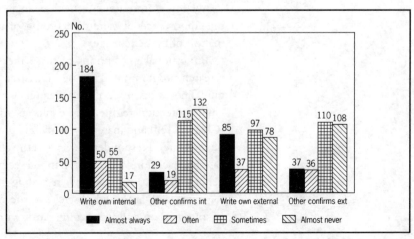

(N = 289 - 306)

agencies are recorded even less frequently; only 29% almost always write those down and nearly as many almost never do. When it comes to receiving a confirmatory note from the other party, fewer than one in six say this happens often or more in the case of communications within their own agency. The report regarding dealings with external agencies is not much better; only a quarter say outside agencies often or almost always write to confirm and rather more say they almost never do. Figure 6.1 displays the data, which is summarised in Table 6.12 in the statistical appendix. Despite the shortfall in all these reports of recording behaviour, it is evident that people have a more favourable perception of their own performance than of others. Therefore, at least as regards exchanging notes if not as regards their own case records, the answers must err on the side of optimism.

Differences in the practices of the various professions were obvious and are compared in Figure 6.2 below.

Figure 6.2: **An interprofessional comparison of respondents' recording behaviour and expectations of others regarding internal and external communications in child protection cases**

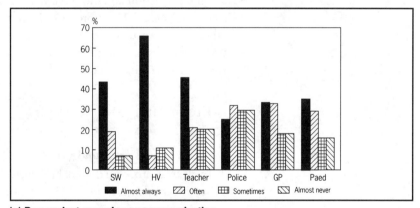

(a) Respondent records own communication

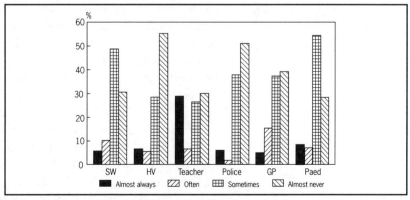

(b) Respondent expects to receive confirmation from others
(N = 289-306)

Given their centrality in the network and their vulnerability, it is surprising and worrying that less than two thirds of social workers are careful to record their intra-agency messages often or almost always. Health visitors appear to be the most punctilious in recording internal messages, with 90% scoring 'almost always', and they are also most likely to record others' messages. Around half of all the other professions scored 'almost always' about internal messages. However, no social workers or health visitors report almost never making such notes but a few of all the others did. General practitioners are least prone to record internal communications but the police stand out from everyone else with not one respondent claiming to record often or more regarding either their own or other agencies' messages. While teachers report a low level of recording their own communications, they most often said they receive written confirmations. In contrast, health visitors say they receive few confirmations.

Respondents' locality is an insignificant variable in all these aspects of recording practice. Few experience and training factors appear to have any bearing; those that do are contrary to expectations, with more specialisation in child protection and more relevant training correlating with less frequent recording oneself. The more specialised staff also have more sceptical views of others' confirmatory behaviour. Supervisors are significantly more likely than principals to note their own internal messages but no other significant variations by rank are reported.

Procedural guidelines

Access to local procedural guidelines

In all areas procedural guidelines were circulated to individual work units either direct by the Area Child Protection Committee or by the constituent agencies. However, there was some question in one authority as to whether, due to financing problems, every general practice had actually received a copy. Just under two thirds of the sample reported owning a personal copy of the child protection guidelines. As Table 6.1 shows, almost every social worker and between 70–80% of health visitors, paediatricians and police have their own copy whereas under half the general practitioners and even fewer teachers have.

There are 51 people, that is around 60% of those teachers, general practitioners and (junior) paediatric staff who do not own a copy themselves, who have never seen the guidelines; a third of the non-owners say the guidelines are easily accessible but 15% say they are 'elsewhere', sometimes entailing a visit to the local social services department. Full details can be found in Table 6.2 and in Table 6.14 in the statistical appendix. Greater experience of child protection training correlates significantly with owner-

Table 6.1 Interprofessional comparison of rates of ownership of the Area Child Protection Committee's procedural guidelines

Respondent	SW (N = 62)		HV (N = 68)		Teacher (N = 76)		Police (N = 22)		GP (N = 58)		Paed'n (N = 39)		Total (N = 325)	
Own guidelines	N	%	N	%	N	%	N	%	N	%	N	%	N	%
No	2	3.2	13	19.1	47	61.8	6	27.3	31	53.4	11	28.2	110	33.8
Yes	59	96.7	55	80.9	29	38.2	16	72.7	26	46.6	28	71.8	214	66.2

Table 6.2 Interprofessional comparison of respondents' access to the Area Child Protection Committee's procedural guidelines

Profession	SW (N = 62)		HV (N = 68)		Teacher (N = 76)		Police (N = 22)		GP (N = 58)		Paed'n (N = 39)		Total (N = 325)	
Where	N	%	N	%	N	%	N	%	N	%	N	%	N	%
Never seen them	0	0.0%	1	7.7%	26	59.1%	0	0.0%	18	60.0%	7	63.6%	52	49.1%
Same building/same floor of large building	2	100.0%	8	61.5%	15	34.1%	3	50.0%	7	23.3%	2	18.2%	37	34.9%
Elsewhere	0	0.0%	3	23.1%	3	6.8%	3	50.0%	5	16.7%	2	18.2%	16	15.1%
Don't know	0	0.0%	1	7.7%	0	0.0%	0	0.0%	0	0.0%	0	0.0%	1	0.9%
Total	2	1.9%	13	12.3%	44	41.5%	6	5.7%	30	28.3%	11	10.4%	106	100.0%

ship of the procedures – a factor that may have been confounded with the owners' professional identity or an independent correlate. People may either have heard about them in training or their presence at training events may reflect the value they place upon interprofessional cooperation and their prior acceptance of the relevance of the procedures. There was little variation between areas; City respondents, however, are least likely never to have seen them but most likely to say they are in some other establishment, which may suggest that more staff are coping with the heavier local caseload with more adverse resources.

Use of guidelines

There are no simple patterns of usage of the guidelines. Some commented that the procedures are engraved on their memory so they do not need to check them; others (13%) cannot remember when they last had occasion to refer to them. It was to be expected from their degree of involvement in child protection that social workers are much the most likely to have used the guidelines very recently, a quarter within the previous 24 hours and over half within the past week; only 5% have not referred to them in the last 6 months. Just under a quarter of health visitors and police but only a handful of general practitioners have looked at the procedures within the week. A third of general practitioners say they have never used them but another third have used them within the year. Whereas a third of head teachers have referred to them within the month, 80% of class teachers never have. The frequency of use among paediatric staff is scattered but a quarter have never used them. Fuller details are in Tables 6.15 to 6.16c in the statistical appendix. As expected in the light of their more frequent involvement in different cases, managerial grades in most services refer to them more frequently than individual field workers and first line managers predominate. More inter-disciplinary training correlates with greater usage and this remains true even when social workers are excluded. Whether this signifies that more training simply correlates with more case involvement or that it also encourages a greater respect for the guidelines is unclear.

Attitudes to guidelines

Nearly two thirds of respondents say the guidelines are helpful in clarifying their own part in child protection procedures and only 8% disagree but a significant number (29%) do not know. A similar pattern emerges as to whether the guidelines help people to understand others' roles but there are slightly fewer negatives, more than a third are agnostic and nearly 10% non-respondents. There are no significant differences of attitude between the three core areas but again more training correlates with a higher valuation.

There are evident attitudinal variations between the professions (see Table 6.3 below). Social workers overwhelmingly (97%) feel the procedures governing their own work are helpful and none gave a negative answer; 85% of health visitors agree but 10% are unsure. The great majority of these two professions and of the police also find the guidelines helpful in dealing with others' roles. In contrast, substantial minorities of some professions have a negative view. Even among the other two core professions, a quarter of the police and 40% of consultant paediatricians find the guidelines relating to their own role unhelpful. So do nearly a tenth of general practitioners. This could be either because they occupy roles with a high degree of autonomy and relative freedom from or resistance to written instruction about the handling of cases in general or because of the specific content of the child protection procedures. 18% of the paediatricians are equally sceptical about the guidelines' value in helping them to understand others' roles. It is disconcerting that well over a quarter of the senior house officers and head

Table 6.3   **A comparison of different professions' opinions of the helpfulness of procedural guidelines**

Profession	Guildelines helpful		Guidelines unhelpful		Don't know		TOTAL	
	N	%	N	%	N	%	N	%
Social workers:								
Own role:	59	96.7	0	00.0	2	3.3	61	18.9
Others' role:	48	87.3	1	1.8	6	10.9	55	17.9
Health visitors:								
Own role:	57	85.1	3	4.5	7	10.4	67	20.8
Others' role:	52	80.0	4	6.2	9	13.8	65	25.1
Teachers:								
Own role:	30	39.5	2	2.6	44	57.9	76	23.6
Others' role:	26	35.6	1	1.4	46	63.0	73	23.7
Police:								
Own role:	15	68.2	5	22.7	2	9.1	22	6.8
Others' role:	19	86.4	1	4.5	2	9.1	22	7.1
Gen Practitioners:								
Own role:	23	40.4	5	8.8	29	50.9	57	17.7
Others' role:	20	35.7	3	5.4	33	58.9	56	18.2
Paediatricians:								
Own role:	19	48.7	10	25.6	10	25.6	39	12.1
Others' role:	20	54.1	5	13.5	12	32.4	37	12.0
Total:								
Own role:	203	63.0	25	7.8	94	29.2	322	100.0
Others' role:	185	60.1	15	4.9	108	35.1	308	100.0

(Own role: N = 322; Others' role: N = 309)

teachers do not know about the relevance of the procedures to their own or others' roles. However, given their low involvement in child protection work, it is not surprising that very few class teachers and less than half the general practitioners know whether the procedures are helpful on either their own or others' score; between them, they comprise over 75% of the 'don't knows'.

The poor rate of ownership and knowledge of the guidelines among class teachers and senior house officers raises the question of how much they need to be involved in their current rank. Is it sufficient that they refer all cases of concern to their superiors and thereafter work, if at all, under their instruction? There are indications in the vignette data (Chapter Ten) that they and others would appreciate their greater involvement in the system. The question of how they learn to collaborate is also raised in Chapter Five, in relation to the junior doctors.

Compliance with guidelines

People were asked on a four-point scale from 'almost always' to 'almost never' whether they themselves and all others could fully adhere to their part in the guidelines; as before it seemed pointless to offer 'always' and 'never' for such a question. It is a matter of concern but not surprising that almost half the respondents say they do not almost always fully adhere to the procedures. Inquiry Reports and official inspections (DH SSI 1990a–j, 1991) indicate frequent omissions or failures to comply fully with official procedures; sometimes the official reports acknowledge that overstrained resources

Figure 6.3: **A comparison of professionals' perceptions of their own and other members of the child protection network's compliance with the Area Child Protection Committee's procedural guidelines**

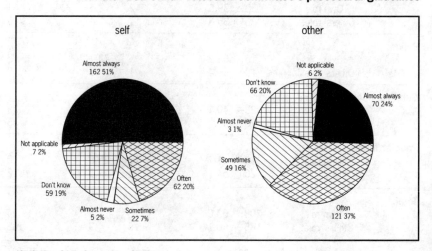

(Self: N = 317; Other: N = 315)

contribute to the lapses and recurring items in the professional press give a compelling picture of chronic overload. In this context, it is more surprising to find that as many as 51% of respondents claim that they (and their subordinates if they have any) can almost always comply and only five say almost never; almost another fifth felt they often can; however, nearly as many say they do not know. Given the reported shortfalls in recording and the poorly informed responses to questions about criteria for case conferences (Chapter Seven), it seems probable that people's self-reported full compliance is over-optimistic and possibly ill-informed. Figure 6.3 compares people's responses about their own compliance with their perceptions of others' and, as with the data about recording practices, shows a significantly greater scepticism about colleagues' performance than their own.

These perceptions vary noticeably between the professions and are compared in Figures 6.4(a) and 6.4(b) below. Over 75% of health visitors and police but fewer (69%) social workers claim they almost always comply with the guidelines. One social worker dared to assert almost never, as did two teachers and two general practitioners; they were all in City. Less than half the paediatricians think they comply almost always; while they and general practitioners are most prone to respond 'often', the latter along with teachers most frequently score 'don't know'. As regards respondents' views of other members of the network, around 40% of police and health visitors see their colleagues as almost always compliant. General practitioners are the most sceptical on this point. Perhaps realistically in view of their position in the network, social workers are most likely to score their colleagues' performance as either often (53%) or sometimes (20%) compliant; few think others almost always follow the guidelines and they are least likely to say they do not know about others' compliance. Of the core professions, paediatricians most often do not know. People in City are most doubtful of their colleagues' capacity to follow the guidelines.

Reasons for non-compliance

As already noted, around half the sample claim they almost always totally follow the guidelines themselves but rather fewer believe their colleagues do. The 151 respondents who confessed their own imperfections and 203 sceptical observers of others were offered a list of possible reasons for non-compliance. A number of 'other' answers have been recoded into the categories offered but the category 'value conflicts' in Table 6.4 below was added because it seemed conceptually valuable although rarely used; it may be that more would have responded thus if the option had been offered. It seemed likely that respondents who perceive themselves and others as failing to follow the guidelines fully on a significant number of occasions might identify different explanations from those who believe the rules were almost

Figure 6.4: **An interprofessional comparison of respondents' view of their own and others' compliance with the Area Child Protection Committee's procedural guidelines**

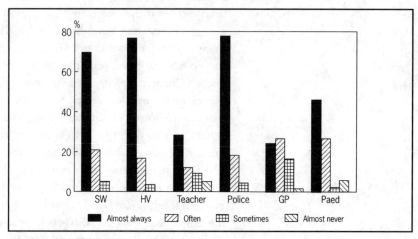

(a) Respondents' views of own compliance

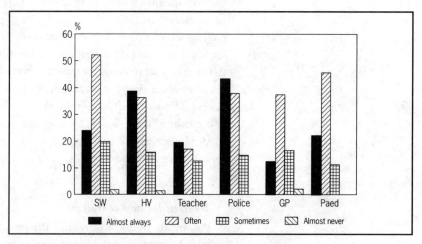

(b) Respondents' views of others' compliance

(N = 317, 307)

Notes: Non-substantive responses are not displayed in these barcharts, so the percentages for each profession do not sum to 100%. The significant excluded groups are (a) 42 teachers and 27 GPs (51.9% and 40.9% of the populations respectively: (b) 46 teachers and 29 GPs (56.8% and 43.9% of the populations respectively

Table 6.4 **Reasons for partial compliance with the guidelines ascribed by respondents to themselves and others**

Subject	Self (N = 151)		Others (N = 203)	
Reason	N	%	N	%
Not publicised	30	19.9	54	26.6
Not well-taught	26	17.2	55	27.1
Not well-enforced	24	15.9	54	26.6
Too busy	24	15.9	43	21.2
Unclear	24	15.9	30	14.8
Unrealistic	24	15.9	25	12.3
Not always relevant	23	15.2	21	10.3
Value conflict/distrust	4	2.6	0	0.0
Avoidance of the issue	0	0.0	10	4.9
Other reasons	6	6.7	12	6.0

always obeyed. The two sets of responses are therefore compared in the text although the table only displays the more numerous responses regarding the partially compliant.

Regarding the partially compliant, the rank ordering of problems is very similar in the columns for 'self' and 'others' but there are some suggestive differences. People are not only more inclined to ascribe nonconformity to others but they are also readier to identify more problems for others more often than for themselves. Fairly even numbers of respondents cite all the reasons in the top half of the table as applicable to themselves whereas noticeably higher numbers think issues about publicity and enforcement apply to others. It seems evident that a more vigorous publicity and training policy might be useful. This could be organised more easily than enforcement within all agencies, although it could only be a partial solution without the latter.

Interestingly, people see being 'too busy' as an explanation for others' non-compliance more often than for their own. However, in the middle of the list where issues of relevance and realism occur, people begin to perceive more problems for themselves than for others. Only two respondents identify confidentiality as an obstacle to cooperation, in both cases imputing it to others and not to themselves. It should be noted that this issue was not selected by any respondent as a barrier to attending case conferences (see Chapter Seven) but it was cited much more often when obstacles to coordination were directly explored (see Table 6.10 below).

When reasons were sought for the occasional lapses of the almost always conformist groups and compared with the above reasons for only partial compliance, some interesting differences emerged. Not surprisingly, fewer problems were attributed overall to those who almost always comply and a lack of publicity features much less prominently among them. However, while teaching and enforcement are still seen as significant issues, pressure of work is more often put forward as a reason for not following guidelines that they obviously know about and believe the others know about. Questions about the relevance or realism of the guidelines in all situations also come more to the fore, particularly to explain the respondent's own occasional defaults.

Although the majority of respondents claim a high degree of compliance, the table shows that a minority identify clear reasons for non-compliance. Almost every point shows significant interprofessional variations in reportage of self and perceptions of others, but these were mainly due to teachers' and general practitioners' numerous 'don't knows'. When responses were reduced simply to 'Yes' or 'No', a few factors remained significant. Whereas social workers and the police are least likely to say the guidelines are poorly publicised to themselves, 42% of general practitioners make this comment. In view of a considerable degree of dissatisfaction in the network about general practitioners' participation, there seem to be grounds for more energetic action to promulgate the procedures among them. Almost half the social workers blame others' non-compliance on poor enforcement. Although the 'other' responses are few and scattered, it is perhaps noteworthy that health visitors are most likely to impute 'avoidance' to medical colleagues and three of the four 'value conflicts' are responses from paediatric staff.

Rank affects a few perceptions; maingrade staff are the most likely to say the guidelines are not well publicised, and this remained significant even when general practitioners were excluded from the analysis. Principals are not only the most satisfied with publicity; they are also the least likely to say the guidelines are unrealistic for themselves or others. It is not unusual for senior ranks to have a more optimistic view of their organisational machinery than their subordinates have. However, other experience factors generally point the same way, with a lot of relevant practice apparently increasing people's confidence that the guidelines are realistic but not always sufficiently enforced. For instance, while those with a little interprofessional training or limited case experience are most prone to see the guidelines as unrealistic for themselves or others, more case involvement and training correlate with increased scepticism about their enforcement.

Importance of non-compliance

A few people appeared to consider a question about the importance of non-compliance irrelevant in the light of their earlier optimistic answers about their own and others' compliance but over half do think there are deviations from the guidelines by members of the child protection network.

Very few think these cause major problems but social workers are most concerned about this. In fact, over half the social workers deem the infractions moderately important and health visitors (37%) follow them in rating the deviations moderately serious or worse. Together, these two professions give 50% of the responses about major problems. It is interesting that the other two core professions, the police and paediatricians, express much less concern. Part of the explanation for this difference may lie in their more bounded and self-contained roles in handling a child protection case; less sustained dependence upon others' inputs goes along with that more limited role.

If that were an adequate explanation one would expect health visitors also to show less concern because they do not carry the full formal responsibility for child protection cases but they do, of course, have a responsibility for promoting the continuing welfare of children or families. They can be seen in that light as being as equally concerned and dependent on others' cooperation as social workers. However, that continuing responsibility is also shared to some extent with other front line professionals who express less concern about the deviations. Over half the teachers and a third of the general practitioners do not know whether non-compliance is an important issue. Another 30% of general practitioners are prepared to score the deviations as 'moderate' but it may be that these relatively high measures of unawareness and deviance together signify more about their general indifference to the procedures or perhaps to the issue of child protection rather than self-criticism. The overall findings of this study suggest that teachers and general practitioners are less troubled about maintaining the network than either social workers or health visitors.

Besides social workers' need for others' support in managing child protection cases, additional explanations seem necessary to account for this complex pattern of reactions. The health visiting service has emerged in many parts of the data as an important and extensive bridge between the core and frontline professions and, by implication, as gatekeepers for the families themselves. General practitioners and teachers have remained peripheral to the child protection system, despite their extensive contact with children. There are suggestions in the literature (Hallett and Birchall, Chapter 8), in their opinions on case conferences in Chapter Seven below and in Phase Three findings, that health visitors carry a lot of anxiety.

Social workers and health visitors, and indeed other nurses sometimes, may all perceive themselves as having responsibility without power. The continuing salience of institutionalised and ascribed status is illustrated by a recent informal communication to the author, quoting the following exchange on a paediatric ward:

Social worker: 'However did that baby get all those bruises on her face?'

Ward sister: 'Oh dear, don't let the consultant know I told you'.

Yet the social workers' capacity to fulfil a primary and legally mandated agency function and the health visitors' and nurses' capacity to carry out their professional functions to their own satisfaction require a sense of trust, mutual respect and collegiality in their dealings with doctors. They need the doctors' diagnostic expertise and willingness to step beyond the normal boundaries of confidentiality. This position of 'resource dependency' (Hallett and Birchall 1992, chapter 2) and unequal status is probably a potent source of anxiety for both the professions of health visiting and social work. If, as it appears, health visitors are even more anxious than social workers, this may relate to their more severe appraisal of cases, as indicated in Chapter Eight below, and the fact that they are also in a situation of resource dependency vis-a-vis the social workers.

Views of coordination regarding actual case interventions

Respondents were asked a series of questions about their perceptions of local coordination of case interventions in child protection, in the assessment phase and in ongoing case management. Opinions were also sought regarding facilitators and obstacles to success in both phases. Up to four free-ranging responses were coded regarding facilitators and a four-point scale was offered covering specific potential obstacles. In addition to these professional factors, another series of closed questions investigated people's perceptions of a number of practical and logistical issues which were deemed potentially relevant. Four-point scales were provided to discourage fence-sitting responses but a very small number of respondents insisted on asserting a mid-point either because their experience was too varied or because they felt the general level was middling. Quite large numbers have no relevant experience, particularly regarding continuing coordination, and significant numbers either have 'no opinion' or failed to answer, 9% regarding assessments and 13% regarding continuing work. The differential response patterns between the initial and continuing stages confirm the view that the active continuing network is smaller and responsibility is concentrated in fewer hands.

Given the cumulative total of nonsubstantive responses, it seems important to identify them more closely before evaluating the concrete answers. Nearly half the teachers claim no experience of either assessment or ongoing work and they comprise the bulk of those responses (55% and 65% respectively); only one and two social workers respectively say they have no experience of such work and the remainder of the responses are evenly scattered across the professions. Non-respondents and those with no opinion are also thinly scattered except for general practitioners' recurring tendency to contribute a disproportionate number (10% of their own number; 50% and 33% respectively of the responses) of the 'no replies'. There are some inter-area variations, with a quarter of Metborough respondents reporting no experience of the assessment stage compared with only 11% of the City sample; however, the gap narrows to 28% against 18% in the continuing phase of work. It seems likely that these differentials simply reflect the different child protection registration rates between the research areas.

Once the above processes had located the non-substantive responses, the remainder represent the views of informed respondents; around two thirds are reasonably satisfied with coordination in both assessment and ongoing work but only one fifth rate the former 'very well' handled. Overall, people are less satisfied with ongoing work; less than 10% give it top rating and over a quarter are positively dissatisfied. The results are summarised in Table 6.5 below.

No statistically significant relationships were found between respondents who give substantive evaluations of local coordination and other hypothetically relevant individual variables: profession, rank, length of time in the locality, degree of specialisation or experience of cases or conferences or inderdisciplinary training. It is interesting that none of these experience factors, including profession which has proved to be the main determinant of experience and correlate of most other observations, has any effect on the fairly high level of general satisfaction with case coordination. Metborough respondents are, however, the most likely to be highly satisfied with the coordination of assessments and City staff most dissatisfied. As this satisfaction rating correlates with the above finding about the smaller number of people involved, it may be that both stem from a more manageable amount of child

Table 6.5 **Respondents' opinions of the general level of coordination in case management in their area, at the assessment stage and in ongoing work**

Rating	Assessment phase (N = 254)		Ongoing Work (N = 224)	
	N	%	N	%
Very well	56	22.0	21	9.4
Rather well	154	60.6	140	62.5
Midpoint demanded	5	2.0	6	2.6
Rather badly	35	13.8	54	24.1
Very badly	4	1.6	3	1.3

Notes: No response: 12 and 20 respectively. No opinion and no experience 73 and 95 respectively.

protection work in Metborough and/or that the smaller network there inculcates closer working relationships.

Factors seen as enhancing coordination

There were 394 specific ideas from 192 respondents about factors that enhance coordination in assessment. Four fifths of the non–responses are from people who had already declared they had no experience or opinion or who think coordination works badly. The substantive responses therefore represent the positive opinions of the majority of informed participants. The most frequently recurring values in Table 6.6 below were crosstabulated with people's profession. Although most had cell counts too small to support a chi-square test, there were some tentative pointers. Health visitors and general practitioners are most likely to stress good communications between workers while social workers more frequently emphasise personal relationships. Both social workers and health visitors contribute a disproportionate number of the responses stressing mutual respect for professional functions, once again suggesting the real problem they have in asserting their roles in this network of unequal statuses. A wide range of 'other' comments were made, ranging

Table 6.6 **Respondents' opinions of the factors deemed conducive to coordination in case management at the assessment stage**

Factor	Number of Responses	Percent of respondents
Good communication among practitioners	71	37.0
Good managerial/policy coordination	44	22.9
Good personal relationships among practitioners	40	20.8
Shared goals among practitioners	33	17.2
Manageable size of local network	26	13.5
Mutual respect for professional functions	21	10.9
Role clarity	18	9.4
Appropriately skilled practitioners	18	9.4
Good use of case conferences	17	8.9
Appropriate training in co-working	17	8.9
Adherence to Guidelines	16	8.3
My (or my agency's) personal effort	8	4.2
Good organisational resources for co-working	6	3.1
Low turnover in local network	3	1.6
Keyworker's commitment	2	1.0
Generalisations re goodwill or good structures	32	16.7
Miscellaneous other	16	8.3
Total number of responses	394	100.0

Note: Percentages do not total 100% due to multiple responses.

from thorough consultation in the formulation of the guidelines so that staff feel a sense of 'ownership', through a drive to share anxiety and responsibility in handling difficult work, to the feeling that coordination is led by particular individuals or agencies who might be described as 'product champions' or as 'reticulists' (Hallett and Birchall 1992, chapter 4).

Although the range of 'other' comments is wide, the table shows that they are relatively few. Thus, very few respondents highlight the value of the proactive role of any individual or profession or identify the 'key worker' as fulcrum; in fact, when identified, these product champions are located in diverse professions or subsets of agencies. This suggests that the key proactive role is not clearly imputed to social services staff although many responses throughout the study indicate that their importance is recognised. However, it is noteworthy that, across the two questions covering initial and continuing coordination, almost all the 20 people who claim that coordination rested on 'my (or my agency's) personal effort' are from social services and represent 32% of the social work population. Just one respondent commented appreciatively on a mechanism in a neighbouring authority that probably should have been called a 'strategy discussion', indicating that they convene an initial conference to allocate tasks and then reconvene to deliberate on the information gathered.

There were also 286 proposals regarding factors that supported continuing coordination. One fifth of responses relate to good communication between practitioners. Core group meetings come second, being mentioned by 27 respondents, but only five people mention review conferences. Good personal relationships and shared goals come high up the list and the majority of items follow in approximately the same order as in the table above. However, good coordination of policy and management is a much less prominent factor in ongoing collaboration, rating only ninth. Surprisingly, skilled practice does not feature in responses to the second question. Social workers are the most likely to identify the importance of shared goals and teachers particularly unlikely to.

For both assessment and ongoing work, these values were then collapsed into a short series and are displayed in Table 6.7 below. 'Adherence to guidelines' and 'managerial/policy coordination' were grouped into the 'policy, management and procedural' item; 'practitioners' roles, goals and skills' covers the fourth, sixth, seventh and eighth factors above; 'communication and relationships' includes the first, third, twelfth and fifteenth; the size of and turnover in the network and the provision of relevant training were all grouped into 'resources' along with the supply of material or administrative facilities for coordination. Where it was possible to discern the bias of the generalisations or the miscellaneous answers, they were allotted to one of the above categories but about 10% remained vague or unclassifiable and have been omitted from the table.

Table 6.7 **Broadly categorised factors deemed conducive to coordination in case management at the assessment stage and in ongoing work**

Factor	Assessment phase (N = 192)		Ongoing Work (N = 155)	
	N	%	N	%
Communication, meetings, relationships	145	75.5	120	77.4
Practitioners' roles, goals, skills	92	47.8	55	35.5
Policy, management and procedures	64	33.3	23	14.8
Resource factors	54	28.1	24	15.5
Total number of responses	355	100.0	222	100.0

Note: Percentages do not sum to 100% due to multiple responses.

There were many fewer responses regarding continuing work but the same broad factors appear in the same order as facilitators regarding both stages; however, there are some interesting comparisons. It is not unexpected that communication and relationship factors are most often mentioned in both phases, as successful communication is a sine qua non for the coordination of any activity. This question cannot show whether the lesser emphasis on professional practice factors reflects a moderate degree of satisfaction with one another's ongoing performance or whether people see the processes of coordination as separate from the content and quality of what each is contributing. However, further exploration of possible obstacles to coordination with closed choice questions (see Table 6.10 and discussion below) suggests that there are significant tensions around roles and skills. There is markedly less emphasis on policy and procedural issues or the various resource factors in relation to continuing coordination, and this may reflect the well known fact that interagency protocols, administrative support, training and other facilities have been largely invested in investigative processes rather than in supportive or therapeutic programmes. Since the question addressed beliefs about current realities, it is likely that the much smaller number of responses in relation to coordination of ongoing work and the different balance between the factors both reflect current habits of mind, which are heavily focused on investigation and assessment, rather than a critical appraisal of the ongoing needs of the children.

Interprofessional variations in choice of factors conducive to coordination

Most professional groups identify the factors in the same order as one another and this order remains consistent at both stages so the commentary will therefore generalise across both stages. Table 6.8 consolidates the results

Table 6.8 **Overall frequency of different professions' selection of broad factors conducive to coordination in assessments and ongoing work**

Profession / Factor	SW (N = 62)		HV (N = 68)		Teacher (N = 81)		Police (N = 22)		GP (N = 66)		Paed'n (N = 40)		Total (N = 339)	
	N	%	N	%	N	%	N	%	N	%	N	%	N	%
Communication	73	40.6%	71	50.4%	38	48.1%	21	46.7%	47	57.3%	15	30.0%	265	45.9%
Practitioners, roles, etc	55	30.6%	31	22.0%	22	27.8%	13	28.9%	9	11.0%	17	34.0%	147	25.5%
Policy, etc	29	16.1%	21	14.9%	15	19.0%	4	8.9%	7	8.5%	11	22.0%	87	15.1%
Resources	23	12.8%	18	12.8%	4	5.1%	7	15.6%	19	23.1%	7	14.0%	78	13.5%
Total No of responses	180	100.0%	141	100.0%	79	100.0%	45	100.0%	82	100.0%	50	100.0%	577	100.0%

in terms of that rank order. However, the groups vary markedly in the number of concerns they express. Overall, social workers make many more responses pro rata than other professions, twice as many as the doctors and three times as many as teachers. Generally, teachers give few responses. Health visitors and the police lie between. These results are congruent with social workers' function as key worker and the accumulating evidence of the slender involvement of teachers in the network. However, the marked contrast between the doctors' and social workers' overall rates of response reflects not only their different roles but also suggests that they may have different degrees of anxiety about and commitment to making the network work.

Despite the similarities in rank ordering of the factors, there are significant interprofessional differences in the frequency with which particular factors are highlighted by each profession and these differences are more clearly displayed by expressing the factors as percentages of the number of respondents in each group, as shown in Table 6.9 below. Communication factors emerge as more valuable to some professions than others, despite being top of every group's list. Around half the social workers, health visitors and police make propositions about the importance of communications, meetings and relationships. Of these social workers, a third mention more than one of these items. In contrast, few teachers mention them and rather few doctors. Paediatricians may generally only be involved in the initial diagnosis and are therefore understandably less interested in continuing communication. Given their continuing contact with children, one might have expected more interest from general practitioners and teachers in maintaining the supportive and observational network; however, their encounters with child protection cases prove to be so rare that this would have a lower priority in their overall conception of their own work. Practitioners' roles, goals and skills are rated

Table 6.9 **Broad factors selected as conducive to coordination in assessments and ongoing work, averaged across the two stages and expressed as percentages of the respondent professions**

Factor	SW (N = 62) %	HV (N = 68) %	Teacher (N = 81) %	Police (N = 22) %	GP (N = 66) %	Paed'n (N = 40) %	Total (N = 339) %
Communication, etc	58.9	52.2	23.5	47.7	35.6	18.8	45.9
Practitioner roles, etc	44.4	22.8	13.6	29.5	6.8	21.3	25.5
Policy, etc	23.4	15.4	9.3	9.1	5.3	13.8	15.1
Resources	18.5	13.2	4.9	15.9	14.4	8.8	13.5
Total number of responses	27.6	20.0	9.5	19.0	11.4	12.4	100.0

second in importance in both phases by every group except general practitioners; however, social workers mention them particularly frequently and general practitioners much less than others. Apart from teachers who may be insufficiently involved in the network to be immediately aware of the issue, paediatricians least often highlight the importance of the whole range of resource factors.

Other variables affecting choice of factors conducive to coordination

Greater experience, measured by the number of case and child protection conference involvements, and greater seniority broadly correlate with an increased identification of all factors. Also the more interprofessional training people have, the more they mention all the factors. However, length of career and of service in the locality shows no correlation with any factor. There were a few statistically significant results which appear to be merely quirks but there are some apparent trends. Not surprisingly, senior ranks tend to identify policy, procedural and management factors more often than other staff. People with a rather heavy involvement in cases (10–39 in the year) have most to say about the importance of all factors in continuing case management but people who have attended that number of conferences and encountered even more cases put forward most comments about policy and resource factors at the assessment stage. There are no inter-area variations.

The numbers are insufficient for more sophisticated analysis and the experiential factors obviously overlap considerably with one another and with professional identity without coinciding. It seems probable that greater exposure to the network heightens people's awareness of the importance of several factors to its effective functioning, regardless of their professional locus. However, the patterns of interdisciplinary training and of case involvement of different ranks cast a possible light on this intricate data. Specialist training is most prevalent in the middle rank. As regards case exposure, once teachers and general practitioners who form the largest proportion of uninvolved staff are excluded, the biggest single cohort in the sample are maingrade staff handling 1–9 cases in the year; next come maingrade staff handling 10–39 cases. Senior ranks feature disproportionately among those handling large numbers of cases but for most of them this contact will obviously be more distant. It may be that awareness of the importance of all the factors increases with deeper case involvement but that a greater preoccupation with procedural issues characterises the role and function of staff in the principal ranks.

Factors seen as obstacles to coordination

Professional obstacles

There was a series of scaled questions about possible obstacles, derived from issues identified in the literature review, but definite answers were sparse (approximately 50% about assessments and slightly fewer about continuing collaboration). It was therefore important to examine the large number of indefinite or non-responses and the relatively few answers to the 'unimportant' end of the scale before considering the value of the clear responses in order to establish whether the non-substantive responses suggested satisfaction with the system, boredom at a late stage in the questionnaire or non-involvement in the network. A very large proportion could be clearly accounted for by reference to responses to the initial general questions. Nearly all (around 90%) the hundred or so who failed to reply or to whom the questions were rated 'not applicable' had already declared themselves reasonably or very well-satisfied with coordination; seven eighths on average of around another 80 had already declared their inexperience or lack of opinion. The remainder who gave substantive responses therefore are more knowledgeable but also tend to be the more critical respondents.

There are evidently real strains around many of these topics, with large percentages of informed members of the network identifying several factors. The obstacles were identified in a similar order for both the assessment phase and regarding continuing collaboration, so responses regarding the assessment phase alone are summarised in Table 6.10 below. The only difference between the two phases is that 'incompatible methods' are mentioned as

Table 6.10 **Perceptions of obstacles to coordination of assessments**

Obstacle deemed important or rather important	Responses		Total no. of respondents	
	N	%	N	%
Different overall workload priorities	150	85.2	176	100
Conflicting values about goals of intervention	144	82.2	175	100
Different case evaluations	132	81.0	176	100
Insufficient knowledge of each others' roles and skills	130	73.9	168	100
Incompatible methods or timescales	123	73.2	163	100
Concerns about confidentiality	87	50.3	173	100
Occupational rivalries	55	32.5	169	100
Other	20	90.9	22	100

important problems in relation to ongoing cooperation more often than 'insufficient knowledge of each others' roles and skills'. There were also slightly more 'other' responses.

Differences in the different agencies' and professions' workload priorities are particularly prominent with almost equal numbers rating them 'important' and 'rather important', and one teacher mentions this point '+ + +' as a source of tension. Conflicting values and different case evaluations are mentioned nearly as often as workload priorities and around three quarters of respondents also identify mutual ignorance and incompatible methods. However, in contrast to workload priorities, these four factors are more often rated as important rather than very important.

It is interesting that, when given these closed questions about obstacles to collaboration, a significant number of people acknowledge confidentiality as an issue although it was hardly raised in response to earlier questions. Even so, it is less prominent than several other factors mentioned above. In assessment work, respondents are very evenly split as to whether it is a problem or not but fewer are concerned about it in relation to ongoing case management. Only a third say occupational rivalries are a significant issue in the assessment phase but another third say guardedly that they are 'rather unimportant'. The slightly smaller number (152) responding about ongoing work show a modest shift in their rating of such rivalries to a higher point on the scale, with only a quarter now deeming them 'unimportant' as an obstacle to continuing cooperation. Under 'other' factors, a small and mixed group of respondents complain of lack of relevant skills in a variety of other members of the network; another small number say various colleagues are difficult to locate. Responses which specifically mention time and resource shortages have been recoded into the next question regarding logistical obstacles.

Bearing in mind that, for the reasons previously discussed, the respondents to these questions are the more involved and critical members of the network, it seems worth looking at their views in rather more detail even though small cell sizes often rule out statistical testing. A few factors seem noteworthy. In confirmation of the interpretation offered earlier for general practitioners' and teachers' low interest in maintaining the network, people with little or no recent case involvement are the most likely to see conflicting workload priorities as an important obstacle to continuing collaboration. Confusingly, however, those with most interprofessional training are divided between thinking such priority conflicts are important and unimportant. Rivalries about occupational status and power appear to cause most concern to those with no interdisciplinary training, suggesting that such training is important to the resolution of process issues in cooperation.

In the assessment phase, interprofessional differences seem evident regarding the importance of awareness of each others' roles and skills; teachers and the police most frequently mark this as a problem, perhaps levelling up with the social workers and paediatricians who accented this topic in their open-ended replies to the previous question about facilitative factors. General practitioners reinforce the impression from the previous question that they are least concerned about this. With teachers, the latter are more likely to worry about confidentiality; no police officers deem this important and, interestingly, 80% of paediatric respondents consider it unimportant.

Few people identify 'other' problems but general practitioners most often volunteer comments about resource problems under this heading in both assessment and continuing collaboration, again responding in a way that reinforces their free form answers. It is difficult to deduce the reasons for this as each individual general practitioner meets very few cases. It may be that other medical problems appear far more pressing upon their attention because of the very rarity of their involvement in child protection but they are no more likely than other professions to raise the issue of conflicting priorities. It may be that they were feeling particularly disaffected at the time of the fieldwork; a number of them expressed deep concern about the implications of their new contract and its effect on their workload but in fact teachers, social workers and paediatricians were also showing similar perturbation about new legislation and government policies affecting their settings.

Practical obstacles

Whereas most responses to the free form question about facilitative factors concentrate on professional issues and rather few identify resource obstacles, when people were directly asked to consider such practical matters, they emerge very clearly. It seems as though workers in the different professions may be so inured to such shortfalls in practical arrangements that they are not on the top of their mind when reflecting on the job but this does not make them any less important and inhibiting to efficiency. The large majority of respondents, ranging from four fifths of social workers to half the teachers, think there are practical and logistical obstacles which make it 'extremely difficult' to keep in touch with other key professionals. Only 17% said 'No'. Teachers again contribute the bulk of the 'don't knows' and, when these are excluded, there are no statistically significant variations between professions in the proportions of 'Yes' and 'No' answers. This global question elicited no inter-area variations.

The 297 (88%) who responded positively to the general question were asked to indicate on four-point scales which of several factors appeared important to them, and the answers are summarised in Table 6.11. Given the high level at which the question was pitched – that people were responding about 'extreme difficulty' in keeping in touch with others in the network – the frequency of these responses reveals serious and widespread problems across all the professions and there are no signficant inter-area variations.

Table 6.11 **Summary of practical and logistical items rated as important or rather important obstacles to cooperation**

Obstacle deemed important or rather important	Responses (N = 297)	
	N	%
Other agencies' time	209	70.1
Own (or subordinates') time	207	69.7
Size of network	176	59.3
Staff movements	169	56.9
Secretarial support	140	47.1
Telephones	112	37.7
Other admin factors (specify)	43	14.5

Time factors, one's own and others', are clearly very important issues and both were rated at the top of the scale slightly more often than 'rather important'. Most other responses were more often deemed rather important. Maintaining contact with a large and changing network is a problem for many. Nearly half note the inadequacy of secretarial support and well over a third complain about access to telephones for this high priority work.

When these responses were analysed by profession, a few appeared to vary substantially although short cell counts on the 'unimportant' side of the scale precluded chi square tests in most cases. Concern about one's own time is very evenly distributed but teachers are the most likely and paediatricians the least likely to deem others' time an 'important' obstacle. However, one paediatrician remarked that 'a history of working well together – with increasing demands and falling resources – will not last'. Secretarial problems do not vary noticeably but status protects people from the mundane problem of access to telephones. The higher the respondents' rank the less aware they are of an issue which affects 55% of the sample. Few doctors find this a problem but over three quarters of health visitors note difficulties over telephones. In particular contrast to general practitioners, health visitors appear most troubled by staff movements and, like social workers, by the size of the network; this may well reflect their respective roles, with the general practitioners relying very much on health visitors to find and sustain the links with the rest of the network.

Summary and conclusions

This chapter has explored respondents' use of written communications in child protection, their access to, use and appreciation of the local procedural guidelines and their general views of the functioning of the local network. The general picture regarding recording gives grounds for concern. Many exchanges apparently go unrecorded even on people's own case notes. Athough they claim a better record than some agencies, it seems particularly disturbing that social workers, key workers in the whole network and repeatedly exposed to hostile media attention, should allow much information to go unrecorded and unconfirmed. The reasons for widespread failures in record-keeping deserve more detailed examination in their own right.

The above finding and data that emerge in other parts of the study suggest that the following claim, though modest, is over-optimistic. Only half the sample report that they fully adhere to the local child protection guidelines in all cases. Accessibility of the guidelines and knowledge of their contents varies widely; almost all social workers have their own copy and refer to it frequently but at the other extreme many general practitioners and teachers would not know where to find one. A significant minority believe they would have to go to another building or to the social services department to see a copy. Some professions find the procedures more helpful than others. A number of people in all professions doubt the relevance and realism of the guidelines either because of their own busyness or because cases vary in ways that procedures cannot encompass.

Social workers and health visitors are the most appreciative of the guidelines and make the most complaints about others' serious lapses. In contrast, paediatricians are the most sceptical about their value. General practitioners most often complain they have been poorly publicised while social workers more often believe they are poorly enforced in other agencies. The gap between doctors' views and those of social workers and health visitors suggests there is a power dynamic involved, with the former affording to be more indifferent to compliance and the latter more reliant on the procedures to induce cooperation. There are grounds for recommending more active promulgation of the guidelines but it is more difficult to resolve the problem of enforcement.

While the majority of informed respondents think interprofessional coordination works reasonably well, only a fifth believe it works very well in the assessment phase and over a quarter consider ongoing coordination is poor. Of the factors that are identified as conducive to case coordination, the most frequently mentioned are good communications and good relationships between practitioners and good policy coordination. Such observations are very unspecific and somewhat tautologous, but specific proposals were less frequent. Formal meetings – case conferences and core group meetings – are mentioned less often. Social workers' and health visitors' wide range of responses indicated most awareness of relevant issues and perhaps most interest in making the network function but the data suggest that teachers and doctors are less concerned. Informed respondents identified many real obstacles to cooperation, ranging from conflicting priorities in different agencies and other professional tensions to shortage of time. Keeping in touch with the numerous and frequently changing staff in the network is a greater problem for social workers and health visitors and this would appear to reflect the social worker's official responsibility as key worker and the role that health visitors actually occupy as a crucial link between the frontline agencies and the child protection services. A large number of main grade staff in these two less prestigious professions are handicapped by prosaic problems like shortage of secretarial support and telephones. It should be a matter of great concern that the key worker in particular is deprived of the tools for communication and recording.

Chapter 7

Experience and perception of child protection conferences

Introduction

Case conferences have been recognised as the cardinal formal mechanism for achieving interprofessional cooperation in the management of child abuse cases ever since the early 1970s. In fact, the use of interagency conferences for families in difficulty was recommended by the government several years earlier and such meetings were occasionally called in the 1950s by the then Children's Departments. Many official circulars and the two editions of the authoritative central government guidance, *Working Together* (1988 and 1991), have stressed the crucial importance of this mechanism. The professional literature has also generally endorsed their value and they have clearly become increasingly used but there have been occasional openly dissenting voices and other signs of subversive agendas. The topic is explored more fully in the literature review (Hallett and Birchall 1992, chapter 13) but the revision of *Working Together* in 1991 makes some updating necessary.

There has been some confusion about the nomenclature and the content of different meetings to discuss children's welfare but also about a proliferation of meetings with overlapping agendas which may lead staff to see them as an administrative chore rather than as an aid to good practice (FRG 1986). When such meetings are called formally to consider a suspected or actual case of child abuse and to reach certain decisions (eg regarding the need for registration) and recommendations for action, they are now specifically designated 'child protection conferences' to distinguish their purpose from any other discussions between workers about any case which might require interdisciplinary cooperation. They are also to be distinguished from the statutory review of a child being looked after under the Childen Act 1989, although the new guidance suggests that the two meetings may be combined so long as both purposes are fully met. Both editions of *Working Together* also mention 'strategy discussions' as a preliminary exchange by professionals regarding the information they hold and the way they might proceed with the first stages of an investigation of alleged abuse. Another concept of increasing prominence in the child protection field is the 'core group'. It is briefly acknowledged in both editions of *Working Together* as a formally identified body of professionals coordinated by the key worker, who will work with the case and report back to periodic review conferences. The fieldwork for this research was carried out before the latest guidance was issued and the data is sometimes written up below, for ease of reading, in terms of the conference or case conference but the whole context of the research and the specific questions limit the topic to child protection conferences or core group meetings.

Working Together (1991) says the child protection conference is

> *the prime forum for professionals and the family to share information and concerns, analyse and weigh up the level of risks to the children and make recommendations for action (p. 31).*

The guide continues that this conference

> *provides them with the opportunity to exchange information and plan together. The conference symbolises the inter-agency nature of assessment, treatment and the management of child protection. Throughout the child protection process, the work is conducted on an inter-agency basis and the conference is the prime forum . . . (p. 41).*

Its functions are to

> *share and evaluate the information gathered during the investigation, to make decisions about the level of risk to the child(ren), to decide on the need for registration and to make plans for the future. If a decision to register is made, it will be necessary to appoint a named key worker and make recommendations for a core group of professionals to carry out the inter-agency work (p. 42).*

The guide stresses that the only decision of the conference is about registration but indicates that the discussion and recording of a proposed plan of action is important to all concerned and that this would normally be the basis of a contract between the various professionals, their agencies and the family.

Attendance at child protection conferences

Numbers of conferences attended

Of the total sample, 266 (78%) respondents reported involvement in at least one possible child protection matter in the preceding year but just under two thirds have attended one or more case conferences or core group meetings in that period. The two types of meeting were not differentiated in the question as it was assumed that few people would have been involved in the latter and the primary research interest was in the degree of interprofessional cooperation rather than the precise designation of the forum. Table 7.1 summarises the range of attendances.

Table 7.1 **Number of child protection conferences and core group meetings attended by all respondents in the preceding year**

No. of conferences attended	N	Respondents %
Over 40	16	4.8
20–39	23	6.9
10–19	38	11.3
5–9	45	13.4
1–4	82	24.5
None	124	37.0
Don't know	7	2.1
Total	335	100.0

More than a third of the sample have attended no conferences in the period, a similar proportion have attended between one and nine such meetings but few have attended over 20 within the year. In the light of one general practitioner's response to another question about reasons for non-involvement in conferences in general, not just during this census period – 'My car broke down on the way' – it would have been interesting to ask at least the non-attenders how many they had ever attended.

Different professions have very different degrees of involvement. Approximately two thirds of teachers and general practitioners attended none in the surveyed period and only 5% and 6% respectively attended between five and nine conferences. Even though social workers, health visitors, police and paediatricians are more heavily involved, their attendance pattern is diverse. Social workers and the police are in the majority among those attending ten or more in the year while paediatric consultants are more likely to have attended up to nine conferences. These more heavily involved professions are compared against the average in Figure 7.1 below. The few social workers who had no attendances are staff with only peripheral involvement in child care and the absent paediatric staff are junior doctors.

It is not surprising that every individual working in largely or exclusively specialised child abuse units attended conferences in the preceding year but 28% of the 276 working in general settings have not. The more child protection training people have had, the more conferences they attend. As previously noted, such training and specialisation in child protection and profession are overlapping variables but the factors do not coincide completely. To the extent that more training may correlate independently with

Figure 7.1: **A comparison of frequency of child protection conference attendance in the last year among the four professions most frequently involved**

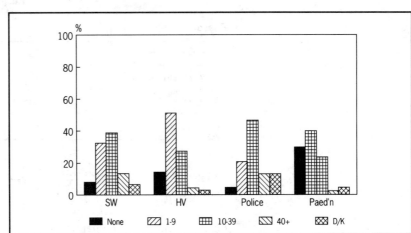

N = : SWs 62; HVs 68; Police 22; Paediatricians 40.

conference attendance, it is possible that training stimulates people's interest in conferences or vice versa. Social work team leaders and first line managers of health visitors dominate the small group who have attended more than 40 in the year. Principals from a wider range of agencies feature most often among the moderate attenders (five to 19) and, not surprisingly, main grade staff attend relatively few, only when directly involved with the particular case.

Reasons for non–attendance

Respondents who had attended none were asked to choose their main reason from a precoded list. In fact, a few respondents gave two reasons and, since there was no way of knowing which was the stronger, both have been scored. The total responses were therefore 160 reasons from 132 respondents, including a few excusing what they felt were their insufficient attendances. The most frequent reasons are that none were held involving any child in their domain or a belief that no conferences had been held in the area. Other significant categories comprised those who say it is not their role to attend and those who plead that time pressures prevent them. Interestingly, not one respondent chose confidentiality as a barrier. The following table summarises the main reasons as percentages of the relevant population only.

The main reasons cited were also examined for any relationships with respondents' profession, area and nature of work unit. It appears, as hypothesised, that the professions most likely not to have had any cases were teachers

Table 7.2 **Main reasons given by respondents for non-attendance at child protection conferences**

Reason	Respondents (N = 132)	
	No.	%
No case involvement known	78	59.1
Not important/not my job	39	29.6
Time barriers	23	17.4
Other reasons	20	15.2

and general practitioners. Most professions are aware that conferences occur in their area even if they are not involved. Teachers were the most likely to say that attendance was not their concern or to assert that no case conferences occurred in their catchment area. The first reason mainly comes from class teachers and reflects their customary duty to report and leave such matters to the head teacher but the second response from all teaching ranks adds to the sum of indications that teachers are the least aware of child protection issues. No significant variations occurred between areas as to level of awareness.

Timetabling conference attendances

Well over half those who are or feel they ought to be involved in case conferences find timing 'difficult' or 'extremely difficult' and less than 13% have 'no problem'. Because they had not perceived any occasion or role for themselves in case conferences, this question was deemed inapplicable to 15% of the sample, (42% of the non-attenders). The remainder are divided into attenders and potential attenders and compared in Figure 7.2. It can be seen that the percentages of the two groups who find timetabling case conferences either 'difficult' or 'possible' are similar but marked divergences exist at the extremes. About 15% of attenders say timing is 'no problem' compared with under 6% of potential attenders, while over 18% of the latter report 'extreme difficulty' compared with 11% of attenders. There is no significant difference between specialised and other work units in ranking the feasibility of fitting in conferences.

Over a third of general practitioners say timing presents extreme difficulties and another 40% say it is difficult. Similarly in a recent Scottish study (Bisset and Hunter 1992), 52% of those invited said they could not attend; they asked for more notice, more convenient timing and in some cases a fee. Although one of the respondents to the present study remarked that short notice gave them a problem in rearranging their surgeries, it seems reasonable to question whether at least those in group practices have greater difficulties

Figure 7.2: **How easy was it for relevant respondents to fit child protection conferences, etc., into their timetable**

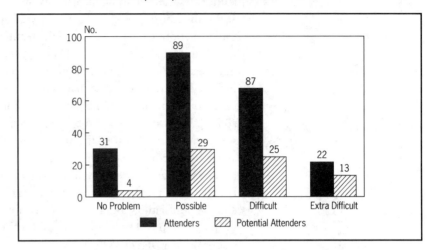

N = 209 attenders; 71 potential attenders; 52 not applicable; 3 non-respondents.

in arranging cover than several other professions. The turnover of children on the national register represents around one case per annum for the average general practitioner (DH 1991c, Gabe et al 1991) and their slight involvement is manifest from other data in this study. Only a fifth of social workers say timing is no problem and 40% of paediatricians and police say it is difficult. When the scale was reduced to 'possible/difficult' a number of other dimensions became evident and statistically significant. Staff of principal rank and those who handle most cases most frequently find timetabling difficult even though the burden of most frequent attendance falls most heavily on the intermediate rank. People with the most interdisciplinary training report least difficulty; this remains true even when social workers who most commonly have the most training were excluded, which would seem to signify a willingness among other professions with such training to give conferences a greater priority in their overall workload. The respondents' location is not a significant variable.

Seeking child protection conferences

Three questions sought to elicit respondents' awareness of local guidelines regarding the convening of conferences. The first was worded 'Please tell me if you can (in paraphrase) what are the criteria for holding an initial case conference'. The second asked whether criteria exist for subsequent conferences and the third sought a paraphrase of any such criteria. Only responses from the three main research territories have been included in this analysis because only their guidelines were obtained for comparison. Guidelines had lately been updated or were currently in process of revision in all three authorities, causing some uncertainty about the edition in widest circulation at the time of this fieldwork, but they all appear to be very similar in their categorisations of abuse: one used the term 'physical injury' where the others used 'physical abuse'; two put 'failure to thrive' in a separate category while one specified it as an aspect of 'neglect'; one stipulated 'physical neglect'; all included emotional and sexual abuse. The most difference lay in the last category; all mentioned 'the same household (as a registered child or known abuser)' but two used it as a sub-category of 'at risk' while another made it the sole premise; another used the *Working Together* (1988) phrase 'grave concern' as a sub-category.

The three areas reveal less differences in their definition of abuse categories than have been reported in the past (see Hallett and Birchall 1992, chapter 13) and the similarities should make it easier for mobile professionals to assimilate in new locations. However, thresholds of suspicion remain difficult to spell out – *Working Together* (1991) says

> *the starting point is that any person who has knowledge of or a suspicion that a child is suffering significant harm, or is at risk of significant harm, should refer their concern to one or more of the investigating agencies . . . It is essential that professionals . . . should be alert to the signs of child abuse . . . The balance needs to be struck between . . . protect(ing) the child from abuse . . . and the family from harm caused by unnecessary intervention (p. 27).*

All three local procedures made similar general remarks about individuals' need to report situations of concern but the further guidance was handled rather differently. All gave some guidance (but it varied) about recognition of suspicious situations; however, two said staff should consult a senior colleague before invoking the procedures while the third implied immediate referral to the social services department. Two stipulated that social workers would investigate the case. Two said any professional may request a conference but there were apparent divergences as to whether a conference would ensue. One categorically stated that 'arrangements for convening a conference should be started' upon first referral, another said one would be called in all cases which appeared to meet the criteria and the third said a social work principal would decide, giving reasons for any refusal. All said a conference should meet within five working days of referral although the official 1988 guidance said that timing would vary, sometimes after a strategy discussion, initial investigations and protective action had occurred and sometimes earlier to pool information and consider ways in which the case might be investigated. *Working Together* (1991) says that the initial conference should not 'result in premature and disorganised action' because it was convened too hastily but the pace should not slacken and the meeting should normally occur within eight working days of referral.

The questions about the procedures elicited a particularly high level of non-response and the responses obtained were generally limited. In order to be coded 'accurate', the following factors were looked for in accordance with the respondent's local guidelines: all case categories, individual professional power to seek a conference, time limits. It may be that people resisted a question that perhaps felt like an examination or that it was not expressed clearly enough to elicit all those factors. In fact, nobody gave an accurate answer to the question about registration criteria; many respondents made very general replies such as 'suspicion of child abuse' but a fair number stipulated all or most of the categories. A few specifically alluded to their individual professional power to request a child protection conference. Almost nobody specified any time scale as laid down in local guidelines. Just over half did not know whether any criteria were set for further conferences and only 27 (9%) answered accurately.

Teachers and others with little involvement in child protection were the most likely to say they did not know the criteria for convening an initial conference; health visitors and social workers gave the fewest poor answers. People in 'County' were better informed than other areas about follow-up conferences. Someone commented on the confusing terminology in the field: 'Review conferences may be called 'case discussions'; case conferences tend to have more weighty implications, e.g. new or continuing abuse'. The poor quality of nearly all responses was disturbing if the question did accurately tap the level of awareness of the circumstances in which individual professionals should activate and sometimes put pressure on the child protection system, as the answers to the next point do suggest.

The guidelines say that anyone in the professional population may initiate requests for conferences and there obviously could be more than one person proposing that a conference is desirable in any particular case. However, it is apparent that only a small percentage actually do so and almost 20% deemed themselves not relevant to this question. Among recent attenders, 42% answered 'almost never' and an equal number 'sometimes' seek the convening of conferences in which they are involved. Only 15% answered 'almost always' or 'often'. Nearly all the initiative appears to come from the social services department; around a third of social workers say they almost always propose the convening of conferences, compared with only six other respondents. They also dominate the 'often' category. It seems likely that the other professions pass on their concerns to social workers rather than explicitly suggest a conference and maybe a more informative question would have been to ask respondents how often they have referred cases to social workers that are then conferenced and, if not conferenced, whether they are satisfied with social services' handling. However, around half the health visitors and paediatricians sometimes initiate the request but 81% of general practitioners say they almost never do. Just four people who have not recently been present claim they almost always seek such conferences as they do attend; over 70% of those with no recent involvement or relevant training scored 'almost never'.

Once again, greater involvement in child abuse work or specific training all correlate with increased initiatives. Staff in the largely specialist units are more likely to request a conference than those in general occupations or those in exclusively child protection settings. This presumably coincides with the greater propensity of social workers and paediatricians, although not police officers, to initiate the suggestion of a conference. Not surprisingly, the most frequent attenders are the more frequent seekers of conferences. There is obviously an overlap between the factors of profession, extensive involvement in child protection and frequent attendance but it would seem probable that members of any profession who are frequently involved would see more utility in requesting a conference in cases of concern. Perhaps surprisingly but reassuringly, maingrade staff in the heavily involved professions are as likely to initiate a request for a conference as their supervisors or managers. It seemed possible that variations in the guidelines might be reflected in inter-area differences in the responses but there were none.

In summary, these questions indicate that many professionals appear to have only a vague grasp of this important aspect of the child protection machinery and rarely see themselves as initiators of conferences. There is some fairly widespread sense that a child whose well-being worries them might be subject to the procedures but there is less clarity about how to activate them. If everyone were clear that they should always tell the social services department and furthermore were satisfied that the latter would always act appropriately, this poor grasp of the procedures might be sufficient. However, there are indications in the literature, in other answers to this survey and in informal communications (including a number of pilot interviews) that other agencies are not always satisfied. In such cases, one would wish to see more of the front line professions confident of their right and duty to seek a child protection conference.

Attitudes to child protection conferences

Are conferences helpful to the child?

The question was addressed to everyone, not only those who see themselves as actual or potential attenders. As Figure 7.3 shows, most respondents believe conferences are generally helpful to the child and there were too few dissenters to test by profession. Recent attenders are markedly more often optimistic than non-attenders (80% compared with 47%)

Figure 7.3: **Are child protection conferences generally helpful to the child?**

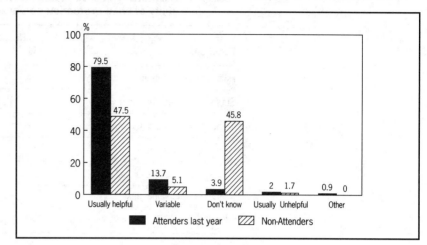

Attenders: N = 205; Non-attenders: N = 118.

although they are not uncritical; a significant number also consider the consequence for the child are variable. This research cannot identify whether optimists are more ready to attend or are convinced by their attendance. Only two respondents think conferences are usually unhelpful, both recent attenders, but many of the non-attenders had no opinion either way.

A minority of respondents (22%) volunteered additional opinions about the utility of conferences. They cannot be assumed to be representative of the sample as a whole and a much larger proportion (36%) gave specific critical comments than had given a negative overall appraisal. However, favourable comments predominate, with 46% considering they help case decision-making. The particular ideas respondents put forward are featured in Table 7.3.

There were a few particularly piquant remarks which will ring bells for some practitioners and illustrate points around which conflict may arise. One teacher said 'At best, the case conference leads to a coherent approach . . .; at worst to protecting your own backside', but another remarked with desperation that 'the more people there are involved, the more likely something will get done by somebody!'. One paediatrician highlighted 'too much concentration on police action' and another commented that paediatricians contribute as experts on children and not just child abuse. A social worker felt conferences were 'often fraught with the conflicting opinions of other professionals and the theoretical views of managers'. Only four respondents commented on conferences as a forum affected by professional anxieties, with two asserting that they helped to manage anxiety and two that they fostered it.

Table 7.3 **A summary of respondents' comments on the utility of child protection conferences**

Functions	Respondents	
	N	**%**
Help plan interventions	24	31.6
Success depends on other work	15	19.7
Trade in unsubstantiated opinions	12	15.8
Help case assessment	11	14.5
Foster/indulge professional anxiety	2	2.6
Manage professional anxiety	2	2.6
Other	10	13.2
Total	76	100.0

Attendance of parents or child

Partly in response to an adverse European Court ruling, there has been increasing interest among policy-makers and practitioners over the last few years in the issue of client participation in child protection conferences. Several recent Social Services Inspectorate reports have indicated that parental attendance is spreading (eg DH SSI 1990d,i). Nevertheless, the matter has proved controversial but, as discussed in the literature review, a number of local empirical studies of the development have given generally favourable reports (Hallett and Birchall 1992, chapter 13). At the time of the fieldwork, all the local guidelines stressed the importance of representing the parents' views and keeping them fully informed. However, only one authority's guidelines stipulated that parents should be invited and then only to part of the conference. The other areas expressly opposed the idea of parents' presence at initial conferences and all stated that the child's views should be presented by the social worker.

Respondents were asked whether they favoured clients' attendance and a comparison of the results from recent attenders and non-attenders regarding parents and children are displayed in Figures 7.4 and 7.5.

Four fifths think parents should be invited but the large majority only want their partial involvement. The favourable responses are very similar from both recent attenders and non-attenders but, as Figure 7.4 displays, the remainder diverge markedly. A significant minority (16%) of those with recent experience oppose parents' presence whereas a similar proportion of non-attenders simply do not know whether parents should be there. A majority (60%) also favour children's attendance, at least in part, if they are of age to understand, but only 7% desire their full attendance and a quarter do not think they should be there at all. Although the majority is smaller than that in favour of parents' involvement and twice as many were uncertain about children, the pattern of responses is very like the above. The results appear in Figure 7.5. Similar percentages of both recent attenders and non-attenders give positive

Figure 7.4: **Should parents be invited to child protection conferences? A comparison of professional views between recent attenders and non-attenders**

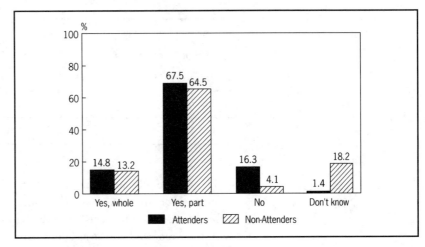

Recent Attenders: N = 209; Non-Attenders: N = 121.

Figure 7.5: **Should children of an age to understand be invited to child protection conferences? A comparison of professional views between recent attenders and non-attenders**

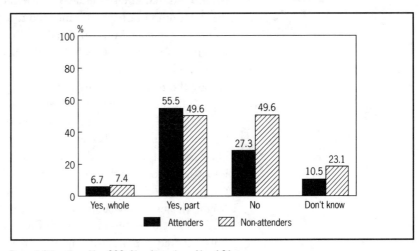

Recent Attenders: N = 209; Non-Attenders: N = 121.

responses but almost a third of the attenders oppose the child's presence while the non-attenders are more likely to have no opinion.

The following table summarises answers from the total sample to the two questions.

Table 7.4 **Respondents' Attitudes to Involvement of Parents and Children in Child Protection Conferences**

Respondents' attitude to:	Parents' attendance		Children's attendance	
	N	%	N	%
Yes, whole of the conference	48	14.4	23	6.9
Yes, part of the conference	219	65.8	177	53.2
No	39	11.7	83	24.9
Don't know	27	8.1	50	15.9
Total	333	100.0	333	100.0

Despite the substantial majorities in favour of at least partial attendance by parents and children, there are some noticeable variations in attitude between different groups. Full details are in the statistical appendix, Table 7.13. In line with their reported concerns about parents being drawn into incriminating admissions, the police in this study show the greatest opposition to family involvement at conferences; indeed, they are four times as likely as others to say 'No' to parents and nearly two thirds also oppose children's attendance. The opposite is true of social workers; twice the average number support parents' and children's full attendance and only one opposes parents being there. Health visitors are also inclined to support both parents' and children's attendance. General practitioners are almost as strongly in favour of parents' presence as social workers but paediatricians are more often in opposition about both. A convergence of views between the former and a divergence among the doctors is thought-provoking. Social workers have long upheld ideals of 'clients as fellow-citizens' and of 'empowerment' even though practice may somtimes fall short, whereas doctors are often portrayed as paternalist. It could be speculated that general practitioners are more libertarian in their values than the more bureaucratically structured groups or it may be, as some of the literature portrays, that they find it difficult to accept the primacy of the child's needs over their loyalties to the parents whereas paediatricians' child-centredness is strongly evident. It was interesting to receive a late communication from one authority that, since they had implemented a policy of parental involvement, general practitioners had begun to attend more frequently.

Senior staff are more hostile than maingrade practitioners to the attendance of either children or parents at case conferences. It is not simply a question of age or experience bringing more old-fashioned or guarded attitudes, as staff with over 10 recent attendances support parents' presence throughout more than those with less practice. On the other hand, those who spend most of their time on child abuse work are split between full supporters and outright opponents while people with no recent case or conference involvement take a middle of the road attitude by favouring parents' partial attendance. These experience factors do not apply to the question of children's presence. Joint training has no bearing on either issue and there are no inter-area variations. Staff who are parents themselves are divided as to whether children should be present but childless respondents are more inclined to say they 'don't know'. Once the 'don't knows', mainly teachers, were excluded, the following results are statistically significant. Women are more likely to favour the partial attendance of both children and parents. Except among general practitioners whose attitudes are more favourable regardless of their gender, men tend to oppose family involvement more often than the women. However, men are more divided between opposition and full involvement regarding parents. Male police and paediatricians voice the most opposition to the attendance of either parents or children.

Attitudes are more often favourable than hostile to the family's presence and this appears to represent a substantial movement of professional opinion in recent years but it should be recognised that many reservations remain. Some respondents fear that children will be less protected and one remarked that she was 'following the party line' in favour of parents' presence even though she had serious doubts. Others suspect that the system will be unmanageable; a paediatrician said

> *I give the diagnosis and all the time they need to question it; I've been assaulted three times . . . (the conference takes) much longer and I can't afford so much time.*

Several studies cited in the literature review suggest that familiarity with parental involvement leads professionals to value it positively (Hallett and Birchall 1992 chapter 13, Burns 1991), but these findings indicate that there is still considerable ground to cover before staff feel really confident in handling the processes or about outcomes for the child. Thoburn's research is an important contribution to the debate.

Potential sources of disagreement in case conferences

Four questions were asked on a four point scale 'Almost always; often; sometimes; almost never' about possible sources of disagreement between workers in conferences. They addressed the salience of different beliefs and values about child abuse matters and of role conflicts, and the possibility of conflicts over the literal interpretation of the guidelines or rigidities in their application. Approximately 250 respondents gave substantive answers to these questions but around a quarter of the sample said they did not know whether any of these issues mattered. In marked contrast to social workers and police who almost always have an opinion, teachers comprise around half the 'don't knows' on every factor. People with no relevant training and no experience (recently, at least) of cases or conferences are also, as one would expect, least able to express opinions. As Table 7.5 shows, most respondents do not see disagreements as a major problem. Only a minority deny conflict arises from these sources but most say it only occurs sometimes. However, over a third of those with definite opinions say there are frequent conflicts arising from practitioners' different beliefs and values and between 20 and 30% say the same regarding the other factors.

Table 7.5 **Respondents' perceptions of the frequency and source of conflicts in child protection conferences**

Conflict due to	Almost always		Often		Sometimes		Almost never		Don't know		Total	
	N	%	N	%	N	%	N	%	N	%	N	%
Roles	22	6.8	53	16.3	134	41.2	36	11.1	80	24.6	325	100
Beliefs and values	19	5.8	69	21.2	146	44.8	20	6.1	72	22.1	326	100
Literal interpretation of guidelines	6	1.9	47	14.6	144	44.6	47	14.6	79	24.5	323	100
Rigid application of guidelines	6	2.0	53	17.5	125	41.3	39	12.9	80	26.4	303	100

After the exclusion of the 'don't knows' described above, only a few inter-group differences were statistically significant on the full four-point scale but more became apparent when the values were collapsed to 'Often' and 'Seldom'. The two sets of results will therefore be discussed together.

Interprofessional differences arise regarding the frequency of conflicts about all four topics but health visitors most consistently deny conflicts on any factor. Half the general practitioners see divergent beliefs and values as an issues whereas 43% of social workers perceive role conflict as a problem. General practitioners are also more concerned about matters relating to the guidelines; over half expect conflict over their rigid application and they share with teachers the most concern about literal interpretations. It is noteworthy that the two professions most concerned about possible misuse of the guidelines are those least involved in the network. The fact that general practitioners are also most concerned about differences over beliefs and values as well as the application of the guidelines suggests that they may impute to the network an unwontedly bureaucratic approach.

A moderate amount of specialised training and of case and conference experience all correlate with maximum awareness of conflict whereas, apart from the general practitioners, those with minimal experience and training who express any concrete opinions tend to deny conflict. Very heavy involvement correlates with a recognition that disagreements do arise on all points but only sometimes. The people who have more than a week of interdisciplinary training and a lot of experience are most prone to say rigid and literal interpretations are almost never a problem. Whether fear keeps the general practitioners away and they remain unaware of the flexibilities that exist or whether those in closer touch have become desensitised and dominated by procedures remains unexplored.

Some response patterns were bipolar, with a heightened awareness of conflict among those with most and least interdisciplinary training or most and least case conference experience. Experienced workers' concern about value conflicts appears to be located mainly but not exclusively among social workers (as most of these effects become statistically insignificant or extinguished when they are excluded). On the other hand, it is general practitioners who have least interdisciplinary training and very limited involvement in child protection and who have already been noted as frequently concerned about value conflicts. Men are evidently more likely to complain about rigidities and marginally more aware of role conflict but, in view of results already noted, both these findings probably derive from the extreme gender imbalance between general practitioners and health visitors. Response patterns were all very similar when analysed by area. Evaluations of two factors seem to be affected by the content of the long vignette which had preceded these questions, so that those respondents who had been thinking about sexual abuse (Jane, see Chapters Nine and Ten) were more inclined to think the guidelines are difficult to interpret and are too rigidly applied, an effect that is consonant with some respondents' more guarded attitudes towards referring her to social workers and to her registration.

Professionals' positive and negative perceptions of conferences

Respondents were presented with a list of positive and negative statements about case conferences, exploring points derived from the researcher's experience and from the literature review. Not surprisingly, most respondents make positive responses about the possibly beneficial characteristics of conferences, between 80% and 92% agreeing with them all. Despite a small strand of critical literature discussed in Hallett and Birchall (1992, chapter 13) and most emphatically expressed by Chapman and Woodmansey (1985), it would be rather like voting against mother and apple pie to disagree. However, the majority is smaller when it comes to rejecting the detrimental propositions in the list. Although the headline question asked for the score that 'best indicates your views' on a four point scale, one person sums up a very few equivocal voices by commenting 'All the negatives and all the positives *can* happen'. A larger majority replied that they have no relevant experience or opinion.

However, appreciation of the plus factors is not unconditional. Far more people agree than strongly agree with all the virtues. Very few deny that sharing information helps in everyone's assessment processes but 10% of respondents positively disagree that conferences contribute to planning their own intervention. Also, over 12% do not see the conference as helping them to know who is responsible for the case; a number say they would know anyway and others emphasise that 'responsibility is shared'. Tables 7.6 and 7.7 below summarise all the responses.

Fifty respondents identify 'other positive values', many of them being elaborations or a re-emphasis of concepts already listed. Examples which

Table 7.6 Percentage responses to a range of questions relating to possible positive values of child protection conferences

Item	Strongly agree	Agree	Response Disagree	Strongly disagree	Don't know
Sharing information helps clarify my diagnosis/assessment	30.1	61.4	2.1	0.0	6.4
Sharing information helps others clarify . . .	26.6	64.2	2.8	0.0	6.4
Sharing information enables me to plan my own intervention	20.5	62.4	9.0	0.9	7.1
Sharing information enables me to mesh . . . with others	23.1	64.0	6.2	0.0	6.8
It lets me know who is responsible for the case	25.7	51.9	11.5	0.6	6.5
It helps me to share anxiety and get a balanced feeling for the case	23.4	59.6	8.8	1.2	7.0
It helps others to share anxiety and get a balanced feeling for the case	17.4	70.6	5.2	0.0	6.7
I find the shared information and discussion generally educative to me	17.5	67.2	7.7	0.0	7.7
Such sharing is generally educative to the participants	13.6	71.5	6.8	0.3	7.7

N = 322 – 329.
The very few who insisted on a mid-position have been categorised among the 'Don't knows'.

relate to assessment or treatment planning are 'gathering and clarifying facts' and 'discovering or defining roles'. Several emphasise sharing decisions and 'not being alone'. Ten specifically draw attention to the importance of meeting and getting to know colleagues as an aid to communication but one person notes that conference members are 'not a regular team and therefore relationships are not developed'. A few identify the child protection conference as a warning shot across the bows of errant parents and one remarks that parental attendance has tightened the quality of information submitted.

A larger number voiced dissident opinions when offered the negative propositions about conferences although a majority rejected most of them. Over half say crucial people were too often missing and, when respondents identify these absentees, they are invariably general practitioners. By virtue of their episodic nature, cases conferences cannot keep in touch with families' changing needs; around 30% of respondents feel they therefore cannot keep plans sensitively up to date and that this unhelpfully constrains future action.

Table 7.7 **Percentage responses to a range of questions relating to possible negative values of child protection conferences**

Item	Strongly disagree	Disagree	Response Agree	Strongly Agree	Don't know
They waste time	22.2	59.1	7.7	0.6	10.5
They fudge individuals' responsibilities.*	15.9	61.9	9.8	1.0	6.4
Crucial people are too often missing.	2.5	33.0	46.6	6.5	11.5
Too many people who don't know the case or haven't the right skills are influencing the outcome.	5.6	56.8	23.0	3.4	11.1
People work up each others' anxiety unnecessarily.	5.3	66.9	16.7	0.9	10.3
Recommendations/decisions made at the Case Conference can be overturned too easily.*	7.1	58.3	21.5	0.0	13.2
Families' needs change from day to day. Case Conferences cannot keep intervention plans sensitively up-to-date.*	4.7	55.0	28.9	1.9	9.4
They are too long for participants to concentrate.	6.8	60.8	18.2	2.2	12.1

N = 312 – 329; missing values exceeded 5% only in those items marked with a *
The very few who insisted on a mid-position have been categorised among the 'Don't knows'.

Over a quarter think too many extraneous professionals influence decisions or recommendations can be too easily overturned by individual agencies.

'Other negative values' were identified by 51 respondents. As with the positive values, some reiterated concepts already included in the table. Pressures on practitioners' time and other resources have already been discussed in Chapter Six, so it is not surprising to find the issue spontaneously raised (This question preceded the above in the order of the questionnaire). People also volunteer concerns about the availability of appropriate services to follow up on conference plans. Just three people from different professions raise 'confidentiality' as a problematic issue. One respondent draws attention to the lack of 'criteria . . . for evaluating the effectiveness of conference decisions'. Several note a possible abuse of power in conferences: they are 'subjective', 'judge and jury', 'record the negative and not the positive aspects about families'; the partial involvement of parents is 'a charade'; there is a risk of the conference being dominated by strong personalities; three of the four respondents who were specific about interprofessional conflict are health visitors who feel undervalued. Many commented on the importance of good chairing to manage the conference, holding participants to task and minimising hidden agendas and abuses of power such as the above. 'A good chairperson is essential. A poor one can be a disaster'.

Interprofessional variations in perceptions of conferences

It is evident that most workers assert positive attitudes to conferences but there are many variations between the different occupations' valuations overall and of specific items. Dissenting responses were scattered and generally too few to reach levels of statistical significance. The scores were therefore consolidated by excluding the non-substantive responses, collapsing the categories into rather unfavourable, favourable and very favourable ratings, and aggregating the series. This reveals greater and lesser degrees of satisfaction.

Based on the aggregate scores, health visitors' appreciation of conferences stands out above all other groups, with police officers next in disagreeing with the negative factors. When teachers have clear opinions they also tend to be strongly positive. Doctors, including nearly half the general practitioners, are most frequently critical or least likely to make strong positive comments. Over one third of social workers come out with 'rather unfavourable' ratings on the positive factors although they cluster around the neutral point on combined scores of both positive and negative factors. Interprofessional differences reached levels of statistical significance on some factors and, despite the statistical problems caused by small cell counts, trends are discernible when combinations of the fewest strongly supportive scores and the most negative scores, or vice versa, are compared.

On the individual factors, health visitors most often agree that conferences help them mesh their own interventions with others, let them know who is responsible for the case and manage anxiety factors helpfully. They are also particularly unlikely to agree that conferences waste time or are too long. Among the minority holding negative views, general practitioners are most numerous and consistent; they most often believe conferences are too long and time-wasting, do not educate them or help others' assessments. Almost half of them think families' needs change too much for conference plans to be sensitive. Nearly half the social workers think that people without the right skills or knowledge of the case have too much influence and a third think recommendations can be too easily overturned.

Tables 7.8 and 7.9 highlight the professions most clearly polarised on each factor. For each item, reading vertically within a cell shows some discrepancy between the groups but reading horizontally across the columns shows the most dissonant views within or between groups and reading diagonally reveals the most convergence. Where the same or kindred profession(s) feature diagonally there is a particular coherence within the group but those displayed in parallel are the most divided among themselves. When general practitioners and paediatricians hold very similar positions they are grouped together as doctors but if their responses diverge they are reported separately. In the main, different professions' responses are scattered between the extremes. Because they are the most appreciative of conferences, health visitors are thus most often polarised from other professions, in particular from general practitioners and from social workers with their more sceptical evaluations.

Some of the most positive concordances are between health visitors and paediatricians regarding conferences helping their own plans and others' assessments. Among the more sceptical attitudes, social workers are most prone to share general practitioners' doubts about the meeting's contribution to others' diagnosis and meshing their own activities. With the police, general practitioners most often disagree about conferences' helpfuness in planning their own interventions. Doctors are least reliant on the conference to let them know who is responsible for the case. Social workers and general practitioners are least likely to agree about conferences' capacity to attune to families' changing needs but doctors' views on that point are complex. While 45% of general practitioners consider family circumstances are too labile, paediatricians least often positively assert that. But no doctors strongly refute the possibility whereas 12% of social workers do. It seems probable that social workers' and paediatricians' greater faith in forward planning relates to more involvement in child protection and a deeper immersion in the belief that families must be challenged to accept responsibility for their children's welfare or face the inevitability of alternative plans. However, this must be a tentative interpretation of the doctors' divergence in particular, in view of their mixed

Table 7.8 **A summary of the most favourable and unfavourable responses to possible positive values of child protection conferences, classified by profession**

Item	Strongly Agree			Disagree/Strongly Disagree		
Response	Profession	N	%	Profession	N	%
Sharing information helps clarify my diagnosis/ assessment (SC)	HVs	29	42.6	All	Negligible	
	GPs	11	16.7			
Sharing information helps others clarify their diagnosis/assessment (SC)	HVs	23	33.8	SWs	4	6.5
				GPs	3	4.5
	Doctors	19	17.9	Paed'ns	0	0.0
Sharing information enables me to plan my own intervention (SC)	HVs	20	29.4	Police	4	18.2
	GPs	8	12.1	Paed'ns	2	5.0
Sharing information enables me to mesh my interventions with others (SC)	HVs	24	35.3	SWs	5	8.1
				HVs	2	2.9
	GPs	8	12.1	Paed'ns	1	2.5
It lets me know who is responsible for the case (p = <.005, CC.28256)	HVs	24	35.3	GPs	17	25.8
	Paed'ns	8	12.1	HVs	3	4.5
It helps me to share anxiety and get a balanced feeling for the case (p = <.0001, CC.40650)	HVs	25	36.8	SWs	20	32.3
				Paed'ns	2	5.0
	SWs	4	6.5	HVs	2	2.9
It helps others to share anxiety and get a balanced feeling for the case (p = <.0001, CC.40680	HVs	20	29.4	SWs	9	14.5
	GPs	6	9.1			
	SWs	3	4.8	HVs	0	0.0
I find the shared information and discussion is generally educative to me (SC)	HVs	20	29.4	Police	4	18.2
				GPs	9	13.6
	Doctors	13	12.3			
	SWs	6	9.7	HVs	1	1.5
Such sharing is generally educative to the participants (SC)	HVs	15	22.1	SWs	12	19.4
	SWs	5	8.1	HVs	0	0.0

NB. Percentages have been worked out against the base populations; there were very few non-respondents.

SC signifies that numbers were too small in some cells for chi-square tests.

For each item, reading vertically within a cell shows some discrepancy between the groups but reading horizontally across the columns shows the most dissonant views within or between the professions and reading diagonally reveals the most convergence.

Table 7.9 **A summary of the most favourable and unfavourable responses to possible negative values of child protection conferences, classified by profession**

Item	Response	Strongly Disagree			Agree/Strongly Agree		
		Profession	N	%	Profession	N	%
They waste time (p = <.02, CC.26269)		HVs	24	33.3	Doctors	16	15.1
		GPs	7	10.6	Others		Negligible
They fudge individuals' responsibilities (p = <.02, CC.26630)		HVs	19	27.9	GPs	11	16.7
		Paed'ns	1	2.5	Police	1	4.8
Crucial people are too often missing (NS)		HVs	4	5.8	All		Over 50%
Too many people who don't know the case or haven't the right skills are influencing the outcome (SC)		HVs	7	10.3	SWs	26	41.9
		GPs	2	3.0	Police	3	13.6
People work up each others' anxiety unnecessarily (NS)		HVs	7	10.3	SWs	21	33.9
		SWs	2	3.2			
		Paed'ns	1	2.5	HVs	7	10.3
Recommendations/decisions made at the Case Conference can be overturned too easily (SC)		Police	4	18.2	SWs	21	33.9
					HVs	6	8.8
		GPs	0	0.0	Police	2	9.1
Families' needs change from day to day. Case Conference cannot keep intervention plans sensitively up-to-date (SC)		SWs	7	11.3	GPs	29	43.9
		Doctors	0	0.0	Others		Over 25%
They are too long for participants to concentrate (SC)		HVs	7	10.3	GPs	28	42.4
		SWs	6	9.6			
		Police	2	9.1			
		GPs	1	1.5	HVs	6	8.8

NB. Percentages have been worked out against the base populations; there were very few non-respondents.
SC signifies that the results were not statistically significant and SC signifies that numbers were too small in some cells for chi-square tests.
For each item, reading vertically within a cell shows some discrepancy between the groups but reading horizontally across the columns shows the most dissonant views within or between the professions and reading diagonally reveals the most convergence.

attitudes to the 'confrontation versus support' question discussed in Chapter Five.

Apart from the practical contributions that conferences may make to case management, another function that receives some attention in the literature is that of relieving practitioners' anxieties. As noted earlier, this function was raised by only four respondents in free comments on the utility of conferences, two thinking conferences alleviated anxiety and two thinking they provoked it unnecessarily. Two positive statements and one negative featured in the schedule under discussion here. Of all the professions, social workers most frequently deny that conferences manage affective tasks well; only 7% strongly agree that it helps them to share their own anxiety and, indeed, over a third feel that conferences 'work up anxiety unnecessarily'. When the three anxiety factors in the two schedules were combined in Table 7.10, health visitors and teachers most often value these functions highly whereas, after social workers, general practitioners have least confidence in them.

Table 7.10 **A comparison of professional perceptions of child protection conferences as a help in bearing anxiety**

Profession Rating	SW %	HV %	Teacher %	Police %	GP %	Paed'n %	Total %
Very positive	5.1	27.1	23.2	20.0	10.5	15.1	16.8
Positive	67.0	68.2	71.8	70.8	76.2	75.5	71.4
Negative	27.8	4.7	4.9	9.2	13.3	9.4	11.9
Total	19.5	21.3	20.1	7.2	20.1	11.8	100.0

The results from this series of questions suggest a number of issues. They show a disturbing level of distrust among social workers of the recommendations and commitments made at conferences and that these key workers are least likely to find the forum supportive. Responses to this question give no information about whether this is because they think others will renege on appropriate contributions or will impose unwanted interventions; either way, the finding resonates with Weightman's (1987) concerns about social workers' difficulties in 'managing from below' and their own concerns, reported above, about interprofessional role conflicts. It is also interesting that polarisations occur most frequently within the primary health care team, between health visitors and general practitioners. These arise over the utility of the conference in diagnosis or assessment and in working out their own inputs; not surprisingly, therefore, they are most often out of step on the question of time wasting. On the other hand, health visitors and social workers diverge most about management of anxiety, contributions to others' diagnosis and mutual education. It is unclear whether health visitors' marked appreciation of conferences reflects their traditionally subordinate nursing role, depending on the meeting to clarify their contribution to the case, or whether it signifies a highly developed sense of cooperation or teamwork. Many of the responses from significant minorities of general practitioners clearly indicate their distance from the notion of shared responsibility for child protection and resonate with others' critical views of their performance evidenced in other parts of the study.

Other factors correlating with perceptions of conferences

Experiential factors show no consistent relationships but a limited amount of post-qualifying training, whether interdisciplinary or not, correlates with the greatest satisfaction. Interprofessional training was strongly associated with positive attitudes to several factors: those with such training are much more likely (one and a half times or twice as likely) to agree strongly that sharing information helps in their own and others' case assessments and interventions, and to disagree strongly that conferences waste time, fudge responsibility or cannot cope with families' changing situations.

One third of principals strongly agree that conferences help them to plan their own intervention and none dissent, whereas subordinate staff are less appreciative about this factor. Principals and supervisors unite in strong agreement (37%) twice as often as maingrade staff, that conferences help them to mesh their own interventions with those of colleagues. Along with the finding that maingrade staff give a rather lower favourable rating to the aggregated list, these two specific findings suggest that conferences tend to serve organisational rather than practice needs. Further development of the core group system may be particularly important to maingrade practitioners. For no apparent reason, MetBorough staff are more satisfied about conferences' contribution to their own plans and the stability of conference conclusions and least likely to feel that extraneous people influence matters.

It seemed possible that there might be some generational differences in respondents' attitudes to interprofessional conferences, with older staff more used to working independently and less appreciative of the forum but this was not borne out. Perhaps nearly 20 years since the Tunbridge Wells Group has achieved a secular change. Age was not significant on aggregated scores, except that the inevitable overlap between youth and inexperience led to a higher rate of 'don't know' responses from people under 30. In fact, the oldest were the most likely to feature among the minority giving strongly favourable ratings to particular factors. Gender correlated with several items. Men are more likely to agree that conferences waste time and provoke unnecessary anxiety, and to disagree that they let them know who is responsible. It seems likely that these age and gender factors are confounded with the professional variables of health visiting and general practice respectively although the gender factor appears to be operating independently in the differential attitudes to talk as a problem-solving mechanism.

Proposals for improvements to child protection conferences

Respondents were asked whether they could think of improvements in the conduct of conferences and, if so, to choose five priority items from a predetermined list of 16 options. Discounting 11% of the sample (38 respondents) who had said conferences are never their business, two thirds (204) of the remainder had attended within the preceding year and another third were past and/or potential attenders. Four fifths of the former and over a quarter of the latter feel improvements could be made. The specific proposals of the recent and potential attenders are compared in Table 7.11 below. There were just three votes for longer or larger meetings which have been omitted.

The rank order of results is quite similar for both groups, apart from the relatively greater prominence of 'shorter meetings' in the potential attenders' group. However, much higher proportions of the recent attenders express concern about all the factors. Absenteeism concerns a significant majority but, in the abstract, a significant minority would welcome smaller meetings. There is an obvious but not necessarily irreconcilable tension between the two points, if there were a consensus that some attenders could be excused but others should be persuaded to come. However, this seems unlikely in view of the results arising from the conference episode in the long vignette

Table 7.11 **Priority proposals for improvements in the conduct of child protection conferences, made by respondents with actual recent experience or with past and potential involvement in such conferences**

Respondent Item	Recent attenders (N = 204)		Other Possible Attenders (N = 97)	
	N	%	N	%
Better attendance by crucial people	121	59.3	15	15.5
Prior written information	102	50.0	12	12.4
Timetabling of meetings	69	33.8	16	16.5
Better chairing	57	27.9	5	5.2
Content of discussion	57	27.9	6	6.2
Agendas on arrival	54	26.5	6	6.2
Follow-up of recommendations	54	26.5	7	7.2
Shorter meetings	49	24.0	15	15.5
Having a Minutes Secretary	46	22.5	4	4.1
Organisation of review conferences	40	19.6	4	4.1
Better minutes	36	17.6	8	8.2
Smaller meetings	35	17.2	5	5.2
Accommodation for conferences	17	8.3	1	1.0
Other (please specify)	19	9.3	1	1.0

(Chapter Ten), where respondents tended to want more attenders than they expected.

Many people make suggestions for the more purposeful conduct of meetings. A fifth of recent attenders feel that the organisation of review conferences should be better managed. A number were concerned about inadequate accommodation. The most frequent 'other' response referred to more involvement of families. Next came further comments about general practitioners' absence and two doctors suggested timing conferences to suit their attendance while one sought payment. A paediatrician said conferences in hospital premises would make it easier for them to attend and a social worker made the same recommendation in order to involve paediatric nurses. One person remarked that issues of ethnicity needed more attention and a health visitor commented on doctors' problems of confidentiality.

When 'don't knows' are excluded and the professions compared, two groupings are evident. Confirming the picture above, doctors, particularly general practitioners, most often propose improved timetabling, shorter and smaller meetings. They are least concerned about absenteeism whereas 70% of social workers want better attendances by crucial people. Otherwise, social workers lead on a wide range of issues concerning the conduct of conferences; two thirds want prior written information, half want better chairing and large minorities want a minutes secretary, agendas and a better standard of discussion. Social workers also made two thirds of the complaints about accommodation for meetings. Different professions' proposals are compared in the following Table 7.12.

Nearly one third of principal officers, most commonly but not exclusively those from the social services department, raise the problem of a minutes secretary. One third in the supervisory rank are concerned about follow-up of conference recommendations but only one of these is a social work senior, suggesting that other agencies may have less confidence in the social services department's future conduct of the case than the key worker's own superiors. Correlations between experience factors and conference concerns are complicated. The degree of specialisation in child protection, the number of cases dealt with and conferences attended, all increase the demand for better chairing but the number of cases handled does not affect people's desire for better discussion. Greater involvement in conferences increases people's concerns about having a minutes secretary, even when the discontents of social work principals are excluded. More interdisciplinary training appears to correlate with concerns about absentees and better accommodation but these results disappear when social workers are excluded. Locality affected two factors, with 36% of County staff concerned about the quality of discussion compared with only 13% in City. Over a quarter of city staff want a minutes secretary whereas less than half that number share this concern in the other areas. Whether this signifies that the problem is nearer resolution

Table 7.12 **Priority proposals for improvement of child protection conferences, crosstabulated by respondents' profession**

Profession / Suggestion	SW (N = 59)		HV (N = 58)		Teacher (N = 34)		Police (N = 20)		GP (N = 44)		Paed'n (N = 30)		Row Total (N = 245)	
	N	%	N	%	N	%	N	%	N	%	N	%	N	%
Better attendances	41	69.5	25	43.1	16	47.1	9	45.0	16	36.4	14	46.7	121	49.4
Prior written information	38	64.4	18	31.0	15	44.1	5	25.0	14	31.8	12	40.0	102	41.6
Timetabling	12	20.3	12	20.7	6	17.6	4	20.0	22	50.0	13	43.3	69	28.2
Content of discussion	21	35.6	6	10.3	7	20.6	8	40.0	8	18.2	7	23.3	57	23.3
Better chairing	29	49.2	4	6.9	5	14.7	4	20.0	9	20.5	6	20.0	57	23.3
Follow-up	12	20.3	17	29.3	7	20.6	2	10.0	11	25.0	5	16.7	54	22.0
Agendas on arrival	19	32.2	7	12.1	5	14.7	5	25.0	12	27.3	6	20.0	54	22.0
Shorter meetings	8	13.6	1	1.7	4	11.8	3	15.0	22	50.0	11	36.7	49	20.0
Minutes Secretary	24	40.7	6	10.3	5	14.7	3	15.0	3	6.8	5	16.7	46	18.8
Organisation review conferences	13	22.0	6	10.3	6	17.6	2	10.0	5	11.4	8	26.7	40	16.3
Better minutes	11	18.6	9	15.5	3	8.8	1	5.0	8	18.2	4	13.3	36	14.7
Smaller meetings	13	22.0	2	3.4	3	8.8	0	.0	8	18.2	9	30.0	35	14.3
Better accommodation	11	18.6	4	6.9	0	.0	0	.0	1	2.3	1	3.3	17	6.9
Total No of proposals	252	100.0	127	100.0	82	100.0	46	100.0	139	100.0	101	100.0	737	100.0

outside City or that fewer of the others have visualised the possibility of such a resource is an open question.

Summary and conclusions

The majority of respondents have attended child protection conferences but the range of experience is very wide. As expected, staff from the more specialised agencies and senior ranks have the greatest involvement. Teachers and general practitioners attend very few. Junior paediatric staff and class teachers are particularly likely to say it is not their role to attend, although there are indications in other parts of the study that they and others would welcome their greater involvement. Respondents are unclear about their local guidelines on the circumstances in which a conference should be sought and most people appear to leave to social services staff not only the convening but also the proposal of a conference. This appears less than satisfactory in the light of other data within this study and other sources which suggest that other agencies are sometimes dissatisfied with social workers' response to their concerns.

Many respondents find it very difficult to fit conferences into their timetable, with general practitioners reporting extreme difficulty despite their slender involvement. Other workers with a heavy burden of cases or of conference attendance also find it problematic, although there are indications that inter-disciplinary training increases these groups' readiness to prioritise conferences more highly in their total workloads. There is significant concern about the absence of important contributors, particularly general practitioners.

A majority of respondents favour parents' and children's partial attendance but there are significant numbers of opponents and doubters. Respondents' profession is a significant factor, with social workers, health visitors and general practitioners most supportive and paediatricians and the police most opposed, but the divisions of opinion also appear to relate to other more personal factors, with greater experience hardening both the favourable and unfavourable responses and generally more men in each profession opposed to their involvement. The large majority of all the professions view case conferences as usually helpful to the child concerned.

To a very large extent, participants consider conferences useful to themselves, particularly in clarifying professional assessments but also in serving a number of other purposes. However, ratings are much more often favourable than very favourable and significant numbers acknowledge weaknesses and even detrimental factors. Frequent conflict is acknowledged by a significant number of respondents on matters of professional role, beliefs and values, and also around the interpretation and application of the procedural guidelines. The absence of crucial members has already been noted but substantial minorities are also concerned that the wrong people may influence decisions and that conferences' inability to keep up with families' changing needs undermines their value. There are cross-cutting interprofessional differences regarding several of these evaluations. Health visitors have the highest opinion of conferences but general practitioners are the most guarded on many points. Social workers are much more likely than anyone else to have a negative view of conferences' capacity for managing professional anxieties and to perceive role conflict between workers. More interprofessional training correlates with a higher appreciation of conferences' contribution to case management, more confidence that disputes are manageable and strong disagreement with the notion that they waste time.

Four fifths of recent attenders and some other possible attenders at case conferences feel they could be improved. The leading proposals were for better attendance by crucial people and for the circulation of prior written information. However, significant numbers also made various other adminis-trative suggestions. Doctors emerge as more concerned about timetabling, smaller and shorter meetings but much less concerned than social workers about absentees. Social workers make most suggestions about improving the administration of meetings, and it may be that the specifics they suggest would go at least part way to meeting the doctors' superficially different preoccupations. However, there remains a serious time problem for many participants and there is a tendency for the different professions to say their lot would be eased if only the conference would meet on their premises. It appears that conferences are more valuable to senior than to maingrade staff, perhaps serving organisational functions slightly better than practitioners' needs. If this inference is true, it would suggest that the emergence of the core group meeting is an important development for the hands-on collaborators.

Chapter 8

Perceptions of the severity of child abuse in a series of brief vignettes: Implications for action

Introduction

The definition of child abuse is elusive; much has been written about the diversity of the situations concealed under the blanket term and about the difficulty of defining the thresholds of unacceptable parental behaviour. The Children Act 1989 requires that 'significant harm' to the child, or the risk thereof, be established before legal intervention is possible. At the time of fieldwork in this study, the relevant statute required proof that the child's 'proper development is being avoidably impaired or neglected or he is being ill-treated' and that 'he is in need of care . . . which he is unlikely to receive unless the court makes an order . . .' (Child Care Act 1980). Neither statute defines what is significant harm or the level of care required. A number of writers have pressed for tighter legal definitions but the matter remains a chimera (see, for instance, Nagi 1977, Geach and Szwed 1983, Adcock and White 1992). Others have argued that it is both inevitable and desirable that judgments are situational and socially constructed (eg Dingwall et al 1983). These dilemmas are more fully discussed in the literature review, where it is suggested that:

> *Every encounter between the family, the professional network and the court is a fraught negotiation of subjectivities where specialised occupational theories and commonsense judgments may clash (Hallett and Birchall 1992, p.106).*

Yet it would seem important that professionals should share a common understanding about what constitutes child abuse if they are to cooperate satisfactorily. Their views of the situation will affect their overall priorities, specific action plans and choice of professional contacts.

One way of investigating the degree of consensus or divergence between practitioners on this topic was pioneered by Giovannoni and Becerra (1979). They used a long series of brief vignettes to explore variations in workers' ratings of diverse incidents in the USA. Their approach was adapted and used on a smaller scale for this aspect of the research. Twenty of their vignettes were replicated, with the addition of three devised from the long vignettes which feature later in this study and a third used in pilot work. Their original study was exclusively concerned with the problem of defining child abuse, investigating both professional and lay reactions to a long series of vignettes and also the professionals' definitions in practice. In the present research programme, the objective of this particular piece is simply to investigate whether professionals report similar views of the severity of the same incident.

Methods in the brief vignette sequence

The original authors' detailed validation of the vignettes was accepted in this study, as in the other derivative projects cited below, but their acceptability was tested with a range of undergraduate and postgraduate students, and professional and academic colleagues in the relevant disciplines at the preliminary stage and in the pilot phase. It seemed important to test whether UK respondents were as willing as the US subjects to rate such brief and decontextualised vignettes and this proved to be the case. In fact, during the main phase there were single complaints about three vignettes and a maximum of four (1%) about a few others. In common with the other derivative studies (Snyder and Newberger 1986, Fox and Dingwall 1985), there are a number of detailed differences from Giovannoni and Becerra in this exercise. These concern the number of vignettes used, the selection criteria, the method of administration, the age of the child concerned and the composition of the professional population.

The original American study used 78 paired vignettes, each pair comprising an event or circumstance with or without its consequence being stated. Avoiding whole pairs, 60 cases were then randomly selected from the series for each respondent. Snyder and Newberger replicated their study with four paediatric hospital professions, using a fixed series of half the original vignettes. In an exploratory British replication, Fox and Dingwall used a fixed series of 20 vignettes. The present study also employs a fixed series of 20 of the original vignettes, with equal numbers concealing or revealing the consequence, plus three more devised from the long vignettes. The single series was necessary in order to obtain comparative data from a wider range of professionals while using few vignettes and also to cope with the constraints of a postal questionnaire.

Secondly, the vignettes were selected somewhat differently from those three studies. Giovannoni and Becerra started with thirteen categories of abuse derived from American legal and professional standards and subsequently collapsed these into nine categories by cluster analysis. The present study restricted the categories to those used in the UK. Although it might be ideal to establish categories by fresh cluster analysis in the UK, this was impossible in a small replication. Secondly and pragmatically, case descriptions have to be fitted into the *Working Together* categories if they are to be handled within the child protection machinery at all. With a limited number of vignettes, a further valuable consequence of using the fewer UK categories is to enlarge the range of cases tested in each category. This seems more likely to reveal whether any particular categories are more problematic than others or more problematic to particular professions.

In some cases Giovannoni and Becerra referred to prior expert standards as to the relative severity of particular vignettes within a category and in others they made reasoned assumptions about different severities. They pretested their vignettes and eliminated those 29 that received uniformly very low or extremely high ratings: examples of each were 'ill-fitting clothing' and 'physical assault and sexual molestation' or 'physical injury leading to death' (1979, p. 106). The two other studies selected the particular vignettes which had previously thrown up the greatest interprofessional variation. Fox and Dingwall took their 20 cases from all Giovannoni and Becerra's nine final categories and chose those which most sharply separated medical and social work opinions in order to contrast health visitors' and social workers' ratings. For their hospital study, Snyder and Newberger (1986) also selected those vignettes which had caused greatest variation. The present study, investigating a wider range of professions than earlier studies and as interested in convergent as divergent opinions, drew cases from the whole range of severity weightings in the original.

At first it seemed to the present researcher as though Giovannoni and Becerra's exclusion of the 29 totally consensual vignettes from their initial series would be a distorting influence, eliminating areas of agreement and accentuating disagreements. This would have mattered if the important findings depended on some absolute quantitative measure of how much consensus or dissensus existed but, on further reflection, it appears that findings of practical importance were derived from the spectrum they used. Moreover, it may be redundant to the point of provoking hostility to ask how people rate such situations. It is also impracticable for this research to draw cases from those extremes as full details of the eliminated vignettes were not given.

Bearing all these considerations in mind, the original 156 vignettes were grouped into the then current five categories of UK child protection registers (ie physical abuse, sexual abuse, neglect, emotional abuse and grave concern). Several vignettes, eg those describing parental sexual mores which had no direct impact on the child or difficult housing conditions with no apparent element of parental irresponsibility, were rejected as falling outside British child protection practice. Finding that the UK categories of 'neglect' and 'grave concern' overlapped ambiguously when applied to the vignettes, those groups were then combined. The resultant categories were physical abuse, sexual abuse, neglect and emotional abuse. At first it seemed appropriate to draw a sample in ratio to the number of vignettes in each category but this grossly overweighted the total list with neglect type cases for reasons which Giovannoni and Becerra did not apparently spell out. Neglect or 'failure to provide' in various forms are believed to be relatively prevalent but professionals' neglect of neglect is also noted in the literature (Wolock and Horowitz 1984, Birchall 1989, DH 1989). In their chapter which studied real cases, Giovannoni and Becerra found less than 15% of cases were initiated on the grounds of failure to provide alone, although it was noted as a supplementary factor in many cases. On balance, it seemed preferable to select fewer neglect vignettes and a more even number of cases from each category were selected for this exercise.

A second step was to obtain a full range of severity scores from the series of vignettes by stratified random sampling, to maximise the opportunity of testing the degree of consensus at the extremities as well as the problematic grey middle in each category. Table 8.1 compares the full range of ratings given in the original study to those vignettes from which the current selection was drawn with the range given to those actually selected and it can be seen that they are very similar.

Table 8.1 **A comparison of the original mean ratings of the total pool of vignettes used by Giovannoni and Becerra and of those drawn for the current study**

Abuse Category	Full range of means of the pool of vignettes	Mean for the category	Full range of means of the selected vignettes	Mean for the category
Sexual abuse	8.33–5.10	6.95	8.15–6.97	6.86
Physical abuse	8.53–1.62	6.24	8.35–3.18	6.27
Emotional abuse	8.36–4.35	5.46	8.31–4.35	5.46
Neglect	7.59–1.93	4.55	7.59–1.93	4.76

The third methodological difference from the original study was that Giovannoni and Becerra administered their vignettes face-to-face, delivering them in random order to each respondent with a written and an oral instruction about scoring. Originally it had been hoped to use the same methodology in this study and the pilot sample was approached in this way. However, as a postal questionnaire has been used exclusively for the main sample, the method was necessarily modified. The instructions were slightly altered to take account of written presentation. The list of vignettes was printed in random order, as in the listing below, but there was no way of reinforcing an independent as opposed to a comparative ranking of the vignettes on the page nor was it possible to randomise the order of presentation for different respondents.

Fourthly, respondents in this study were asked to 'assume the child in question is five years old unless otherwise specified', whereas the American study stipulated a uniform age of seven. The reason for specifying the age of five was to maximise the salience of the topic both to health visitors who generally have less contact with children of school age and to teachers who less often have contact with them earlier. Clearly, the younger age of the subjects might be expected to increase the severity rating ascribed to many if not all the incidents, and this was borne out. However, the main purpose of this piece of the current study was parallel to that of Giovannoni and Becerra and any direct comparisons are subsidiary.

Lastly, while the number of participants is similar, with 339 respondents in the current study and 313 in Giovannoni and Becerra, the professional composition is somewhat different. Both studies cover social workers, paediatricians and police, but this study also includes general practitioners and teachers while omitting lawyers.

The vignettes

As in the three previous studies, respondents in this study were asked to rate the vignettes on a scale of one to nine with one as the 'least serious' and nine as the 'most serious' score.

1 The parents constantly compare their child with the younger sibling, sometimes implying that the child is not really their own. The child continually fights with other children.

2 The parents always let their child run around the house and garden without any clothes on.

3 On one occasion the parent and the child engaged in sexual intercourse.

4 Although clean, the baby has a sore bottom and is difficult to feed. The toddler is poorly clad and difficult to control but healthy.

5 The parents immersed the child in a tub of hot water.

6 On one occasion the parent fondled the child's genital area.

7 The parents fail to prepare regular meals for their child. The child often has to fix his own supper. The child has an iron deficiency.

8 The parents ignore their child most of the time, seldom talking or listening to her.

9 The parents burned the child on the buttocks and chest with a cigarette. The child has second degree burns.

10 The parents usually punish the child by spanking with a leather strap, leaving red marks on the child's skin.

11 The 8 year old girl has recently become distressed at school and is showing an interest in smaller boys' genitals.

12   The parents live with their child in a small rented house. No one ever cleans up.

13   A child has severe behaviour problems. The parents have allowed the child to undergo treatment but refuse to cooperate themselves.

14   The parents regularly left their child alone inside the house after dark. Often they did not return until midnight.

15   The parent and child repeatedly engaged in mutual masturbation.

16   Today the child was found wandering two streets away from home across a main road in a town.

17   The parents usually punish their child by spanking with the hand, leaving red marks on the child's skin.

18   The parents regularly fail to feed their child for at least 24 hours. The child was hospitalised for 6 weeks for being seriously malnourished.

19   The parent repeatedly showed the child pornographic pictures. The child suffers recurring nightmares.

20   The parents let their child sip out of their glasses when they are drinking whisky. The child has become intoxicated.

21   The parents ignored their child's complaint of an earache and chronic ear drainage.

22   The parents have kept their child locked in since birth. They feed and bathe the child and provide basic physical care.

23   The parents hit the child in the face, striking with the fist.

Results

As shown in Table 8.2 below, most of the ratings are markedly more severe than those in the original study and this could be due to any combination of the younger age of child that was specified, secular change in attitudes, transatlantic cultural differences or the impact of legislative and agency contexts.

The greatest change is in the uprating of the less serious incidents of physical abuse and neglect from base scores of 3.18 to 6.07 and from 1.93 to 3.34 respectively, but the narrower span and lower ceiling on the ratings of emotional abuse are also interesting. In both studies, the sexual incidents receive the most severe and uniform mean ratings but the present results, while notching up the severity, somewhat widen the range of means. However, this study is more concerned with workers' convergences and conflicts in the UK in the 1990s than with comparisons with Giovannoni and

Table 8.2 Current respondents' range of mean ratings of vignettes in each category compared with the ratings of the 20 common vignettes in Giovannoni and Becerra's original study

Abuse Category	Ratings in the original study	Mean for the category	Ratings in the current study	Mean for the category
Sexual abuse	8.15–6.97	6.86	8.87–7.44	8.43
Physical abuse	8.35–3.18	6.27	8.85–6.07	7.90
Emotional abuse	8.31–4.35	5.46	7.69–5.22	6.26
Neglect	7.59–1.93	4.76	8.61–3.34	6.29

Becerra's findings in the USA in the 1970s. Unfortunately, because of Fox and Dingwall's use of only two professions and the limited overlap in the vignette series used, it is not useful to compare their category means with these results. It may be that the generally narrower as well as higher span of scores than in the original reflects greater consensus within the contemporary UK network.

In all the studies there has been a reluctance to use the bottom of the scale, despite Giovannoni and Becerra's preliminary validation of the vignettes and rejection of some that had proved unanimously to fall below the threshold. Maybe, examples should have been offered of an unambiguously non-abusive situation and of a very mild example of poor parenting to illustrate the baseline and to encourage people to use the full scale in the way spelt out by the introductory rubrics, with a score of one as the 'least serious' point on a scale of abuse. The almost total refusal to give any of the incidents a rating of one seems to imply that the lowest points used in fact signify that fuzzy threshold of behaviour that professionals actually deem abusive. Various studies of professional gatekeeping in practice, such as Dingwall et al (1983) and Packman et al (1986) and the agency case study phase in Giovannoni and Becerra's own research, as well as the theoretical arguments about problems of definition, would support this interpretation.

Miscellaneous variables

Before discussing interprofessional differences and similarities which form the main focus of this sector of the data, other potentially pertinent variables are briefly considered. Respondents' ratings were tested against a number of personal characteristics: gender, age and their experience of bringing up children. In addition, their locality, their recent case and child protection conference experience and whether they had received interdisciplinary training were all examined. It seemed reasonable to hypothesise that much professional experience or common local policies might lead to a convergence of views between workers. It is also frequently regarded as very important that staff should experience some measure of interdisciplinary training in order to develop a shared professional culture, although the literature on this topic is sometimes contradictory (Hallett and Birchall 1992). In almost all cases these variables proved to be insignificant. Giovannoni and Becerra found staffs' experience of child-rearing had virtually no effect and this study found none. They did not test locality, age or experience as factors but Snyder and Newberger found few effects; nurses alone were affected by increased experience, becoming less severe in their rating.

While most of these factors appear to have no salience in this study there were, as in the original, several vignettes in which gender was significant with women always rating them more seriously than men did (vignettes 5, 6, 13, 14, 20 and 21). There seems to be no common thread running through these vignettes whereas, when Giovannoni and Becerra found differences, they found women more concerned about those regarding basic physical care. Snyder and Newberger found similar gender effects only among physicians in relation to physial abuse and psychologists regarding vignettes of neglect. A number of other studies have found gender a significant variable in both lay and professional definitions of social problems (Hallett and Birchall 1992 chapter 6, Bisset and Hunter 1992). However, the differences are here confounded with the gender imbalance of the different professions and it seems probable that, as the original study and previous replications found, professional identity is far more pertinent and relates to health visitors' more severe pattern of ratings.

Professional ranking of categories of abuse

The data was analysed in several different ways and the broadest view, in Table 8.3, derives from a comparison of the mean scores given by each profession to the batch of vignettes in each category of abuse. This reveals that their rank ordering of the categories of abuse is almost the same, with general practitioners making only a marginal reversal of the ranking of neglect and emotional abuse.

All professions in this study clearly rate sexual and physical abuse higher than the other categories. In their schema of nine categories, Giovannoni and Becerra did not find total concordance between social workers, paediatricians, lawyers and police in ranking the categories but all were agreed in placing physical and sexual abuse within the top three categories. Snyder and Newberger found their diverse paediatric professions ranked the categories in the same order with physical abuse rated highest.

Even though the various professions in this study rank the categories in a similar order, the different means in Table 8.3 reveal differences in the ranges they use. Although the point is debated, it is widely accepted that a long scale may be treated as an interval scale (Berger and Patchner 1988b, Bryman and Cramer 1990). It might be argued that health visitors' and teachers' use of a rather higher band of values for all the abuse categories simply indicates different interpretations of a scale which has no absolute zero but, in fact, a judgment of 'no maltreatment whatsoever' is a zero for every respondent. Since variations of range exist within each professional group as members rate different cases from different categories but their ratings also overlap with other professions in different ways within a given category, this suggests that the differences in respondents' evaluations are substantive.

Table 8.3 **Comparisons of different professions' mean ratings of vignettes in each category of abuse**

Category	All	SW	HV	Profession Teacher	Police	GP	Paed'n
Sexual Abuse	8.09	7.90	8.37	8.23	8.09	7.94	7.92
Physical Abuse	7.90	7.73	8.25	7.95	7.92	7.74	7.71
Emotional Abuse	6.26	6.07	6.94	6.49	5.90	5.85	5.84
Neglect	6.04	5.46	6.52	6.49	4.89	5.88	5.70

Despite the similarities noted above between these results and Giovannoni and Becerra's overall rankings, when the three professions in common between the two studies are compared (social workers, paediatricians and police), different rankings of every category emerge. In both studies, the police gave the highest ratings to sexual and then to physical abuse, as do social workers and paediatricians in the present study, but in the original the paediatricians rated physical abuse most severely. Social workers gave comparatively higher ratings to emotional abuse than the police and paediatricians in both studies, but in this study everyone rates emotional abuse more severely than neglect. It is not possible to say from these data whether the discrepancies between the studies are due to different professional cultures in the two countries or to secular changes in attitude on the part of one or more professions but rising concern about sexual abuse has been obvious in recent years.

Two further levels of analysis are probably more important, in that the severity of any incident would seem likely to be only partly dependent on its formal categorisation as sexual or physical abuse, etc., but also dependent on its particular content. The first is to establish whether individuals within a profession have a consensual view of the severity of each vignette and the second is to investigate whether any such consensus is shared interprofessionally.

Intraprofessional variations in ranking individual vignettes

Neither Giovannoni and Becerra nor Snyder and Newberger discussed the degree of consensus within groups but Fox and Dingwall reported considerable differences. They argued that these were greater among social workers than health visitors but, in fact, their results for the two groups were extremely similar. Social workers varied more than health visitors just 11 times out of 20 and actually showed a smaller sum of standard deviations. A greater homogeneity among health visitors would have been, as they argued, surprising. Although a more managerialist culture is now encouraged in the health visiting service, the then prevailing structure allowed a high level of autonomy and 'independent practitioner' status was often asserted. As they suggest, this would be expected to produce more individual variation in their ratings.

The present study found that there are differences in the homogeneity of different professions' judgments but these vary from incident to incident and range from an extremely tight standard deviation of 0.16 among the teachers on vignette 3, (sexual intercourse) to a rather wide 2.49 among the police on vignette 12 (the unkempt house). Overall, despite the apparently marked contrast between their organisational structures, in this study the health visitors do prove to have least intra-group variation and the police most. This would suggest that there is a common professional culture among health visitors which they sustain in their individual decisions, whereas, at least in specialised units such as child protection, the apparent 'command' structure of the police does not impose uniformity upon the 'street level bureaucrats' (Lipsky 1980). Social workers are the second most diffuse group overall, showing wide deviations on half the series. They have least scatter on only one incident, a serious neglect (vignette 18). The paediatricians are also quite diffuse and are the most homogeneous on only one matter (vignette 6, genital

Table 8.4 **A comparison of each profession's standard deviations in rating the severity of vignettes in each category of abuse and over the whole series of vignettes**

Profession	Mean SDs for each category				Mean SDs for whole series	Sum of SDs for series
	SA	PA	EA	N		
Health Visitors	0.87	0.95	1.49	1.54	1.26	28.95
Teachers	0.90	1.41	1.56	1.61	1.34	30.85
General Practitioners	1.25	1.51	1.82	1.56	1.46	33.56
Paediatricians	1.26	1.63	1.70	1.60	1.48	33.95
Social Workers	1.18	1.33	1.81	1.70	1.53	35.10
Police	0.93	1.38	2.16	1.56	1.55	35.72

fondling), rating it less severely than any other group. While quotation of the mean figures for each category of abuse inevitably reduces the appearance of diversity, the standard deviations summarised in Table 8.4 indicate the general pattern.

Despite these differences, within each profession almost all the variances of rating on every vignette fall within two standard deviations and a very few outliers do not distort these results in any group. Indeed, many vignettes reveal a much closer occupational consensus. This result does indicate a more homogeneous view of the incidents within each profession that might be expected across them all or across a general population. It is this degree of internal consensus which makes the later interprofessional comparisons meaningful.

However, the variety of response patterns across the different professions and across the series of vignettes, which is only suggested by the spread of the standard deviations for whole categories, can be graphically illustrated by the contrasting bar charts below. The first is a fairly typical distribution, the second and third show the most diffuse and the tightest distributions in the

Figure 8.1:   **Barcharts of severity ratings of brief vignettes selected to illustrate the diversity of response patterns**

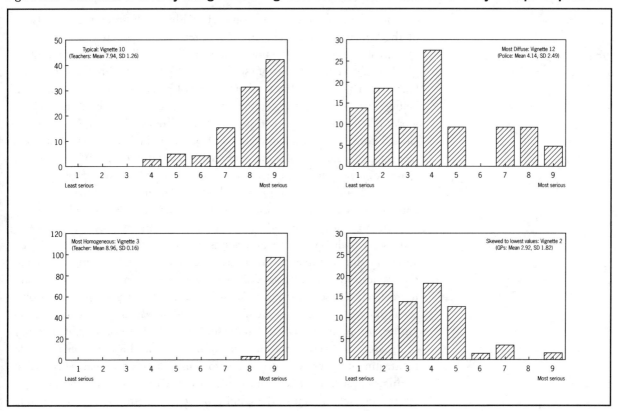

series and the last represents a not untypical pattern of responses to a low-scored neglect incident.

Discussion of intraprofessional results

The differences in variation can be classified in three ways. Sometimes there is an extremely tight consensus around a similar severity rating by every respondent in every profession. Sometimes uncertainties about the rating of particular incidents are more localised in particular professions and sometimes all the professions have equally amorphous attitudes. A close look at the patterns around individual vignettes suggests that they relate to:

consensual human outrage about extremely severe incidents;

clearer attitudes within one group or more about matters perceived as within their particular domain of skill or ideology, whereas the other groups may have more diffuse attitudes, as in the next typification;

diffuse attitudes among many groups over less severe matters, perhaps raising doubts about whether they should be construed as abuse or whether intervention may do more harm than good.

There is an extremely close consensus within each group regarding three of the sexual practices (vignette 3 – intercourse; vignette 15 – repeated masturbation, vignette 19 – nightmares after repeatedly being shown pornographic material) and one physical abuse (vignette 9 – multiple cigarette burns). On vignette 3 the teachers' dispersal is remarkably tight. Table 8.5 below shows that these vignettes all received extremely high ratings and the scores fall around or well within one standard deviation. There is nearly as close a consensus about most items of physical abuse but only about one neglect case (vignette 18 – the malnourished child in hospital). The clearest examples of attitudes that are similarly diffused within every profession are vignettes 2 and 17, relating to the child with reddened slap marks and the child allowed to run around naked in the garden, the first one given a very low mean rating and the other a rather low one on the prevailing scale.

Cases which divide the professions between homogeneous and diffuse views are more complex to discuss because they sometimes seem to represent the application of a particular skill or knowledge base and at others they seem more likely to be a matter of personal attitude and perhaps professional acculturation. These cases are also quite widespread in their overall mean ratings, spanning 3.00 to 8.48 on the severity scale. It is noteworthy that four of the nine in this class are incidents of neglect and this is an arena of child maltreatment which is known to be problematic to professionals. It is hard to distinguish cause and effect; one could speculate that the dissensus minimises referral of such cases into the child protection system where a moderating influence might be brought to bear or, alternatively, that the system is so preoccupied with physical and sexual abuse that the dissensus is tacitly encouraged to survive (the continuing neglect of neglect).

Health visitors hold the most consensual and severest views about a child being left alone in the dark (vignette 14) or having an unattended problem with his or her ears (vignette 21), both of which fall within their domain although not exclusively. One would also have expected the doctors' reactions to vignette 21 to be as consistent. Health visitors and teachers have the most united views and the highest degrees of concern about the possibly sexually abused eight year old (vignette 11). One might have expected social workers to share the same professional ideology and interest in the psycho-emotional welfare of children and to view vignettes 14 and 11 with a similarly coherent standpoint, perhaps in contrast to the preoccupations of the police and the more biotechnically oriented doctors, but this proved not to be so. It has been argued that social workers' concentrated experience of families in difficulties raises the threshold of their concern above that of other groups (Giovannoni and Becerra 1979, Stevenson 1989), which might cause them to pitch their scores at a lower level but does not explain why as a profession they make less consistent evaluations than the teachers and health visitors.

For no evident reason, the police are remarkably consensual in their horror over a single incident of genital fondling (vignette 6) when everyone else is less clear. It is not surprising that the police have the most dispersed attitudes about the child getting his own supper (vignette 7), the untreated ear (vignette 21) and the unkempt house (vignette 12), none of which is likely to fall within their professional province. However, they are also quite diffuse in their attitudes regarding a small child at large on main roads (vignette 16), whom one might expect them to worry about, and give this incident a considerably lower mean rating than general practitioners who give it both the tightest range and the highest score. On a matter which would seem to be the stock in trade of both groups, it is strange that health visitors have the most diverse views while general practitioners are relatively homogeneous in their level of concern about the baby with the sore bottom and the unruly toddler (vignette 4).

Among all the groups, health visitors have the tightest dispersion on over half the series and the lowest aggregate dispersion. With the partial exception of the neglect cases, there is a clear tendency for increasing consistency within a group to accompany a more severe rating of any incident. There seems no obvious reason for health visitors' particular homogeneity unless it is their tendency to severity, which in itself may reflect the prevalence of anxiety among them. It has been one of the stereotypes of interprofessional relation-ships that health visitors cannot get social workers to accept their concerns or, on the other hand, that they make too many trivial referrals. The field interviews in Phase Three of this study have found a high degree of anxiety among health visitors. As argued earlier, their organisational locus is fairly independent while their ideologies about children's emotional needs are probably akin to those of social workers and the primary school teachers in this sample, both of whom have quite dispersed attitudes. In contrast, the police have the most diffused attitudes overall and they are polarised from health visitors on this measure of homogeneity on almost a third of the series. It seems probable that the heterogeneity among the police is because they have no specialised knowledge base relevant to child development and child welfare as opposed to investigation and control.

A few comparisons can be made between the health visitors and social workers in the present study and in Fox and Dingwall's study in the early 1980s. The explosion of awareness and concern about sexual abuse in recent years is evident in both the professional and public presses. Although the Cleveland Inquiry (1988) arose from public fears that professionals had become over-excited about its prevalence and seriousness, there is no doubt about its continuing high profile in recent professional thought and practice. It is interesting to note the remarkable hardening and convergence of social workers' and health visitors' opinions about the two sexual abuse vignettes common to the two studies (vignettes 15 and 19) since Fox and Dingwall used them. Their ratings have gone up around two whole marks and the standard deviations have changed from 2.37 to 0.47 and from 1.55 to 0.21 respectively about vignette 15, while health visitors' opinions about vignette 19 closed from 1.62 to 0.52 standard deviations. It is difficult to deduce any particular pattern regarding the other vignettes common to the two studies, the ratings have varied slightly over time but the internal spread of opinions remains quite closely comparable. Health visitors now rate the neglected ear much more severely but social workers' opinions are rather more spread regarding that child and the one with behaviour problems. In the third severe and fully consensual case discussed above (vignette 9), social workers' views are now marginally more diffused than they were in the earlier study.

Interprofessional comparisons of individual vignette ratings

Each professional group ranked most of the incidents within each category in the same order. With marginal exceptions among social workers and health visitors, everyone ranked the sexual abuse cases in the same order. Everyone agreed the ranking of the emotional abuse cases. In ordering the vignettes of physical abuse, four professions agreed overall and there was total agreement in the top ranking of vignette nine; however, social workers disagreed with the others on the ranking of one item and health visitors gave a very discrepant order. There were more dissonances in the neglect series with social workers giving the order most divergent from anyone else. However, some broad patterns were apparent when the list was divided into three bands; this showed a unanimous ranking of the two top cases and everyone agreed in placing the remainder in the same middle and bottom bands.

This rank ordering of individual vignettes varied in several instances from that in the original study. All but the paediatricians in the original study disagree with their UK peers and with the prevailing order found here regarding sexual abuse cases. US social workers alone positioned the physical abuse group in the same order as the generality of the present respondents but a little differently from UK social workers. There was no consensus between the American professions in ranking the emotional abuse vignettes but there were very few dissents in the present study. US and UK paediatricians scored them differently although American social workers agree with social workers in the current study. Every group in both studies agrees in ranking the case of serious malnutrition (vignette 18) highest in the neglect category but there was consensus over less than half the remainder. Fox and Dingwall (1985) found only one significant difference between UK social workers and health visitors in the rank ordering of their series of vignettes, despite choosing incidents that had most sharply discriminated medical from social workers' ratings in the orginal study. They suggested that their finding related to overlaps in their professional roles. It may also be that issues of social status and gender, which were more homogeneous in their sample than in the original US sample of social workers and paediatricians, had some influence on their findings. These comparisons generally suggest considerable fluidity in such judgments of ranking between the two countries or over the intervening years.

However, despite the similarities within this study in ranking the individual vignettes, like the original study, this survey found little consensus between all the professions in rating the severity of individual vignettes, there being complete consensus on only three of the 23 items, two relating to sexual abuse and one physical and all rated as very serious. Giovannoni and Becerra found statistically significant disagreements on 88% of their series but when they applied the Newman-Kuels test, many agreements between subsets of the professions became apparent. The same was found in this study but it is not always the same groups who agree. Insofar as the groups overlap with the other previous studies, neither do the results accord with those in Snyder and Newberger or Fox and Dingwall. Snyder and Newberger found social workers and nurses converged in rating cases more severely than other professions. Fox and Dingwall's more closely comparable study of English health visitors and social workers also found no significant disagreements between the two groups whereas this study finds them in least agreement.

Table 8.5 **The vignettes and ratings by six groups of professionals**[1]

Vignette	Overall rating[2]	Group ratings					
		SWs	HVs	Teachers	Police	GPs	Paedns
Sexual Abuse (8.09)[3]							
3 On one occasion the parent and the child engaged in sexual intercourse.	8.85	8.76	8.92	8.97	8.82	8.86	8.76
15 The parent and child repeatedly engaged in mutual masturbation.	8.84	8.81	8.95	8.81	8.77	8.72	8.73
19 The parent repeatedly showed the child pornographic pictures. The child still suffers recurring nightmares.	8.35	8.44	8.77	8.75	8.23	8.52	8.45
6 On one occasion the parent fondled the child's genital area.	7.77	7.24	7.70	7.51	8.48	7.15	7.13
11 The 8-year old girl has recently become distressed at school and is showing an interest in smaller boys' genitals.	6.08	6.24	7.49	7.11	6.14	6.44	6.51
Physical Abuse (7.90)							
9 The parents burned the child on the buttocks and chest with a cigarette. The child has 2nd degree burns.	8.65	8.76	8.92	8.86	8.95	8.94	8.80
5 The parents immersed the child in a tub of hot water.	8.81	8.23	8.68	8.65	8.59	8.24	8.25
23 The parent hit the child in the face, striking with the fist.	8.58	8.34	8.73	8.41	8.09	8.17	8.08
10 The parents usually punish the child by spanking with a leather strap, leaving red marks on the child's skin.	7.44	7.50	8.17	7.94	7.91	7.59	7.40
11 The parents usually punish their child by spanking with the hand, leaving red marks on the child's skin.	6.76	5.95	6.75	5.92	6.05	5.75	6.03
Emotional Abuse (6.26)							
22 The parents have kept the child locked in since birth. They feed and bathe the child and provide basic physical care.	7.69	7.67	8.14	7.77	7.59	7.23	7.28

Vignette	Overall rating[2]	SWs	HVs	Group ratings		GPs	Paedns
				Teachers	Police		
8 The parents ignore their child most of the time, seldom talking or listening to her	6.58	6.31	7.27	6.77	6.18	6.09	6.53
13 A child has severe behavioural problems. The parents have allowed the child to undergo treatment but refuse to cooperate themselves.	5.54	5.11	5.29	5.84	4.77	5.38	5.10
1 The parents constantly compare their child with the younger sibling, sometimes implying that the child is not really their own. The child continually fights with other children.	5.22	4.98	6.06	5.56	5.05	4.71	4.45
Neglect (6.04)							
18 The parents regularly fail to feed the child for at least 24 hours. The child was hospitalized for 6 weeks for being seriously malnourished.	8.61	8.6	8.80	8.67	8.14	8.53	8.45
14 The parents regularly left their child alone inside the house after dark. Often they did not return until midnight.	7.67	7.23	8.35	7.91	7.18	7.44	7.38
20 The parents let their child sip out of their glasses when they are drinking whisky. The child has been intoxicated.	7.06	6.23	7.70	7.43	6.64	7.14	6.68
21 The parents ignored their child's complaint of an earache and chronic ear drainage.	6.92	6.50	7.60	7.37	6.86	6.58	6.15
16 Today the child was found wandering two streets away from home across a main road in a town.	6.58	5.50	7.21	6.82	5.91	7.03	6.34
7 The parents fail to prepare regular meals for their child. The child often has to fix his own supper. The child has an iron deficiency.	7.69	6.05	7.08	6.71	6.45	6.56	6.25
12 The parents live with their child in a small rented house. No one ever cleans up.	3.89	2.84	4.24	4.68	4.14	3.70	3.55

Vignette	Overall rating[2]	SWs	HVs	Group ratings			
				Teachers	Police	GPs	Paedns
4 Although clean, the baby has a sore bottom and is difficult to feed. The toddler is poorly clad and difficult to control but healthy.	3.77	3.44	3.95	4.82	3.68	3.03	3.18
2 The parents always let their child run around the house and garden without any clothes on.	5.22	2.69	3.71	4.03	3.00	2.92	3.30

[1] Underlining indicates groups who agreed – that is, indicated no significant difference in ratings based on the *Student Newman-Kuels test*
[2] This is the mean rating of all groups combined
[3] THe number in parentheses is the overall category rating

Table 8.5 above shows the results from this study, the underlinings displaying the linkages of opinion on individual cases and the shifting alliances throughout the series of vignettes. The matrix below summarises the number of disagreements between each pairing of professions.

Table 8.6 Matrix of statistically significant interprofessional disagreements in rating the 23 brief vignettes of possible child abuse

No. of disagreements between	HVs N	HVs %	Teachers N	Teachers %	Police N	Police %	GPs N	GPs %	Paed'ns N	Paed'ns %
Social Workers	13	56.5	9	39.1	3	13.0	5	21.7	0	0.0
Health Visitors			3	13.0	6	26.1	4	17.4	2	8.7
Teachers					6	26.1	10	43.5	9	39.1
Police							2	8.7	0	0.0
General Practitioners									0	0.0

Discussion of interprofessional results

Across the whole series, social workers give the lowest ratings and health visitors the most severe, so it is not surprising that these two professions provide the most numerous dissonances on the individual vignettes, on over half the series. The relative severity of teachers' ratings means they are most frequently in agreement with health visitors, disagreeing in only three cases. Teachers and health visitors are markedly different from the rest, with health visitors discrepant from at least one other profession in 18 cases. Teachers frequently disagree with social workers, general practitioners and paediatricians, and also with the police quite often. Disagreements between general practitioners and the police are rare, as they are between paediatricians and anyone else except teachers. Despite the dissonances, it should be noted that there are agreements between at least two groups in over two thirds of the possible permutations even though there is total consensus in only three cases. What would seem to matter most is whether the professions most involved and mutually dependent in specific situations give convergent or divergent ratings.

Superficially, the present findings seem to contrast with those of Giovannoni and Becerra, where police officers and social workers agreed more often that either did with paediatricians. Social workers and paediatricians agree in all the cases here and so do paediatricians and the police. Social workers also agree with the police in all but three cases. In fact, this represents a higher percentage of convergence between all three together than was found in the original and it may mean that the three investigative professions in the UK can now agree in practice when they are rating real cases. In this study as in Giovannoni and Becerra, the paediatricians as a group most frequently give a medium rating to incidents, scoring them in ways that are not significantly different from the varying coalitions of low and high scorers on both extremes. However, it would not necessarily follow from their statistically median position that the paediatricians can draw the extreme opinions together in reality. Sometimes the apparent overlaps are an artefact of relatively diffuse intra-group scores rather than rooted in a high degree of homogeneity among and between them all. This would simply indicate that the dispute is about personal values rather than professional ideologies or skills, which might, of course, then engage the paediatric consultant's political weight in any case conference in favour of his or her interpretation of the event. At other times, when the division of opinon is between front line agencies and the social worker, it might prevent the child being admitted to the interprofessional scrutiny of the child protection system.

Giovannoni and Becerra found their sample's responses cross-cut in complex ways across four professions and the different vignettes. They offered tentative rationales for some of the agreements and disagreements, based on the different professions' roles. Snyder and Newberger and Fox and Dingwall also interpret the convergences they found between nurses or health visitors and social workers as due to overlap in their work roles but the explanation seems inadequate in view of the divergence found here. The permutations of six groups in the present study are even more difficult to categorise in themselves and made even more difficult in view of results that conflict with those earlier rationales. As already noted, there is most unanimity on the most severe ratings. Among the less consensual, are there any common threads linking specific cases that unite particular coalitions or cause particular disputes?

Comments and suggestions are made on those where a pattern seems reasonably clear. Many other aspects of the study have shown health visitors to be willing and accessible cooperators and it may be their generally high level of concern about cases which motivates this. However, teachers respond strongly to these vignettes but appear generally quite distanced from the world of child protection, so the same argument does not apply to them. If it is high concern that motivates health visitors to seek cooperative efforts but their evaluations are so often at odds with others', particularly those of the social workers, they may frequently find themselves in the role of Cassandra. Acting as a crucial link between the core professions and others in the front line and peripheral professions, (see Chapter Nine) and appearing more appreciative and uncritical of interprofessional relationships than the other parties (see Chapters Six, Seven and Eleven), they may indeed find themselves doing others' 'dirty work' (Dingwall 1980) and carrying a heavy burden of anxiety.

Teachers and health visitors rate the sexualized behaviour of the 8 year old girl (vignette 11) more seriously than other professions. There is no way of knowing whether they would wish any investigative or enforcement actions to ensue at this stage (although Chapter Nine shows teachers' responses to the more contextualised version of this vignette to be distinctly low key) but the investigative agencies clearly rate the case less severely. As in Giovannoni and Becerra, the professions split differently in their comparative attitudes to fondling and pornographic pictures, with police taking vignette six most seriously and vignette 19 least seriously. One wonders whether the police have an ideology of outrage about any sexual contact whatsoever while the professions more oriented towards psychological and emotional content can be more flexible about the first incident and more disturbed by the second. These both seem to be situations where conflict could arise about appropriate responses.

Within the physical abuse category, health visitors disagree over three 'punishment' vignettes, with social workers over vignette ten and with doctors over vignettes 23 and 17. Professionals' difficulties about rating physical chastisement as a matter for official intervention are well-known, and it is perhaps for this reason that social workers give the lowest rating to one of these. In contrast to Giovannoni and Becerra's finding and interpretation, the paediatricians are relatively less concerned than the other professions about the strap and the fist and do not apparently infer potentially serious harm.

There is most confused overlap of different professional groupings in the other two categories. Health visitors agree with teachers about all four cases in the emotional abuse group but both disagree with doctors and/or with social workers about three of them, always expressing greater concern. Once again, one cannot know what intervention they would seek. It is not surprising and may be of little consequence that the police appear least attuned to emotional abuse. Although they would be likely to be informed and asked to contribute available information if a child protection conference were convened, they would be unlikely to be concerned in direct investigation of most such cases or to come into conflict over their management.

Among the neglect incidents, the police are polarised from social workers, health visitors and teachers in rating the child hospitalised for six weeks following negligent if not wilful malnutrition rather less severely (vignette 18). Interestingly, the doctors take the middle ground on that case, suggesting that the situation was not as devastating to the child's physical well-being as the others thought. Perhaps they were also less concerned about the emotional implications of being deprived of food by one's parents. This may be a case in which respondents' gender played a part. Only social workers and health visitors polarise in their views of the child getting his own supper (vignette 7). Health visitors disagree with everyone but teachers in their serious opinion of the child left unattended after dark (vignette 14). Social workers and doctors are less disturbed than others by the neglected ear problem (vignette 21). It seems likely that social workers have more flagrant situations to worry about and, as Giovannoni and Becerra argue, doctors can make the most informed and less anxious appraisal of the outcomes of such neglect.

Social workers and the police are least worried by the wandering child but this is a case where these two groups displayed quite large intra-professional differences. In respect of vignette 4, it is surprising to find general practitioners most distant from health visitors regarding a family situation that must be commonplace business for both groups. Teachers take the unkempt house and the unclothed child (vignettes 12 and 2) somewhat more seriously than social workers. While the first may be less familiar to school-based staff than to social workers, the discrepancy over the second feels more surprising. One might have assumed that primary school teachers, particularly if they are acquainted with nursery classes, might be accustomed to small children running around undressed at times. Poor housekeeping standards are very familiar to social workers and it has been argued (Dingwall et al 1983, Stevenson 1989) that they become undesirably inured to them and this could explain their rating of vignette 12. However, Giovannoni and Becerra argue the obverse from some of their results, that social workers and the police are alert to the harm done by poor environments and careless supervision.

Previous studies concluded that respondents' different attitudes to diverse situations reflected their agency function or professional expertise and not idiosyncratic factors. For instance, Giovannoni and Becerra found paediatricians making more discriminating and sometimes less serious assumptions about medical conditions than other groups but having little sensitisation to poor home environments. They argued that lawyers give parsimonious ratings out of respect for family rights while social workers and the police share an ideology of protective responsibility over a wide range of children's situations. Snyder and Newberger and Fox and Dingwall similarly argue that training and work roles offer the most promising explanation of the rating patterns. Professional identity emerges as the dominant variable in every other aspect of this research project; this segment also shows greater homogeneity of attitudes within than between the professions but it has also revealed enough variations from the coalitions found in the previous studies to cast doubt on the specific interpretations they offered for the agreements and disagreements. It would seem probable that none of the work roles is so one-dimensional as to support one unequivocal conclusion about the reasons for consensus and conflict in particular cases. Furthermore, the moderate measures of intra-professional dispersion also suggest that personal values have some salience.

Summary and conclusions

The small scale replication of Giovannoni and Becerra's (1979) original vignette study investigated the degree of consensus between individuals and professions in rating the severity of various incidents of possible abuse. Physical and sexual abuse are evidently rated more severely than the other categories by all the professions. Within the categories, it is clearly more difficult to establish either internal or interprofessional consensus about cases deemed less severe. This must cause problems in establishing a baseline for protective intervention. As was expected, cases of neglect and emotional abuse cause most dissensus. There is total interprofessional consensus in only a minority of cases but there are many areas of agreement within and between the professions which should support a considerable degree of consensual action.

The coalitions of view vary from case to case but it may be reassuring that there are relatively few divergences between the core investigative professions. There are no divergences between general practitioners and the police or paediatricians and few between teachers and health visitors. As a group, paediatricians most often give median ratings which appear to be consensual with outlying groups on either side but the degree to which that statistical finding indicates that they can draw the other professions' views into harmony is unexplored. The most numerous disagreements are between health visitors and social workers, the two professions who are most frequently interweaving their continuing support and observation of the same families. Other data support the view that teachers are little involved in the network but, if their ongoing pastoral role were exploited more systematically, the discrepancies between their ratings and social workers' might also assume more importance in practice.

These observations do suggest real tensions between the frontline and the core professions around thresholds of concern and intervention. There is some support for the stereotypical view of overanxious health visitors and teachers pressing impassive social workers who will not be moved. Conflicts between doctors and social workers, prominent in Chapter Eleven, however, seem more likely to relate to discrepancies of status and organisational structure than to disputes about the rating of cases. The particular patterns of agreement only sometimes replicate those in the previous studies and therefore cast doubt on the adequacy of the rationales, rooted in professional skill or role, offered by them.

It is worth considering whether more interprofessional training and joint rating exercises, backed up by some common education in child development, could reduce these discrepancies. Some are no doubt inherent in the different personal and cultural values of each individual in this society. It seems pertinent to echo Kempe and Helfer (1972) on the importance of essentially different people providing interpersonal data for the assessment, and Dingwall et al (1983) on the protection of families from monolithic professional control that such diverse views offer.

Chapter 9

Proposals for intervention in a developing case vignette:

Introduction

This chapter and the next explore interprofessional cooperation and coordination in more specific terms than have been reported so far, by discussing the responses given to a developing case vignette and a sequence of questions about what respondents would do. The reasons for incorporating this approach are more fully discussed in Chapter Two. The main strengths of vignettes as a research technique are that they offer respondents concrete stimuli which would seem to be easily related to their everyday professional responsibilities and to decisions they may have made in the past. In the context of this total research programme, a major virtue is that one can thus explore the understandings and intentions of a large random sample, regardless of their present participation in the network, in contrast to Phase Three which is restricted to a smaller number of those currently involved in cases.

The main theoretical weaknesses of vignettes arise from their hypothetical nature and the unknown load of meanings attributed to them by respondents. However, the two problems of action and meaning are not exclusive to vignettes but affect all research which utilises people's reports rather than direct observation, and the triangulation of different methods is designed to reduce any distortions that may arise between people's hypothetical actions and actual behaviours. The second problem of meaning would appear to affect much wider fields of life than the research activity alone. Meanings inferred from personal values and experience inevitably impinge on many professional judgments. Most often the way a child protection career begins is by one professional evaluating someone else's unease, frequently conveyed briefly in words, about a possible case of child abuse. Even at the stage of the child protection conference, the interprofessional discussion is still somewhat abstracted from the total reality and remains subject to a whole range of participants' unarticulated assumptions. The literature review (Hallett and Birchall 1992) discusses the salience of many such unspoken values and the apparent impossibility of elucidating them all in practice. Therefore, although the vignette format is an abbreviation or representation of reality, in many respects it would seem to be a reasonable surrogate.

Two vignettes, one further subdivided to feature either a black child or one of unspecified race, were alternately distributed to the sample in 50:25:25 proportions. Response patterns matched this distribution closely, with 85 responses to the black variant of vignette A, 85 to the other and 167 to vignette B. Each vignette unfolded through three different stages culminating in a child protection conference. Identical questions were asked at the first two stages to explore the extent to which people varied their response patterns in the light of added information; the third stage explored their expectations of attendances at the conference and their opinions about future plans for the children.

Stage One

Vignette A. Stage 1.

> *In the course of your duties, you hear that a neighbour has said the six month old baby next door has chilblains on her hands and is often crying. The mother is a 19 year old (Black Caribbean) and has a toddler. She lives on Social Security and her fuel has been cut off.*

(NB. to simplify the commentary, the report will call this family the Youngs when there is no need to differentiate between the black and unspecified variants).

or Vignette B. Stage 1.

> *Eight year old Jane, one of three children, had been a happy and confident child. Father is a local businessman and active in Rotary. Mother is a schoolteacher. There are now marital problems and mother is starting divorce proceedings.*
>
> *In the course of your work you observe or are told by someone you respect that this child has recently become miserable and secretive with grownups. She seems now to be rather hostile to men. She plays with smaller boys and is said to show a lot of interest in their private parts. Her schoolwork is deteriorating.*

Initial thoughts and action proposals

The first few questions explored people's initial reactions in the light of the given information. Two were open-ended and designed to tap their free and spontaneous assessments of the situation and of the response they would make. Up to nine answers were coded regarding such reactions and a further two reasons for taking no action were noted, if applicable.

All but one of the respondents acknowledge some concern about the situations initially outlined; the single exception related to the child expressing sexual curiosity. While the majority express their concerns in varied or general terms, 38% specifically raise a consideration of child abuse. Only nine people (less than 3%) say they would take no action, mainly regarding Jane. This level of concern and active intention is somewhat surprising but it would perhaps be difficult for respondents to admit to unconcern or to ignore the suspicion of child abuse in the context of this research programme. One wonders whether as many people would translate their concern into concrete activity in the course of everyday work. In fact, 8% of respondents go on to offer reasons why they might not react in any way at this stage; over half of these say the story does not warrant it and nine each also suggest another agency might already be involved or it was not their responsibility. These negative responses came from all areas and all professions but the police.

Answers varied considerably in length and specificity and may not all have been comprehensive. For instance, thoughts ranged from 'Contact the health visitor' to 'Single parent mother under stress because of financial problems; ?not coping with care of two young children; ?child neglected; ?neighbour influenced by racial prejudice; mother unsupported'. Consequential actions vary from 'Ask the health visitor to do a routine visit' to 'Check records in SSD; speak to neighbour who referred and ascertain whether any concerns re parenting; ?visit; negotiate with gas/electricity boards/DSS (either self or HV)'. People's responses to these two unstructured questions did not always draw a distinct boundary between thoughts and action proposals but the content was classified and coded according to whether they referred to perceptions and evaluation of an approach to the case or whether they indicated some concrete activity.

An extended coding of the positive responses is summarised in Tables 9.1 and 9.2, generally in descending order of frequency, except that three responses applying only to Jane are grouped at the foot of Table 9.1. The first level of analysis is simply to explore the range of ideas and action proposals presented by the sample as a whole; in this form, the discrete answers are generally too few to test again most independent variables and so the thoughts and actions were then combined and collapsed into broader categories for the bulk of the analyses reported later. As can be seen, the most frequent responses signify a feeling that the situations depicted are unsatisfactory and 'something ought to be done'. A quarter of respondents initially think in terms of supporting the mother, but otherwise many different ideas are expressed. In view of the prevailing emphasis in recent years on the starting point of 'protecting children' (Dale et al 1986, DH 1988), it is interesting that no respondent used this phrase in their initial thoughts. It is also interesting to note that nobody, not even the police respondents, started with the notion of a criminal offence.

Some differences in thoughts about the different vignettes are significant, mainly distinguishing Jane from the Young family. However, there are a few differences between the racial variants; just two respondents remark on the need for racial or cultural sensitivity in dealing with the black family and nobody queries the ethnic background in the two vignettes where it was unspecified. Fewer people propose some non-specific follow-up of the black family but they are offset by the greater number proposing support to the

Table 9.1. **Respondents' initial thoughts on reading stage one of the vignettes**

Thoughts	Respondents (N = 328)		Responses (N = 553)
	N	%	%
Concern – general	176	53.7	31.8
Concern – child abuse?	121	36.9	21.8
Mother needs support or help	79	24.1	14.3
Situation needs unspecified follow-up	58	17.7	10.5
Either parent abusive?	19	5.8	3.4
Child – assess/observe/interview/examine	13	4.0	2.5
Situation needs inter-agency approach	13	4.0	2.5
Could be malicious or baseless story	12	3.7	2.2
Assumption/probably child abuse	11	3.4	2.0
Concern – other siblings	8	2.4	1.4
Not my (agency's) responsibility	6	1.8	1.1
Situation needs CP investigation	4	1.2	0.8
Multi/subcultural sensitivity	2	0.6	0.4
Unconcerned	1	0.3	0.2
I ought to have been told	1	0.3	0.2
I ought to have spotted this	0	0.0	0.0
Protect child	0	0.0	0.0
? offence	0	0.0	0.0
Interest in genitalia – ? insignificant	5	1.5	0.9
Interest in genitalia – ? sexual abuse	2	0.6	0.4
Exclude father	1	0.3	0.2
Other	18	5.5	3.3

Notes: Respondents were allowed multiple responses and therefore the first column sums to more than 100%.

mother. Only 10% explicitly raise the question of abuse in either variant of that vignette. The pattern of responses is quite different as regards Jane, with over a third directly querying abuse. Of the 19 explicit questions about possibly abusive parenting, 18 relate to her but only one of the 12 suggestions that the story could be baseless. A more active investigative approach is immediately in mind, with nearly two thirds of the proposals to examine or interview the child referring to her. Very few people commented on her interest in little boys' genitalia but most of these consider this inconsequential.

In Table 9.2 below, a wide array of specific action proposals have been grouped into 23 fairly fine categories. Different disciplines have different modes of investigating but it is important to distinguish front line screening from specific investigation. For instance, when social workers and other core professions have said they are undertaking a child protection investigation, or the police that they will interview the family or a paediatrician examine the child, it is clear that specialist evaluation of a suspicion of abuse is in hand, and likewise if another discipline refers the case explicitly to one of the investigative agencies for this purpose. All such initiatives have been grouped under the heading of 'Child protection investigation; special medical; interview family'. In contrast, when a non-specialist says they will check the story,

Table 9.2. **Respondents' initial action proposals on reading stage one of the vignettes**

Action proposals	Respondents (N = 332)		Responses (N = 568)
	N	%	%
Exchange evaluation/planning with other agencies	99	29.8	17.4
Actively initiate help	93	28.0	16.4
Gather information from other agencies and/or Child Protection Register	70	21.1	12.3
Refer/leave issue to other agency/discipline	50	15.0	8.8
Advocate/arrange (non-CP) services	40	12.0	7.0
Inform other agency/discipline	28	8.4	4.9
Report situation to superior/specialist	26	7.8	4.6
CP investigation; specialist medical: Interview the family	25	7.5	4.4
Note information/observe/talk to peers	24	7.2	4.2
Talk to family or child opportunistically	22	6.6	3.9
Ask another agency to assess and report back	20	6.0	3.5
Check own agency records/knowledge of case	18	5.4	3.2
Consult superior/specialist within agency	18	5.4	3.2
Check story with child/PHCT examination	9	2.7	1.6
Seek report from subordinate	9	2.7	1.6
Write inviting parent to office, clinic, etc	5	1.5	0.9
Joint visit with other agency	5	1.5	0.9
Write parents/child to seek help	4	1.2	0.7
Seek child protection conference	4	1.2	0.7
Give background information to other discipline/ agency	1	0.3	0.2
Await instructions	1	0.3	0.2
Other	4	1.2	0.7
Nothing	9	2.7	1.6

Notes
1. Abbreviations used in the table: CP is child protection; PHCT is the primary health care team including general practitioners, community nurses and health visitors.
2. Respondents were allowed multiple responses and therefore the first column sums to more than 100%.

examine the child or invite the parents in, this primary level assessment has not been classified as a child protection investigation. A wide range of practical services like advocacy with fuel boards or arrangement of a day nursery place have been categorised as 'arranging other (non-CP) services'.

It is noteworthy that the most frequently proposed action is an actively cooperative one, to exchange evaluations and planning with other agencies, a purpose that would inevitably entail the gathering of information from one another. However, it is equally noteworthy that only one fifth of respondents (at the maximum) spontaneously propose to collect information from the child protection register and even fewer explicitly propose a child protection investigation at this stage. Many varying ways to follow up the case are put forward, most frequently by some personal commitment to initiate help oneself but also in a significant number of cases by referring the situations to another agency.

As before, only a few of the proposals for action differentiate the black variant from its pair but they are all in the direction of more active intervention. Three staff would consult a superior about the black toddler but none in the other version. While only nine respondents would explicitly assess child protection issues at this stage, six of these are in relation to the black family. A slightly higher proportion (21% against 18%) would exchange information and plans with other agencies and almost twice as many (16%) would advocate or arrange other services to support the family. Action proposals for Jane are markedly different. Staff are over six times as likely to say they would note and observe the situation and would more often talk to the child, either opportunistically or deliberately planning to explore the story, and are also more likely to discuss it in a supervisory setting. There would be more gathering of information and less inclination simply to notify or leave the case to another agency at this early stage. This may reflect either people's simple fear of intervention after the Cleveland affair or a wholesome recognition that a more gradual unfolding of the truth may be more effective than hasty action in such situations.

Further analysis of thoughts and action proposals

A descriptive analysis was made of a few values that appeared particularly discrete or interesting but where numbers were too small for statistical tests. Eight of the 11 respondents who start with an assumption that abuse was occurring are doctors. More than half the concerns about siblings come from teachers. The six responses indicating that the case is 'not my responsibility' come from every profession but health visitors. All these responses were scattered through the areas and the ranks. As already noted, people make multiple and often overlapping responses but it is possible to rank them approximately according to the degree of activity entailed. As displayed in

Table 9.3, concepts were grouped together for further analysis and the following commentary uses only the discrete responses or the most 'active' of overlapping proposals (e.g. where a respondent has said they would inform another agency and collect information from others and/or act concurrently and in liaison with them, only the last item is scored). Combining the thoughts and actions makes a negligible difference to the balance, as reported earlier, between a predisposition to approach the case as possible child abuse or with more varied concerns but 29% of respondents are found to express both approaches.

Table 9.3. **Broad categorisation of initial responses to Stage One of the vignettes: frequency of responses**

Action proposals	Respondents (N = 332)		Responses (N = 1121)
	N	%	%
Non-specific concern	175	51.6	15.6
Initial focus on child abuse issues	130	38.3	11.6
Initiate help (not explicitly re CP)	115	33.9	10.3
Act in liaison or jointly with other agencies	106	31.3	9.5
Handle the situation myself	84	24.8	7.5
Gather outside information	79	23.3	7.0
Inform other agency/discipline	72	21.2	6.4
Initial focus on helping mother	69	20.4	6.2
Non-specific follow-up	57	16.8	5.1
Discuss with own management/specialists	54	15.9	4.8
Investigate CP issues	25	7.4	2.2

Notes
1. Respondents were allowed multiple responses and therefore the first column sums to more than 100%.
2. The percentage of response is worked out against the sum of all the responses (1121) in the initial listing; as some minor categories and miscellaneous answers have been dropped from this table and subsequent analyses, they do not sum to 100%.

The large majority of people (90%) are concerned about the situations outlined but, in these open-ended answers, diverse patterns of activity are put forward. A third propose some form of liaison and concurrent action, involving a degree of joint discussion and joint decision making or, in a few cases, seeking a case conference. Only five, one social worker and four police officers, visualise any form of joint activity and in their case it means a joint interview. Almost all those who would both gather information from and give it to external agencies would also act in liaison in some respect. Another 12% indicated they would simply inform another agency but also follow up the situation in some way themselves. Relatively few (7%) would do no more than inform another agency. Only three indicated they would simply report the situation to a management or specialist colleague. A closed question elicited that 14% would not contact any other agency or discipline at this point. The general picture is of a large majority engaging in discussion with other agencies in deciding what to do about the children but, when the case is labelled 'suspected child abuse', only the social workers and the police mentioning joint action (focussed on the forensic task). It seems as though there may, pro rata, be more hands–on cooperation between agencies in delivering services other than child protection investigation.

As expected, people's perceptions and intentions varied on several points, depending on the vignette they were given, and Table 9.4 shows the statistically significant variations.

Table 9.4. **A comparison of significant variations between responses to the different vignettes at stage one**

	Vignette				
	U.R.*	**Black**	**Jane**	**Total**	
	(N = 87)	**(N = 85)**	**(N = 167)**	**(N = 339)**	
Action orientation	**%**	**%**	**%**	**N**	**%**
Non-specific concern	40.2	48.2	56.2	175	51.6
Initial focus child abuse					
issues	18.6	18.6	58.7	130	38.3
Initiate help (not explicitly CP)	42.6	40.0	26.3	115	33.9
Inform other agency/					
discipline	33.3	25.8	16.8	79	23.3
Handle the situation myself	16.1	11.8	28.7	72	21.1
Initial focus on helping					
mother	39.1	41.2	0.0	69	20.4
Non-specific follow-up	26.5	17.6	11.3	57	16.8
Discuss with own					
management/specialist/					
subordinate	4.6	10.6	24.6	54	15.9

Note:
1. *Family of unspecified race
2. Respondents were allowed multiple responses and therefore the first column sums to more than 100%.
p = <.02, CC.15937; p = <.0001, CC.38101; p = <.02, CC.15685; p = .02, CC.16260
p = <.005, CC.18159; p = <.0001, CC.44612; p = .01, CC.16367; p = .0002, CC.23278

Three main points seem to emerge about Jane. Overall, she arouses much more concern than the Young family but twice as many people see her situation as one they can handle within their own agency despite the comparatively high level of awareness that it might be a case of sexual abuse. Secondly, a quarter would consult their own management or specialist colleagues about her whereas few would be immediately thinking of the need for such support in dealing with the Young family. Thirdly, in Jane's case nobody articulates an approach based on supporting the mother and there are far fewer helping initiatives of any kind. As one would expect, there is less clear distinction between the variants of the Young family but there were some differences which have no foundation in the story as presented. While it is hard to see any particular meaning in the greater use of referral to another agency and unspecified follow-up for the family of unspecified race than the black family, the smaller likelihood of handling it alone and greater recourse to management or specialist colleagues about the latter does suggest a higher degree of anxiety in dealing with them. These varied reactions to the different vignettes are interesting and suggest that respondents were thoughtfully engaged in the research process. However, the issue that arises for this research is not that different cases elicit different responses but whether there are discrepancies between the professions or any other groupings or respondents in the way particular cases are perceived and which might therefore create conflict or friction in their interventions. This was borne out regarding several factors.

Action proposals analysed by profession

From the responses in Table 9.3 above regarding all the vignettes, only those which revealed professionally distinctive patterns are discussed. An initial orientation towards the information as 'possible/probable abuse' varied across the professions, from 49% among general practitioners, closely followed by social workers, to around a quarter of police and teachers. Among those who proposed one or more of a bundle of activities that constituted handling the situation themselves, the numbers also varied significantly, from 5% of paediatricians and police to 29% of social workers and 36% of teachers. Only 5% of teachers would gather information from other agencies compared with 50% of social workers. Between 20% and 30% of most professions would 'initiate help' but this varied from 18% of paediatricians to 66% of health visitors. Teachers are the most likely to discuss or report the situation to their heads, few of whom suggest contact with social services. Health visitors are also likely to discuss the case with their superiors or specialist colleagues but none of the police would report up.

Only these significantly different response patterns were then compared in relation to the individual vignettes. See Table 9.5 for a summary. The much higher overall index of suspicion regarding Jane's case as possible child abuse nevertheless varies widely from a third of teachers to three quarters of social workers. The professions also vary in their readiness to manage Jane's case themselves or inform another agency, and about whether to initiate help or to consult within the agency. There are no consistent interprofessional differences in proposals for the racial variants and fewer significant variations between them regarding the Young family at all, but they do arise regarding

Table 9.5. **Interprofessional variations in response to the different vignettes at stage one**

Approach		SW N	SW %	HV N	HV %	Teacher N	Teacher %	Police N	Police %	GP N	GP %	Paed'n N	Paed'n %	Total N	Total %
Suspicion of child abuse	1. Young family					Not significant								32	18.6
	2. Jane	24	75.0	23	69.7	14	33.3	5	45.5	20	64.5	12	66.7	98	58.7
Mother needs help	3. Young family	14	46.7	20	57.1	18	46.2	4	36.4	7	20.0	6	27.3	69	40.1
	4. Jane					Not significant								0	0.0
Handle it myself	5. Young family					Not significant								24	13.6
	6. Jane	12	37.5	4	12.1	23	54.8	1	9.1	7	22.6	1	5.6	48	28.7
Inform other agency	7. Young family	4	13.3	5	14.3	16	41.0	8	72.7	9	25.7	9	40.9	51	29.7
	8. Jane	6	18.8	5	15.2	2	4.8	5	45.5	7	22.6	3	16.7	28	16.8
Discuss with superiors/ specialists/subordinates	9. Young family					Not significant								13	7.4
	10. Jane	4	12.5	11	33.3	25	59.5	0	0.0	0	0.0	1	5.6	41	24.6
Initiate help to family	11. Young family	17	56.7	30	85.7	8	20.5	5	45.5	9	25.7	2	9.1	71	41.3
	12. Jane	1	3.1	15	45.5	13	31.0	0	0.0	10	32.3	5	27.8	44	26.3

Notes:
N for the three vignettes: Family of unspecified race 87; Black family 85; Jane 167. Percentages relate to the population for each vignette and not to the total population in each profession.
Each respondent was allowed multiple answers; therefore the percentages do not sum to 100.

2. Jane: p = <.005, CC.31191; 3. Young family: p = <.001, CC.31191; 4. Jane: p = <.001, CC.26339; 4. Jane: p = <.0002, CC.37251; 5. Young family: p = <.001, CC.33397; 6. Jane: p = <.05, CC.25615; 7. Jane: p = <.0001, CC.47549; 8. Young family: p = <.0001, CC.47952; 9. Jane: p = <.002, CC.32756

informing another agency, helping the mother and initiating other forms of help.

Some variations appear to relate simply to different professional functions. For instance, in relation to the Young family health visitors are particularly likely to speak in terms of 'mother needs help' or to propose a variety of directly helping initiatives; social workers take similar standpoints but doctors are least likely to do so. However, other variations seem also to suggest attitudinal or perceptual differences towards the situations which then lead to different judgments about the appropriate response. This is particularly clear in the matter of construing a case as probable abuse or not. The majority of teachers do not construe Jane's situation as an abuse query and therefore propose neither to gather information from nor to involve other agencies. The non-labelling of the case implies an underlying perceptual difference from which the other two points derive; teachers might well deem information-gathering an inappropriate function for themselves but referral to an investigative agency would seem a necessary alternative once they cross a threshold of suspicion. The other front line agencies, health visitors and general practitioners, see the case and also react more like the social workers and paediatricians. But interestingly, among the investigative professions, the police react differently to both vignettes; the paediatricians and social workers are, as expected, more likely than others to 'investigate child protection issues' in all of them but none of the police would take up any of the cases at this stage. The contrast between the key professions is clearest in the case of Jane where, taking a position closest to the teachers, less than half the police suspect abuse; it seems that they would consider the story too slender to suggest the need for their attention at this stage and they are rather unlikely to seek any other intervention for her. To take this paragraph full circle, neither teachers nor the police appear to have any more of a role 'helping mother' or 'initiating help to the family' than the doctors but the former much more frequently conceptualise the needed interventions in those terms. It may be that this split follows gender lines rather than professional postures.

These variations in unstructured responses suggest a complex cross-cutting of people's professional task orientations and personal views in relation to the different cases and different proposals. This is not a surprising finding but it does mean that much cooperative activity in the child protection network is situationally specific, probably extremely difficult for the practitioners to articulate into generalised rules and certainly difficult to conceptualise theoretically. Few other personal variables appeared to correlate significantly with these action choices but these are covered later, together with those that impinged at stage two of the vignettes. The next passage considers people's spontaneous proposals for initial interventions at stage two, which are discussed in the same format as stage one.

Stage Two

Vignette A. Stage 2.

> You now learn that the baby Sarah is below the third centile in weight and
> height. Margaret, the mother, says she is difficult to feed and is anxious
> about her. She is clean but has a sore bottom.

> The toddler Jimmy is robust though not very warmly dressed. He is very
> active and rather rough with his toys and his mother.

> Sarah has a bruise on her lower cheek.

or Vignette B. Stage 2.

> Mother says that Jane talks with other girls about big, stiff penises/willies
> with white stuff. Mother says she has started bedwetting and her vulva is
> sore.

> Mother is very upset about the breakup of the marriage, blames her
> husband and is determined to win custody of all the children and deny him
> access. She says the child is afraid to be near him sometimes but at others
> wants to climb on his lap and stroke him. She has always been Daddy's
> favourite. Mother now suggests he has been sexually abusing her.

Initial thoughts and action proposals

The data for this stage were analysed in the same way as that for stage one
and the extended coding of people's multiple positive responses is found in
the Statistical Appendix (Tables 9.23 and 9.24). Only a few more action
proposals in aggregate emerge at stage two but a comparison of detailed
responses at the two stages shows several markedly different choices. Spontaneous reactions to these stories are more frequently explicitly oriented to the
issue of child abuse. Although the numbers querying the possibility of abuse
remain similar, far fewer now express non-specific concern and 22% instead
of 3% make a positive assumption that abuse is probably occurring. However,
eight teachers still consider the story warrants no response. 10% of the total
sample are now querying whether a parent is implicated although a significantly greater number (18%) also note that the story could be malicious.

There is a major shift away from support and service approaches towards a
planned and purposeful investigation of suspected abuse. Four times as many
are considering the need to help the children directly, to assess them more
formally and to pursue an abuse investigation. Only half as many mention
helping the mother. The question of 'protecting the child' emerges for the
first time but only explicitly from six respondents; still nobody talks in terms
of any criminal offences. The need for an explicit interagency approach to
investigation and management is more often expressed, although still by only

11% of respondents. While the proportions who would inform or exchange information with other agencies remain similar, fewer would gather information for themselves and more would work in continuing liaison with other agencies or, particularly in Jane's case, refer the case out. Table 9.6 compares the frequency and rank ordering of proposals across the two stages, listed in descending order of frequency at the second stage.

Once again the important question for this research is whether respondents' views and intentions towards each vignette or to the different stages

Table 9.6. **A comparison of action proposals at stages one and two, featuring any actions mentioned by over five respondents at either stage**

Action proposals	Stage 1 (N = 332) %	Stage 2 (N = 324) %
Exchange evaluation/planning with other agencies	29.8	33.2
Child protection investigation; specialist medical; interview family	7.5	28.3
Refer/leave issue to other agency/discipline	15.0	25.8
Actively initiate help	28.0	12.9
Report matter to superior/specialist within agency	7.8	9.5
Consult superior/specialist within agency	5.4	9.2
Inform other agency/discipline	8.4	8.9
Gather information from other agencies and/or Child Protection Register	21.1	8.9
Joint visit with other agency	1.2	8.6
Seek child protection conference	1.2	6.5
Check story with child/PHCT examination	2.7	5.5
Advocate/arrange (non-CP) services	12.0	4.9
Note information/observe/talk to peers	7.2	2.5
Ask another agency to assess and report back	6.0	2.2
Check own agency records/knowledge of case	5.4	1.8
Seek report from subordinate	2.7	1.8
? PSO, Care proceedings, Child Protection Registration	0.0	0.9
Talk to family or child opportunistically	6.6	0.6
Write inviting parent to office, clinic, etc	1.5	0.6
Give background information to other discipline/agency	0.3	0.6
Other	1.2	1.5
Nothing	2.7	2.2

Notes:
1. Abbreviations used in the table: PSO in Place of Safety Order, now designated an Emergency Protection Order; PHCT is the primary health care team including general practitioners, community nurses and health visitors.
2. Respondents were allowed multiple responses and therefore the first column sums to more than 100%.

vary on any identifiable group variable or whether they are expressions of individual choice. The detailed responses were grouped into the same categories as at stage one and are displayed in Table 9.7 below.

Table 9.7. **Broad categorisation of initial responses to stage two of the vignettes: frequency of responses**

Action proposals	Respondents (N = 324)		Response (N = 1210)
	N	%	%
Initial focus on child abuse issues	195	57.5	16.1
Act in liaison with other agencies/ disciplines	144	42.5	11.9
Inform other agency/discipline	106	31.3	8.8
Investigate child protection issues	91	26.8	7.5
Non-specific concern	85	25.1	7.0
Discuss with own management/specialists/ subordinates	67	19.8	5.5
Initiate help (not explicitly re CP)	53	15.6	4.4
Non-specific follow-up	40	11.8	3.3
Initial focus on helping mother	38	11.2	3.1
Gather outside information	36	10.6	3.0
Handle the situation myself	32	9.4	2.6

Notes:
1. Respondents were allowed multiple responses and therefore the first column sums to more than 100%.
2. The percentage of response is worked out against the sum of all the responses (1210) in the initial lining, some minor categories and miscellaneous answers having been dropped from this table and subsequent analyses. Therefore, they do not sum to 100%.

Again, there are few distinctions between detailed responses to the variants of the vignette regarding Jimmy and Sarah but such as there are signify greater concern about the black family (25% compared with 20% querying abuse and slightly higher proportions mentioning generalised concern, the need for an interagency approach and the children's need for help) and the action proposals for the black variant perhaps show a harsher approach. Nine fewer would initiate help to the black family although equal numbers would advocate for supportive services to either family. At stage one, 12 people (14%) were classified as simply 'notifying' another agency of the black family's situation but only two would do so now. Such an action might have been support-oriented or investigative, but at this stage those 12 intentions have shifted to initiating an explicit child protection assessment. The same shift has not occurred in relation to the family of unspecified race.

Several detailed reactions to Jane are different. Four fifths of the assumptions of abuse and all of the few concerns about possible siblings relate to her. Her story gives rise to 90% of the suspicious fingers pointed at a parent but also to all the queries that the story could be malicious. Nobody suggests the matter is not their responsibility; fewer indicate they would assess the situation personally, more would refer the case away and more are also thinking about an interagency approach. As at the first stage, most supervisory discussions relate to Jane and most of the proposed formal interagency activity refers to her rather than to Jimmy and Sarah (66% of the proposals of interagency planning and 86% of the joint investigations). The two mentions of criminal investigation also arose from this case.

However, when respondents' detailed proposals were grouped into the broader categorisations of Table 9.7, interventions for the three vignettes varied less than they did at stage one. This finding is not surprising and confirms the pattern in the brief vignettes, where there was greater convergence of views where the cases were more severe and clearcut. These few variations are summarised in Table 9.8 below.

Table 9.8. **A comparison of significant variations between responses to the different vignettes at stage two**

	Vignette			Total	
	U.R.*	Black	Jane		
	(N = 87)	(N = 85)	(N = 167)		
Action orientation	%	%	%	N	%
Initial focus child abuse issues	37.9	56.5	68.3	195	57.5
Non-specific concern	35.6	50.6	6.6	85	25.1
Discuss with own management/specialist	11.5	16.5	25.7	67	19.8
Initiate help (not explicitly CP)	31.0	20.0	5.4	53	15.6
Initial focus on helping mother	17.2	23.5	1.8	38	11.2

Notes:
1. *Family of unspecified race.
2. Respondents were allowed multiple responses and therefore the first column sums to more than 100%.
p = <.0001, CC.24469; p = <.0001, CC.40110; p = <.02, CC.15281; p = <.0001, CC.28583; p = <.0001; CC.28950.

To summarise, amid a generally higher level of suspicion of abuse, the family of unspecified race is least likely to be so labelled and managed and Jane most likely. General expressions of 'concern' and proposals of 'help' are markedly fewer for Jane.

Action proposals analysed by profession

Not only are there fewer variations between the vignettes; the different professions have more convergent views of how to handle them. Among the generally fewer proposals to handle the situations themselves, there are now no significant variations between the disciplines. More would inform other agencies, three times as many as at stage one (45%) in the case of health visitors. Only those variables which reveal professionally distinctive patterns of response or which are notably different from those in stage one are discussed. Although the general level of suspicion has risen, professions again vary in their initial orientation towards 'possible/probable abuse' but the pattern is now different. Now two thirds of social workers, paediatricians and health visitors, and nearly as many police, see the case in this light; 44% of teachers now consider this issue but only two more of the general practitioners.

Altogether fewer 'helping' initiatives would now occur but the pattern of such responses has also changed a little since stage one. Although only half as often, health visitors remain the most likely to proffer help but the police are now the least likely to do so. More respondents, particularly among the health visitors, would consult their own managerial and specialist colleagues. Fewer intend simply gathering information from other agencies; police, paediatricians and social workers in particular are turning their attention to explicit child abuse investigation. 61% of social workers, 82% of the police and half the paediatricians would now be seeking to act concurrently and in liaison with another agency.

Some discrepancies continue between the professions in their responses to the individual vignettes but fewer than at the first stage. Although responses were sometimes too few to be statistically tested, those that suggest clear differences are shown in Table 9.9. Strangely, rather fewer general practitioners than at stage one (16 compared with 20) label Jane as 'suspected child abuse' but notably more teachers, paediatricians and police do. It seems as though the general practitioners who have dropped the abuse suspicion may be more sceptical of the mother's motives and story than the other professions. There is no significant interprofessional variation in the much greater prospensity to consider the black family as possibly abusive, whereas the attitudes of everyone but the doctors to the other family are less suspicious. Interprofessional differences emerge regarding the mother's need for help only in respect of the black family. The contrast is particularly strong between the police, two thirds of whom think she should be helped, and general practitioners, none of whom propose such an approach. There seems little consistency in people's attitudes to 'initiating help' in relation to both variants of the Young family, either across the vignettes or according to their professional role, but small numbers of health visitors and teachers are almost alone in proposing such initiatives with Jane. They are also much the most likely to seek intra-agency support in dealing with her.

Table 9.9. **Interprofessional variations in response to the different vignettes at stage two**

Approach		SW		HV		Teacher		Police		GP		Paed'n		Total	
		N	%	N	%	N	%	N	%	N	%	N	%	N	%
Suspicion of abuse	1. Family of U.R.*	4	30.8	4	25.0	4	20.0	2	33.3	13	59.1	6	60.0	33	37.9
	Black family					Not significant								48	56.5
	Jane	25	78.1	25	75.8	23	54.8	8	72.7	16	51.6	17	94.4	114	68.3
Mother needs help	Family of U.R.*					Not significant								15	17.2
	Black family	6	35.3	4	21.1	4	21.1	3	60.0	0	.0	3	25.0	20	23.5
	Jane					Not significant								3	1.8
Discuss with superiors/ specialists/subordinates	Young family					Not significant								24	14.0
	Jane	2	6.3	18	54.5	20	47.6	0	.0	1	3.2	2	11.1	43	25.7
Initiate help	Family of U.R.*					Not significant								27	31.0
	Black family	2	11.8	9	47.4	1	5.3	1	20.0	3	23.1	1	8.3	17	20.0
	Jane	1	3.1	3	9.1	5	11.9	0	.0	0	.0	0	.0	9	5.4

Notes:
1. N for the three vignettes: *Family of unspecified race 87; Black family 85; Jane 167. Percentages relate to the population for each vignette and not to the total population in each profession.
2. Each respondent was allowed multiple answers; therefore the percentages do not sum to 100.
3. Only two of these interactions could be statistically tested, due to small cell counts in the others.
Suspicion of CA: Jane: p = <.01; CC.29220
Discuss with superiors: p = <.0001; CC.46169.

Action proposals at both stages analysed by other variables

The personal variables of age and gender and those relating to professional locus and experience were tested against the same range of action choices. Very few appear to correlate significantly.

Gender correlated with seven variables across the two stages. Although fewer at the second stage, women are twice as likely as men to 'initiate help' at both stages. At stage one, a quarter of women are twice as likely as men to 'initiate help' at both stages. At stage one, a quarter of women respondents also would propose 'helping mother' compared with 14% of men; this is not fully explained by (the almost exclusively female) health visitors' strong role bias towards this approach because teachers also score relatively highly on this proposed approach. Men are more likely to seek interagency action at both stages, which seems more likely to relate to doctors' extensive use of colleagues and 'ancillaries' whereas primary interventions of a counselling and supportive nature, when appropriate, are important parts of the role of the predominantly female professions of social work and health visiting. Women's over-representation in seeking internal consultation also seems likely to relate to their preponderance in the two professions most frequently referring up, teaching and health visiting. As discussed in the literature review (Hallett and Birchall 1992, chapter 8) the interconnections between gender, status and semi-professional occupations are well-documented and classically explored in Etzioni (1969).

Over half the respondents in the supervisory grade (two thirds of social work seniors and senior teachers and nearly as many paediatric registrars but none of the few senior police ranks) start from an initial orientation towards the abuse content, compared with 28% of principals and 38% of main grade staff. It is interesting and puzzling that, in most professions, the principal and main grades are closely comparable with one another on this point. Main-grade staff might be loath to label the case because of inexperience or for pastoral motives but it would not seem that the same explanation could be postulated for principals. Neither does it seem likely that the supervisors identified share similar functions either in managing their subordinates in this field or in conducting interagency negotiations. The workload implications of labelling a case as child protection and having to follow through all the procedures have been noted as a deterrent factor in some authorities (eg DH SSI 1989). Not surprisingly in view of their role, the rank most likely to speak in terms of 'initiating help' at stage one are maingrade staff but principals are the least likely to (4%) at stage two. On the other hand, principals most often mention 'following up' in unspecified ways.

The amount of case experience and of specialised training, particularly interdisciplinary training, also correlated with several choices. People holding the 'responsibility first' orientation (see Chapter Five) are more likely to consult the child protection register than those with a 'support first' approach, although other variables signifying deeper engagement in child protection are not statistically significant. Neither does this preference show any correlation with other labelling or action orientations, except that the 'responsibility first' group would more often adopt an information-gathering approach at stage one. Around half the respondents who have dealt with any child protection cases or conferences in the year are likely to consider the vignettes as child abuse, whereas only a fifth of the inexperienced start with that orientation. At stage two, the pattern is the same although the index of suspicion is considerably higher for everybody. The more experience and specialised child protection training people have, the more likely they are, not only to approach the case with that label at both stages but also to adopt an information-gathering and investigative rather than a helping method at the second stage. Evidently, there is scope for raising professionals' thresholds of awareness with regard to case recognition and intervention and also about the procedures, through training and case discussion.

However, it is those with some (less than a week) specialised training who would most frequently initiate some helping activity at both stages. Similarly, people who have dealt with only a few cases are the most likely (43%) to speak in these terms. It seems likely that these results are confounded with profession and that they reflect health visitors' choices. More training, case and conference experience also correlate significantly with more frequent proposals of interagency action. Staff working in specialised child protection units are half as likely to 'inform' other agencies but much more likely to 'investigate' and to seek interagency activity.

Those in specialist units are mainly police and are the least likely to seek intra-agency consultation. In tune with their less experience in general, the 'support first' school and junior ranks other than the police would turn more often to senior colleagues for consultation.

Contacts with other agencies at stages one and two

Not only people's views of how to approach and handle cases but also whom they select to work with and their respective perceptions of one anothers' roles are essential ingredients of coordination and collaboration. A range of closed questions explored proposed interactions within the child protection network at stages one and two. Many of these results have been averaged over the two stages of all the vignettes, thus offering a cross-section of contacts in the network which should be representative of cases akin to these.

In answer to a general question, most people (86% and 90% at the two stages) say they would contact some colleague in another discipline or agency but there are some interprofessional variations. At both stages, all the police would make external contacts and 90% or more of most other professions; however, at stage one 14% of health visitors say they would manage the case themselves, and at both stages few class teachers would make outside contacts although a high proportion of head teachers would. There are no other significant variations by rank and none by locality.

At the first stage, around half the respondents name two contacts but only 5% would communicate with five others; at stage two people proposed 52 more contacts overall but the tail-off in range is similar. There is a steady pattern that more initial and continuing contacts are made by people with more interdisciplinary training, and this remains broadly true of each separate profession. The exceptions are health visitors, who retain the same pattern of contacts regardless of training, and paediatric staff, who show no clear pattern but are probably more influenced by the role belonging to their rank. Eight professions were nominated by over 5% of the sample at either or both stages but, in addition, there were another 62 contacts at stage one and 48 at stage two with up to a dozen other professions.

Of those to be contacted within the agency or without, social workers and health visitors dominate the scene. It had seemed possible that they might be alternative choices but similar numbers contact either or both at stage one and a third of respondents choose neither. It also seemed possible that the selection might depend on whether people approach the cases with a child abuse orientation or more generalised concern and this was partly borne out, particularly at stage two with twice as many referrals to social workers coming from the abuse oriented. However, the obverse is not true; those who express generalised concern are equally likely to involve a social worker or not. If this signifies that the professional network still regards social workers as sources of general help and support to families and not just as child protection investigators, it is a reassuring finding.

Teachers are also a prominent point of contact and, in this population of primary schools, the head is most frequently proposed. School nurses are more frequently cited than had been envisaged and they are sufficiently prominent to suggest they should have been included in the research design. Eight professions were nominated by at least 5% of respondents at one stage or the other of the vignettes. Other professions or agencies more occasionally mentioned at either stage included welfare rights advisers, social security, fuel boards, and day care facilities. Not surprisingly, police surgeons, psychiatrists, psychologists and accident and emergency doctors are very rarely mentioned. These contacts at stages one and two are summarised in Table 9.10.

There are some interesting changes of order between the stages. While recourse to health visitors remains identical, social workers become significantly more prominent as the stories have developed. Teachers, school nurses and education welfare officers are seen as less relevant at the second stage but

Table 9.10. **Professions identified as immediate points of contact at stages one and two of the vignettes**

Respondents at Profession to be contacted	Stage 1 (N = 339)		Stage 2 (N = 335)	
	N	%	N	%
Social workers	141	41.6	186	55.5
Health visitors	144	42.5	141	42.1
General practitioners	45	13.3	73	21.8
Teachers	109	32.2	67	20.0
Paediatricians	16	4.7	51	15.0
Police			48	14.3
School nurses	18	13.6	25	7.5
Education welfare officers	46	5.3	10	3.0
Other	62	18.3	48	14.3
Total of proposed contacts	597	100.0	649	100.0

Note: The percentages do not sum to 100% because respondents made multiple responses.

paediatricians and general practitioners considerably more so. The police also come more to the fore. Fewer 'others' are involved. Responsibility is becoming concentrated into fewer hands.

The pattern of interprofessional contacts

The above has described the gross number of contacts but has not indicated whether any particular linkages are more salient to some disciplines than others. The research includes only two stages of basically two case scenarios; only six respondent professions are included in the sample and only the eight commonest contacts are presented. The real world would be much more complex, involving from time to time many different individuals from each profession and a wide range of peripheral professions (Hallett and Birchall 1992, chapter 14). Within the limits of the study, which has in fact embraced the most salient groups, this section explores the interactions proposed by the respondent professions. Although the data arises from a very simplified world, the pattern of interactions is very complex. The pattern is examined in two ways: first from the point of view of individual actors and secondly as linkages within the network as a whole. The first arises from direct comparisons of the percentages in each profession making particular links but the second requires the research responses to be extrapolated to the number of practitioners in each profession in the research areas. For the second purpose, in fact, the class teachers and paediatric staff below consult-ant rank have been deleted, since their roles in the communication network are slight.

The range of interactions is immense, from 96% of police officers communicating with social workers to no paediatricians proposing contact with education welfare officers. An alternative measure is to note that the interchange between all respondents and social workers represents 28% of the total activity while that with education welfare officers is 0.9%. The data are fully summarised in Tables 9.16 and 9.17 below and in Table 9.28 in the statistical appendix but it is probably more helpful to unravel some of the complexities first and then attempt to build up a model of the system in stages than to attempt to grasp it all at once. The detail is thus presented in four different stages, comparing where appropriate the individual practitioners' view of what is important to themselves and an overview of how large an element they contribute to the whole network. Who were the people most frequently turning to colleagues within their own agencies? Are any sub-systems evident? If so, are they detached from or well-integrated into the child protection system? Can the network be modelled?

Intra-agency contacts

Table 9.11 shows the markedly different patterns of intra-agency contact.

Table 9.11.   **Frequency of respondents' recourse to colleagues within their own agency**

Profession	N	%
Teachers	41	50.0
Health visitors	31	45.6
Social workers	26	40.3
Paediatricians	9	22.5
Police	2	13.6
General practitioners	3	4.5

It emerges that teachers relate to their own colleagues noticeably more often than the other professions; nearly half their communications would be with their own colleagues and represent 9% of the postulated exchanges in the identified network. Health visitors and social workers also use intra-agency contacts quite frequently. Given their occupational structure, it is unsurprising that general practitioners turn to their peers very little. What does seem surprising but consonant with their earlier responses is the relatively high degree of autonomy asserted by police constables in these circumstances.

Contacts with the core professions

Table 9.12 shows how often the different professional groups propose contact with the core professions, comparing the interactions between those

Table 9.12. **Proposed contacts by respondents with the three core professions, expressed as percentages of the total, comparing interactions between them with the number of contacts initiated with them by other respondents, averaged across the two stages of the vignettes**

Contacts By	SW (62 = 18.3%) %	Cons't Paed'n (40 = 11.8%) %	Police (22 = 6.5%) %	Other (233 = 63.4%) %	Total (339 = 100%) %
With					
Social Worker	11.8	18.3	28.0	12.5	70.6
Paediatrician	3.1	6.6	0.7	2.4	12.7
Police	9.0	2.9	4.0	0.8	16.7
Total	23.8	27.8	32.6	15.7	100.0

three professions with those emanating from other front line professions.

This shows the prominence of social workers in the whole system but also the importance to police officers and paediatricians of communicating with social workers. To a less extent, it also shows that intra-agency contacts are more important to the latter than to the other core professions. Proportionally, the police would turn to social workers in these cases far more often than other groups would.

When these contact patterns are extrapolated to the professional population at large, as shown in Table 9.13, social workers' prominence in the network remains very similar. Due to their smaller numbers, the other core professions appear rather less prominent and the large front line groups come more to the fore in the whole system of child protection. Although the next block suggests that many general practitioners use health visitors extensively as intermediaries with social workers, nearly half the general practitioners and nearly two thirds of the health visitors would contact social workers. General practitioners dominate the relatively few contacts with paediatricians. Teachers, including head teachers, propose far fewer contacts with social workers than any of the other professions would and, less surprisingly, schools have negligible contact with others in the core group. However, because

Table 9.13. **Proposed contacts with the three core professions, extrapolated as percentages of the total interactions in the real world network dealing with cases similar to the vignettes, comparing interactions between the core professions with the number of contacts initiated with them by other professions, averaged across the two stages of the vignettes**

Contacts By	SW (62 = 18.3%) %	Paed'n (22 = 6.5%) %	Police (22 = 6.5%) %	Others (251 = 68.7%) %	Total Contacts (339 = 100%) %
With					
Social Worker	13.1	5.9	4.8	45.9	69.7
Paediatrician	3.3	2.1	0.1	11.9	17.5
Police	9.8	0.1	0.7	2.3	12.8
Total	26.2	8.1	5.6	60.1	100.0

schools are so much the largest sector of the professional network for children, they do in fact emerge as an important source overall. Nevertheless, as one would expect, the core professions continue to contribute more pro rata than any of the front line professions. While the police are slightly less prominent, the paediatricians are still slightly more evident than numbers alone would warrant.

These tables show the central place of social workers in the child protection network more clearly than Table 9.10, suggesting that their role as key contact is widely recognised. Almost three quarters of the interchanges with the core professions are addressed to them, with the police being the most frequent initiators. Although social workers make many contacts, they initiate fewer than they receive whereas, pro rata, the police and paediatric staff originate over twice as many as they receive. This suggests that the latter are referring cases or seeking action from social workers more often than social workers invoke their assistance. This is not surprising, given social workers' preventive and supportive role with families as well as the investigative task the three professions share. Social workers do, however, propose more contacts with the police and paediatricians than the latter make with one another direct.

Sub-systems

The third dimension is to locate any sub-systems which may function outside the core system or in contact with a particular sector of it. Individual teachers' low profile as initiators of contact with the core group reinforces the picture given in the literature (Hallett and Birchall 1992, chapter 7) and by their basic orientation to the vignettes, reported above. All these sources indicate that teachers, including heads, may have a lower index of suspicion or that they use other resources when they are considering a question of possible child abuse. General practitioners' links with the paediatricians and the very high interchange they have with health visitors suggest there may be a medical network which screens cases of concern before making referrals to the child protection system. The stress laid upon immediate communication with social services and prompt case conferences in earlier government guidance appeared not to sanction any diversion, although it must always have occurred. Such screening and possible diversion may not be inappropriate and, in fact, some recent Social Services Inspectorate reports have suggested that too many children have reached the case conference stage (DH SSI 1989, 1990h). What degree of imperative is needed before workers break out of their known relationships and make referrals to a more distant and formal system? The latest edition of *Working Together (1991)* adopts the standard set by the Children Act 1989 – suspicion of 'significant harm' – as the threshold of referral to the system and it remains to be seen whether a practical consensus develops about that threshold. This survey cannot test the point directly but the data above and in the previous chapter suggest that there are different thresholds. Two sub-systems can be delineated in which cases are likely to be sifted and sorted, as shown in Tables 9.14 and 9.15 below.

Table 9.14. **Proposed contacts with workers in the school sector, comparing rates of initiation by teachers with those initiated by non-teachers, averaged across the two stages of the vignettes**

| Contacts   By | Teacher (81 = 23.9%) % | Other (258 = 76.1%) % | Total (339 = 100.0%) % |
With			
Teacher	50.0	18.4	68.4
School nurse	11.7	10.1	21.8
Education Welfare Officer	11.7	1.7	13.4
Total	43.3	56.7	100.0

It has already been noted that teachers turn most frequently to other teachers but Table 9.14 also includes the most frequently identified professions ancillary to schools. Teachers comprise 24% of the respondent population but, averaged across the two stages, propose less than one sixth of the communications in the system. However, as discussed earlier, half these contacts are with their own colleagues and subordinate teachers rely largely on their heads to make external contacts; they also contribute 43% of all contacts with the school-related professions. Their communications with education welfare officers in connection with child protection are few but they outweigh all those proposed by the rest of the sample. However, when the figures are extrapolated to the total population, social workers emerge as having more contacts with education welfare officers in this context. Teachers propose far less contacts with school nurses than health visitors in the sample and the latter still have marginally more contacts with them than the schools in the extrapolated totals. Others' initiatives towards teachers are quite limited, ranging from 39% of social workers at stage one to 2% of general practitioners at stage two. Whereas 26% of the sample would make contact with teachers, the extrapolated total is only 17%.

A similar comparison can be made of the medical sector, as shown in Table 9.15 below. Two thirds of the nominations of health staff come from other personnel within the sector.

Health visitors' cardinal position in the eyes of individual practitioners in the medical network in relation to child protection is clear in the above Table 9.15. Over two thirds of general practitioners would contact them. In the

Table 9.15.   **Proposed contacts with workers in the health sector, comparing rates of initiation by medical personnel with those initiated by non-medical personnel, averaged across the two stages of the vignettes**

| Contacts   By | HV (68 = 20.1%) | GP (66 = 19.5%) | Paed'n (40 = 11.8%) | Other (165 = 48.7%) | Total (339 = 100%) |
With	%	%	%	%	%
Health Visitor	45.6	68.2	40.0	30.6	52.6
General Practitioner	49.3	4.5	17.5	9.4	21.8
School nurse	27.9	2.3	3.8	8.2	13.1
Paediatrician	2.2	24.2	22.5	4.2	12.4
Total	31.4	24.2	12.4	32.0	100.0

total system, over half the proposed contacts with the medical sector and 44% of general practitioners' contacts with the system are addressed to health visitors. Although much less frequent, general practitioners propose far more initiatives than other professions towards paediatricians but the latter turn to health visitors more often than to general practitioners. Health visitors also propose much more communication with school nurses than anyone else, even including teachers.

Integration of the sub-systems into the total network

The last questions posed above were whether these sub-systems are well-integrated with the core professions or not and whether the whole system, even with this simplified data, can be modelled? The two questions are posed together because it appears that two professions are the crucial links in the larger network, social workers and health visitors. More communications flow into the core professions than out but they are mainly into the social work sector. Given their role as lead agency in child protection, it is not surprising that social workers are so prominent and that around half the respondents would name them as an immediate point of contact. Indeed, one would expect even more unless a considerable amount of prior screening were accepted as desirable.

The important communication flows as perceived by the initiators are displayed in Figure 9.1 and Table 9.16 below. These show that the health visitors initiate more communications than anyone else in the sample, closely followed by social workers, but that pro rata the police initiate more communications with any single professional group (social workers) than anyone else. The average range of contacts proposed by individuals varies from two by social workers and health visitors to 1.2 by teachers. Taking an overview of the system again and extrapolating to total population figures changes the picture slightly, as seen in Figure 9.2 and Table 9.17. The position

Figure 9.1   **A simplified sketch of the reciprocal importance of contacts between the six respondent professions and salient others in the child protection network in relation to the two vignettes, as proposed by respondents**

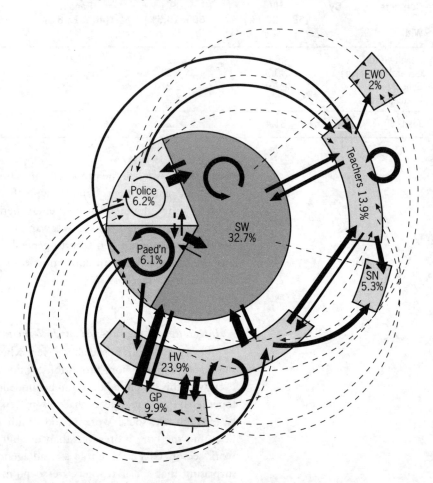

This sketches the flow of communications within and between the six research professions and two others in the child protection network regarding cases such as the vignettes. Communications from school nurses and education welfare officers are unknown. Several other professions which proved to be more peripheral are omitted entirely.

It represents the network from the viewpoint of individual respondents, showing the relative frequency with which individuals in each professional group initiate contacts with others. The size and positioning of the shaded blocks approximates to their salience in the network and the relative thickness and direction of the arrows approximates to the reciprocal flow of reported communications. An alternative and more comprehensive way of viewing the network is given in Figure 9.2.

of the core professions and the relative salience of the professional sectors in the total system remain fairly similar but the communications within the core group appear a much smaller part of the whole. Health visitors are slightly less prominent and teachers a little more so. From this perspective, general practitioners emerge as proposing the most contacts with particular groups, namely with health visitors but also very significantly with social workers.

Looked at from the individual respondent's perspective, the most frequent and fairly mutual interactions flow between social workers and health visitors. There is also a strong reciprocal link between health visitors and general practitioners and many of the latter would contact social workers. Although there is quite a high degree of reciprocity in teachers' and social workers' proposals they only involve about a quarter of each group. That so few teachers would involve social workers in these cases suggests that many do not observe the formal procedures and may prefer other ways of handling children in difficulty. Head teachers are not much more prominent than their subordinates in making this particular link although they have been observed to make the majority of contacts with external agencies. There are also significant links between health visitors and teachers and from health visitors to school nurses. While health visitors are the most likely to involve school nurses, teachers are the only other significant users of them and the other school ancillary, the education welfare officer. Paediatricians would more often call on health visitors than vice versa. A fair degree of reciprocal interest but less frequent contact occurs between general practitioners and paediatricians.

The prominence of the interaction between the front line professions themselves and between them and social workers is evident from Figure 9.1. There are many intersecting communications between them and a scattering of occasional contacts. The other core professions' dependence on the social workers in dealing with cases that are labelled child protection is evident from the arrows within the core. Nearly three quarters of paediatricians would invoke social workers but only 10% of the latter would call on paediatricians for these vignettes. A similar disproportion occurs between the police and social workers, reflecting the particular content of the vignettes.

Looking at Figure 9.2, suggesting the weight and flow of communications in the real world, the picture does not change greatly but the communications between the front line professions themselves and with social workers are even more prominent and interactions within the core group recede. It would thus appear that many cases like the vignettes are filtered and cared for outside the child protection system but that health visitors as well as social workers emerge as a fulcrum between children's wider world and the world of child protection.

Table 9.16.　**Frequency of proposals for interdisciplinary contact between the respondent professions and significant target professions, averaged across stages one and two of the vignettes**

Contacts By / With	SW (62 = 18.3%)		HV (68 = 20.1%)		Teacher (81 = 23.9%)		Police (22 = 6.5%)		GP (66 = 19.5%)		Paed'n (40 = 11.8%)		Row Total (339 = 100%)	
	N	%	N	%	N	%	N	%	N	%	N	%	N	%
Social Worker	25.5	40.3	42.0	61.8	19.0	23.5	21.0	95.5	31.0	47.0	25.0	62.5	163.5	48.2
Health Visitor	33.5	54.0	31.0	45.6	13.0	16.0	4.0	18.2	45.0	68.2	16.0	40.0	142.5	42.0
Teacher	18.5	29.8	16.5	24.3	40.5	50.0	4.0	18.2	3.0	4.5	5.5	13.8	88.0	25.9
General Practitioner	13.0	21.0	33.5	49.3	1.0	1.2	1.5	6.8	3.0	4.5	7.0	17.5	59.0	17.4
School Nurse	3.5	5.6	19.0	27.9	9.5	11.7	0.5	2.3	1.5	2.3	1.5	3.8	35.5	10.5
Paediatrician	6.5	10.5	1.5	2.2	0.0	0.0	0.5	2.3	16.0	24.2	9.0	22.5	33.5	9.9
Police	19.0	30.6	2.0	2.9	2.0	2.5	3.0	13.6	2.0	3.0	4.0	10.0	32.0	9.4
Education welfare officer	3.0	4.8	0.5	0.7	9.5	11.7	0.5	2.3	0.5	0.8	0.0	0.0	14.0	4.1
TOTAL	122.5	21.6	146.0	25.7	94.5	16.6	35.0	6.2	102.0	18.0	68.0	12.0	568.0	100.0

(N = 331 to 337 but all responses are percentaged against base populations).

Figure 9.2   **A simplified sketch of the volume of contacts between the six respondent professions and salient others in the child protection network in relation to the two vignettes, as proposed by respondents and extrapolated to the size of the respondent professions in reality**

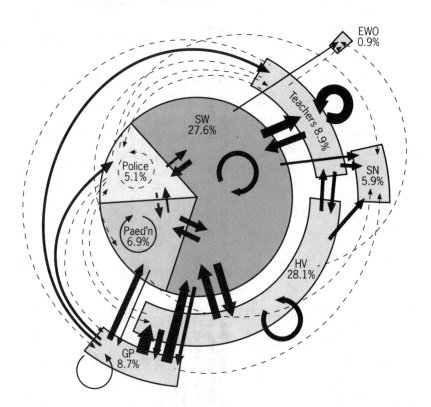

This sketches the flow of communications within and between the six research professions and two others in the child protection network regarding cases such as the vignettes. For the purpose of this model, only head and senior teachers and consultant paediatricians are included, since their subordinates are little involved. Communications from school nurses and education welfare officers are unknown. Several other professions which proved to be more peripheral are omitted entirely.

It represents this network as a whole by extrapolating from the response patterns of each professional group to the size of that group in reality in the research areas and thus approximates the total flow of communications between the groups concerned. The size and positioning of the shaded blocks approximates to their salience in the network and the relative thickness and direction of the arrows approximates to the reciprocal flow of reported communications. An alternative and more individualised way of viewing the network is given in Figure 9.1.

Table 9.17. **Proposals for interdisciplinary contact between the respondent professions and significant target professions, weighted and extrapolated as percentages of the total interactions in the real world network dealing with cases similar to the vignettes, averaged across stages one and two of the vignettes**

Contacts By / With	SW (62 = 23.1%)		HV (68 = 25.4%)		Snr Teachers (32 = 11.9%)		Police (22 = 8.2%)		GP (66 = 24.6%)		Cons't Paed'ns (18 = 6.7%)		Total (268 = 100.0%)	
	N	%	N	%	N	%	N	%	N	%	N	%	N	%
Social Worker	144.6	5.2	146.3	5.2	116.6	4.2	53.4	1.9	244.1	8.8	65.2	2.3	770.2	27.6
Health Visitor	190.3	6.8	108.0	3.9	79.7	2.9	10.2	0.4	354.3	12.7	41.8	1.5	784.3	28.1
Teacher	105.1	3.8	57.5	2.1	248.5	8.9	10.2	0.4	23.6	0.8	14.4	0.5	459.3	16.5
General Practitioner	73.9	2.6	116.7	4.2	6.1	0.2	3.8	0.1	23.6	0.8	18.3	0.7	242.4	8.7
Paediatrician	36.9	1.3	5.2	0.2	0.0	0.0	1.3	0.0	126.0	4.5	23.5	0.8	192.9	6.9
School Nurse	19.9	0.7	66.2	2.4	58.3	2.1	1.3	0.0	11.8	0.4	3.9	0.1	161.4	5.8
Police	108.0	3.9	7.0	0.3	12.2	0.4	7.6	0.3	15.7	0.6	1.0	0.0	141.5	5.1
Education welfare officer	17.0	0.6	1.7	0.1	3.1	0.1	1.3	0.0	2.6	0.1	0.0	0.0	25.7	0.9
TOTAL	695.7	24.9	508.6	18.2	524.5	18.8	89.1	3.2	801.7	28.8	168.1	6.0	2787.7	100.0

(Note: In view of the slender involvement of class teachers and paediatric staff below consultant rank in the communication network according to the survey responses, they have been discounted in the calculation of this table.)

The purposes of interprofessional contacts

The previous sections discuss the frequency with which different professions propose contact with other members of the network, highlighting
changes between stages one and two of the vignettes and also identifying the
interactions within the whole system and two sub-systems. The purposes of
such contacts were explored next through a fixed choice question, as
displayed in Table 9.18. Once again, if respondents offered multiple answers
regarding any one contact, only the most 'active' of the proposed interactions
was scored. For instance, only the second interaction would be coded if a
respondent proposes both to give information to another party and also to
decide jointly with them how to react. It can be seen that the largest number
of responses involve cooperative rather than unilateral activity. However,
nearly all of this cooperation comprises exchanges of information and
opinion about the case; even when people propose joint action they generally
mean continuing liaison rather than hands-on collaborative activity. It is
evident that the cooperation is largely at a verbal level and confirms the
picture of a network rather than the therapeutic teams and mutual support
groups that several writers have commended as invaluable (Hallett and
Birchall 1992, chapter 11). The anxieties expressed by health visitors and
quite often felt by social workers to be unresolved or even exacerbated by case
conferences might indeed be better managed if more elements of interprofessional teamwork could be enhanced, at least among the core professions.

Table 9.18. **Purposes of immediate contact at stages one and two of the
vignettes**

Respondents at	Stage 1 (N = 298)		Stage 2 (N = 294)	
Stated purpose	**N**	**%**	**N**	**%**
Pass case on only	65	10.9	69	10.4
Seek/give info only	143	23.9	124	18.7
Seek advice/direction	65	10.9	91	13.7
Discuss and decide jointly	201	33.6	204	30.7
Act jointly	123	20.7	176	26.5
Total of proposed purposes	598	100.0	664	100.0

Generally, respondents sought contact with the target professions for the
full range of purposes in rough proportion to the overall number of contacts
with them but a few differences in expectations were very evident. A number
of shifts also occurred between stages one and two of the vignettes. (See
Tables 9.26 and 9.27 in the Statistical Appendix). At both stages, people were
much more likely to make simple referrals to social workers (average 40%)
than to anyone else, although at stage one nearly a quarter of referrals would

go to health visitors. Teachers and health visitors are important sources of information. At stage two, more social workers and police would be involved, with a noticeable shift towards joint action. Fewer people would simply pass the case on to health visitors but information would more often be sought from general practitioners at stage two. More referrals would be made to paediatricians, and they would be approached more often for advice or joint action. In some agencies, there would also be rather more internal communication about the case. Whereas two thirds of social workers and health visitors would act independently at stage one, the numbers now drop to about half. Paediatric staff would make much more use of outside agencies at stage two, shifting from 87% to only 33% independent interventions at stage two.

The above discussion has presented the frequency of proposed contacts and their purposes in terms of the target professions but it is also important to differentiate the initiators of specific interactions. The other core professions would be more likely than others to refer the cases to social workers at stage one but also much more likely themselves to seek joint decision-making or concurrent interventions with them (70% of the police and a third of the paediatricians). Over a quarter of the health visitors would also be seeking joint decision-making with social workers at stage one and a third at stage two. By then even more of the police and paediatricians would be looking to act jointly with social workers. Very few general practitioners would simply refer the case but 26% would wish to discuss and decide or act jointly with social workers at stage one, and rather more at stage two. Four out of five teachers would make no contact regarding stage one and less than 30% at stage two; hardly any would seek advice or give information, but 6% would be interested in collaborative action at stage two.

The police are hardly evident at stage one but a few social workers would contact them for information or joint decisions and two paediatricians would seek advice; at stage two, a third of the social workers and three paediatricians would be looking for joint action. Ones and twos of other professions propose contacting them for varied purposes. The only people contacting paediatricians at stage one are junior paediatric staff or general practitioners, mainly for collaborative action. At stage two, a fifth of social workers would be variously seeking advice, joint decisions or joint actions with them; rather more medical colleagues would also be looking for similar support.

Over half the social workers would contact health visitors, in almost equal numbers for information or joint decisions at both stages; however, 15% would seek to act in conjunction with them at stage two. Paediatricians would use health visitors, mainly for information, more frequently at stage one. Less than a fifth of teachers would contact them. As already noted, general practitioners and health visitors have most reciprocal contacts but there appears to be an asymmetry in their mutual expectations (or their choice of language for their transactions). A few of the general practitioners would be simply referring the problem but 40% say they would be discussing and deciding jointly with health visitors and another third acting jointly with them at stage one, slightly fewer at stage two. Significant numbers of health visitors, on the other hand, say only that they would be exchanging information and a few would be seeking advice or direction from the general practitioner. A few more would be seeking joint decisions but few expect there to be any joint action, many fewer than the doctors themselves propose. (See Table 9.19 below).

Table 9.19.   **Contrasting expectations between health visitors and general practitioners regarding cooperative transactions**

Profession	Purpose	Joint Decision %	Joint Action %	Other %
Health Visitor proposes		17	8	32
General Practitioner proposes		40	33	17

It is not possible to say whether this imbalance indicates that health visitors are failing to claim a partnership role that is being offered or whether the doctors are less ready to share responsibility in practice than they say they are seeking. But the reported mismatch fits in well with the literatures on problems in collaboration between doctors and others and on gender relations. These topics are explored more fully in the literature review (Hallett and Birchall 1992, chapters 8, 12 and 14).

15% of social workers and of paediatricians would contact general practitioners initially and a few more at stage two, mainly for information and a few for joint decisions. Other professions' contacts with them were negligible. Mainly, social workers, police and health visitors would contact teachers to seek information from them but at stage one 15% of social workers would wish to make joint decisions with them. With the exception of one social worker seeking to make joint decisions, only doctors would contact psychiatrists. Of all the professions in the sample, health visitors are the most likely to contact school nurses and to seek joint decisions with them. Otherwise, the fringe groups are named by disparate respondents.

The commentary above derives from respondents' proposals about contacts upon first receiving the information in the vignettes. The same professions predominate when people were asked about any continuing liaisons they might seek and therefore those results are not reported in detail. These interactions appear partly to reflect the particular needs of the different cases and the differential exercise of appropriate professional roles, as becomes clearer when the vignettes are analysed separately. However, they also reveal some sub-networks that may have more to do with proximity or status than with the functions and skills of those concerned.

A comparison of different contact patterns for the different vignettes

There are several differences in respondents' proposals for contact with other disciplines for each vignette, as shown in Figure 9.3 below. At stage one, social workers and health visitors are similarly prominent in relation to both variants of the first vignette. Since health visitors function as school nurses in some areas, it is possible that their involvement with Jane reflects local division of labour; when the two groups are aggregated, very similar numbers of community nurses are involved in all three vignettes. Given her age and presenting problems, it is not surprising that teachers are particularly important in Jane's case. Significantly less respondents propose to involve social workers with her than with the Young family, a finding that accords with most teachers' preference for managing her situation themselves at this point. On the other hand, a few more would seek paediatric attention for Jane than for the Young family; all these bids come from general practitioners and paediatric juniors and clearly indicate a more cautious or anxious approach to suspicions of sexual abuse than to other forms.

Figure 9.3: **Interprofessional contacts at Stage One: the three vignettes compared**

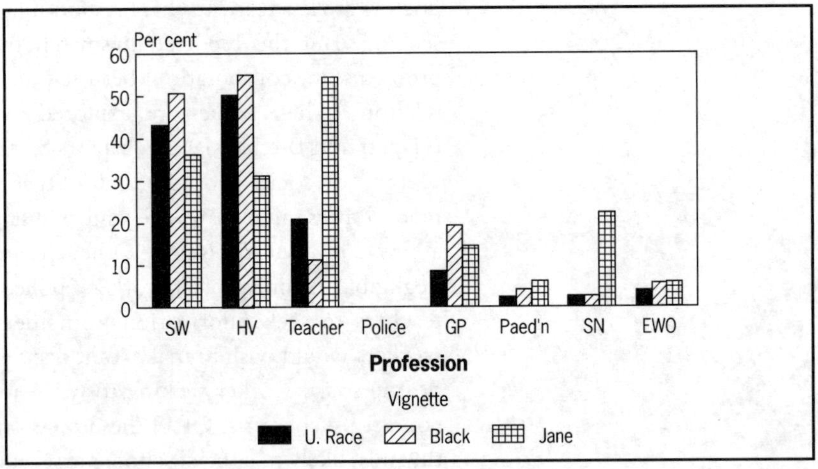

In the discussion of follow-up contacts and at Stage Two, however, social workers are heavily involved on behalf of Jane and nursing staff less. Police are also brought into Jane's case more often at these points. General practitioners are approached more often on behalf of the Young family. There are a few strange anomalies between the variants of the Young family. The differential recourse to teachers and general practitioners at Stage One seems inexplicable and may simply be a random result of no real significance. However, significantly fewer respondents would seek a paediatrician's attention but more social workers for the black family, and, as Figure 9.4 shows, the

Figure 9.4:   **Interprofessional contacts at Stage Two: the three vignettes
compared**

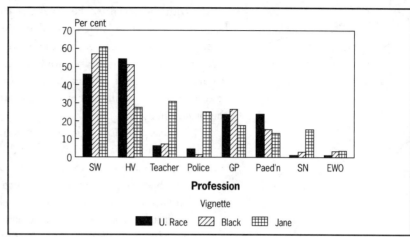

recourse to social workers regarding the black family becomes even more
marked at Stage Two.

Particular professional interactions at stages one and two

The last section compared the overall patterns of respondents' contacts for
the different cases. However, different professions' contact patterns vary.
Their particular desires for different liaisons and varying content in their
interactions regarding the different vignettes are examined next. The most
heavily involved groups (social workers and health visitors at both stages and
the police and general practitioners at stage two) were more specifically
analysed as to the reciprocity of their expectations regarding joint decisions or
joint action (see Tables 9.26 and 9.27 in the statistical appendix).

The more active concern in respect of the black family than the other one
has been noted. Health visitors are more than twice as likely to involve social
workers and six times as likely to seek joint decisions with them rather than
some lower key exchange. Social workers also would more often involve
health visitors. General practitioners would be more likely to seek joint
action with social workers for the black family but be twice as likely to discuss
the other with the health visitor. Rather more teachers would also involve
social workers on behalf of the black family. The police also show marked
differences, involving social workers very little regarding the family of
unspecified race but seeking a similar pattern of contact over the black family
as they would over the sexual abuse query.

At stage two, health visitors would be twice as likely to wish to discuss the
black family with both the social worker and the general practitioner whereas

the latter would then be less interested in discussion and wanting more joint action with them. In contrast, health visitors would be proposing more joint action with the social worker over the family of unspecified race than the black one; it is not possible to tell from these data whether this is a counter-trend in the general heavier drift of interventions with the black family or is in fact an avoidance of 'joint holding' activity on their behalf. Whereas paediatricians would involve health visitors equally in joint decisions or actions over both families, they would more often involve social workers with the black one.

In Jane's case it is not surprising that nearly three quarters of social workers and nearly half the paediatricians would be in touch with teachers at stage one; it is, however, noteworthy that only three teachers would initiate contacts with social workers and, less surprisingly, none with paediatricians. Despite their limited role in relation to a child of school age, over two thirds of health visitors would contact teachers and the school nurse. Significant minorities of social workers and teachers would also contact the school nurse. Health visitors are the most likely to involve general practitioners, although around a fifth of paediatricians and social workers also would. Most general practitioners would immediately involve paediatricians to act jointly regarding Jane and the majority would also collaborate with health visitors.

Only 39% of health visitors would involve social workers at stage one but almost all at stage two, most with a view to joint decision-making or joint action. Only a third of general practitioners would involve social workers at stage one but twice as many at stage two. Teachers remain surprisingly insulated from the child protection system at stage two. Over two thirds of subordinate staff would refer up their concerns about her but, although the majority would make a miscellany of other contacts, only 37% of the heads would involve social workers. Two thirds of paediatricians would involve social workers at both stages, mainly in joint decisions or action, but the balance in making the links shifts from juniors to consultant paediatricians between stages one and two.

Whereas none of the police intend direct investigation at stage one, some of them would seek information from most professions; however, they propose almost no contact with the same people at stage two and it seems probable that they feel they have already collected their information and their task at this stage is more direct. Particularly at stage two, Jane's case is distinguished by numerous police proposals of joint action with social workers. In contrast, more of the latter are only wanting to share decisions and apparently do not feel the time is ripe for joint interviews.

In summary, it does seem that the black family is receiving lower status services than the other one and/or is perceived as having problems of functioning that require social rather than medical intervention. In combination with previous findings that they are more likely to be perceived as abusive, there is an obvious risk of less effective or more disruptive interventions occurring to them. Such an outcome appears to be attested in the literature regarding black families' treatment by the care system (Ahmed et al 1986, Dutt undated) although there is unresolved debate about the statistics (Bebbington and Miles 1989; Loughran, informal communication). In Jane's case, most professions are alert to the need for active investigation and the core professions propose a high level of interaction, particularly at stage two, but the majority of teachers remain unwilling to refer her for investigation.

Attitudes to coordination in managing cases similar to the vignettes

As already discussed, the great majority of respondents say they would contact their own colleagues or other professions in the situations described. Almost all respondents with any relevant experience think the stories were 'typical' although a few think them too florid or severe.

People were asked whether they would contact other agencies regarding other cases such as those described in the vignettes. There is a very close correlation between the responses to the earlier vignette-related question and this more generally phrased enquiry, with 15% at stage one and 7% at stage two seeing no need for any liaison in kindred circumstances. Reasons for not cooperating are featured in Table 9.20, including some that had been assumed by the researcher to be conceptually important but in fact very rarely used. For instance, the literature review (Hallett and Birchall, chapter 8) found some concern, particularly among health visitors and teachers, about the difficulty of getting hard-pressed social services departments to accept their

Table 9.20. **Reasons, if applicable, for not contacting other agencies in situations similar to those depicted in the vignettes**

Reason	Responses Stage 1 (N = 313) N	%	Stage 2 (N = 311) N	%
I/my agency can manage	19	6.1	6	1.9
Story doesn't justify action	10	3.2	3	1.0
My superior/specialist would decide/ act	9	2.9	9	2.9
Not my/agency's job	3	1.0	1	0.3
Not priority for other agencies	2	0.6		
Another agency already involved	1	0.3	3	1.0
Other	4	1.3	1	0.3
Don't know/no experience	5	1.6	3	0.9
Not applicable	260	83.1	285	91.6
Total	313	100.0	311	100.0

worrying cases as of sufficient priority. Only two respondents at stage one deem other agencies' priorities an obstacle and none at stage two. In fact, health visitors contribute the bulk of the 'my agency can manage' responses, five of the six at stage two, and teachers are the most likely to say their superiors would decide.

Those people who would contact another agency were asked whether they would simply exchange information in hand or whether they would seek some continuing joint collaboration. The responses for the two stages of the vignette have been aggregated and are shown in Table 9.21 below. Around 15% failed to answer these questions, mainly teachers and general practitioners, and another 10%, mainly teachers, said it was not their role to do either. Many more people would almost always exchange information than would almost always maintain collaboration but over one third of respondents say they would sometimes do the latter. A few more respondents proposed that they would almost always exchange immediate information at stage two than at stage one but over twice as many said they would almost always intend to continue collaboration. Those who would often collaborate at stage one moved to almost always doing so at stage two; the number who would seldom collaborate remains very similar at both stages.

Table 9.21. **Professionals' proposals to exchange information in hand compared with proposals to continue some form of collaboration in cases similar to the vignettes**

Purpose	Stage 1				Stage 2			
	Exchange Information (N = 286)		Continue Collaboration (N = 293)		Exchange Information (N = 280)		Continue Collaboration (N = 282)	
Frequency	N	%	N	%	N	%	N	%
Almost Always	99	34.6	33	11.3	113	40.4	72	25.5
Often	97	33.9	73	24.9	65	23.2	70	24.8
Sometimes	51	17.8	126	43.0	59	21.1	94	33.3
Almost never	5	1.7	25	8.5	19	6.8	22	7.8
Not my role	32	11.2	33	11.3	23	8.2	23	8.2
Don't know	2	0.6	3	1.0	1	0.4	1	0.4

This pattern of responses thus shows a significant move towards closer collaboration at stage two among the staff who already see themselves as cooperators but the non-cooperators generally do not see the worsening situation as affecting their role or response. The professional network that would be activated remains similar to that described earlier. Social workers are relatively more prominent and teachers less so, although slightly more senior staff in schools say they would be communicating with other professions at this point.

Particularly at stage two, there is a clear bias towards a greater degree of continuing involvement regarding cases like Jane's.

Respondents' perceptions of autonomy, advice and direction

A number of questions explored practitioners' views of their professional autonomy and whether they would seek advice and direction from anyone or give it to anyone in the conduct of these cases. Respondents who had indicated they would not make any contacts or pursue the case in any way are excluded from the following report. Generally, there was a somewhat higher expectation of support when dealing with stage two of the vignette, but this commentary averages the results across the two stages unless a striking anomaly occurs.

Over three quarters of respondents say they would need no authorisation from superiors for their initial proposals. Perceptions of autonomy vary between ranks, with just one principal feeling the need to consult at stage two; what is more surprising is that the supervisory rank feel no more autonomous than their main grade colleagues. There are, however, significant variations between the professions. Given their occupational structure, it was to be expected that no general practitioners would refer up, but it was unexpected that all the police would act without hierarchical consultation at either stage. When the groups with mixed views of their autonomy were separately analysed, professional variations were significant. Among main grade and supervisory staff, two thirds of teachers would seek higher authority and around a third of social workers and paediatricians but only 10% of health visitors. This suggests that health visitors still maintain an independent role despite the increased emphasis in recent years on management structures in the service.

Whatever their responses had been to the question of formal autonomy, at least one third of all respondents would nevertheless look for 'advice or direction'. The greatest proportion would be teachers and the fewest general practitioners, a finding that appears to mirror the hierarchical structure above but in fact the picture is different. With the exception of social workers at stage one, the majority of these respondents would seek such guidance from external colleagues rather than superiors. This was particularly marked with the police, almost all of whom would want advice at stage two but none would turn to senior officers. No staff ranked as principals would look for guidance within their agency but 25% would turn to external colleagues. Supervisors and main grade staff were equally likely to seek external support at stage one but an increased majority of maingrade staff would do so at stage two.

A further question explored the type of support respondents would be seeking and this evoked an even higher response. Just under half the sample want 'professional or clinical ideas' and there are no significant interprofessional differences. About a third would look for 'procedural guidance', most often teachers and least often police or social workers. Only around 15% would seek 'authorisation to act' but at stage two significantly more of these would be social workers. This suggests that the actions people have in mind are generally within their delegated powers but that at stage two some social workers are beginning to contemplate more stringent interventions. These might be formal child protection investigations in which they would usually if not always involve their managers to share the decision-making and quite often the tasks; possibly some are thinking of legal proceedings, for which they would need formal authorisation.

Respondents were also asked whether they would give advice or direction with regard to interventions in these cases, to external colleagues or peers, within their agency. Approximately 40% of respondents would do so. Police and doctors, particularly paediatricians (45% at stage two), were the most frequent donors of such advice. Over four fifths of senior ranks from all professions but teaching would do so, half the main grade social workers and 41% of general practitioners; small proportions of other main grade staff would do so. There is a tendency for various experience factors to increase the advice-giving initiatives but this is not entirely consistent. There is a considerable overlap between the factors of profession and experience of child protection cases or related training although the factors have proved to be not completely confounded. Staff in the more specialised units are around twice as likely as the generalists to proffer advice, as are those with moderately heavy case involvement at stage one. However, at stage two the advice is tendered most often by respondents with the most case and conference experience. Those with most case experience or most interdisciplinary training are the most likely to offer advice to social workers.

Around 18% of the total sample would address advice to social workers and health visitors; that is approaching half the respondents who would proffer advice at all. In contrast, only 1% of the sample or 3% of the advice-givers would offer advice to paediatricians. The pattern remains similar at both stages, except that school nurses are mentioned half as often and the police twice as often at stage two as recipients, mirroring their changing degrees of involvement. Table 9.22 reports the average of the two stages.

Where cell sizes were sufficient to be tested, there were statistically significant differences as to who gave the advice to whom. A third of general practitioners would advise health visitors but paediatricians would intervene more frequently with the latter at stage two. Nearly a third of social workers would be advising health visitors and teachers at stage one but far fewer at stage two. This changing interaction between paediatricians and social workers on the one hand and health visitors on the other suggests that there is

Table 9.22. **Addressees of advice or direction, which would be given by 40% of the sample, in relation to interventions with the vignettes, averaged across stages one and two**

Addressee	Respondents (N = 339)	
	%	%
Health Visitor	64	18.9
Social Worker	56	16.5
Teacher	42	12.4
General Practitioner	18	5.3
School Nurse	18	5.3
Police	17	5.0
Paediatrician	4	1.2
Others	19	5.6

less of a primary supportive role being 'delegated' by social workers while paediatricians are tightening the core professions' grip through advice at stage two. Very few teachers of any rank would give advice or direction to external colleagues and it is surprising, given class teachers' relatively high demand for internal consultation, that only one in three of their superiors said they would proffer it; more support or advice would be offered to class teachers by health visitors and the police. There were several 'don't knows' regarding advice to the police but almost all the positive answers came from a fifth of social workers. General practitioners and school nurses also provoked several 'don't knows' but social workers, health visitors and paediatricians (8–13% respectively) were the only significant advisers of general practitioners. Health visitors (15%) would advise school nurses and so would 8% of social workers; otherwise, only two paediatricians and two teachers would offer them guidance. Paediatricians were the least likely to be offered advice, by less than 5% of social workers, police and general practitioners.

Summary and conclusions

Case vignettes explored respondents' views of appropriate professional interventions for children in situations of some difficulty, in relation to their immediate thoughts, action proposals and contacts on receiving two stages of information. Thus data were gathered on their convergent assumptions and mutual expectations as well as points of friction between them. The vignettes were deliberately ambiguous, particularly in the initial stages, although the total research focus provides an unavoidably leading context in which the stories were evaluated. Therefore, although the majority did not instantly query child abuse, the virtual unanimity of concern may overstate the judgments respondents would make in real life. Moreover, the coding policy was to select the strongest or most active expression in people's free form answers, so the results will err on the side of exaggerating people's commitments to intervention and to collaborative actions.

As evidenced in the responses to the brief vignettes, there was an obviously higher index of suspicion and greater anxiety regarding the case with sexual content (Jane) than about the Young family in difficulty. To a less marked degree but significant and troubling nonetheless, people also reacted more suspiciously and anxiously, perhaps harshly, to the black variant of the Young family than to the one of unspecified race. There was a greater readiness to label the case as suspected abuse, confirming data from the USA (Nalepka et al 1981), and fewer proposals of direct help or medical attention, particularly at stage two. People proposed more reference to social work agencies than to paediatric help. Although one variant of the vignette did not refer to any specific ethnic origin, it appears that respondents assumed the family was white. These are findings of considerable significance for black families, the child protection system and for strategies to combat racism in the health and welfare services.

The very large majority of respondents proposed some intervention and also some inter-agency contact about all the vignettes at stage one and even more at stage two. Nearly all felt the stories and their responses were typical of real life. The purpose of such contacts was generally to exchange evaluations and to plan with other agencies, very rarely to work conjointly on a task. It is evident that the cooperation envisaged is that of a communications network and not a team giving close collaboration and emotional support, although there were indications that many people would turn to colleagues in other agencies for advice and guidance sometimes in preference to their own management.

Within these broad outlines, however, there were many differences. In their free form answers people expressed their concerns in diverse ways and proposed diverse interventions. Even when poposals were collated into larger conceptual categories, the specific categories were nominated by only a minority of the total sample. Some of the divergences, whether in perception or proposed intervention, could be related to people's occupational roles but this was often not evident. For instance, at stage one, the greatest degree of unanimity on any point was among social workers, three quarters of whom construe Jane's case as possible sexual abuse, a point about which another core profession, the police, were fairly evenly divided. At stage two, there was more consensus about this but teachers and general practitioners remained split. There was total unanimity on only one point, a negative one, at stage one; nobody proposed that Jane's problem should be approached through 'helping mother'. Thresholds of referral to the investigative agencies vary, as do preferences for managing the case oneself; while the former imply different perceptions, the latter sometimes relate rather weakly to people's professional tasks. Even at stage two, nearly two thirds of head teachers were not referring Jane to the social services department but preferred a miscellany of other contacts. Most suggestions either produced significant inter-professional variation and/or little consensus within any particular professional group.

The language of 'protecting children' and 'risk assessment' is conspicuously absent, and few propose to check the child protection register or seek a conference even at stage two. Notions of care or criminal proceedings are negligible. However, those who construe the cases as 'query child abuse' are rather more likely to initiate or pursue an investigative approach than those who express miscellaneous or generalised concerns. Readiness to consider the possibility of child abuse was not consistently related to people's professional locus but greater experience of child protection issues was broadly correlated with it.

There are problems in interpreting an aggregate of open-ended responses when people's proposals are not necessarily comprehensive or mutually exclusive but may sometimes even be conflicting. However, the differences do reveal the lack of any established technical consensus within or across the professions as to the best approaches to such situations. That there is a complex cross-cutting of respondents' tasks and roles and varied perceptions in relation to different cases, which then lead to different proposals, is not a surprising finding but it does mean that much cooperative activity in the child protection network is situationally specific, probably extremely difficult for the practitioners to articulate into generalised rules and certainly difficult to conceptualise theoretically. It would seem that particular action plans will often depend on individual preferences or, when they are opened up for discussion, are still to a large extent the outcome of the fundamentally moral and political processes of interprofessional negotiation that Dingwall et al (1983) analysed.

Respondents' proposed contact patterns were then explored in detail and, even within the grossly simplified confines of the research data, the network is complex. It comprises the key worker and core investigative professions (social workers, paediatricians and police); front line agencies (schools, health visitors and general practitioners and, in many cases, also the social workers); peripheral contact professions (school nurses and education welfare officers); case-specific professions (lawyers, psychiatrists and many others). There were marked interprofessional variations in the frequency and scope of contacts at both stages of the different vignettes. The findings affirm social workers' key role in the network and a high level of interaction between them and the other two investigative professions, the police and paediatricians. However, social workers also have many more contacts than the latter with the rest of the network. Health visitors also emerge as an equally important resource, particularly at stage one of the vignettes and particularly in relation to the Young family. It would seem that they are a crucial link in the mesh of front line observation and support services in which teachers and general practitioners normally and social workers sometimes go about their business.

Many other professions appear fitfully, school nurses and education welfare officers to a limited extent in the front line and psychiatrists or psychologists sometimes being used as specialist resources apparently as an alternative to child protection interventions. There do appear to be sub-systems around the school and the medical centre which probably contain many cases appropriately. However, the generally low level of child protection awareness displayed by teachers and general practitioners, revealed in this chapter and others, suggests that the sub-systems may sometimes inappropriately divert cases from child protection investigation. Health visitors appear to have a critical role as a fulcrum between those sub-systems and the sphere of child protection in which social workers, the police and paediatricians have very specific roles.

A few differences were evident in people's purposes in contacting different professions, and there were a number of shifts in these purposes between stages one and two of the vignettes. Social workers were the most likely target of simple referrals, particularly at stage two. Teachers and general practitioners were more often involved in information exchanges than other transactions. Paediatricians were not prominent at stage one but at both stages they were the target of referrals and a source of advice. The police were most often sought for joint action, that is sharing interviews with social workers. The core professions were the most likely to perceive their interactions as joint decision-making, although general practitioners and health visitors have many such interactions and also seek them with social workers. Paediatricians generally make most use of external resources. In general, people reported more intentions to exchange information in hand than to maintain a collaborative relationship, although the patterns of collaboration among those who would do so were similar to those that were reported in detail.

There were obvious discrepancies of bureaucratic and professional organisation but not all were in the expected direction. Apart from teachers, few said they would need formal authorisation to follow through their proposals and the police claimed total autonomy in this context. Many more would look for advice or support, generally in the area of professional or clinical interventions and mainly from external colleagues rather than their own hierarchy. The professions and the ranks with most experience of child protection were the most likely to offer advice but, echoes of Cleveland, few would offer advice to the paediatricians.

As a general conclusion, these interactions appear partly to reflect case needs and professional functions but some may have more to do with easy access or status than with the functions and skills of those concerned.

Chapter 10

Proposals for Intervention in a developing case vignette:

Introduction

In addition to the matters of professional judgment and practice discussed in the previous chapter, another group of questions explored people's procedural responses to the vignettes at the first two stages. At stage three, their assumptions regarding appropriate attenders at a child protection conference were also explored, as were their opinions about ensuing interventions with the children. Almost all respondents said their sequence of responses was typical of their general pattern of decisions and actions in such cases; at stage two, just five said their proposals were uncharacteristic because they considered the vignettes atypical and 3% did not know what would be typical. This handful of responses was scattered across the professions except that the bulk of the 'don't knows' were teachers. It may therefore be assumed that responses about the formal mechanisms and respondents' proposals for the children's future care are also typical.

Use of formal mechanisms

The Child Protection Register

Although few spontaneously volunteered the idea, in response to a direct question the majority of people say they would find out the family's status on the child protection register on hearing the first stage of the vignettes; however, while over two thirds of most professions would enquire, the range is from one third of teachers to over 90% of the police. A greater number but in similar proportions would check at stage two. Among those who would contact the register, the reasons are very similar at both stages with almost all deeming it relevant information. Of the 7% who say it is 'routine', the largest group are social workers. In some of the authorities at least, the register status of the family is automatically revealed by the computer record when prior information is checked at the time of any referral to the social services department.

The prevailing reason among the third who would not check the information on the register is that the story does not justify it (40%) but there are some interesting interprofessional variations. Of those who say they would already expect to know the child's status, 44% are health visitors. Almost all the paediatric registrars would ascertain this information but about a third of the consultants and even more juniors say it is not their job; despite the careful wording of the question to include getting someone else to inform you, it is difficult to take this apparent degree of paediatric indifference literally and it seems more probable that the information would be passed on by the registrars. Over two thirds of those who are unaware of the register are teachers but half the senior and head teachers would check. Over 10% of those who checked at stage one would not do so again, a few rather curiously saying the stage two story does not justify it. Mainly, the reason is that they believe they would already know what was on the register. The belief that previous knowledge is sufficient or accurate denies one of the purposes of the register, which is to act as a constantly-updated pool of information about children acknowledged to be at risk. More interprofessional training correlates with greater use of the register (over and above the prevalence of 'don't knows' among the untrained).

Child protection conferences

Few (7%) respondents would seek a child protection conference on the basis of the initial story, but by stage two a larger number would. This would still only be a third of the sample, with another quarter uncertain and 45% still definitely not. At both stages, most proposals of conferences relate to Jane.

Table 10.1 **Reasons given by respondents for not seeking a child protection conference at stage one and stage two of the vignettes**

Reason for not seeking CP Conference	Stage 1 (N = 329)		Stage 2 (N = 321)	
	N	%	N	%
Story doesn't indicate need	213	64.7	94	29.3
Not my job, expect other to seek it	19	5.8	46	14.3
Depends on outcome of others' actions	25	7.6	24	7.5
Don't know about case conferences	21	6.4	19	6.0
Not my job, my agency would	14	4.3	22	6.9
Depends on outcome of my actions	7	2.1	6	1.9
Care plan in hand, no need for conference	0	0.0	2	0.6
Other	8	2.4	7	2.1
NA, I already have sought one	22	6.7	101	31.5
Total	329	100.0	321	100.0

The main reasons for not seeking a conference are tabulated above, led at both stages by the opinion that the story does not justify one. The only significant change in the order of reasons between the two stages is that at stage two over twice as many respondents would be feeling that a conference should be sought by someone else. Just four people baldly asserted that it was 'not their job'. Among those who would await the outcome of current activities before deciding whether a conference is justified, four times as many are depending on others' rather than their own inputs.

At both stages, there are significant variations between professions in their conference-seeking intentions. Over 10% of paediatricians and health visitors would seek a conference at stage one whereas less than 2% of social workers would, with other professions clustered around 5%. At stage two, however, the pattern is different, with similar numbers (around a third) of social workers, health visitors and general practitioners saying they would seek a conference compared with nearly half the paediatricians but only a quarter of the police. These intentions contrast sharply with responses in Chapter Seven, where the initiation of child protection conferences appears to be very largely left to Social Services. It may be, particularly at stage one of the vignette, that the cases straddle an uncertain threshold in respondents' minds. However, if that were an adequate explanation of the proposed initiatives by the non-social workers, one would either expect that the social workers would feature more frequently here or that the other professions would make many more proposals than they indicated in Chapter Seven (even though the paragraph here below suggests they might fall on resistant ears). It seems that the direct question in the context of these vignettes stimulated an unrealistically positive response from some professions at least.

Among those who would not seek a conference, there are evident differences in professions' choice of reasons, although cell counts were generally too small for tests of statistical significance. While the commonest overall reason and the commonest for every profession at stage one is that the story does not justify one, this is almost the only reason given by social workers (87%) but by just over half the teachers. Health visitors are almost the only people to say the decision would rest on the outcome of their own activity whereas most professions mention others' activities as a consideration. Teachers are almost the only respondents to give the reason that they know nothing about conferences. Although the question was about seeking and not about convening a conference, teachers are, with the police, the most likely to say it is 'not their job'. At stage two, the commonest reason among social workers, health visitors and general practitioners is that they still think the story does not justify a conference but the other professions give more diverse reasons. Social workers are the most likely of all the professions to say at stage two that their decision would rest on the outcome of current activities.

Although only a minority would seek a conference, a large majority say they would attend if one were convened and less than 15% would refuse. There is a greater readiness to attend regarding Jane than the young family at stage one. There is considerable variation between professions, with nearly 90% of health visitors, about half the paediatricians but around two thirds of the other groups proposing to attend at stage one. The health visitors' exceptional commitment is in accord with the high valuation they put on conferences, as reported in Chapter Seven. The 55% police attendance would be concentrated, although not exclusively, on Jane. At stage two, the teachers would not have changed their intentions but significantly higher proportions of social workers and paediatricians would attend. Evidently, two of the core professions feel the cases now warrant more priority but the police have not changed their intentions. Although more class teachers than heads do not know whether they would attend, equal numbers of both ranks gave positive replies. It is surprising and interesting that so many class teachers would expect to attend, as it has often been asserted that schools cannot release them from classroom duties. Along with data presented in Tables 10.2 and 10.3 below showing that respondents in general have both a greater desire for and expectation of class teachers' attendance than their head teachers', these responses suggest that schools are adapting to meet the need.

While there are no inter-area differences in intentions to seek a conference at stage one, there are at stage two; County staff are readiest to seek a conference and City least likely, with a greater number of 'don't knows' in MetBorough. Intentions to attend also vary significantly, with 20% of City staff refusing at stage one compared with less than 5% of MetBorough respondents. The pattern remains very similar at stage two. This suggests that a higher threshold of concern operates in the area with the highest case bombardment and highest registration rates. The greater the degree of interdisciplinary training, the greater the readiness to seek a conference at stage two and to attend at either stage.

Expectations regarding professional attendances at a child protection conference

Respondents were presented with the following third stage of their vignette, outlining additional information gathered at a case conference.

Vignette A. Stage 3.

> *At Case Conference it emerges that Margaret has been depressed since Sarah's birth. Sarah's father walked out on her just before and left a pile of debts. He still comes back about once a week for the night and they sleep together. Margaret would like him back even though he sometimes beats her for not keeping the children quiet.*

Margaret is not cooking or feeding herself very well. She gives Jimmy fish and chips and apples, which he eats wandering about outside the house.

At times she says she gets very angry with the children's 'whining' demands and crying. Two days ago the Day Nursery noticed that Jimmy had red weals on his calves and fingertip bruises on his upper arm. He has several bruises around his lower legs and on his forehead. Margaret admits she wallops him on the bottom and calves but denies she ever bruises him or hits his head. Jimmy says she did hit his head when he wet his pants.

The baby's weight has fallen from the 25th centile at birth to the 3rd now. She has had several minor chest infections and a recent diarrhoea.

Margaret had a child by another father. This child was adopted after strong suspicions that he had broken her arm and ribs when exasperated with her crying at night. She parted from this man when she was expecting Jimmy because she did not want any further difficulties with Social Services.

The social worker and health visitor have been visiting weekly since the first message 2 months ago. Margaret has been willing to talk to them but finds it difficult to follow their advice on the children's needs. She has not told either of them much of this history which has been collated from agency records. She says she intends to attend a psychiatric outpatient clinic soon.

Or   Vignette B. Stage 3.

At Case Conference it is reported that Jane has now been interviewed jointly by a policewoman and social worker. At one stage she said Daddy asks her to do rude things. She said he sometimes came into her room at night to kiss her and say he loved her very much, and he'd made her touch his penis. Sometimes it got stiff and he poked it at her and 'wriggled like they do in the videos'. Later she said she'd made all this up.

She is very angry that Daddy has left them and made them all very sad. She says he wants her and her 5-year old sister Julie to live with him and Mummy wants them to live with her, and she wants them all to live together and be happy. Mummy and Daddy keep saying nasty things about each other.

Father adamantly denies to the police that any sexual abuse ever occurred and says his wife has been putting malicious ideas in Jane's head. Mother offers no explanation of how she suspected this was happening and didn't report him or seek help sooner, but 'he's not going to see them again now'. On forensic medical examination, Jane showed some vulval redness which could be due to her bedwetting but also possibly consistent with sexual interference. There were no other physical signs of sexual abuse. Julie has not been medically examined.

People were asked to indicate from a list of 34 possible attenders whom they would wish to be present at the child protection conference to consider that information and whom they would expect, from experience in their locality, actually to be present. Around 13% of respondents to each vignette claimed insufficient experience to say whom they would want and around 16% did not know in practice whom they should expect; the bulk of these answers came from teachers. Substantive answers regarding wanted and expected attenders are compared in Table 10.2 and 10.3. The average positive respondent nominated 8.9 attenders, a figure very much within the normal range from various surveys of conference attendance patterns (Hallett and Birchall 1992, chapter 13). Not surprisingly, there were many more nominations in response to this question than had been proposed by respondents as contacts they would initiate for themselves at earlier stages of the vignette. Partly, this seems likely to be a reaction to the direct cue list presented here but it is also reasonable to infer that at this stage people would be interested in the views of a wider range of professionals than those they have a direct relationship with.

The general picture is that more people are wanted at case conferences than are actually expected. Earlier responses about possible improvements to conferences in general revealed that people were concerned about absenteeism although nobody wanted larger meetings and 8% wanted them smaller and 23% wanted them shorter. This ambivalence about the size of conferences suggests a conflict between a resistance to conferences in the abstract, as typified in John Cleese's well-known film 'Meetings, bloody meetings', and a recognition of the number of people who have valuable contributions to make in the particular.

Corporately, social services staff dominate the list but it was surprising to find that thirteen people (6% of the relevant substantive respondents), scattered through the other professions and through the different vignettes, wanted no social services participation in the conference. Social workers and seniors were wanted twice as often as their area managers (or equivalent) and rather more often than specialist advisers, but the different ranks were only occasionally sought in tandem by other professions. Individually, main grade health visitors and general practitioners were most frequently wanted, by over three quarters of respondents. As a group, school/nursery staff were also prominent, with class teachers nominated much more often than their superiors. Whereas nearly as many respondents would want both class teacher and head as class teacher alone, only a quarter would want the head alone.

Table 10.2 **Respondents' wants and expectations regarding professional and family attendances at a case conference to consider the Young family at stage three of the vignette, ranked in agency groups**

Person nominated	Wanted (N = 160)		Expected (N = 161)	
	N	%	N	%
Social worker (area)	103	62.0	90	56.3
Senior social worker	101	60.8	85	53.1
SSD CP specialist adviser	85	51.2	61	38.1
NSPCC	71	42.8	61	38.4
SSD line manager/P.O.	41	24.7	38	23.8
Social worker (hospital)	34	20.5	25	15.7
Health Visitor	145	87.3	126	78.8
Nurse manager	58	34.9	61	38.1
School nurse	32	19.3	22	13.8
Nursery staff	104	62.7	87	54.4
Class teacher	50	29.1	40	25.0
Head teacher	32	19.3	24	15.0
Educational Welfare officer	31	18.7	29	18.1
Educational psychologist	15	9.0	14	8.8
General practitioner	130	78.3	63	39.4
Paediatric consultant	90	54.2	60	37.7
Paediatric junior doctor	15	9.0	12	7.5
Paediatric ward sister	21	12.7	13	8.1
Adult Psychiatrist	56	33.7	27	17.0
Community Psychiatric nurse	54	32.5	27	16.9
Child Psychiatrist	25	15.1	11	6.9
Police senior officer	64	38.6	57	35.6
Police constable	44	26.5	36	22.5
Mother	71	42.8	37	23.1
Father	39	23.5	16	10.0
Child	6	3.6	3	1.9
Clinical medical officer	57	34.3	47	29.4
Accident & Emergency consultant	26	15.7	12	7.5
Accident & Emergency junior doctor	10	6.0	10	6.3
Local Authority solicitor	45	27.1	31	19.4
Probation officer	20	12.0	19	11.9
Court welfare officer	9	5.4	4	2.5
Housing department	13	7.8	5	3.1
Other	3	1.8	2	1.3

Table 10.3 **Respondents' wants and expectations regarding professional and family attendances at a case conference to consider Jane and her family at stage three of the vignette, ranked in agency groups**

Person nominated	Wanted (N = 160)		Expected (N = 161)	
	N	%	N	%
Social worker (area)	87	55.1	82	54.3
Senior social worker	86	54.4	83	55.0
SSD CP specialist adviser	84	53.2	65	43.0
SSD line manager/P.O.	49	31.0	48	31.8
NSPCC	44	27.8	39	25.8
Social worker (hospital)	16	10.1	14	9.3
Health Visitor	118	74.7	106	70.2
School nurse	82	51.9	63	41.7
Nurse manager	50	31.6	56	37.1
Class teacher	113	71.5	190	59.6
Head teacher	66	41.8	69	45.7
Educational Welfare officer	62	39.2	56	37.1
Educational Psychologist	29	18.4	22	14.6
Nursery staff	12	7.6	9	6.0
General practitioner	118	74.7	58	38.4
Paediatric consultant	92	58.2	70	46.4
Paediatric junior doctor	12	7.6	7	4.6
Paediatric ward sister	12	7.6	9	6.0
Police senior officer	73	46.2	70	46.4
Police constable	58	36.7	51	33.8
Child Psychiatrist	54	34.2	21	13.9
Adult Psychiatrist	6	3.8	0	0.0
Community Psychiatric nurse	6	3.8	4	2.6
Mother	50	31.6	24	15.9
Father	50	31.6	23	15.2
Child	10	6.3	3	2.0
Clinical medical officer	37	23.4	24	15.9
Accident & Emergency consultant	10	6.3	6	4.0
Accident & Emergency junior doctor	1	0.6	1	0.7
Local Authority solicitor	44	27.8	30	19.9
Court welfare officer	16	10.1	7	4.6
Probation officer	13	8.2	13	8.6
Housing department	0	0.0	2	1.3
Other	7	4.4	6	4.0

The particular structure of hospital medicine is reflected in the prominence of the consultant paediatrician and the small proportion of proposals for the attendance of junior doctors or ward sisters. More police senior officers than constables are both wanted and expected but rather more constables would have been welcomed. A few choices regarding the attendance of senior ranks correlate with the respondents' own rank but these are statistically significant only as regards head teachers and social services area managers.

More principal grade respondents than subordinate ranks want head teachers' presence whereas more middle ranks want the area manager. When these differences were examined in terms of intra-agency relationships, evidently more social workers want their seniors and the latter want their principals. This is far less obvious in relation to school staff but a very high proportion of health visitors look for the nurse managers' attendance. Two thirds of police constables want to attend themselves and do not want their senior officer, a finding that accords with their other responses around questions of autonomy and suggests a desire among the investigating constables for a deeper involvement in the follow-through of their work; there were too few members of senior ranks to test the obverse. While over four fifths of paediatric consultants do not want their juniors to attend, more of their juniors would want to go; again, some numbers were too small for statistical tests but the pattern is consistent. Senior house officers are most in favour of ward sisters' attendance. It seems probable that consultants would be worried about cover on their wards if ward staff were to be present but the subordinates evidently feel they have something to contribute. Given their very limited exposure to interprofessional training and their rapid turnover, they may also feel they have little opportunity to learn about either the membership or the formal operation of the local network until, as consultants, they dive in at the deep end from a high board.

As discussed in Hallett and Birchall (1992, chapter 13), conferences have complex functions which are sometimes poorly defined and understood and may indeed be difficult to integrate with one another. *Working Together* asserts that their functions are: to share and evaluate information prepared in advance by the key worker and other investigating staff as well as that contributed at the time by other members; to decide the level of risk in the family and the need for registration; (ambiguously) to appoint a key worker or see that one is appointed and recommend core group membership; to propose case management plans to the individual agencies. It also says the members of the conference should be those with a need to know, those with a contribution to make (plus administrative back-up) and that they should be 'representatives' of the main agencies and others as needed. It leaves the decisions about appropriate representation to local agencies and it offers little guidance on the balance between the tasks of the conference. To what extent is the conference a place in which 'raw work' is done between professionals and with the family? Should the discussion and evaluation and formulation of opinions have been completed beforehand so that the direct practitioners come to the conference to report their considered, mutually informed and, hopefully, shared conclusions? Is the conference primarily an expert forum which criticises or confirms the practitioners' conclusions? Is it a bureaucratic institution which applies procedural judgments to the proposals? Is it a managerial mechanism to allot the moral commitment and resources of agencies to the agreed plans? How well can it manage all these tasks? How do they all articulate with the direct roles of the practitioners at the preparatory stage and with the direct case business of the continuing core group?

The overall impression is that most people have a simplified conception of the conference and mainly want the attendance of those with immediate knowledge of the child or family for a collegial, intervention-focused discussion. Maingrade professionals would like more opportunity to contribute their own observations and opinions to the forum. The findings suggest that the need for complex organisations to acknowledge 'ownership' of the case problem may be undervalued by some members of the network. They also suggest that the particular diversity of social services' roles in relation to case management and the proper conduct of the child protection register may be insufficiently understood. There is an important political dimension in addition to the complexities of task outlined above. The social worker as key worker and his or her supervisor apparently feel the need for support in inter-agency negotiations, an interpretation that accords with the extensive literature on inter-professional power relations (Hallett and Birchall 1992, chapters 8, 11 and 13). So also do health visitors. The interprofessional discrepancies of status and of hierarchical accountability as well as the gender factor are perhaps underestimated by some others. On the other hand, the emphasis by these principal and subordinate staff alike on bureaucratic support and control structures when they meet other professions may itself inhibit the development of a robust and more fitting collegial structure for such negotiations.

There is a strong expectation that social services staff and health visitors would be present but six professions are wanted more than twice as often as they are expected. As in other surveys and in other data from this study, the most frequently noted absentee is the general practitioner but psychiatric staff are also conspicuously absent. Although the gap is narrower, another very important mismatch arises regarding paediatric consultants who are also wanted considerably more often than expected, particularly in the case of the Young family. Small numbers would like to see more of the A&E staff and of probation or court welfare officers. People are twice as likely to say they want parents to be present as to expect them. However, in the context of these vignettes, only 42% say they want the mother's attendance and a third want the father there, a finding that contrasts sharply with the 80% who favoured parents' partial attendance when responding to the earlier abstract question.

The above gaps represent shortfalls between desired and expected attendances, which are particularly serious in relation to the medical professions. There are a few instances where more people are expected than wanted. Nurse managers, head teachers, NSPCC and education welfare officers are expected but unwanted by over 10% of respondents. While the shortfalls indicate a measure of disappointment in the potential of the conference, the latter seem to present some possibility of actual conflict and, as suggested above, to reflect some confusion about the relevance of these attenders' roles.

Interprofessional variations in assumptions about case conference attendance

Significant differences arise between professions regarding their wants in relation to two thirds of potential attenders and, perhaps more surprisingly, there are also different expectations about half of them. The expectations appear to parallel respondents' wants as often as not, rather than reveal clear views of local practice. It therefore seems more interesting as well as valuable to analyse people's pattern of desires. Where the interprofessional differences are significant, the positive wants are summarised in Table 10.4 below. Again, 'don't knows' have been excluded and the percentages are derived only from the substantive answers. It seems important to the interpretation of these responses to note that the question simply asked whose input into the discussion would be welcomed, not whom the individual would expect personally to invite.

Amid the generally high level of demand for field social workers' and seniors' attendance, teachers and general practitioners were the least interested. The highest demand for area managers comes from health visitors and, as already discussed, from social workers themselves. Around a third of paediatricians want hospital social workers to be there; so do a similar proportion of the police and a quarter of social workers but few others. Paediatricians' and social workers' interest in the hospital social workers' attendance is more self-evident than the police's. That social workers themselves are the least likely (15%) to seek NSPCC attendance suggests a measure of domain conflict between the two agencies, while other agencies may be more appreciative of the additional pressure or presumed expertise the NSPCC may apply to the system.

Health visitors are sought by almost everyone but only by 72% of teachers. Besides the many health visitors who want their managers' support, few others except for a large minority of social workers look for the latter's attendance. Doctors are least interested in school nurses' contribution but general practitioners have previously indicated (Chapter Nine) that they rely very heavily on health visitors. Perhaps surprisingly but again in accordance with Chapter Nine, teachers score health visitors more frequently than school nurses. As noted previously, in some areas the two nursing roles are combined, so the relatively low profile of school nurses may reflect organisational factors. General practitioners are over three times as likely to want class teachers as their principals. Education welfare officers appear salient to teachers and, less explicably, even more so to the police; they are, however, less important to the health professions. Very few people other than teachers mention educational psychologists.

General practitioners are wanted by the very large majority of respondents but expected by few. Only they themselves and teachers have a reasonably high expectation of their participation. Child psychiatrists would be welcomed by half the teachers and a third of general practitioners and police, but only the teachers expect their involvement. Teachers' optimism about the attendance of these two medical professions may be a naive reflection of their own slender experience. Most demand for community medical officers comes from health visitors and teachers and least from general practitioners.

Paediatricians highly desire and expect their own involvement; while three quarters of social workers also seek their attendance only half expect it. Few people seek paediatric junior doctors or ward sisters except the junior paediatric staff themselves. More respondents want the attendance of senior police officers than of constables although, as already noted, the latter would like to be present. However, a fifth of non-police respondents also wish for constables' attendance. Teachers and general practitioners are the least interested in involving the police, and social workers and health visitors the most. Nearly two thirds of social workers and substantial minorities of the other core investigative professions, paediatricians and police, would want the local authority solicitor but social workers are least optimistic about his/her attendance.

As already reported, fewer people say they want the parents to be there than had in principle favoured greater parental involvement (Chapter Seven) but the interprofessional variations parallel the earlier result, with social workers the most likely to seek parents' participation, followed by teachers and general practitioners. Very few police and only 20% of paediatricians want either parent to attend.

Overall, social workers seek the widest range of professions more frequently than others; health visitors mostly involve social services or colleagues in the primary health care team; general practitioners nominate the narrowest spectrum and teachers depend heavily on the education network. These conclusions also mirror those arising from the proposed pattern of contacts at earlier stages of the vignettes, as reported in Chapter Nine.

Table 10.4 **Summary of statistically significant variations between professions in their wants regarding attendances at a case conference in relation to stage three of the vignettes**

Respondent Profession	SW		HV		Teacher		Police		GP		Paed'n		Row Total	
Profession Wanted	N	%	N	%	N	%	N	%	N	%	N	%	N	%
Social Worker	46	76.7	49	72.1	23	46.0	18	81.8	31	56.4	23	63.9	190	65.3
Senior Social Worker	42	73.7	45	67.2	17	37.0	13	59.1	29	65.9	22	75.9	168	63.4
NSPCC	9	15.3	33	48.5	22	45.8	9	40.9	28	50.9	14	37.8	115	39.8
SSD Area Manager, etc	30	50.8	34	50.7	2	4.3	3	13.6	9	16.4	12	34.3	90	31.6
Hospital Social Worker	16	26.7	3	4.5	3	6.4	7	31.8	8	14.5	13	36.1	50	17.4
Health Visitor	53	88.3	64	94.1	36	72.0	22	100.0	52	94.5	36	97.3	263	90.1
Nurse Manager	26	44.1	58	85.3	8	17.0	3	13.6	5	9.1	8	22.2	108	37.6
School Nurse	22	36.7	31	46.3	27	54.0	11	50.0	14	25.5	9	25.0	114	39.3
Class Teacher	36	60.0	34	50.7	35	72.9	17	77.3	23	41.8	18	50.0	163	56.6
Head Teacher	22	36.7	23	34.3	30	61.2	7	31.8	7	12.7	9	25.7	98	34.0
Educational Welfare Officer	25	41.7	17	25.4	22	45.8	12	54.5	11	20.0	6	17.1	93	32.4
Educational Psychologist	8	13.6	7	10.4	21	43.8	0	0.0	4	7.3	4	11.4	44	15.4
General Practitioner	55	91.7	60	88.2	30	60.0	17	77.3	52	94.5	34	91.9	248	84.9
Paediatric Consultant	46	76.7	43	64.2	17	35.4	11	50.0	32	58.2	33	91.7	182	63.2
Paediatric Junior Doctor	7	11.9	3	4.5	3	6.4	0	0.0	1	1.8	13	36.1	27	9.4
Paediatric Ward Sister	6	10.2	6	9.0	4	8.3	0	0.0	5	9.1	12	33.3	33	11.5
Child Psychiatrist	9	15.3	12	17.9	24	51.1	8	36.4	18	32.7	8	22.9	79	27.7
Clinical Medical Officer	18	30.0	32	47.8	16	34.0	7	31.8	11	20.0	10	27.8	94	32.8
Police Senior Officer	37	61.7	42	62.7	9	19.1	9	40.9	24	43.6	16	44.4	137	47.7
Police Constable	24	40.0	24	35.8	14	29.8	14	63.6	13	23.6	13	36.1	102	35.5
Local Authority Solicitor	37	61.7	18	26.9	4	8.3	9	40.9	7	12.7	14	40.0	89	31.0
Mother	36	61.0	22	32.8	27	34.0	3	13.6	25	45.5	8	21.6	121	41.9
Father	27	45.8	17	25.4	21	55.1	1	4.5	16	29.1	7	19.4	89	31.1

Note: N varies from 265 to 291, from a potential of 301 respondents. Area SW: $p = <.005$; CC .23900; Snr SW: $p = <.002$; CC .25932; NSPCC: $p = <.002$; CC .25184; SSD area manager: $p = <.0001$; CC .37646; Hosp. SW: $p = <.0001$; CC .29607; HV: short cells; Nurse man.: $p = <.0001$; CC .51482; School nurse: $p = <.02$; CC .21913; Class teacher: $p = <.01$; CC .22790; Head teacher: $p = <.0001$; CC .30044; EWO: $p = <.002$; CC .25716; Ed psychol.: $p = <.0001$; CC .34355; GP: $p = <.0001$; CC .32026; Paed cons:: $p = <.0001$; CC .33094; Paed jnr dr: short cells; Paed ward sister: $p = <.001$; CC .26134; Clinical MO: $p = <.05$; CC .19684; Child psychi.: $p = <.0005$; CC .27049; Police snr O: $p = <.0001$; CC .29325; Police const.: $p = <.05$; CC .20185; LA solicitor: $p = <.0001$; CC .38306; Mother: $p = <.0001$; CC .29907; Father: $p = <.002$; CC .25926.

Other variables influencing choice of attenders

Significant inter-area variations regarding which personnel are appropriate attenders occur in a third of the list. As expected from local administrative arrangements, City staff have more involvement with the NSPCC. They also have more to do with school nurses and are three times as likely to expect a child psychiatrist. Social services area managers and specialist advisers are both more involved in MetBorough, as are a spread of other professions – clinical medical officers, nurse managers, educational psychologists and solicitors. Probation officers are most often wanted in County, whereas they and court welfare officers hardly appear in MetBorough. Senior social workers are most often expected but least often wanted in County. There would seem to be no professional rationale for such variations in the network and it must be assumed that many reflect local resource patterns which then shape people's assumptions about what is desirable.

There is a general tendency for more child protection experience, measured by case and conference exposure and relevant training, to increase the range of people's desires for others' attendance but, as has been noted elsewhere, there is considerable overlap between experience and profession. Social workers are prominent among those with extensive experience and want the widest range of attenders at the conference, so it seems probable that professional role is confounded here. Particular correlations of limited experience and specific choices also closely follow the professional patterns already explored.

As regards parental attendance, the picture is complicated. Those with no recent case experience most want both the mother (60%) and the father (52%) to be present. However, those with very limited or maximum case exposure are much less interested in mother's presence while no conference experience or the maximum correlate with a greater interest in her presence. Interest in father's attendance diminishes steadily as case experience increases but bottoms out among those with even a little conference experience. While there is an innocent welcome for parents from those with least experience on both counts, it seems that the greatest experience of conferences is more important than maximum case experience in increasing respondents' confidence that they can manage the tensions aroused by parents' presence.

Comparisons across the vignettes

Responses were evenly distributed across the different vignettes and there were many similarities, some more surprising than others, in people's choices of attenders in all three cases. However, what is interesting and particularly surprising in view of respondents' widespread alertness to the question of sexual abuse is that notably fewer respondents wanted social services staff involved with Jane.

Community nursing staff are as prominent in all cases, with rather fewer health visitors counterbalanced by more school nurses in Jane's case. Nursery staff and teachers counterbalance according to the children's ages, and the education welfare officer and psychologist would be sought twice as often for Jane. Police officers are wanted by substantial majorities in all cases although rather more in Jane's case. Solicitors are equally wanted and probation or court welfare officers similarly. The adult psychiatrist and community psychiatric nurse are more prominent for the Young family, which accords with the story given, but a third of respondents would want to involve a child psychiatrist with Jane.

There are several disturbing discrepancies between people's views of appropriate attendances regarding the racial variants of the Young family. Some of the choices here (as in Chapter Nine) suggest that the black family is ascribed a lower status than the other one; for instance, a child psychiatrist would be both wanted and expected significantly more often for the family of unspecified race and a community psychiatric nurse and educational psychologist more often for the black family. However, the obverse is true as regards the paediatric input, where the consultant would be relatively more often expected for the black family and the junior doctor for the other. Similarly, the social services department special adviser in child protection would be expected more often for the black family but the hospital social worker would be wanted more often for the other. As in Chapter Nine, these two results suggest that another mechanism may also be at work, ascribing a more problematic as well as a lower status to the black family.

As noted earlier, large minorities of respondents want parents to attend. In view of the different content of the vignettes, it is not surprising that the mother's attendance is wanted more often than the 'father's' in the case of the Young family. It is interesting, however, that people are apparently equally ready to deal directly with the mother and the suspected father in Jane's case.

Desired Outcomes for the Children

A series of questions then explored respondents' views of appropriate future plans for the children and whether they thought there would be agreement or not regarding case conference decisions and recommendations, and lastly what they would do if there was dispute about desired outcomes.

For all the vignettes, a large majority think the index children's names should be put on the child protection register but a greater number would register the baby Sarah (85%) than Jane (76%). The gap is more marked when their siblings are considered although still a considerable majority would register in both cases; 88% would register Jimmy but only 63% think it necessary for Julie. Over three quarters want police investigation of the sexual abuse query but a sizeable minority also think this appropriate for the Young family, more particularly for the variant of unspecified race. This is contrary to the tendency to treat the black family more stringently and may reflect some anxiety about police interventions with black people. People's recommendations regarding future care or oversight of the children are diverse and overlapping. Few want any of the children admitted to care (average 14%) under any rubric but only the same number exclusively propose support and services at home with no form of compulsion. Many respondents do not know what they would recommend, some indicating the data was insufficient or the timing premature and others apparently unable to decide what would be best. The gross responses are summarised in Table 10.5 below.

Table 10.5 **Comparison of Total Responses regarding Appropriate Future Plans for the Children**

Proposal	Response	Yes %	No %	Don't Know %
Register index child		80.5	4.9	14.6
Register sibling		75.6	8.8	15.5
Police investigation		53.5	29.2	17.2
Home Support Services		52.6	32.4	13.8
Supervision order		58.9	22.4	17.8
Voluntary admission to care – index child		11.9	72.0	16.1
Voluntary admission to care – sibling		10.7	72.2	17.1
Interim Care Order – index child		22.8	51.1	26.1
Interim Care Order – sibling		20.1	52.9	27.1
Care order – index child		7.0	64.4	28.6
Care Order – sibling		5.8	65.3	28.9
Order expected – index child		10.6	49.5	39.9
Order expected – sibling		6.2	52.0	41.7

As in reality, the options are not mutually exclusive and some people signify a logical sequence of positive choices; others make somewhat conflicting or muddled proposals. In fact, 69% favour home supervision; the largest exclusive vote in the whole range of options is for supervision orders over the children but many more are willing to accept either voluntary or court-mandated supervision, occasionally concurrently with proposing some form of admission to care. A fifth think interim care orders might help but less than 7% favour full care orders and hardly any more believed a court would grant them. These recommendations and expectations are presented as a matrix in Table 10.6 below.

There are several significant variations in response to the different vignettes. Voluntary support is more often deemed a possibility for Jane and

Table 10.6 **Matrix of Positive Respondents' Views of Appropriate Future Plans for the Children**

	Home Support services	Superv. Order	Vol. adm. to care – index	Vol. adm. to care – sib.	Int. care order – index	Int. care order – sib.	Care order – index	Care order – sib.	Care order – index	Care order – sib.	Total Positive Responses
Home Support Services	47	106	3	3	18	14	5	4	10	5	172
Supervision order		75	27	13	42	34	8	6	19	7	192
Vol. admission to care – index			30		27		13		9		29
Vol. admission to care – sib.				29		23		9		8	35
Interim Care Order – index					4		19		19		75
Interim Care Order – sib						12		16		12	66
Care order – index							9		15		23
Care Order – sib								9		12	19

Note: n = 318–329. The rows and columns in this table do not aggregate, as many respondents made overlapping and sometimes contradictory proposals.

Julie than for Sarah and Jimmy. Despite the large majority rejecting admission to care for any of the children, 30% would favour interim care orders for Jimmy and Sarah and 20% would consider voluntary reception into care for them (now 'accommodation' under the Children Act 1989). Only 6% expect that care orders would be granted over Jane and even fewer for her sister, but 10% think magistrates would commit the Young family to care. However, significant majorities think either scenario could be managed by supervision orders. Among those favouring court-mandated interventions, it is worrying that there is again a small but consistent trend to propose heavier plans for the black than the other family. Fewer supervision orders or voluntary admissions are proposed but there are more thoughts of care orders and more people believe that the courts would accept such recommendations.

Interprofessional variations in proposals for the children

A few of the positive choices for the children vary markedly by profession, as shown in Table 10.7, although in some instances small numbers precluded statistical testing. However, most differences occur in the distribution of 'don't knows', with teachers (48–62%) most prominent. Teachers and doctors least want police involvement in the investigations whereas a large majority of social workers and the police themselves consider this desirable. There is little disagreement about the need to register the children although social workers are least and paediatricians most in favour of registering the non-index child.

The two professions with least experience of the child protection system, general practitioners and teachers, are prominent among the small number who think the children should be removed from home. They most often believe that care proceedings are appropriate and also most often expect a court to grant care orders. When all the legal options for admission to care are aggregated, general practitioners are twice as likely as social workers or police to seek this for one or other of the children. It has often been asserted that both teachers and general practitioners are particularly reluctant to risk their other primary roles with families by antagonising parents with allegations of child abuse (Hallett and Birchall 1992, chapter 8), so it is interesting that they should take the hardest line on this point, particularly the doctors who come out rather strongly in favour of parents' presence at the conference. Health visitors and social workers are least in favour of voluntary admissions to care but the police have least faith in care proceedings.

Significant relationships between other variables and proposals for the children

There is a strong tendency for the youngest staff and for workers not specialising in child protection not to know what to propose for the children

Table 10.7 **Summary of Respondents' Views of Appropriate Future Plans for the Children, crosstabulated by Profession**

Profession Option	SWs N	SWs %	HVs N	HVs %	Teachers N	Teachers %	Police N	Police %	GPs N	GPs %	Paed'ns N	Paed'ns %	Total N	Total %
Police Investigation*	46	75.4	40	61.5	31	38.8	17	77.3	23	39.0	17	43.6	174	53.5
Registration of index child	48	78.7	52	80.0	60	75.0	18	81.8	51	86.4	35	89.7	264	80.5
Registration of sibling*	42	68.9	51	76.1	57	71.3	17	81.0	48	80.0	33	84.6	248	75.6
Home support services	40	65.6	35	52.2	33	41.8	13	59.1	29	49.2	22	56.4	172	52.6
Supervision orders	19	31.1	51	76.1	46	57.5	12	54.5	43	72.9	21	56.8	192	58.9
Vol. admission to care – index*	5	8.2	3	4.5	12	15.0	3	13.6	13	21.7	3	7.7	39	11.9
Vol. admission to care – sibling	5	8.2	4	6.0	9	11.3	2	9.1	10	16.7	5	13.2	35	10.7
Inter care order – index	10	16.4	16	23.9	17	21.3	4	18.2	20	33.3	8	20.5	75	22.8
Interim care order – sibling	11	18.0	12	17.9	16	20.0	3	13.6	16	26.7	8	20.5	66	20.1
Care order – index	4	6.6	3	4.5	9	11.3	0	0.0	5	8.3	2	5.1	23	7.0
Care order – sibling	3	4.9	4	6.0	6	7.5	0	0.0	4	6.7	2	5.1	19	5.8
Order expected – index	6	10.0	2	3.2	12	15.4	0	0.0	10	16.7	4	10.5	34	10.6
Order expected – sibling	3	5.0	3	4.8	7	9.0	0	0.0	5	8.3	2	5.3	20	6.2

N = 321–329, mainly 329.
* statistically significant results, with data dichotomised into Positive choice versus No or Don't know;
$p = <.0001$; CC .29780. $p = <.0001$; CC .30187. $p = <.05$; CC .18199.

but what is more interesting and unexpected is that maingrade and principal staff are often equally uncertain in their views. Those in the middle grade are much clearer in saying what they do not want. However, there are very few differences between respondents on several dimensions of experience regarding what they do want. The only apparent differences in positive choices by rank are that main grade staff (4%) are more reluctant than senior ranks (12%) to recommend care orders. When allowance is made for the fact that half of these few 'maingrade' recommendations come from general practitioners who have already been noted to be more in favour of strong soluctions, other ground level professionals' resistance to care orders becomes even more pronounced. In line with other findings reported above, three quarters of staff in partly or fully specialised units favour police involvement compared with less than half the staff with no specialisation in child protection. Similarly, staff with greater case or conference experience more often want police involvement. Not surprisingly, staff who stress the importance of intervening in a family on the footing of parents' initial recognition of responsibility for the situation would favour police involvement more often than those who start with a 'professional acceptance first' orientation (See Chapter Five above) but it is interesting that this difference of orientation has no impact on any of the other proposals for the children.

Table 10.8   **Selected future plans for the children, crosstabulated by the amount of respondents' interdisciplinary training in child protection**

Amount of training	None		Less than 1 week		More than 1 week		Total	
Proposal for the child	N	%	N	%	N	%	N	%
Involve the police*	68	43.0	69	57.5	37	82.2	174	53.9
Home support services*	82	51.9	56	45.9	33	73.3	171	52.6
Supervision orders*	104	65.8	69	57.0	18	40.0	191	59.0
Voluntary admission to care – index	21	13.1	16	13.1	2	4.4	39	11.9
Voluntary admission to care – sib	15	9.4	18	14.8	2	4.4	35	10.7
Interim care order – index	36	22.5	32	26.2	6	13.3	74	22.6
Interim care order – sib	29	18.1	29	23.8	7	15.6	65	19.9
Care order – index	12	7.5	8	6.6	3	6.7	23	7.0
Care order – sib	9	5.6	7	5.7	3	6.7	19	5.8

Notes: N for the series varied between 319–327, and for the individual columns as follows: No training 157–160, Under 1 week 118–122, More than 1 week 44–45.
Statistically significant results marked*; $p = <.0001$, CC .25600; $p = <.01$, CC .17265; $p = <.01$, CC .17259

Nearly two thirds of the non-specialists would propose supervision orders whereas only 40% of the more specialised staff would. This finding is also endorsed by the preference of staff with less case involvement or conference experience for supervision orders. Since these experience factors and more interdisciplinary training all correlate fairly closely with one another, it is not surprising that the amount of such training correlates with these proposals in the same way. The most-trained staff also least often propose voluntary admission to care or interim care orders but they are not perceptibly more in favour of care orders. They are significantly more likely than the untrained or less trained to favour support services to the families at home, voluntarily accepted and not under supervision orders. The relationship between the amount of training people have had and their preferred options for the children are highlighted in Table 10.8.

Expectations of agreement and handling of disagreement

The strong emphasis on cooperation in the literature and official policy makes it important to know how frequently people expect disputes and how they deal with them. Two questions therefore addressed people's views as to whether they would expect an easy consensus at this conference and whether they think others would agree with their own proposals. Responses regarding each of the vignettes make it clear that disagreements and frictions do occur significantly often, with only a minority expecting the conferences to come easily to consensual recommendations or to agree with the respondent's own proposals. However, it is interesting to note that, among the 60% who do not expect consensus in the abstract, the responses are fairly evenly divided between an expectation of active disagreement and 'don't knows'. More people sit on the fence as 'don't knows' and fewer are prepared to expect conflict directly with themselves when the question is more particularised. There are also several interprofessional differences. Teachers are significantly different from the other professions, least expecting consensus in general or agreement with themselves in particular. In line with earlier observations (Chapter Seven), health visitors least expect conflict on either measure. There

Table 10.9 **A comparison of different professions' expectations of general consensus**

Variable	Profession	SW N	SW %	HV N	HV %	Teacher N	Teacher %	Police N	Police %	GP N	GP %	Paed'n N	Paed'n %	Total N	Total %
Expect consensus		28	46.7	33	51.6	19	23.8	9	40.9	29	49.2	16	42.1	134	41.5
Expect agreement with me		23	37.7	33	50.8	24	30.0	10	45.5	24	40.0	19	48.7	133	40.7

N = 321; p = <.0001; CC .32188. N = 323; p = <.005; CC .27430.

is, not surprisingly, a large overlap between people's expectations regarding general consensus and agreement with their own views but there are some clear tensions between the two questions. Nearly three times as many would expect people to agree with their views despite lack of consensus, compared with the number who would expect to be disagreed with while expecting consensus to emerge. Despite their relatively high expectations of consensus, social workers and general practitioners are the most prone to see conflict focused on their own views; the reverse is true of paediatricians who expect less easy consensus but more compliance with their opinions.

There is a significant tendency for more of the senior ranks than of maingrade staff to expect consensus but other experience factors point in both directions. More specialised workers and those who have handled more cases or attended more interdisciplinary training expect both consensus and conflict more often than the generalists, the latter being less sure what to expect. However, it is encouraging that increasing experience specifically of child protection conferences steadily correlates with an increased conviction that consensus would be easy, from 30% among those with no recent attendances to 60% of those with over 40 attendances.

All the consultant paediatricians expect others to agree with them, regardless of whether they are specialising in child protection. Such an expectation would be compelling if the issues in question related to medical diagnostic factors but the options presented were all about the child's career in the child protection and care system. Among the core specialists, only social workers (28%) positively expect their views to be disputed and even more of the fully specialised social workers (55%) expect conflict. Once again, questions of occupational status and of perceived skill seem evident but so does the issue of role encroachment (Hallett and Birchall 1992, chapter 11). Not surprisingly, a lot of case and conference experience reduces the 'don't knows', but this not only leads to an increased majority of staff expecting that they would be agreed with but also enlarges to around a quarter the minority who would expect to be disputed with. So, although the general trend is that more specialisation and experience led to a higher expectancy of agreement there are pockets of tension, particularly around social workers' own proposals.

Lastly, people were asked how they would deal with unresolved disputes. Many declined to answer but 75% of these either expect no dispute or do not know what to expect. The positive responses in the following table therefore seem likely to be representative of how involved and informed members of the conference network would handle such conflicts as occur. *Working Together* and official policy documents acknowledge that, although conferences should seek to agree their recommendations and coordinate their services to the child, each agency has the legal responsibility to decide how to fulfil its specific duties. Conferences hold no executive power other than over the decisions about registration and future conferencing.

Table 10.10 **Respondents' proposals for dealing with disputed outcomes at case conferences**

Action proposed	N	%
Nothing but put my views	55	16.2
Accept case conference recommendation	47	13.9
Minute my dissent at the conference	47	13.9
Record my dissent on my file	10	2.9
Refer problem to my superior	8	2.4
Seek reconvening of the conference	13	3.8
Refer problem to Area CP Committee	2	0.6
Go my own/agency's way	19	5.6
Other	39	11.5
Don't know	16	4.7
No reply	136	38.9
Total	339	100.0

There are few noticeable differences between the professions in their declared attitudes to acceptance of conference conclusions or active dissent. However, social workers are most numerous in the small group who indicated that they would go their own or their agency's way. As the group charged with making the full family assessment and responsible for the child's possible career in care but also experiencing most dissent from their views, it is perhaps surprising that they report taking unilateral action so infrequently. Among those going their own way, there are significantly larger proportions of senior staff; the only main grade staff are police and social workers. These findings fit in with the roles of the departments. That health visitors are the most likely to get their dissent on record accords with their punctiliousness about recording observed in Chapter Six. None of these choices showed any significant inter-area differences.

Summary and conclusions

The developing vignettes explored workers' use and perceptions of the child protection register and the child protection conference and also their assumptions about appropriate outcomes for the children.

With direct cues, the majority of respondents indicate they would ascertain the register status of the family because they deem the information relevant. However, substantial minorities including half the head teachers would not do so. In accordance with the case perceptions reported in Chapter Nine, the commonest reason for not checking the register or seeking a conference is that the stories do not justify it. However, there was also an implication that the register is seen by some as an inert bureaucratic device rather than a source of dynamic information, a significant minority from various professions indicating they would already know what was on the register.

Even at stage two, less than one third of respondents would actively seek a child protection conference although another 20% rely on the belief that somebody else would initiate it. 40% still think it premature or unnecessary. Among the active minority, paediatricians most frequently and social workers least frequently propose it and general practitioners are surprisingly prominent. These findings conflict with those in Chapter Seven and may be idealised.

At the postulated conference, on average people seek the attendance of more other professionals than they would expect in reality but the numbers proposed are very similar to those found in other empirical research. The particular choices are in line with the multi-layered pattern of front line, core and peripheral agencies and sub-systems identified in the previous chapter. Social workers and, broadly, those with most experience of child protection make most nominations. Once again, the most frequent dissatisfaction is about the absence of general practitioners but other doctors, although nominated less frequently, are wanted conspicuously more often than expected. Parents' attendance was less often proposed in these concrete circumstances than in respondents' answers to the earlier abstract question about their involvement. There were some variations between the localities which suggest that local resources and habits to some extent condition staff's assumptions about the appropriate network.

There is a general preference for less managerial and more main grade participants, from subordinate ranks themselves and from other agencies, but rather less self-immolation from the upper ranks. This highlights ambiguities and dilemmas about the complex functions of conferences.

When proposals for the children came to be considered, there was a high level of agreement that their names should be placed on the child protection register but very few wanted the children admitted to care. Many people made alternative and sometimes contradictory recommendations for them, revealing the genuine difficulties of the job. Social workers, and others with much relevant experience, most favoured supporting the children at home on a voluntary footing whereas two other front line professions would much more often prefer supervision orders. On the whole, the higher up the tariff of options, the more people of all ranks and professions said they did not know. Sometimes this related to their feeling that decisions were premature. Others, particularly the teachers, felt insufficiently experienced to answer and one may infer that in reality they would leave the judgment to other members of the conference. However, despite their limited experience in this field, general practitioners were the group most likely to favour the children's removal from home.

The widespread uncertainties and the evident conflicts between these various recommendations are mirrored in the fact that only a minority expect consensus to be easily achieved in a conference dealing with such case material. Social workers most frequently expect to be disagreed with while paediatricians least expect it.

The general conclusions of this chapter are that there are significant individual and interprofessional differences in use of the register and that agencies need to publicise its dynamic function more energetically. Similarly, it seems appropriate to stress more strongly to all staff that they have a personal responsibility to suggest, whether it be direct to the convener or via their own hierarchy or the key worker, that a conference be convened whenever they perceive the need. Different perceptions of the children's vulnerability and thus the need for continuing education and equalisation of standards were further confirmed.

There was much common ground about appropriate conference attenders but there needs to be more thought about the primary functions and the processes of the meeting and the appropriate balance of different ranks from the different agencies. Although less than in earlier accounts, there still appears to be significant domain conflict between social workers and paediatricians.

Chapter 11

Experience and perceptions of interprofessional relationships

Introduction

In addition to the questions discussed in Chapter Six regarding people's general views of procedures and of the network, four schedules explored respondents' views of other possible members of the child protection network. Besides those enrolled in the research project, six other professions were listed in the light of the literature review and from experience as likely or potentially important members of the child protection network. The two groups are as follows:

general practitioners;	accident and emergency doctors;
health visitors;	lawyers;
paediatricians;	psychiatrists;
police;	psychologists;
social workers;	school nurses;
teachers;	school social workers or education welfare officers.

Other professions could have been seen as relevant but it was felt that this was already quite a demanding list. At the time these were deemed probably the most salient to most of the occupations in the research sample and also to the general focus of the questionnaire on children at the beginning of their school careers. Too late to be incorporated in the design, the recent summary of inquiry reports identified nurses (unspecified) and midwives as involved more frequently than psychiatrists or school nurses (DH 1991b). School nurses have proved to be more prominent than education welfare officers or psychiatrists in the present study.

Respondents were asked on four point scales whether, in handling child abuse cases, they found cooperation with each other easy or difficult; whether the roles of others were clear or unclear; whether they thought the roles important or unimportant; and whether they thought the roles were well or poorly performed. Slots were also provided for no experience or no opinion regarding each particular item. It is important that the whole of this chapter and indeed the whole report is read as an analysis of respondents' views and experience of their own role and performance and that of their colleagues only in the context of child protection work. It is self-evident that, throughout this schedule of questions, the target and respondent professions are both important variables in investigating the salience of each group. There may be a high degree of reciprocity in some professions' views of one another and asymmetries between others. However, such mutual information is only available for the professions participating in the research and there is only a one-way view of the other group.

A general overview of reported experience of interprofessional cooperation

Nearly everyone replied to the four schedules but significant numbers reported having no experience of some relationships. There were, not surprisingly, many more clear opinions about some professions than others, ranging from 310 (91%) opinions on the importance of social workers to only 175 (52%) on the role performance of solicitors. On most counts, however, the levels of non-response and of 'no opinion' were satisfyingly low. In general, more people were prepared to express views about the clarity and importance of different professions' roles than could report any experience of cooperating with them or would stake an opinion on their performance. A negligible number of responses (0.6%) insisted on creating mid-points on some scales, either signifying that cases and practitioners vary and no generalisations are possible or expressing a midway evaluation of their colleagues. These have been discounted from subsequent analyses.

Non-substantive responses

Before exploring the positive data in more detail, the non-substantive answers were examined more closely. Although the same groups tend to give most 'no experience', 'no opinion' and 'no replies' across all four topics, there were sufficient differences to suggest that people generally discriminated between their concrete practical experience of cooperation and their perceptions of or presumptions about the role and performance of others. The variety and range of these responses is summarised in Table 11.1 below.

In view of the relatively large numbres giving no judgment on their colleagues' role performance, it was important to establish whether the abstentions reflect a reluctance to comment or a lack of relevant information. In many cases, they prove to be largely due to respondents' inexperience of the particular relationship although there are more evident abstentions regarding a couple of professions. This point is discussed in more detail later alongside the substantive results.

Teachers and, to a somewhat less extent, general practitioners consistently gave high proportions of these non-substantive responses. The other professions contribute a very small and scattered number of 'no replies' and 'no opinions'. This remained true throughout the four schedules despite a generally higher level of uninformative answers about role performance.

Table 11.1   **A summary of the percentage of non-substantive responses to the series of questions relating to perceptions of cooperation and of role salience and performance among twelve professions potentially involved in the child protection network**

Factor Response	Ease of Cooperation (N = 339)	Role Clarity (N = 339)	Role Importance (N = 339)	Role Performance (N = 339)
No reply	4.1–8.3	3.8–5.3	3.5–6.5	4.1–6.2
No opinion	1.8–7.2	1.5–7.7	1.5–7.3	5.6–17.9
No experience	6.9–37.4	6.9–22.9	3.7–16.4	10.5–32.6

Substantive responses

The first and fundamental question was about the ease or otherwise of cooperation with others in the context of child protection work with individual children and families. Since people could hardly have an opinion on this topic without concrete experience at some point in their careers, the total substantive responses should give a good indication of the range of respondents' contacts with the network. The response was surprisingly extensive in view of the limited experience or limited role of many respondents. Chapter Four reports that 18% of the sample have had no case involvement in the last year and many have said such non-involvement was typical; moreover, it seems unlikely that, for instance, a class teacher would have a role with A&E doctors in relation to child protection. The data from this schedule give no indication of the number of dealings between respondents and these target professions and it may be that some of the experience is very slender.

Between 76% and 91% have views about cooperating with social workers, health visitors, teachers, general practitioners, paediatricians and school nurses. It was a surprise to find school nurses relatively prominent; with only 13% of the sample having no experience of working with them, it seems they would have been a pertinent addition to the sample. At the other end of the scale only slightly more than half can speak of working with psychiatrists and lawyers. These data can give no indication of whether other unnamed professions might feature equally frequently but data in Chapter Nine suggest that they would not. The professions are listed in Table 11.2 below in order of frequncy of mention.

The order is similar to that revealed in other parts of the study. Despite social services departments' key role in child protection, the fact that they are not top of the list either here or in Chapter Nine suggests that a significant amount of screening out of cases occurs before others consider discussing

Table 11.2 **Rank ordering of prevalence of experience of cooperation with other professions in relation to child protection cases**

Substantive opinions of cooperation With:	Respondents %
Health visitors	91.2
Teachers	88.8
General Practitioners	86.1
School Nurses	81.4
Paediatricians	80.8
Police	77.0
Social Workers	75.9
Educational Welfare Officer	75.5
Accident & Emergency doctors	74.8
Psychologists	72.6
Psychiatrists	60.4
Lawyers	55.0

Note: N = 301–325; missing values 14–28

concerns with social workers. Not surprisingly, the large professions with routine contact with the whole child population are at the top of the list even though individual members' contact with child protection cases may be infrequent. However, paediatricians, the police and social workers are nearly as prominent, even though they would only come into the arena at the point when the front-line professions feel more searching assessments are called for. There is a high level of concordance between the respondent groups in the rank ordering of the less frequntly mentioned professions. That local authority lawyers are least frequently mentioned here and have a low profile in other chapters, dspite their importance in those cases that go to court, must indicate that the bulk of cases causing concern to field professionals are not at the heavy end of the spectrum of child abuse. This adds empirical substance to Parton's (1986) sceptical rejection of the pivotal role in the system ascribed to lawyers and the law in the Jasmine Beckford Report.

Aggregation of responses to the four schedules generally confirms the prevalence order shown here. Although only an inference, it seems probable that the strongest and most frequent interactions occur between or around those professions about whom the largest number of definite opinions, whether positive or negative, are expressed on all four schedules. Fuller results of grouping all the responses into four quartiles for each profession are available in the Statistical Appendix, Table 11.16, but Table 11.3 shows the relative prominence of the professions in a simplified form.

The top quartile of responses from the total sample span from 71% with opinions on general practitioners' performance to 92% with opinions on teachers' importance. The top quartile of responses from individual pro-

Table 11.3 **A summary of substantive responses to the series of questions relating to perceptions of cooperation and of role salience and performance among twelve professions potentially involved in the child protection network, grouped into quartiles to differentiate clusters of greatest and least salience to the respondent professions**

Respondents	Frequency of responses			
	First quartile	Second quartile	Third quartile	Fourth quartile
All	SWs, HVs, Teachers, GPs	Police	Psychologists	Psychiatrists, Lawyers
Social workers	Police, Paed'ns, HVs, Teachers, GPs	Lawyers	School nurses	Psychologists, Psychiatrists
Health visitors	SWs, Paed'ns, GPs, School nurses	Educ. Welfare Offs		Psychiatrists, Psychologists
Teachers	EWOs, School nurses, HVs, SWs	Gen. Practitioners		Psychiatrists, Lawyers, A&E
Police	SWs, Teachers, Paed'ns			Educ. Welfare Offs. Lawyers
General practitioners	Paed'ns, HVs, SWs	Acc. & Emergency	School nurses	Psychologists, Lawyers
Paediatricians	SWs, HVs, GPs, Teachers	Acc. & Emergency		Educ. Welfare Officers

Note: Fuller statistical data from which this table is derived can be found in the Statistical Appendix, Table 11.16.
The groupings were calculated with responses about one's own profession excluded. It is probable that respondents would put their own profession in the top quartile.

fessions vary from 63% of teachers having opinions on the clarity of social workers' roles to 100% of the police expressing opinions about several other professions on most factors. Most responses in the top quartile relate to social workers, health visitors, teachers and genral practitioners, confirming them to be the most prominent members of the network. Response rates are not only lower overall in the other quartiles but vary much more between the respondent professions regarding the target professions, suggestive of varying saliences and degrees of acquaintance. Lawyers and psychiatrists are in the lowest quartile for every group but the positions of the other professions are less consistent. The broad pattern suggests that the research sample has tapped the professions most frequently involved.

It had seemed possible that, however relatively infrequent, teachers might have greater contact than other professions with psychologists, education welfare officers and school nurses; likewise, that general practitioners might have greater recourse to other medical colleagues. Chapters Nine and Ten indicate the existence of such sub-networks. Although this appears true in terms of frequency of interactions, this proved untrue in terms of range. There is no significant variation in the prevalence of contact with psychologists; only general practitioners have less contact than teachers with the others in the school sector and most other professions have more. General practitioners prove to have rather less contact with psychiatrists than social workers and less with accident and emergency doctors than the police. They also have less contact with paediatricians than everyone but teachers. However, the quartile positions of the combined answers to all the schedules, not surprisingly, do indicate a separation between the medical and school worlds but once again indicate that the health visitor is a crucial link.

Qualitative responses to the four schedules

The large majority of substantive respondents report generally favourable opinions of other members of the network on all four topics and people tend overall to have rather more positive views of their own colleagues than of other professions. Nevertheless, there are considerable variations both as regards the target professions and also between the respondent professions. The full range of these scores is summarised in Table 11.4 below. Because of the very small number of strongly negative responses, both negative values of each item were collapsed before any statistical testing of individual items was possible. However, a few particular items from the full scale seem worth noting to indicate the extremities.

Among over 5,000 possible substantive responses across the four schedules regarding each profession, health visitors score only five very negative appraisals (0.1%), school nurses only 13 (0.3%) and social workers only 15 (0.3%). With the exception of paediatricians, the medical profession is more critically viewed: 7% of responses regarding general practitioners are extremely negative, as are 6% about accident and emergency doctors and 8% about psychiatrists. Over 5% of the responses relating to lawyers are equally negative. The topics of the schedules are somewhat heterogeneous and therefore these aggregates cannot be taken as exact measures of concord or antagonism in the network but they do suggest which professional roles appear most congruent, comfortable and familiar to respondents.

Table 11.4   **A summary of substantive responses to the series of questions relating to perceptions of cooperation and of role salience and performance among twelve professions possibly associated in the child protection network**

Factor Reponse	Ease of Cooperation N	%	Role Clarity N	%	Role Importance N	%	Role Performance N	%
Very positive	16 –154	5.0– 48.3	30 –187	9.3– 57.4	33 –262	10.4– 80.1	13 –98	4.1– 30.2
Positive	85 –160	26.7– 49.4	75 –132	23.2– 41.0	47 –187	14.4– 57.4	91 –162	28.2– 50.0
Negative	13 –77	4.1– 24.3	6 –95	1.8– 29.3	0 –75	0.0– 23.7	14 –98	4.3– 30.3
Very negative	2 –25	0.6– 7.9	1 –24	0.3– 7.5	0 –9	0.0– 2.8	1 –35	0.3– 10.8

The commentary so far has given a broad view of respondents' awareness of other professions and their apparent salience to them. It seems most appropriate to report the detailed perceptions of practical cooperation and of others' role performance as proportions of those with substantive experience and opinions and to discount those who have none.

However, given that possibly unsubstantiated opinions and assumptions can be important parts of people's perceptions of their potential colleagues' role and functioning, the questions about role clarity and importance are reported as percentages of all responses. The non-substantive responses regarding ease of cooperation are detailed in the statistical appendix Table 11.13. Respondents' views of their own profession have been excluded from the commentary unless the contrary is spelt out.

Detailed data are presented where there are important variations between respondents' views of the target professions and between different respondents' views of the same profession. Other variables of experience or locality are reported only where they seem important. The organising principle behind the subsequent discussion is to divide the professions into four groups:

key worker and core professions—responsible for investigation and assessment, and key worker responsible for coordination of any continuing interventions (social workers, police, paediatricians);

front line professions—in day-to-day contact with children and families and available for identification, assessment, surveillance and continuing support or other purposeful intervention (health visitors, teachers and general practitioners);

peripheral contact professions—with no institutionalised responsibility for universal child or family care but apparently variably used in an intermediary or pastoral role (school nurses and education welfare officers);

case-specific professions—occasionally involved for a particular role or task whether investigative, assessment or therapeutic (lawyers, accident and emergency staff, psychologists and psychiatrists).

Ease of cooperation with other professions

Given their role in the child protection network, it is concerning that nearly a quarter find social workers difficult to work with, even though only just over 3% see them as very difficult. Responses to the police are fairly similar but they receive somewhat fewer ratings as rather difficult. Substantial minorities find both police and social workers very easy. Opinions about paediatricians are varied, with over a quarter finding them difficult and a not insignificant number (8%) very difficult, but another quarter find them very easy, second only to the nurses and health visitors.

Table 11.5 Substantive Responses regarding ease of cooperation with other professions in the management of child protection cases

Rating Of:	Relevant Respondent Population	Very Easy		Fairly Easy		Rather Difficult		Very Difficult		Total Subst. responses		Subst. responses as % of relevant population %
		N	%	N	%	N	%	N	%	N	%	
Social Workers	277	49	21.6	124	54.6	45	19.8	9	4.0	227	100.0	81.9
Health Visitors	271	107	46.7	107	46.7	13	5.7	2	0.9	229	100.0	84.5
Teachers	258	27	12.2	150	67.9	39	17.6	5	2.3	221	100.0	85.7
Police	317	50	21.6	141	60.8	33	14.2	8	3.4	232	100.0	73.2
General Practitioners	273	30	13.3	98	43.6	72	32.0	25	11.1	225	100.0	82.4
Paediatricians	299	59	26.3	105	46.9	43	19.2	17	7.6	224	100.0	74.9
Lawyers	339	16	9.1	85	48.6	53	30.3	21	12.0	175	100.0	51.6
Psychologists	339	35	15.3	132	57.6	52	22.7	10	4.4	229	100.0	67.6
Psychiatrists	339	16	8.5	88	46.8	59	31.4	25	13.3	188	100.0	55.5
Accident & Emergency Doctors	339	27	12.3	116	53.0	53	24.2	23	10.5	219	100.0	64.6
School Nurses	339	127	47.4	118	44.0	18	6.7	5	1.9	268	100.0	79.1
Education Welfare Officers	339	76	31.1	130	53.3	32	13.1	6	2.5	244	100.0	72.0

Notes: Percentages do not coincide with those in Table 11.2 because:
1. In the first six rows of this table, respondents from the same profession are excluded.
2. The final column shows the relationship between the number of substantive respondents and the relevant total population, including non-respondents and other non-substantive respondents. Data about non-substantive responses are detailed in the statistical appendix, Table 11.13.

As shown in Table 11.5, health visitors and school nurses stand out from all others as easy to cooperate with; around half the relevant respondents see them as 'very easy' and almost all the remainder say 'fairly easy'. All the other professions are also rated as fairly easy by 45% to 60% of respondents but there are fewer 'very easy' responses and a number of negative views about these others. Around 20% say teachers are difficult but over two thirds find them fairly easy. Over a third give negative responses about doctors other than paediatricians; general practitioners are seen as difficult to work with by an alarming 43%. Doctors feature consistently and significantly among the very difficult: psychiatrists (13%), accident and emergency (11%) and general practitioners (11%). Less than 10% perceive lawyers as very easy and 12% score them as very difficult. Other groups are hardly ever identified as very difficult.

Interprofessional variations in perceptions of cooperation

Although the majority of substantive responses were positive, experience and perceptions vary markedly across the professions. Social workers (38%) are prominent among those finding paediatricians very difficult. A quarter of the police find paediatricians very easy and an equal number difficult. In contrast, less than half as many paediatricians find social workers difficult and, like most other professionals, they see working with the police as generally easy. The police claim that cooperation with social workers is easy. This is a particularly interesting and apparently significant change since the 1970s, when the involvement of the police in case conferences was deeply contentious.

No social workers or police report working with general practitioners to be very easy. Nearly four fifths of social workers and two thirds of the police find them difficult, with nearly a quarter of the social workers rating them very difficult. In contrast, like paediatricians, general practitioners are significantly more likely to say working with them is easy. Three quarters of general practitioners find working with health visitors very easy whereas less than a third of health visitors reciprocate and 21% find the relationship difficult. Approximately half the paediatricians and health visitors find mutual cooperation fairly easy but almost all the remainder of the paediatricians think the relationship is very easy while a third of the health visitors see it as difficult.

Social workers, the police and paediatricians are most likely to be involved in an initial core group and the health visitor in an ongoing core group. The general practitioner at least might hypothetically be involved with the social worker and health visitor in collaborative, ongoing work with families where children are suffering from poor care or the parents have emotional, psychological or health stresses. The marked imbalance between the doctors' and others' views of these relationships resonates with findings reported in previous chapters and fits in with much that has been written about the difficulties of collaboration and teamwork with the medical profession, due both to their occupational status and professional acculturation to authority and prescription. This topic was explored in the literature review (Hallett and Birchall 1992, chapters 8 and 11).

Regarding the more peripheral professions, social workers and health visitors are also prominent among those who find psychiatrists and accident and emergency doctors very difficult; paediatricians give very mixed responses about them and general practitioners, although still only a minority, are most likely to perceive them as very easy. Whereas generally over half the other professions find lawyers difficult, social workers' responses are more diffuse. Teachers are the most likely to have experience of working with psychologists and over half say this is very easy. Three quarters of the teacher respondents find school nurses very easy, as do a similar number of health visitors. General practitioners are the most likely to report difficulty with education welfare officers, a finding which may be a cause or a consequence of their reported minimal contact with them (Chapter Nine). In contrast, health visitors and paediatricians are among those most likely to find them very easy.

Teachers, police officers and general practitioners are particularly likely to say they find it very easy to cooperate with their own colleagues. At the same time, most professions never score cooperation with their own colleagues as 'difficult' but 5% of general practitioners do.

Other variables

Greater experience and involvement in child protection, measured on all factors (working in a specialist child protection unit, number of cases and child protection conferences in the year, amount of relevant post-qualifying training, interdisciplinary or otherwise), correlates with a sense of greater ease in cooperation with social workers. However, this is not consistently true in relation to other professions. Those spending a small amount of time on child abuse matters or handling a moderate number of cases find more difficulty with the police than the very inexperienced or the most involved, which suggests that an awareness of role conflict develops with greater contact but is then worked through and resolved. The few workers in the totally specialist units most often find cooperation with them very easy whereas others cluster around the 'fairly easy' rating. More training and more case conference experience go with increased ease with lawyers.

In contrast, difficulties with teachers increase with greater case experience and other measures of experience point in the same direction. The same tendency for greater experience to increase tension is evident regarding health visitors and is extremely marked in relation to general practitioners. No total specialists and only 6% of those spending most of their time on child protection rate the latter as very easy to collaborate with. Although more interdisciplinary training correlates with greater ease with paediatricians, more specialism goes with a sense of more difficulty. Consistently inverse patterns between experience and ease are also apparent when considering relations with accident and emergency doctors. There is a similar inverse trend regarding psychiatrists, except that a median amount of interprofessional training correlates with greatest difficulty. Less experience correlates with greater ease with psychologists, both factors associated with teachers and therefore both likely to be dependents of the professional variable.

Since social workers are the professional group with most involvement and specialised training and have appeared quite prominent among those finding interprofessional cooperation difficult, it seemed important to exclude them and recheck the relationships between these experience factors and ease of collaboration. This produced no reversals or marked changes. On the whole, these results suggest that professional proximity is more important than case experience in creating or sustaining easy relationships. This implies that it is important to make time and space for joint training and team-building exercises.

Cooperation with the police varies by area, with greatest ease in County and greatest difficulty in City. Relations with paediatricians are seen as easiest in Metborough and most often difficult in City. Except that the bulk of 'no experience/no opinion' replies come from basic grade staff, there are no significant variations between ranks in perceptions of cooperation. Greater local experience is associated with increasingly easy coopertion only with teachers. Women consistently find it more difficult to relate to all the hospital doctors but the gender imbalance among health visitors and, to a lesser extent, among social workers makes it probable that this factor is confounded with profession. It is an open question whether professional or gender status is the dominant influence but, as evident in the literature on the gender structure of the professions (Etzioni 1969, Dex 1985, see also Hallett and Birchall 1992, chapter 8), they are likely to be mutually reinforcing.

Clarity of professional roles

The large majority of respondents report themselves to be 'very' or 'fairly clear' about the roles of the core professions: social workers, police, paediatricians (See Table 11.6 below). Even though only seven (2.7%) admit to being unclear about social workers another 12% have no view. Those with no view have been found to be predominantly the teachers and general practitioners with little involvement in child protection and it is therefore reasonable to infer that they are likely to be unclear. Regarding the other core

Table 11.6 **Respondents' perceptions of the charity of role of other professions in child protection cases**

Rating / Of:	Relevant Respondent Population	Very Clear		Fairly Clear		Rather Unclear		Very Unclear		Don't Know		Total	
		N	%	N	%	N	%	N	%	N	%	N	%
Social Workers	277	139	52.5	87	32.8	6	2.3	1	0.4	32	12.1	265	100.0
Health Visitors	271	91	35.5	108	42.2	25	9.8	2	0.8	30	11.7	256	100.0
Teachers	258	45	18.5	93	38.8	77	32.1	11	4.6	14	5.8	240	100.0
Police	317	116	38.4	99	32.8	40	13.2	7	2.4	40	13.2	302	100.0
General Practitioners	273	44	16.6	80	30.2	85	32.1	16	6.0	40	15.1	265	100.0
Paediatricians	299	104	36.4	104	36.4	24	8.4	4	1.4	50	17.5	286	100.0
Lawyers	339	80	24.8	75	23.3	52	16.1	16	5.0	99	30.7	322	100.0
Psychologists	339	34	10.6	110	34.3	88	27.4	14	4.4	75	23.4	321	100.0
Psychiatrists	339	30	9.3	83	25.8	94	24.2	24	7.5	91	28.3	322	100.0
Accident & Emergency Doctors	339	72	22.4	116	36.1	50	15.6	13	4.0	70	21.8	321	100.0
School Nurses	339	86	26.5	127	39.2	50	15.4	5	1.5	56	17.3	324	100.0
Education Welfare Officers	339	83	25.6	122	37.7	34	10.5	5	1.5	80	24.7	324	100.0

Notes: 1. In the first six rows, respondents from the same profession are excluded.
2. No replies range from 8 to 18, 2.9–5.3% of relevant populations.

professions, around two thirds feel very or fairly clear about the police and paediatricians' roles but 16% say they are unclear about the former and 10% about the latter and the remainder could give no opinion or have no relevant experience. It is debatable whether 'fairly clear' is good enough in relation to these core investigative professions. That occasional members of the network are less than clear about these two professions is probably unimportant so long as they are very clear that they should always contact Social Services when they are concerned about the possibility of child abuse. The most disconcerting finding, therefore, is that only half are very clear about the social worker's key role in the network.

Regarding the frontline professions, only one third of respondents feel very clear about the role of health visitors and around 10% say they are unclear. There is widespread confusion about teachers' and general practitioners' roles; well over a third feel unclear about them and less than 20% very clear. Despite their less frequent encounters and/or their more peripheral positions, more respondents say they are clear about lawyers, accident and emergency doctors, school nurses and education welfare officers than about general practitioners. Only psychiatrists and psychologists have even foggier roles in others' eyes.

This pattern is paralleled more strongly in the professions' self-perceptions, with the core professions generally having a very clear idea of their own role. The frontline staff, particularly the teachers and general practitioners, are less sure of their function as Figure 11.1 shows. As previously reported, those two professions have only occasional contact with abuse cases; very few have any relevant training and even fewer have trained jointly with others in the network. It is therefore not surprising that so many are unsure of their role.

Figure 11.1: **Respondents' perceptions of the clarity of their own roles in child protection cases**

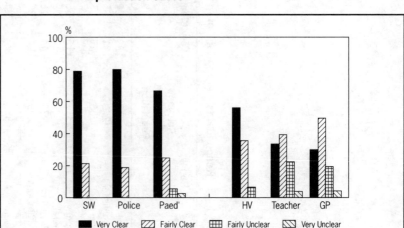

Interprofessional variations in perceptions of the clarity of others' roles

Different professions have varied perceptions of some other members of the network. Paediatricians and the police, the other core professions, are clearest about the social worker's role. Teachers are most uncertain about this: only one respondent in the whole sample, a teacher, deems it very unclear and only just over half the teachers claim to be very or fairly clear about social workers. As would be expected, social workers are clearest and teachers least clear about the police role. Interestingly and surprisingly, social workers follow teachers in being least clear about the role of paediatricians. It is arguable that social workers' confusion, like their difficulties in cooperation, relates to the issue of role boundaries.

There has been considerable discussion over the years about the health visitor's role, whether it is to be primarily preventive, educational and supportive to the whole spectrum of children and indeed to other age groups or whether their energies should be more focused on families in particular difficulty (Hallett and Birchall 1992, chapter 7). It is therefore perhaps surprising that only two people, both social workers, rate the health visitor's role in child protection very unclear. Most teachers are less than very clear about their own role and 29% are positively unclear. Two thirds of social workers and over half the paediatricians are unclear about the general practitioner's role. Although they work with them every day and many are based in health centres and are the profession most often claiming to be clear about the general practitioner's role, still less than a third of health visitors feel very clear about it.

Paediatricians feel clearest about the lawyers' role, with two thirds reporting themslves as very clear. Surprisingly, as many as 17% of social workers are unclear and, less unexpectedly, so are over half the general practitioners. In accordance with earlier evidence of this sub-system, over half the health visitors and over a third of teachers feel very clear about school nurses' role; others, including the core professions, are much vaguer. It is an open question whether the role ascribed to them in this context by the health visitors and teachers is appropriate or whether the sub-system is a distraction from the effective functioning of the child protection network.

Other variables

A few roles are seen more clearly as respondents' experience increases but neither their rank nor their length of local experience shows any relationship with these perceptions. More cases, more time spent on child protection and more interprofessional training are positively associated with increasingly clear views of the social worker's role. All the experience factors are inversely correlated with clear views of general practitioners and it seems that inexperienced people make assumptions about what general practitioners are to do in the network but these assumptions are not borne out in practice. Those who are clearest about psychologists are also those with minimal or no relevant experience; it seemed likely that they would be teachers, who have been shown in Chapters Nine and Ten to use them more frequently than other members of the network do and perhaps to have atypical assumptions about their role in child protection, but this proved not to be the case. It therefore seems probable that there may be naive assumptions about them in the same way as postulated regarding general practitioners. Those with a middling amount of case and conference experience feel clearest about lawyers' roles, which is hard to understand unless those with most experience are most aware of all the cases that do not need legal input and are in fact eliding the question of role clarity with a notion of pervasive importance.

As in the previous section, because of their prominence among the most experienced, social workers were then excluded to establish whether their views were a confounding factor but this made no apparent difference to the above pattern. There were no significant variations between areas. Once again, the bulk of 'no experience/no opinion' replies come from basic grade staff.

Importance of different professions' roles

Generally, people declare others' roles to be important if not essential. Even when the respondent indicates no practical experience of the other's involvement there is a marked reluctance to label anyone's role 'not at all important'. (See Table 11.7 below).

There is a very high consensus (80%) that social workers are 'essential' and few respondents have no view about them; the remainder all see them as 'important'. However, it is evident that respondents in general have a wider view of child protection than the diagnostic or investigative function and give the frontline nearly as much emphasis as the investigative professions. Over half deem both health visitors and paediatricians essential and around a third see general practitioners and teachers likewise. Only 2% consider health visitors 'not very important' and a few more rate these doctors thus; nobody rates any of them as 'not at all important'. About a third also rate teachers and over a quarter rate the police as essential.

As Figure 11.2 shows, all these workers consistently rate themselves as more important than their observers do. The large majority of social workers and police have no doubt of their essential role in child protection but superficially the paediatricians' posture seems more akin to that of frontline workers. However, further analysis shows that their responses split sharply along rank lines. Consultant paediatricians rate their input essential as often as the other investigators do but only a minority of junior paediatric staff see their profession as essential.

Table 11.7 Respondents' perceptions of the importance of other professions' roles in the management of child protection cases

Rating Of:	Relevant Respondent Population	Essential		Important		Not Very Important		Not at All Important		Don't Know		Total	
		N	%	N	%	N	%	N	%	N	%	N	%
Social Workers	277	209	79.2	39	14.8	0	0.0	0	0.0	16	6.1	264	100.0
Health Visitors	271	137	53.1	95	36.8	6	2.3	0	0.0	20	7.8	258	100.0
Teachers	258	67	27.1	155	62.8	13	5.3	1	0.4	11	4.5	247	100.0
Police	317	111	37.4	134	45.1	22	7.4	2	0.7	28	9.4	297	100.0
General Practitioners	273	84	32.2	125	47.9	30	11.5	0	0.0	22	8.4	261	100.0
Paediatricians	299	144	50.5	100	35.1	12	4.2	0	0.0	29	10.2	285	100.0
Lawyers	339	76	24.1	102	32.3	54	17.1	9	2.8	75	23.7	316	100.0
Psychologists	339	46	14.7	149	47.6	59	18.8	5	1.6	54	17.3	313	100.0
Psychiatrists	339	33	10.6	125	40.2	75	24.1	5	1.6	73	23.5	311	100.0
Accident & Emergency Doctors	339	74	23.6	126	40.1	49	15.6	8	2.5	57	18.2	314	100.0
School Nurses	339	76	23.6	152	47.2	50	15.5	3	0.9	41	12.7	322	100.0
Education Welfare Officers	339	84	26.1	139	43.2	38	11.8	3	0.9	58	18.0	322	100.0

Notes: 1. In the first six rows, respondents from the same profession are excluded.
2. No replies range from 11 to 28, 4.3–83% of relevant populations.

Figure 11.2:   **Respondents' perceptions of the importance of their own roles in the management of child protection**

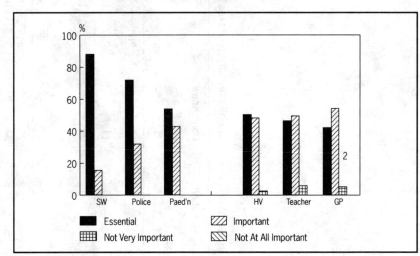

The response patterns about and by these three professions are difficult to interpret. Social workers have an inescapable dual role, investigating all suspicions of any form of abuse and in one way or another helping those children found to be at risk. One therefore wonders why even a few rate themselves as less than essential. In contrast, the police and paediatricians may be characterised as having similar roles in the investigative phase. Both may have pertinent information about past events or kindred risks in the family, which should always be trawled, but the specific investigative/diagnostic skills of either may only be needed in a segment of the cases reported. It would seem that other respondents do perceive them, and indeed social workers, as performing this second function and doing so selectively. While consultant paediatricians appear reconciled to a routine involvement, maybe their ward-weary juniors see the frequently minor injuries and suspicions of child abuse as less crucial than other demands on the paediatric service and, in keeping with other findings reported earlier regarding their exclusion from case conferences and lack of interdisciplinary training, they have less comprehension of their profession's role in the system.

The frontline staff are very evenly split as to whether they are essential or important. Very few deem themselves unimportant, despite the significant amount of confusion they feel, particularly teachers and general practitioners, regarding their role. Only a small minority rate psychologists and psychiatrists as essential but the other professions are so rated by a quarter of respondents. However, between 15% and 25% view six of the listed professions as 'not very important' at most. It seems surprising that 3–4% should rate lawyers and accident and emergency doctors as not at all important when they would seem to have such an obviously crucial role in some cases, particularly when negligible numbers of the other professions were so placed.

Interprofessional variations in perceptions of the importance of others' roles

Although the great majority of all professions deem social workers essential, there was a marked division within primary health care. Only one health visitor but a quarter of general practitioners rate them as merely important. Social workers also frequently rate health visitors (60%) and teachers (43%) as essential. Health visitors are also more inclined than other professions to rate teachers thus. These three professions have the least episodic involvement with the children or families in their domain and are particularly likely to rely on the others for their observation and their pastoral care of children in difficulty but, alongside the importance they attribute to one another, in other data there are indications of some frustration between them. Given their respective roles and the tremendous emphasis in recent years on sexual abuse and collaborative working between them, it was to be expected that social workers most often see the police as essential. In contrast, general practitioners are least likely to consider them important, a finding which accords with their responses to the long vignettes (Chapters Nine and Ten). However, that they should also not rate the lawyers' role very highly is more surprising, in view of their relative enthusiasm for having the children in the vignettes admitted to care. Social workers and health visitors most often rate accident and emergency doctors as essential while doctor respondents more often consider them unimportant. More teachers think general practitioners are essential while the core professions think otherwise. Between a third and a half of health visitors and teachers deem school nurses and education welfare officers essential but around a third of social workers and general practitioners think they are unimportant.

Other variables

Neither rank nor local experience has any bearing on respondents' perceptions of others' importance but greater experience of child protection conferences and more interprofessional training are positively associated with an essential rating of the social worker's role. The same pattern broadly applies to the police and lawyers. Those with a small amount of interprofessional training are most likely to rate accident and emergency doctors important whereas they are most often seen as unimportant by those without any such training. Once again, these results were crosschecked with social workers excluded but with few noticeable results. The importance of the police was slightly uprated, particularly among those with most child protection conference attendance, 71% deeming them essential. General practitioners were also rated a little more often as important or essential, particularly among those with most interprofessional training. The only people who think the health visitors' role unimportant are two social workers and four paediatricians in City. The police were most often seen as very important in County and as unimportant in City, a results that parallels people's responses regarding how easy it was to cooperate with them. That this was the only significant difference suggests that the network is structured in a fairly similar way in all the areas.

Perceptions of role performance

The replies to this schedule seem creditable despite the numbers apparently abstaining from passing judgment on their colleagues' performance, shown in the summary Table 11.1 above. In many cases, the abstentions are due to respondents' inexperience of working with specific groups. The contact patterns, as already reported in the section on cooperation, vary widely across the spectrum of professions. Well over 85% of those with some relevant experience give an opinon about the performance of social workers, health visitors, paediatricians and accident and emergency doctors. Over 80% give a rating of teachers, police officers, general practitioners, lawyers, school nurses and education welfare officers. Table 11.8 summarises these responses. Between 2% and 9% of respondents, depending on the target group, indicate they have no experience of how well they function. This response is not unexpected as some respondents would simply be making a referral and not receiving any feedback on the other practitioner's progress with the case.

Only about 5% on average of respondents with any experience of the relevant relationship say they could give 'no opinion' on their colleagues' role performance. There is a greater reluctance to express opinions about psychologists and psychiatrists than about other colleagues. It seems probable that such clinicians would give others less feedback on their therapeutic handling of the case than others in the network who share, inter alia, a surveillance role. Whatever the reason, only 70% of those with experience respond substantively about them while 13% and 14% respectively choose to give no opinion. While the relatively low rate of encounter with these professions and with accident and emergency doctors and lawyers explains the low number of responses, the poorer rate of response regrding psychologists and psychiatrists must cast some doubt on the representativeness of these particular opinions.

In general, people do not report critically on others' role performance. It may be speculated that the responses tend to blandness but there are sufficient sharper opinions of some professions to suggest that the responses are generally honest. In the light of the explanation offered above for the high proportions of respondents reporting no experience or no opinion of their

Table 11.8 Respondents' perceptions of how well other professions' carry out their role in the management of child protection cases

Rating Of:	Relevant Population	Very Well N	%	Fairly Well N	%	Rather Poorly N	%	Very Poorly N	%	Don't Know N	%	Total N	%
Social Workers	277	58	20.9	127	45.8	16	6.1	5	1.9	52	20.2	258	100.0
Health Visitors	271	70	27.6	117	46.1	13	5.1	1	0.4	53	20.9	254	100.0
Teachers	258	20	8.3	126	52.5	54	22.0	3	1.2	37	15.4	240	100.0
Police	317	54	18.3	135	45.8	29	9.7	2	0.7	75	25.4	295	100.0
General Practitioners	273	10	3.8	68	26.1	82	30.8	35	13.2	66	25.3	261	100.0
Paediatricians	299	65	23.0	127	44.9	21	7.3	2	0.7	68	24.0	283	100.0
Lawyers	339	21	6.7	119	37.9	25	7.9	5	1.6	144	45.9	314	100.0
Psychologists	339	18	5.7	122	38.6	31	9.7	6	1.9	139	44.0	316	100.0
Psychiatrists	339	13	4.1	92	29.2	37	11.6	12	3.8	161	51.1	315	100.0
Accident & Emergency Doctors	339	29	9.1	134	42.3	39	12.1	10	3.1	105	33.1	317	100.0
School Nurses	339	48	15.1	147	46.4	30	9.3	0	0.0	92	29.0	317	100.0
Education Welfare Officers	339	37	11.6	136	42.5	31	9.6	1	0.3	115	33.9	320	100.0

Notes: 1. In the first six rows, respondents from the same profession are excluded.
2. No replies range from 12 to 25, 4.4–7.4% of relevant populations.

colleagues' functioning, it also appears that few are projecting an imaginary or prejudiced perception upon them, favourable or otherwise. The percentages used in the text below are therefore based on the substantive responses only and do not match Table 11.8 which includes both non-substantive responses (no opinion and no experience) in the 'don't know' column. The largest block of responses (55–70%) rate others, with the exception of general practitioners, as performing fairly well. Another block (27–37%) rate social workers, health visitors, the police and paediatricians as fulfilling their function very well. The highest negative scores relate to doctors other than paediatricians. Over half think general practitioners perform poorly, 18% rating them very poorly. Almost a third are dissatisfied with psychiatrists (8% very poor) and a quarter with accident and emergency doctors (5% very poor). A quarter consider teachers' performance in child protection rather or very poor. One fifth rate psychologists and lawyers poorly but few deem their performance very poor. Social workers are thought to perform poorly by 10% but only five people rate them very badly and none of these critical responses comes from the other professions at the core of the assessment process.

Interprofessional variations in perceptions of others' role performance

Because the bulk of responses rate others' functioning 'fairly well' and relatively few responses are negative, statistical testing of interprofessional variations was impossible in most cases but there are some apparent trends in relation to some members of the network. Most professions tend to rate their own performance well but teachers are less inclined to. General practitioners are split; while over half rate themselves very well in fact a mean number also rate themselves poorly.

Social workers are the most frequent critics of others' role performance in this field. They are one and a half times to twice as likely to rate almost all the other professions as functioning poorly in child protection and none think general practitioners, psychologists or psychiatrists do very well. Almost four fifths consider general practitioners function poorly and they are also the most likely to be extremely dissatisfied with psychiatrists; they also give paediatricians the least very good and the most poor ratings. They give average ratings to accident and emergency doctors and one third, a higher proportion than other professions, think very well of the police in this role.

General practitioners (45%) are most likely to rate health visitors' performance very highly. Teachers are most likely and health visitors least likely to score the police as performing poorly. Only 5% of respondents think general practitioners perform their role very well. Not only social workers are very critical of them; no police rate their performance very well and over half, as well as more than two thirds of paediatricians and health visitors, consider it poor. Health visitors most often think highly of teachers and, with teachers, they are notably more likely to rate school nurses as functioning very well. Teachers are similarly appreciative of education welfare officers and psychologists. However, health visitors follow social workers in their low rating of psychologists.

Other variables with a bearing on perceptions of role performance

There is a general tendency, although not always reaching statistically significant levels and sometimes not testable due to small cell counts, for a greater degree of experience, measured severally in number of cases and child protection conferences in the last year and in the amount of interdisciplinary training, to correlate with more sceptical appraisals of colleagues' performance. There is most confidence in social workers and police among those with 10–39 cases in the previous year but this confidence falls off in the topmost bracket of case contact. As experience factors increase, the 'very wells' decrease and/or more 'poor' ratings are given to health visitors, teachers, psychologists, psychiatrists, accident and emergency doctors and school nurses. The diminished confidence in general practitioners is massive: 94% of those who attended over 40 conferences and three quarters of those spending more than a day a week on child protection or with over a week of interdisciplinary training rate their performance as poor. There is no apparent correlation between any of these factors and respondents' assessment of paediatricians, lawyers and education welfare officers.

When social workers' responses are excluded, health visitors' performance is more often highly rated, with 40% saying 'very well'. School nurses are also more highly rated. However, these ratings peak among those with fairly heavy involvement in child protection and are less favourable among the most specialised workers. More critical appraisals of accident and emergency doctors correlate with greater case experience; it seems likely that these coincide with paediatricians' rather sceptical view of them on other factors.

Discussion

Generally, respondents gave positive ratings to other professions on all four aspects but there were sufficient variations between respondents and target groups and the different schedules to indicate that the responses were generally thoughtful and not simply displaying a halo effect from one factor to another. Very positive ratings were more often given to others' importance than to any other factor, the only exceptions being school nurses and education welfare officers. However, when the scales were collapsed, the pattern became more distinctive. Social workers received more positive ratings than anyone else for role clarity but they also scored 100% on importance; the other two core professions, police and paediatricians, were more often rated positively on importance than any other factor, as were teachers and general practitioners. Health visitors were given more positive ratings for easy cooperation than any other factor. Although responses about them were fewer, the peripheral and occasional professions scored higher on ease of cooperation but amidst greater reservations about other factors.

The main factor influencing all these perceptions is the respondent's own profession but the data above are intricate and only the most important points and the clearest relationships are highlighted below. The three investigative professions are discussed first, then the other frontline professions and, lastly, those on the periphery of the network.

Social workers

Over four fifths of the sample have worked with them and most, regardless of profession, find the collaboration very or fairly easy. Nevertheless, nearly a quarter report otherwise and, given social workers' stated key role in the child protection system, this is a matter of concern. The vignette responses showed some reserve about drawing social workers into the arena. It seems important to find out whether this is because other professionals see referral to social workers as stigmatising or an automatic threat to the family's integrity, whether they think social workers have insufficient resources to give a supportive response to families or for other reasons. It is essential that social workers do have the right resources, skills and presentation to offer a supportive and non-stigmatising service and are not cast in the role of 'child snatchers'. Over half the sample think social workers' role is very clear and very few see it as unclear. However, the police and paediatricians are clearest about this, as would be expected in view of their joint responsibility for investigation and assessment of alleged abuse.

Teachers and general practitioners are frequently noted to be well-placed for early identification of children at risk and to make referrals to the investigative services. It is therefore worrying to report that nearly half feel unclear about the social workers' job although it is also noteworthy that, because of their numbers on the ground, both professions emerge from the vignette study in Chapter Nine as prominent referral sources. There is little doubt in people's minds about the importance of social workers' role, with four fifths deeming them essential in child protection and only 6% saying 'don't know'. Nobody says they are unimportant. However, scattered though all the professions, there are more reservations about their role performance; less than 30% of the definite opinions are strongly favourable although the vast majority of the remainder think they function fairly well.

Police

Nearly three quarters of respondents say they have collaborated with the police and rate this marginally easier than with social workers. Overall, one third have no clear view of the police role but teachers are most often unclear. While most think they are important, they are not generally seen as essential. Only a quarter of the definite opinions give them top marks for performance although nearly all the remainder think fairly well of this. Social workers most often claim the clearest view of their role, rate it as essential and their job as very well done.

Paediatricians

Three quarters have worked with paediatricians and a few more find them very easy than so find social workers or the police. However, fewer find them fairly easy and noticeably more find them very difficult. Most respondents feel reasonably clear about their job in child protection and, with no evident interprofessional variation, half the respondents think the role essential and another third think it important. Their performance is rated very much the same as social workers'.

Mutual perceptions among the core professions

The importance of effective coordination between these three professions is constantly emphasised in official policy and the professional literature; they are the inner ring gathering and assessing the initial grounds for concern and social workers are always designated the key worker to hold the responsibility for continuing coordination of work with the child and family. Their relationships have therefore been abstracted from the full data set and separately considered in Tables 11.9 to 11.12.

The majority find cooperation fairly easy. However, there are evident problems. Social workers and the police are both prominent in the whole sample among those reporting difficulty in collaborating with paediatricians. Given the great need for successful coordination within this core group, it is not surprising but even more disturbing that they are particularly prominent among the small number reporting extreme difficulty. Only 12% of social workers find paediatricians very easy and well over a third report difficulty, whereas nearly three times as many paediatricians find social workers very easy and only half as many see them as difficult to work with. There is less imbalance between the police and paediatricians, with similar proportions finding the relationship difficult but more police finding it very easy than vice versa.

Personal, professional and bureaucratic status factors have often been cited as a cause of tension between doctors and others in the human service world

Table 11.9 **A comparison of the perceptions of ease of cooperation between the three investigative professions in child protection cases**

Rating:	By: Of:	Social Work		Police		Paediatrician		Total	
		N	%	N	%	N	%	N	%
Very easy	Social Work	—	—	12	57.1	11	32.4	23	41.8
	Police	14	23.0	—	—	4	12.1	18	9.1
	Paediatrician	7	11.7	5	23.8	—	—	12	14.8
Fairly easy	Social Work	—	—	8	38.1	17	50.0	25	45.5
	Police	36	59.0	—	—	22	66.7	58	61.7
	Paediatrician	30	50.0	11	52.4	—	—	41	50.6
Rather difficult	Social Work	—	—	1	4.8	6	17.6	7	12.7
	Police	11	18.0	—	—	7	21.2	18	19.1
	Paediatrician	23	38.3	5	23.8	—	—	28	34.6

Note: This table compares results from three different variables and the response rates varied slightly regarding each profession (60–61 SWs, 20–22 police and 33–34 paediatricians). Although the results are closely comparable, the percentages refer to the individual response rates and cannot be aggregated.

and it seems reasonable to suppose they are operating here. However, in terms of educational and professional standing one might expect there to be more difficulty between paediatricians and the police than between the former and social workers. It may be that there is less domain conflict between the police and paediatricians, with the police having a clearly circumscribed and generally dependent function in this relationship, simply gathering evidence from the expert diagnostician, even though there are also times when the paediatrician is dependent on the police for scientific and forensic data. On the other hand, social workers and paediatricians may be contesting their expertise and sense of responsibility for the child's total welfare. While the obvious turf fights over who is chairing the conference may well be ancient history (Hallett and Stevenson 1980, Dingwall et al 1983), status as a determinant of the weight given to different participants' opinions is a continuing theme in the literature (Hallett and Birchall 1992, chapter 8). Paediatricians also vary in their degree of interest in psycho-emotional and family dynamics as opposed to a narrower biotechnical focus. Social workers have legal responsibility for the child's longterm welfare but may sometimes have only a limited expertise in the requisite assessment and therapeutic skills (DH 1988). It may therefore not be surprising if there is discomfort in the relationship when, as one of the paediatric respondents explicitly stated 'We attend as experts on the whole child, not just the injuries'.

There is a similar though less marked pattern between social workers and the police, with the majority of social workers having fairly easy relations with the police but a significant minority reporting difficulty. In contrast, most of the police officers claim very easy relations with social workers and only one says the relationship is problematic. There is an extensive literature on the different value systems of the two professions and on the conflict between law-enforcement and therapeutic roles. The power and status relations are by no means one-directional. Although writers like Blagg and Stubbs (1988) and Thomas (1986, 1989) continue to call in question the degree to which social workers and the police cooperate to the benefit of the children concerned, these issues do not seem to be causing much concern to practitioners in 1991. It is perhaps surprising that so little difficulty is reported and it may be, as the example of 'dawn raids' in Rochdale and elsewhere suggests, that social workers have subordinated too much of their own role to police interests. However, the recent empirical study by Brown and Fuller (1991) found that planned cooperation between the two services had not only improved mutual relationships but also their response to children.

Table 11.10 **A comparison of the perceptions of the clarity of roles between the three investigative professions in child protection cases**

Rating:	By: Of:	Social Work		Police		Paediatrician		Total	
		N	%	N	%	N	%	N	%
Very easy	Social Work	—	—	18	81.8	27	73.0	45	76.3
	Police	36	61.0	—	—	16	45.7	52	55.3
	Paediatrician	24	39.3	12	57.1	—	—	36	43.9
Fairly easy	Social Work	—	—	4	18.2	9	24.3	13	22.0
	Police	19	32.2	—	—	13	37.1	32	34.0
	Paediatrician	31	50.8	9	42.9	—	—	40	48.8
Rather difficult	Social Work	—	—	0	0.0	1	2.7	1	1.7
	Police	4	6.8	—	—	6	17.1	10	10.6
	Paediatrician	6	9.8	0	0.0	—	—	6	7.3

Note: This table compares results from three different variables and the response rates varied slightly regarding each profession (59–61 SWs, 21–22 police and 35–37 paediatricians). Although the results are closely comparable, the percentages refer to the individual response rates and cannot be aggregated.

In comparing their views of one another's role, the large majority of police and paediatricians are very clear about the social worker's job and most social workers are clear about the police role. It is unexpected that social workers report themselves less clear about the paediatricians' role. However, it may be explicable in terms of the domain conflict postulated above rather than to doubts about their diagnostic function. Alternatively, it could be because social workers meet a wide spectrum of possibly abusive situations that are assessed by the frontline workers without recourse to hospital specialists, although there would appear to be no reason for this to cause uncertainty about the latter's role in appropriate situations.

When the three views of each others' importance in this sphere are compared, there is a very high degree of consensus between the other professions that social workers are essential whereas only half consider the police essential and around two thirds agree that paediatricians are essential. These measures may again indicate a selective approach to the involvement of paediatricians and police in contrast to the universal requirement for the social work function. A small number of both social workers and paediatricians doubt the importance of the police function.

Table 11.11 **A comparison of the perceptions of the importance of roles between the three investigative professions in child protection cases**

Rating: 	By: Of:	Social Work		Police		Paediatrician		Total	
		N	%	N	%	N	%	N	%
Essential	Social Work	—	—	19	86.4	30	78.9	49	81.7
	Police	33	55.0	—	—	16	45.7	49	51.6
	Paediatrician	37	61.7	16	72.7	—	—	53	64.6
Important	Social Work	—	—	3	13.6	8	21.1	11	18.3
	Police	22	36.7	—	—	16	45.7	38	40.0
	Paediatrician	23	38.3	6	27.3	—	—	29	35.4
Not very important	Social Work	—	—	0	0.0	0	0.0	0	0.0
	Police	5	8.3	—	—	3	8.6	8	8.4
	Paediatrician	0	0.0	0	0.0	—	—	0	0.0

Note: This table compares results from three different variables and 60 SWs and 22 police responded. Paediatricians' response rates varied slightly regarding each profession (35–38 paediatricians). Although the results are closely comparable, the percentages refer to the individual response rates and cannot be aggregated.

Lastly, their views of each others' performance are compared. Although opinions are generally favourable, paediatricians prove to be less ready than social workers to rate the police highly but equally likely to rate them poorly. Social workers are considerably more critical of paediatricians than vice versa.

While strains between these three professions are more worrying, at least in the investigative phase, than any that might arise between the other professions, the majority of responses show convergent attitudes and mutual appreciation. There are many tensions arising from their respective roles within the child protection system and their different responsibilities and priorities outside it (Hallett and Birchall 1992) and it could be argued that relationships are as good as can be expected. However, there does seem to be an important issue about relationships between social workers and the medical profession. This may only be resolved when and if social workers have been helped to achieve more advanced expertise and the concomitant organisational status and when and if some doctors resist the temptation to assert authority and expertise over others' spheres of responsibility.

Table 11.12 **A comparison of the perceptions of role performance between the three investigative professions in child protection cases**

Rating:	By: Of:	Social Work N	Social Work %	Police N	Police %	Paediatrician N	Paediatrician %	Total N	Total %
Very well	Social Work	—	—	9	45.0	10	30.3	19	35.8
	Police	20	36.7	—	—	6	24.0	26	30.2
	Paediatrician	15	25.9	8	40.0	—	—	23	29.5
Fairly well	Social Work	—	—	10	50.0	21	63.6	31	58.5
	Police	30	49.2	—	—	15	60.0	45	52.3
	Paediatrician	33	56.9	11	55.0	—	—	44	56.4
Rather poorly	Social Work	—	—	1	5.0	2	6.1	3	5.7
	Police	11	18.0	—	—	4	16.0	15	17.4
	Paediatrician	10	17.2	1	5.0	—	—	11	14.1

Note: This table compares results from three different variables and 20 police responded. SW response rates varied slightly regarding each profession (58–61 SWs) and remain comparable. However, only 25 paediatricians responded about the police while 33 responded about SWs. This discrepancy makes this one result less comparable than the others. The percentages refer to the individual response rates and cannot be aggregated.

Health visitors, teachers and general practitioners

Almost everyone finds health visitors easy to work with and over half deem them essential but only one third feel very clear about their role. Although general practitioners and social workers equally perceive them as essential, the doctors think more highly of their performance than do the social workers. Nearly everyone but the police deems teachers' role important or essential but significant numbers find teachers difficult to cooperate with. There is also a lot of confusion about their role in child protection, not least among themselves, and nearly a quarter consider their performance rather or very poor.

There is a lot of dissatisfaction around general practitioners' role in this field. Few find them very easy to work with; indeed a large majority of social workers say they are difficult and a quarter very difficult. A similarly large proportion consider they perform this role poorly. Not one social worker or police officer rates them as very easy to work with or as functioning very well, and two thirds of pediatricians and health visitors think they perform poorly. They themselves are even less likely than teachers to rate their own role in this sphere as very clear and over a fifth say it is unclear. It is evident from recent editorials and other items in the medical press that such ambivalence and uncertainty are common (Harris 1991, Lea Cox and Hall 1991, Bisset and Hunter 1992). The core professions are again even more confused about what to expect of them, with over two thirds of social workers and 57% of paediatricians seeing this role as unclear and no police feeling very clear about it. Even among their primary health care colleagues, less than a third of health visitors are very clear about what general practitioners should be doing. In view of such role confusion, it is perhaps not surprising that few people rate their performance favourably.

There is evidently a large unresolved question about the place of the two front line professions of teaching and general practice in child protection. They appear to be well-placed to identify and refer children to the specialist agencies but clearly are not well-integrated into the network. Remarkably few of them have received any training on the topic, a fact which must correlate either with their professions' corporate lack of interest or their own. Cases of child abuse occur as a very occasional interruption of their normal responsibilities and interests and the literature indicates that many are not alert to signs of possible abuse. Teachers vary widely in their attitude to pastoral aspects of their job and general practitioners seem less likely, in a world of high family mobility and increasingly impersonal group practices, to have that intimate and continuing knowledge of families which has been claimed as their invaluable contribution. There seems to be scope for qualitative research focused on members of the two professions who have worked out a valued and active role for themselves in this field.

The peripheral professions

Many people have had contact with several other professions, at least episodically, in connection with child protection work. Again the doctors are seen as presenting more difficulty as collaborators than the other professions. Nearly a third of respondents are unclear about the roles of psychiatrists and psychologists and significant minorities also question their importance. Despite the crucial importance of lawyers in a relatively small number of cases, they have quite a small impact on the system as a whole. Not surprisingly, the frontline have less contact and ease than the core professions with them.

Only a quarter of respondents feel clear about school nurses and education welfare officers even though around three quarters think their input is important. Teachers and health visitors, particularly the former, consider these two groups very important but are no clearer about their role than anyone else. In view of teachers' low profile in child protection, one may speculate that they see them as intermediaries to the social services department. As regards health visitors' view of them, there would appear to be a close professional identity between themselves and the school nurse; in some areas of the country the two roles are held by the same person. Given health visitors' apparent prominence in linking the frontline and the core professions, there may sometimes be informal communications between them and school nurses regarding children causing concern before the latter cross the threshold of referral as suspected abuse. It is harder to hypothesise about health visitors' bond with education welfare officers. However, if these speculations are well-founded, the communication chain would appear to be uncomfortably stretched and insecure. One would wish for more direct discussion between teachers and social workers, particularly as both education welfare officers and nurses have rather a low salience to the core professions and sizeable minorities of social workers rate their performance poorly.

Summary and conclusions

Four dimensions of respondents' perceptions of twelve professions in the child protection network were explored through scaled questions. These covered the ease of cooperating with them, the clarity and importance of their roles and their performance in this field. A very large majority claimed some experience, however limited, of most of the professions named, the lowest response being 55% in relation to lawyers. There were, however, significant numbers of general practitioners and teachers who indicated no relevant experience overall or in relation to specific others; almost everyone else had a wide range of contacts. These questions give no direct information about the frequency of contacts within the network, although the greater readiness to answer the full range of questions about some groups is suggestive of more intimate experience of them, nor can they give any clue to the relevance of other unnamed groups.

The patterns of contact gave further evidence of the relevance of the front line professions of health visiting, teaching and general practice. The core professions of social work, paediatrics and the police were nearly as prevalent and so were the peripheral professions of school nursing and education welfare; a similar number, which seems surprisingly high, say they have had contact with the case-specific professions of A&E, psychology and psychiatry. Despite the wording of the questions, it seems possible that people have drawn on their experience of cooperation with such groups in a wider arena than child protection. However, it is evident that the core professions and health visitors constitute a denser network among themselves but also link with a wider network than the others.

The bulk of substantive responses to all professions rated them fairly positively on all factors but there are some marked variations. There is widespread dissatisfaction with general practitioners' contribution to child protection on all four factors.

School nurses and health visitors are reported to be particularly easy to cooperate with and the balance of opinion about the police is favourable. It seems that the previously prominent concerns about confidentiality and role conflict between the helping agencies and the police have dissipated, although teachers and general practitioners showed a rather guarded attitude towards them through their responses to the long vignettes. All the medical professions are found difficult more often than others and rated as very difficult by significant minorities. However, a quarter find working with paediatricians very easy. Opinions about social workers are also split with sizeable minorities finding them very easy and difficult. Generally, doctors find it easier to work with social workers and health visitors than vice versa and this marked imbalance in the collaborative relationship is familiar in the literature.

A large majority feel very or fairly clear about the role of the core professions but a worrying number, particularly of teachers, only feel fairly clear about social workers. There is considerable confusion about the role of teachers, health visitors and general practitioners, not least among themselves. Few respondents rate any profession's contribution unimportant and there is a high consensus on the essential role of social workers but more rather mixed views of the others. That the front line professions are generally deemed as important as the investigative professions indicates that most members of the network have a wider view of child protection than the merely forensic. As befits their coordinating role, social workers recognise the importance of a wider range of other professions more often than other respondents. Fewer people feel able to comment on others' performance of their roles, apparently due to their limited experience or lack of feedback, but the bulk of responses deem others fulfilled their functions fairly well. Sizeable minorities think the core professions and health visitors perform very well. Social workers were most often critical, particularly of doctors but they thought highly of the police. Generally, greater experience increased people's scepticism about others' role performance but not concerning paediatricians.

Views of the peripheral professions and of those episodically involved are more fragmentary but some indications of sub-networks in the primary health and school spheres, linked to the sphere of child protection by health visitors, add to similar indications in the responses to the long vignettes. This suggests that professional proximity rathr than appropriate roles may influence respondents' choice of relationships and that some communication chains, particularly between teachers and social workers, may be unduly stretched and insecure. The data here also suggest a disturbing distance between social workers and general practitioners although the latter's position in the network appears quite prominent in Chapter Nine. If mutual trust and collaborative relationships depend considerably on proximity, the essential partners must, as the literature argues (Hallett and Birchall 1992, chapters 11 and 14), create and be given the opportunity to invest time with one another and in joint training.

Chapter 12

Conclusions

General observations

A broad sweep of public policy encourages coordination as a means of improving the effectiveness of many services. A strongly mandated official policy requiring interprofessional cooperation in child protection has developed, partly in response to professional precept and partly in response to a series of Inquiry criticisms of poorly coordinated work in this field. Little is known of how it works in practice or of how the professionals themselves value it. The present research programme, through its three phases of literature review, extensive postal survey and case studies, gives a preliminary map of the ground and explores some of the issues.

The most striking impression is that the need to cooperate in child protection is widely recognised and valued. Most respondents with relevant experience assert that the coordinating system works fairly well and the majority report that others in the network are fairly easy to collaborate with. The corollary of this statement is, of course, that only a minority think everything and everyone work very smoothly together. Many diversities with regard to case judgments and the choice of interventions are evident and there are varying and sometimes significant numbers who report substantial difficulties in particular facets of the machinery or in particular interprofessional relationships.

A second general point is that almost all cooperation and coordination comprises the exchange of information and only the police and social workers are doing any significant amounts of 'hands on' joint work. This confirms the continuing primacy of the forensic task and continuing underdevelopment of planned, interdisciplinary therapeutic interventions with the children or their families of the sort occasionally mentioned in the literature (Hallett and Birchall 1992, chapter 12). It also suggests that the professional network is not a 'team' that can give emotional support to the practitioners although there were indications that people often turned to external colleagues for advice and support.

The conclusions of Phase Two are presented under five headings:

Description of respondents and their experience of child protection;

Convergences and divergences in perceptions of cases;

Perceptions and evaluations of the local case management system.

Perceptions of the local interprofessional network

General conclusions.

The underlying interpretive questions for each heading are:

What are the important influences on this issue?

What interpretations can be offered for any important relationships?

What are the implications for policy and practice?

How do these relate to the original algorithm presented in Chapter One?

Important questions about the structure and machinery of the child protection network can be clearly answered with descriptive facts but many subtler issues arise from the perceptions and judgments of workers. A number of more tentative interpretations are offered about their causation and their likely impact on the way the network operates. Some issues can be discussed and recommendations made within the confines of a specific heading but others derive from the overall findings and will be discussed under the heading of General Conclusions. However, the extent and complexity of the practitioner network and the complex nature of the concept of coordination mean that a first study such as this points to more questions as well as suggesting some answers.

Profession is the factor that most affects perceptions and actions in dealing with abused children and their families, not only in the obvious sense of fulfilling a task specific to the person's job but more pervasively in influencing the worker's perception of a case, of the way it should be handled, of the appropriate network to engage with and of his or her place in that network. Clearly personal judgments and values are also significant factors in individuals' decisions and choices in case management in child protection and there are few points on which there is a massive consensus either between the professions or within each group. However, there are consistencies in the data which are best expressed as more or less likely postures.

It had been hypothesised that, given three contrasting locations, local policy and professional and agency cultures might significantly affect people's decisions about cases but the respondent's locality had no effect on these issues and surprisingly little correlation with perceptions of policy and coordinating machinery. Many similarities between the local guidelines plus this finding suggest that a fairly uniform national culture and a common procedural framework of working together has developed over recent years, in marked contrast to the researcher's earlier experience as a practitioner in different locations, although discrepancies between individuals and professions evidently remain. Where area appeared as a statistically significant variable, it was about the availability of and contact with peripheral groups such as clinical medical officers or NSPCC staff and no doubt reflected particular local staffing and resource patterns.

Despite their salience to some issues in the literature, gender, age and child-rearing experience correlate with almost none of the case perceptions in this study. As one would expect from the literature on gender and on the sociology of the professions, it appears that gender may be a pertinent factor in some aspects of interprofessional relationships but it is entwined with a whole bundle of status factors that are associated with different professional roles. In order to study the gender effect independently, a considerably larger sample would have been necessary to obtain adequate numbers of men and women in each of the differently balanced professional groups and, in the case of health visitors, it would be impossible to separate gender from their professional identity. At times and with some groups in this study, it has been possible to distinguish the gender factor but at others it remained confounded with profession. Explanations have then been offered in terms of professional role for some groups and gender for others, for instance in the differential response patterns of the professions and the sexes to the utility of case conferences in handling anxiety.

There were insufficient respondents from ethnic minorities to test the effect of race issues in interprofessional relationships but there was disturbing evidence of different approaches to case management, depending on the race of the child. This is discussed in more detail below.

Apart from the strong and easily explicable correlation between inexperience and 'don't know' responses or 'no replies', various factors relating to respondents' experience of child protection work also prove to be comparatively marginal. Personal, experiential and local factors are therefore only mentioned in the report when they showed a significant correlation or when it seems particularly surprising that they did not.

In addition to the factual findings, most of the discussion therefore relates to individual and professional variations in perception and judgments and their likely impact on cooperative relationships. While such differences are frequent, it is important to stress that most respondents with relevant experience think that the case coordinating system is fairly satisfactory. The majority also think that collaborative relationships are fairly easy. However, only a minority think the people and the system work very smoothly and many frictions are evident.

Some differences are explicable in terms of professional task or agency function and may often be unproblematic. Others, where different workers' tasks and priorities may clash, may be sources of conflict. Others indicate individual opinions in a contentious and uncertain sphere of work or role confusion within and between the professions, any of which may lead to unrealistic or incompatible expectations of what individuals will or should do. When the cogs of the machine begin to grate for any of these reasons and discrepant expectations arise, then it is likely that political factors of power and status and resource dependency will come into play and domain conflicts may also emerge. Such factors were not often overtly acknowledged and are difficult to uncover through a postal survey but, as one would expect from the literature, are strongly suggested by some of the response patterns.

Description of respondents and their experience of child protection

The processes of selection and the structure of the sample are described in Chapters Three and Four. It is a stratified random sample of six professions which were assumed and proved to be particularly salient to child protection case work. Stratification and weighting mitigated the effects of widely varying numbers in the professions and also deliberately biassed the sample in favour of personnel with greater involvement in child protection while still including a substantial proportion of more generalist staff who also have some actual or potential responsibilities in this field.

There was an evident and strong tendency for people who declined to participate in the research to be those with least engagement in child protection, particularly the general practitioners whose overall response rate was low and the teachers and junior paediatric staff whose response rate was generally at a reasonable level but who most often said their refusals were due to lack of any relevant experience or knowledge. This tendency was further accentuated by the preponderance of 'don't knows' or 'no replies' among the actual responses from these groups. Teachers were five times as likely and general practitioners three times as likely as social workers or the police to give 'don't know' responses and both were three times as likely to give no reply. The outcome is that respondents to this survey tend to be those with more than average experience of child abuse issues and the substantive responses are often a further distillation from that pool of greater experience, limited though this sometimes proves to be.

The gender structure of the professions varies predictably, with a heavy preponderance of men among the general practitioners and, to a less extent, among the paediatricians. Almost all health visitors are women and the specialist police are predominantly women and thus very different from other sectors of the police service. Smaller majorities of social workers and teachers are women but the gender balance changes in favour of men among those of principal rank in all groups. The age structure of the professions also varies to a limited extent, although the majority of respondents are between 30 and 44. The bulk of health visitors are over 45 and the police tend to be younger. As expected, age and rank correlate more closely for paediatric staff than any other group. As well as the health visitors, the social workers are older at recruitment than the other professions, belying the stereotype of youth and inexperience that has often been applied to them. The large majority of respondents have experience of child-rearing although few of the police have. There are a small number of ethnic minority respondents, mainly Indian doctors. Variations in educational level are noted simply for descriptive purposes but are so thoroughly confounded with profession that no attempt was made to use educational attainment as an independent variable.

The large majority of the sample have more than ten years' experience in their professions and are also well-established in their locality. However, there were varied permutations of length of service in the profession, the locality and current rank, some of them being expected like the rotation of junior doctors and police officers. Social workers show most mobility on all three factors in combination and therefore may be less embedded in the convoluted strata of the local child protection network as outlined below.

The distribution of child protection responsibilities across the ranks in the different agencies is complex and quite diverse: in this primary school sample, head teachers generally appear to hold the reins quite tightly on matters of interagency communication, as do paediatric consultants regarding assessment and diagnosis; general practitioners' autonomous status is well-known; health visitors, social workers and the police negotiate much everyday liaison and decision-making at ground level but their hierarchies come into the picture at different points and for different purposes. Health visitors appear to turn to their nurse managers primarily for advice and support but not for authorisation. In cases such as the vignettes, the police constables also claim to act without prior authorisation and officers above the level of sergeant in these areas appear to have extensive administrative functions. In contrast, within the hierarchical and specialist structure of the social services department, the diversity of responsibilities it carries in relation to child protection means that several staff of different ranks and with special roles may be operationally involved with a case. Some of the social services' roles are to do with direct work with children and families and some to do with staff supervision and accountability, some with resource-finding or administration. All this means that inter-agency liaison involves a complex mix of staff of different professional seniorities, organisational and personal status and local rootedness.

As expected, the professions have very varied experience of child protection matters. Despite the broad mix of the social work sample, there is strong evidence of the weight of this particular function in the social services department's overall workloads. To a lesser extent, consultant paediatricians in district general hospitals also reveal their heavy involvement. The police, entirely sampled from child abuse and domestic violence units, are inevitably deeply immersed in this work with a massive turnover of cases. Health visitors' engagement is considerably less than the above but much more than that of general practitioners and teachers who prove to be rarely involved. The minimal involvement of teachers remains evident even when only the head teachers are examined. Thus the professions bring very different degrees of familiarity with the shared task of child protection to their cooperative efforts.

It is obvious that the specific tasks of many professions in relation to a family's child protection career are different and these tasks might at first appear simple to aggregate. However, this is not so. Issues of value conflicts are dealt with later but it is also important to the more mechanical consideration of how the network articulates to recognise that the time spans entailed for the achievement of each profession's task vary widely. These are likely to affect practitioners' ability to collaborate, as discussed in chapter 14 of Hallett and Birchall (1992). Some roles, like the police officer's, generally involve only a brief investigative episode; the paediatrician's is likely to be similar unless the child has suffered lasting harm; other roles, like the teacher's or health visitor's and often the social worker's, involve a relationship which may span years of pastoral care. Although there is disturbing evidence that social work resources are insufficient to allocate a key worker to every child on the register (HC 1990–91), if it is to be effective the social worker's role should mean a sustained and intensive involvement throughout the child's career in the child protection system, whether he or she is supported at home or admitted to care. Such different timespans and tempos seem likely to be one feature of the significant number of complaints about differing priorities, time and mutual accessibility as obstacles to cooperation.

Each profession forms its members in very different ways, in terms of educational level, occupational acculturation and the practical content of basic training. It has frequently been found that these factors, combined with different tasks and priorities, lead to incompatibilities between the professions when they attempt to collaborate (Hallett and Birchall 1992, chapter 8). The degree to which any of them enter their professional worlds with a common understanding of child development and shared expectations of family life and of the specific issues of managing children at risk is unclear but it seems likely to be limited.

The fabric of interprofessional cooperation is thus woven of very complex threads and textures, comprised of different experiences, different organisational structures, different statuses, different priorities and tasks and different time orientations. The values that hold it together may be a combination of shared goals for the children concerned, mutual respect for one another's functions and fear of getting it wrong, but there is evidently great scope for confusion and conflict. Although the data from this study suggests much concern for children and goodwill about the professional network, there was also no shortage of evidence regarding frictions in the system and divergent opinions about how cases should be handled.

Much has been written about workers' need for specific training in this field, with two main themes: the need for greater knowledge and skills and a clearer understanding of each others' roles and skills but also the need to learn how to collaborate (Hallett and Birchall 1992, chapter 8). Specifically with regard to the processes of cooperation, the literature emphasises the difficulty of the enterprise and the amount of energy and commitment that has to be invested in organisation maintenance. The structure of the network as outlined in Chapter Nine and displayed in Figures 9.1 and 9.2 would suggest that both tasks are large and important. A very large number of people are occasionally or potentially involved in the system and a significant but smaller number are repeatedly involved.

It seems probable that the former need more information about aspects of child abuse and about various agencies' roles but that the latter need more opportunity for training together in ways that develop mutual trust and collegiality. Yet, as Brill cited from Wise et al (1974):

> *It is ironic indeed to realise that a football team spends 40 hours a week practising for the two hours on Sunday afternoons when their teamwork really counts. Teams in organisations seldom spend two hours per year practising when their ability to function as a team counts 40 hours per week (Brill 1976, p. 45).*

Brunel (1988) suggest that, through their relatively frequent encounters at child protection conferences, senior members of the different professions may develop into a de facto interagency team. The Cleveland Report (1988) commended the development of an interagency team of practitioners or practice consultants. The data here confirms a high level of attendance by, notably, senior social workers and first line managers of health visitors but also fairly high attendances by the principal ranks of social services, police and paediatrics. It may be that they are a small enough group to develop personal relationships and begin to feel a team within a small authority or geographical division. However, it is evident that the burden of national and local policy guidance regarding interagency cooperation has been about procedural matters although the government has given rather more attention to practice issues since 1988. It seems likely that, given the diverse organisational roles these individuals occupy, although difficult it would be rather easier to integrate their activities on behalf of bureaucratic functions than as a practice or consultancy team.

However, significant agencies are left out of the above. Any one of the numerous primary school heads or general practitioners is rarely involved. This research did not include pre-school provisions and secondary schools but it is evident that their incorporation into the picture adds further complexities. Whether the greater personal and institutional distance of teachers and general practitioners from the child protection system adversely affects the welfare of many children is a matter for empirical enquiry into outcomes. However, that distance has been a matter of concern in several of the Inquiries into child abuse tragedies from Maria Colwell onwards. With general practitioners' well-known independence from any managerial organ-isation, it seems doubtful that the occasional participation of an individual makes any significant impact on the profession as a whole. The policy move towards local management of schools is also likely to increase the difficulties of integrating them more effectively into the system.

If cooperation is important to practitioners' effectiveness, both in terms of well-planned care for the children and families and in terms of mutual support and challenge in carrying out a very difficult job, it is clear that there is still plenty of scope for improvement, whether the system is viewed as a network or aspires to be a closer team. The evidence from this survey suggests that specific training is a valued and valuable factor in improving cooperative practice and developing the necessary degree of mutual trust. However, the data also show that training for either the technical tasks or collaborative processes is extremely limited. The facts are grim.

Half the sample have had no post-qualifying training whatsoever or even attended any conference on the subject of child protection (as distinct from case conferences). Only 20% have aggregated more than two weeks of such training and only 14% have received more than five days of interdisciplinary training during their working lives. The pattern varies markedly across the professions, with most of the social workers, police and health visitors having had some such training and as many social workers having had more than a fortnight as the rest of the sample put together. Small minorities of the class teachers and general practitioners and few of the paediatric junior doctors have attended any, and only two thirds of the senior teachers and less than four fifths of the consultant paediatricians.

Most of the people who have had any such training have spent part of it in an interdisciplinary setting but this is even less likely among the teachers and general practitioners. The range of professions encountered varies widely. Social workers and the police are the commonest combination, apparently reflecting the recent upsurge of interest in joint training for sexual abuse investigation. Nearly all the social workers and health visitors have shared some training and significant numbers of them have shared with teachers, despite the small proportion of this much larger profession who have participated. The paediatricians are much more likely to have trained with social workers than vice versa, no doubt partly reflecting the numerical imbalance between the groups but accentuated by the minimal participation of junior doctors in any such experience. Even consultant paediatricians tend to have had less interdisciplinary training than the other core professions or health visitors. Thereafter, the pattern is fragmented but tends to cluster into sub-networks of educational and health personnel.

Generally, respondents valued this slender experience of inter-disciplinary training but open-ended responses suggested that the different professions emphasised different aspects. In view of their slight experience, it is understandable that teachers most often highlighted increasing their knowledge about child abuse and child protection, a matter that might be further addressed within their own profession as some other respondents felt the content of interprofessional courses was too basic for their own needs. Health visitors and the police showed themselves most concerned about improving their understanding of others' technical contributions, apparently viewing cooperation primarily as a resource exchange.

Social workers were the most likely to emphasise the need to improve participants' understanding of the processes of cooperation. This preoccupation may reflect both their professional stance (their concern about feelings, about healing and comforting and also about conflict avoidance: Hallett and Birchall 1992, chapter 11) but also, very importantly, their responsibilities in the child protection network. The few doctors involved in such training showed no particular pattern in their answers. In accordance with an extensive literature, this is only the first of several points where social workers' real problems in fulfilling their coordinating role and doctors' limited interest in the issue of cooperation emerges from the data. The breadth of the general paediatrician's responsibilities is acknowledged and cannot be equated with the much narrower task of the similarly scarce specialist police but the apparent gains in collegial relations between social workers and police officers through their investment in joint training must be compared with the evidence of continuing strains between the doctors and the other professions. Moreover, given the evidence in the literature of doctors' tendency to encroach on others' roles and to claim the leadership in collaborative situations (Hallett and Birchall 1992, chapter 11), it seems important that doctors should invest more effort in wider inter-disciplinary training, preferably in the formative stages of their professional careers, and particularly important that social workers and junior paediatric staff learn to develop a closer working relationship.

Convergences and divergences in perceptions of cases

Debate continues in the professional literature about whether it is more fruitful to approach families with possible problems of child abuse in a basically supportive and unthreatening way or to be more direct with parents about their responsibility, when this is the case, for the child's condition or how effectively the approaches can be combined. Although the new orthodoxy among social work writers in the field of child protection favours directness combined with acceptance of the parents, there appears to be no direct empirical evidence of how widely this has been adopted in practice by social workers nor of how other members of the network may view the question. It seems that these basic stances might lead to conflict over the appropriateness and timing of referrals to the investigative professions but also to confusion and ambivalence in the network's ongoing dealings with the family.

The majority of respondents in this study basically asserted the direct approach, particularly social workers, police officers, paediatric consultants and general practitioners. It is not surprising to find social workers and perhaps paediatricians taking this standpoint in view of the prevailing climate and the police taking it as part of their professional function. However, it is more surprising to hear it from general practitioners as it has often been said, most recently in a Scottish survey by Bisset and Hunter (1992), that they find particular difficulty in risking their friendly relationships with parents, which are normally in tune with the child's needs, and adopting a posture that may alienate the parents in order to protect the child. The other professions and the junior doctors were evenly split on the topic and further exploration revealed more ambiguity in all professions, with some people admitting that the severity of the case or their assessment of the family's total situation would affect their judgment. In the abstract situation of this question, interprofessional consensus was strongest on the need to confront parents over suspicions of sexual abuse but, in fact, the practical proposals in relation to the first stage of the Jane vignette suggest many would be more guarded.

The preference for the more direct approach is not significantly altered by case experience but does appear to be taught to social workers in post-qualifying training; the number favouring the accepting approach falls from 40% to nil after such training. In contrast, nearly half the health visitors continue to favour the accepting approach, despite the same amount of training but perhaps a different curriculum, and they are particularly likely to assert that parents' recognition of responsibility is a developing process. Numbers in the other professions were too few to reveal any trend. Whereas additional probing had revealed a more contingent approach in many respondents, training reduced this malleability regardless of profession; people obviously gained in conviction that directness was necessary even when families appeared fragile or the abuse minor and thus implied that they believed relationships could be successfully sustained through the confrontational process.

However, these data leave an open question as to whether the more fixed postures of the core professions reflect the development of a common ideology between them. It might simply indicate that the front line professions held generally more extreme images of 'the abused child' in mind as they made their initial response and then, in responding to the supplementary questions, began to think more in terms of the 'grey' cases that cause them some anxiety in real life. The long vignettes indicated that many are content to monitor and/or support cases within their own settings for some time longer before referral to the investigative agencies. Thresholds of referral for investigation and confrontation are evidently difficult to define. Nagi observed that

> *to recognize vagueness around the lines of differentiation is not . . . to*
> *sanction apathy and carelessness. Rather, the purpose is to emphasize one*
> *of the major problems underlying difficulties in the delivery of services and*
> *the administration of justice in this field (1977, p. 108).*

A series of brief vignettes, which derived from a study in the USA of definitions of child abuse, was used to explore how severely professionals rate cases of possible abuse and whether their judgments are similar or discrepant. The implication of divergent ratings would be that staff would be unlikely to agree on referral thresholds or action plans. The data indicate that each profession has a rather more homogeneous view of the severity of cases than would be expected from an open population, with scores from most professions regarding most of the incidents falling within two standard deviations. Nevertheless, few cases achieved consensus across all the professions. There was strongest agreement both within and between groups on the cases that respondents rated most severely. The obverse was more individual as well as interprofessional diversity in rating the less severe cases. The greatest dissensus arose about cases in the neglect and emotional abuse categories. These findings confirm the difficulty of establishing a common baseline for referrals to the child protection system and the particularly problematic nature of defining standards for cases of neglect and emotional abuse. It appears to be easier to find a common level of understanding of cases of physical and sexual abuse and the higher anxiety about cases in the latter category is evident.

There was, however, a considerable degree of agreement between different coalitions of professions and a high level of agreement among the core professions in their ratings of the brief vignettes. There were just three statistically significant divergences between the police and social workers and none between either of those professions and the paediatricians. This suggests that the core professions may generally be able to agree in practice on appropriate responses to cases that gain admission to the child protection system. However, social workers generally rated cases less severely than all the other professions and disagreed more than half the time with health visitors, who consistently gave the most severe ratings. Similarly, teachers rated cases severely and were often in disagreement with social workers. These results suggest that there will be considerable tensions between front line agencies and social services about thresholds of referral and adds further weight to other findings in the report which support the familiar stereotypes of over-anxious health visitors and teachers facing impassive social workers. Although it appears that social workers seek more conferences than other professionals, there were indications in data from the long vignettes that others would want a conference when the social workers saw no need. It therefore seems possible that social workers' gate-keeping activities may sometimes prevent these conflicting views reaching the wider interprofessional forum for resolution.

Two different stories, one with a racial variant built into alternative forms, were presented to different respondents. These long vignettes aroused almost universal concern, which might be difficult to deny in the context of research into child protection, but it was interesting that many people did not spontaneously interpret the cases as incidents of abuse or articulate the task explicitly in terms of child protection. It appears that many social workers and other professionals are still aware of a role for social services outside the bounds of child protection. The vignettes appear to have tapped the large grey area in which most decisions have to be made by practitioners.

The ambiguities and conflicts in responses to the research questions add clear empirical evidence to the theoretical discussions of the problematic nature of much decision-making in this field. Few people reacted to the Young family as a case of suspected abuse at the first stage and less than half at stage two but there were several disturbing signs of a more suspicious, more anxious, more stigmatising and perhaps harsher attitude to the black variant. At both stages, the majority of respondents articulated the possibility of sexual abuse in relation to Jane but there were also large minorities who did not. These perceptions varied markedly across the professions, with teachers and the police being particularly unlikely to construe her case as a child protection matter at stage one.

A very large majority of respondents proposed some contact with other agencies to evaluate their concerns and/or to seek help for the children. However, many different agencies and modes of help were envisaged, some of which can be clearly related to differences between the cases and some, sometimes less clearly, to the different agency functions of the respondents. The variety of responses indicates not only that the vignettes explored situations that the individual professions and the network as a whole found ambiguous; it also revealed the lack of any technical consensus on how to handle such presenting problems. Professional discretion is important to many practitioners and competent situational judgments important to the practice. For instance, clinical freedom is a highly-esteemed value among doctors and the inevitability of variable judgements and action choices between 'street level bureaucrats', whatever their profession, is well-documented (Hallett and Birchall 1992). Hallett and Stevenson's (1980) field study confirmed and Phase Three again finds the variability of individuals' commitment to cooperative, multi-disciplinary working. In practice, this sample confirms that individuals would be likely to handle the cases in different ways and their decisions about referral to the investigative professions would vary.

Whether the system should strive for more consensus through, for instance, a massive investment in interprofessional case seminars, including but also reaching far beyond those who already frequently attend child protection conferences, is a debatable point. They could discuss staff's personal values and cultural variations within society; they could offer feedback on the short and longer term outcomes for the children who have been referred to the child protection system. Pawl (1987) asserted that the whole system should resolve its dilemmas and frictions of values but that would appear to be an extremely ambitious and unrealistic aspiration. It can also be argued, and has been by Dingwall et al (1983), that the pluralistic values and human diversity within the network are desirable factors and important safeguards of civil liberties.

At stage three, when a limited range of options for the children's future management was offered following a child protection conference, a large majority agreed that all the children should be placed on the child protection register although social workers and paediatricians disagreed significantly about one of them. Despite their earlier higher thresholds of suspicion regarding Jane, in the end rather more people wanted the Young family on the register than Jane or her sister. This may indicate a greater reluctance to impose sanctions on a middle class family or to risk mis-labelling a suspicion of sexual abuse or, despite the effort to keep both stories ambiguous but anxiety-provoking, some people may have thought the story objectively less threatening than the other vignette; a comparison of only two vignettes leaves many interpretive possibilities open but the more important point is that a significant number of people dissented from the majority opinion.

However, the fact that so many agreed to registration of all the children indicates a broad acceptance of the concept of the register among professionals and no evident concern about the civil liberties or justice issues which have sometimes been raised in the media and the courts. Nevertheless, there was a significant divergence between teachers and doctors on the one hand and social workers and police on the other regarding the appropriateness of involving the police in investigations of these cases, with the former being less willing to do so.

Very few people wanted any of the children admitted to care but many respondents did not know how to respond to the more weighty options of admission to care or care proceedings. In contrast to the notion of authoritarian intervention by social services and the police, these two services consistently proposed fewer admissions to care than the doctors. It was interesting that paediatric registrars appeared more reluctant to say they did not know what was best for the children than the consultants, despite their lack of relevant training or case conference experience; it is tempting to speculate that they have learned the authoritative medical role and not yet confronted the complexities of the child care world. In a similar vein, although the numbers were very small, the general practitioners made more proposals for the children's admission to care than other professions.

Several responses were mutually contradictory, with the same person favouring both support to the family at home and the children's indefinite admission to care. More proposed interim care orders and home support, which may be seen as compatible options. Many others seemed equally happy with either voluntarily accepted support at home or supervision orders. Such results again display the lack of prescriptive certainties in this field but it was noteworthy, if unsurprising, that social workers made many fewer overlapping or conflicting proposals than other professions, suggesting a degree of competence and intra-professional agreement about the best way forward. Among all the options, the highest single vote came from three quarters of general practitioners and health visitors for supervision orders. It was striking that less than a third of the social workers who would have to carry them out were in favour but two thirds would offer voluntary support to the families, and the more experience they had, the more strongly they preferred to give voluntary support.

Few child protection cases involve severe injury and emergency protection orders (formerly place of safety orders) or admissions to care have always been few in relation to the number of children investigated. However, a doctrine of 'protection first' was promulgated in the mid-1980s by Dale et al (1986) and rapid and decisive rescue was recommended by many writers, particularly in the case of children suspected of being sexually abused. These issues are more fully discussed in Hallett and Birchall (1992), particularly in Chapters Nine and Ten. These views appear to have given way to a more gradual and listening approach since the Cleveland Report (1988). The Children Act 1989 has established the criterion that the child's removal from home must be less detrimental than the alternative (which restates and perhaps reinforces the previous requirement that the court had to satisfy itself not only that there were grounds for concern about the child but also that there was need for an order to improve the situation). A number of items in the professional press show that some practitioners fear the pendulum may now swing too far the other way (eg a letter from Tony Bray on 12.9.91 and a news item on 6.2.92, both in Social Work Today).

In exploring the ambiguities and conflicts in responses to the vignettes, the research highlights the problematic nature of much decision-making in this field. It may be that much of the ambivalence and ambiguity would be of no consequence to the formulation of a protection plan (although it may be of profound consequence to the children) if the uncertain or less informed voices leave the child care planning to others. However, only a minority of respondents expect consensus to be easily achieved in the conference and there is a significant though not extreme divergence of positions between the two prime contenders for influence over such decisions. Social workers have a higher expectation of consensus than other professions but even their senior ranks were rather unlikely to expect others to agree with them, whereas paediatric registrars and consultants had less expectation of consensus but more often thought others would agree with their views.

The difficulties the practitioners found in evaluating the cases and the high incidence of expected dissensus sharply reveal the lack of certain and agreed intervention protocols and indicate the need for much careful research into outcomes and more skill development among the practitioners. 'Child abuse' is not a disease but a wide range of interpersonal behaviours, some of which appear to be exacerbated by environmental stresses and some of which appear clearly pathological and all arousing varying degrees of moral outrage or compassion on the part of practitioners and society. While strict treatment protocols in a medical sense are unlikely to be achieved or appropriate for such diverse situations, there may be scope for the development of greater treatment and intervention skills for some of them and further discussion of moral assumptions.

The tortuous process of improving the handling of sexual abuse (the legal issue of removing the alleged perpetrator or the child, the continuing problems of prosecutions dropped because children's evidence is insufficiently credited and, even after the Pigot Report, the court processes remaining so alien to them) nevertheless illustrates that the dilemmas reach far beyond the network of practitioners and deep into society's political fabric and assumptions about justice. As suggested earlier, more systematic inter-professional discussion and exposition of people's criteria for decision-making, away from the urgency of live case conferences and including many of the practitioners who may need to understand the bases of child protection but who are not routinely involved, might gradually develop more convergent standards if these are desired. Given the immensely problematic nature of 'child abuse' and of managing other people's private behaviours, and also given social workers' unique responsibility for and knowledge of the impact of careers in care, an alternative and desirable outcome would be a readier acceptance by and support from other members of the network for social workers' professional opinions regarding appropriate future care of the children.

Perceptions and evaluations of the local child protection case management system

For many years, the strongest theme in official guidance on child protection was the importance of interprofessional coordinating machinery and procedures. This theme has been worked out through a series of government circulars to the key professions in social services, health, education and the police. Inquiry criticisms of poor communication and sometimes a lack of respect or antagonism between the professions have been the goad while the positive convictions of leading practitioners have been the inspiration behind these policy statements. One sector of the present study examines the case coordinating machinery and the collegial network from the viewpoint of average professionals in their everyday work. It highlights four different points in the machinery and also explores four ways of evaluating the network.

Procedural guidelines

With the possible exception of general practitioners in one area, Area Child Protection Committees had arranged the circulation of local guidelines to every relevant work unit in their areas, including all the professions in this study. The majority of respondents report that they have their own personal copy but the stories from different professional groups contrast sharply. Almost all social workers have their own copy but fewer than half the general practitioners and even fewer teachers. It is disturbing that most of these and other non-owners say they have never seen a copy and do not think one would be easily accessible. Patterns of ownership and access clearly mirror different professions' degrees of involvement in the child protection system but it is also probable that non-access unhealthily reinforces non-involvement. The policy makers and promulgators clearly intended that publication of such guidance would have a positive effect on people' case management and collaborative behaviour and this cannot happen if significant numbers do not know where they would look for the document.

Again partly a reflection of the different professions' actual involvement with identified child abuse cases but probably also an unhealthy amplifier of their non-involvement in the network, the different groups vary in their appreciation of the guidelines. Almost all social workers and health visitors find them helpful in defining their own and others' roles whereas other have more varied attitudes. Most of the class teachers, paediatric senior house officers and general practitioners do not know whether they are helpful. However, 40% of the paediatric consultants actually deem the guidelines unhelpful regarding their own role and over a quarter of the senior teachers do not know.

Most owners of the guidelines claim to adhere to them almost always although respondents are more sceptical of others' behaviour than their own. However, other data including the generally vague responses and numerous straightforward 'don't knows' about criteria for convening child protection conferences suggest that informed observance of the procedures is more limited than people are prepared to admit. While it is noteworthy that adherence to the guidelines actually came a long way down the list of factors people spontaneously proposed as important to collaboration, that does not negate the importance of compliance and of the problems that infractions or indifference by some members evidently cause to the coordinating agency.

Social workers, in their key coordinating role, express most concern about publication and enforcement of the guidelines in some other agencies and about sometimes major problems arising from non-compliance. Although health visitors do not hold the same formal responsibility for coordinating child protection work, much of the data in this study suggests they hold a crucial linking role between the front line agencies and the core professions. That they also carry this role with considerable anxiety is also evident. Along with social workers, they also most often express concerns about the impact of others' non-compliance. It seems probable that the security of professional status allows the doctors to ignore or dismiss the guidelines while the social workers and health visitors are striving to draw the network together from a position of limited influence.

Recording

There has been a recurring concern in reports by the Social Services Inspectorate and in Inquiry Reports about the poor quality of case recording and of confirmation of communications between workers in child protection work. This issue was briefly explored by four questions about file notes or written confirmations of messages exchanged between workers. The general result was very disturbing, with well under half the respondents saying they almost always made such notes and only 11% saying they almost always received confirmation from the other party. Only a few more said they often made or received such notes. External communications were even worse recorded than internal ones. Social workers are not alone in ignoring this safeguard although their position in the network and in public esteem may make them the most vulnerable when their practice comes under scrutiny. Health visitors are the most punctilious and, perhaps surprisingly in view of their legalistic training and role, the police reported themselves as the most lax about such notes. Significant numbers of respondents complained of poor administrative facilities and a shortage of secretarial back-up and that may be part of the explanation; time pressures and overwork were also in evidence from people's responses at various points. However, these issues were not directly investigated and, if efficient and accountable conduct of the child protection system is an important policy objective, they deserve research in their own right.

The child protection register

In accordance with *Working Together*, child protection registers list all children in the area who are considered to be suffering or likely to suffer significant harm and for whom there is a child protection plan. An important purpose is that they provide

> *a central point of speedy inquiry for professional staff who are worried about a child and want to know whether the child is subject of an inter-agency protection plan (1991, p. 48).*

In principle, the register is intended to be a perpetually updated, active and accurate source of information to which people promptly refer when concerned about a child. It can tell them whether the child is already registered or whether other members of the network have recently raised queries about the same family. However, other commentators have doubted whether it is frequently used and there is much evidence of its shortcomings and variability between different authorities (Hallett and Birchall 1992, chapter 13). It was noteworthy that few respondents to the long vignette spontaneously proposed to ascertain the child's register status although many more said they would do so when directly cued. However, the professions responded very differently, ranging from half the head teachers and no class teachers to 90% of the police. Some, particularly teachers, were unaware of the register's existence. Others, particularly health visitors, believed they would already know the child's register status and this reason was more prevalent at stage two. These responses indicate that many professionals do not see the register as a dynamic source of information. Yet most people seemed to accept the legitimacy of the concept of registration, judging by the large majority in favour of the children's registration at stage three of the vignette. It seems unlikely that all members of the network, particularly those in the peripheral professions or those with episodic involvement such as hospital out-patient staff, can be informed about child protection concerns regarding individual children without an accurate and actively used register. However, if those with more continuing contact with the children or with each other rest on the faith that they all know the current pool of information, they may be taking substantial risks and are certainly depriving peripheral colleagues of an essential tool. There appears to be a need for reinforcement of the importance of contact with the register, whether this is directly by all field staff or via nominated senior officers.

Child protection conferences

Case conferences have been recognised for many years as the cardinal professional forum for achieving interprofessional cooperation in case management and almost everyone in the sample is aware of this mechanism. However, data about respondents' conference-seeking initiatives are equivocal. Despite procedural guidelines spelling out that any concerned professional can request that a conference be convened, a general question elicited that few respondents other than social workers actually do so with any frequency in relation to the number they attend. On the other hand, social workers indicated far less intention than the other professions to seek a conference at either stage of the long vignette sequence, a finding suggesting that, when and if other agencies do propose conferences, they could in reality be facing a reluctant social services department. There are some other indications in the literature review and elsewhere in this data that sometimes social workers are perceived by others to be too sanguine about cases. If the other professions' more accurate answer is that they seek few conferences and their second in response to the vignettes more idealised, there would seem to be a need to reinforce the message that any professional should take responsibility for proposing a conference whenever they consider it appropriate. If the second answer is the more informative, it would be interesting to know how often other professionals feel frustrated by social services' resistance to such proposals and whether they think the outcome has been detrimental to the child.

Less than two thirds of the respondents have attended even one conference in the year. Once again, the data confirm the wide variation in professional involvement, with about two thirds of teachers and general practitioners having attended none in this period and several signifying that they had never attended one in their whole career. In contrast, most of the social workers and police have attended more than ten in the year. Senior paediatricians' attendance is moderate. Health visitors attend less than the core professions but far more than the other front line professions. It is evident that the conference burden falls very heavily on some groups and particularly on the senior ranks.

In accordance with all other empirical data, general practitioners are the most conspicuous absentees. They are the most likely to say the timing or siting of conferences is extremely difficult for them but it is hard to see that the problems are more intractable for them than for other professionals with very fixed commitments like class teachers or with a much heavier bombardment of cases like social workers and paediatricians. It is in the nature of child protection that case conferences have to be convened at relatively short notice and cover has to be found for other commitments and it is inevitable that convening a large, mixed group of busy staff will cause considerable inconvenience to many if not all of them. Particularly in the light of their overall response patterns, it seems more reasonable to interpret general practitioners' objections as indicative of a lower priority to child protection or to collaboration, for whatever reason, than is common among other members of the network. It was apparent that, of all respondents, they gave the most guarded rating of the value of conferences. It has already been noted that very few have any interdisciplinary training in child protection; such training is a factor that correlates with a greater commitment to and appreciation of conferences. While the factor operates independently of professional identity, it is not clear which is the causal influence or whether both are simply by-products of greater involvement in child protection work.

Child protection conferences are generally valued by the majority of respondents although frequent tensions are acknowledged on a number of scores. Nearly all those with relevant experience believe conferences are helpful to the children concerned but only a minority indicated in their responses to the long vignettes that consensus would be easy to achieve. Most say conflicts arise between professionals in matters relating to their roles and beliefs and also regarding the application of the guidelines, with very substantial minorities reporting that such conflicts are frequent. In what appears to be a significant attitudinal shift in recent years (see Hallett and Birchall 1992, chapter 13), most respondents favour greater involvement of parents and children in the conference although the majority of the police and paediatricians remain opposed to this development. Greater experience of child protection work actually hardened respondents' attitudes in both directions, either favouring or opposing attendance of the family concerned. Reasons for opposition were to do with difficulties of focusing frankly on the child's needs and of getting through the business in realistic timespans if the parents' anxieties and hostilities also had to be managed in the meeting. Clearly, there is still much ground to cover with all professionals in regard to agenda management and fundamentally in convincing them, if it is so, that the outcomes are better for the children concerned. Thoburn's forthcoming research is an important contribution to this debate.

The most frequent and strongest positive ratings were given to conferences in respect of their contributions to case assessment and planning of interventions. However, significant minorities felt that conferences' inability to keep up with families' changing needs limited the effectiveness of the forum and also that the wrong people had too much influence over decisions. The most frequent negative views related to significant absentees, particularly general practitioners. There was some indication from maingrade respondents that they would prefer the attendance of more class teachers and police constables and fewer senior ranks. In contrast, senior ranks gave a higher overall rating to the values of conferences than maingrade staff and were also more in favour of their peers' attendance. These responses suggest an unresolved tension between the organisational and bureaucratic functions of the conference adjudicating on registration and committing agencies to a broad 'protection plan' and the direct practitioners' needs for detailed mutual discussion of their contributions to the case. It seems probable that the recent development of the concept of the 'core group meeting' may clarify the different agendas but it is arguable (for instance, Cleveland 1988) that there is an unresolved need for highly skilled consultancy from advanced practitioners which neither forum can meet at present.

Health visitors were the most appreciative of conferences overall and were the least likely openly to acknowledge conflicts between professionals. These findings add further weight to the view that they are particularly concerned about making the network function from a position of considerable anxiety and no explicit authority. They were shown in the brief vignette series to give consistently higher severity ratings to cases than others and to be frequently polarised from social workers. Yet social workers have most contact and role overlap with them in everyday work and they also have kindred semi-professional status. It is within this context that it is arguable that health visitors may see the conference as an occasion when they can arouse others' interest, lobby for their support and offload some of their anxiety. In contrast, the data show that social workers are the most likely to see the conference as the arena in which anxieties are unnecessarily raised and they feel unsupported.

Perceptions of the local interprofessional network

There were two sources of data on the membership of the local network, one being the pattern of contacts that people proposed in response to the long vignettes and the second being their responses to a series of direct questions about others in the network. A very important finding from both sources and the generally positive responses about case conferences is that, at least among the professions sampled, there appears to be widespread acceptance among those with relevant experience of the need for interdisciplinary cooperation. The long vignettes show that few perceive children in distress as problems they can or should cope with single-handed, whether or not they have construed the situation as possible child abuse. However, the previous section on case perceptions noted the varied ways in which people articulate the children's problems. Their notions of appropriate interventions and contacts were also very variable.

As noted earlier, the proposals to some extent reflect the worker's own role; for instance, a health visitor is most likely to construe interventions to the Young family in terms of helping mother while many teachers would suggest observing Jane. There were, however, many overlaps and ambiguities, with, for instance, health visitors referring Jane for abuse investigation and the police using the language of 'help' when doctors did not. Such open-ended responses are suggestive of different conceptualisations of the problem and of modes of intervention. They reflect the unstructured situation in which workers actually have to interpret the information they receive and make their initial decisions but they may not give the full range of any respondent's intentions. The structured questions about actions and contacts run the obverse risk of evoking more answers than the person would intend in real life.

Besides the general readiness to initiate a cooperative contact, a few generalisations are nevertheless possible amid the welter of detail from the long vignettes. Nearly all proposed contacts are in order to give or exchange information and to some extent to make joint evaluations of that information. Often that exchange would be a one-off discussion but quite often there would be a proposal to maintain liaison and update mutual information. When respondents construe the case as possible abuse, there is a greater tendency to refer the case to social workers, give them information and drop out, whereas those who express generalised concern are more likely to call on a miscellany of services but to continue some form of helping relationship with the child or family themselves.

It is reassuring to those who fear that social work may be reduced to a more residual service dealing with child protection alone that a significant number of other workers who did not label the cases as possible abuse did nevertheless consider it appropriate to seek social workers' supportive interventions. On the other hand, only the police and social workers proposed any 'hands on' collaboration, in joint interviewing regarding the suspected abuse. It was noteworthy that none of the social workers, health visitors or teachers considered the possibility of joint supportive or therapeutic work with either the parents or the children, either between themselves or for instance with specialist therapists or day care settings. Notions of joint work in child protection remain trapped in the forensic framework.

Much the most frequent contacts would be made with social workers and health visitors, approximately equal numbers at stage one of the vignettes but with social workers in the lead at stage two. Over three quarters of others' proposed contacts with the investigative professions would be with social workers, making their key role clearly evident. The two professions of social work and health visiting also initiate the widest range of contacts with others and health visitors dominate the communication network within the medical sector. They appear to be an important fulcrum between the child protection system and the wider network.

There was some tendency for professionals in the medical and school spheres to turn to colleagues within their own systems for discussion or action more frequently than outsiders would, although the numbers of such contacts were much fewer than with the social workers and health visitors. This suggests that cases might sometimes be diverted into the hands of educational psychologists or medical specialists as an alternative to processing as a child protection query and also that sometimes education welfare officers might be used as intermediaries or filters.

Besides the frequency with which other professions are invoked, some evident differences in mutual expectations also emerged. People tended to make simple referrals to social workers and to paediatricians, particularly at stage two of the vignettes. Teachers and general practitioners were mainly involved in information exchanges although general practitioners report that they would be involved in joint decision-making with social workers and health visitors. Paediatricians would offer and be turned to for advice but would turn to others for resources and services.

The general questions gave information about the prevalence of encounters between the respondents and twelve 'target' professions in the network but no direct indication of the frequency of such contacts. These revealed considerable variations in patterns of professional contacts although most respondents with any experience of child protection had encountered most of the nominated others. There was a marked reluctance to label anyone's role as less than important, although the salience of some groups appeared limited and presumably episodic. Health visitors, teachers and general practitioners emerge as universally relevant, suggesting that preventive and supportive services are rather more prominent in others' eyes than the investigative task. Social workers, paediatricians and police are nearly as widely known although the long vignettes indicate they would be brought to the fore when professionals' worries had reached a higher level. School nurses and education welfare officers have also been encountered in the context of child protection by most respondents. However, far fewer people have had contacts with psychologists, psychiatrists, lawyers and accident and emergency doctors.

The patterns of contacts emerging both from the long vignettes and the general questions indicate that the child protection network is a five tier system:

key worker and core profession – responsible for coordination of investigation and any continuing interventions (social workers):

other core professions – with specific responsibilities for investigation and assessment (police, paediatricians);

front line professions – in day-to-day contact with children and families and available for identification, assessment, surveillance and continuing support or focussed intervention (health visitors, teachers and general practitioners);

peripheral contact professions – with no institutionalised responsibility for universal child or family care but apparently variably used in advisory/ consultative and also intermediary or pastoral roles (school nurses and education welfare officers);

case-specific professions – occasionally involved for a particular role or task whether investigative, assessment or therapeutic (lawyers, accident and emergency staff, psychologists and psychiatrists).

The hierarchy may suggest a simpler linear structure than actually obtains. One can begin to understand the potential size of the network in any one locality if one aggregates all the human service professionals who work there and considers their career mobility. Add the number of children causing concern in the course of a year and permutate the inevitability of different coalitions dealing with individual cases. Maher (1987) suggests that the network in a large city may comprise 10,000 workers and Jones et al (1987) list 42 different professionals who might be involved in a single case. In practice, the numbers are generally much smaller; around ten professionals usually attend child protection conferences. However, even within the simplified framework of this research programme (investigating six professions' responses to one case and their perceptions of just twelve other groups), the communication flows between them prove to be complex (see Figures 9.1 and 9.2 for an even more simplified representation).

It was evident and encouraging that respondents' views of others in the child protection network were generally favourable, with most rating the others as fairly easy to work with, with fairly clear and important roles and fairly good performance of those roles. However, only minorities rated others 'very easy' to work with or their performance 'very good'. There were marked interprofessional differences, with people finding school nurses and health visitors easy colleagues but significant numbers finding many doctors, particularly general practitioners, difficult. Among the core professions, paediatricians and social workers received mixed ratings. Somewhat surprisingly and contrary to the early history of the child protection network in the 1970s, the police were seen as easy to work with. Echoing their concerns about others' non-compliance with guidelines and once again indicating their difficult role as key workers, social workers were the most critical of others' performance. It is also noteworthy that greater experience of child protection brought more critical appraisals of others' performance whereas the inexperienced seemed readier to assume the network works efficiently and harmoniously.

It is particularly disturbing that only just over half the respondents feel very clear about social workers' role in child protection. Teachers are least clear. Unless others know the key agency's and key worker's role, they are unlikely to be able to clarify their own either as informants or as monitors or therapists working concurrently with a protection plan. There is obvious need for further development of inter-agency policy information and for interprofessional training.

There was a considerable lack of clarity among and about general practitioners', teachers' and health visitors' roles in this sphere. The literature stresses the potential importance of teachers and general practitioners as identifiers of children who are victims or at risk of abuse. Yet, despite increasing numbers of school-age children on the child protection registers, teachers have appeared to be a diminishing source of referrals (Creighton and Noyes 1989) although the NSPCC's most recent figures suggest this trend may have reversed (Creighton, informal communication). Family doctors' own image of their professional role stresses their continuing, perhaps lifelong, knowledge of families on their lists but other sources suggest they may have little knowledge of these frequently mobile and troubled families (Hallett and Birchall, chapters 7 and 11). It may be that they do not have a crucial role in child protection, despite the customary presumptions.

Teachers are particularly well-placed to observe and evaluate children whose appearance or behaviour may be outside the normal range and to keep the investigative and therapeutic professionals informed. Some teachers might welcome and undertake a pastoral role but not all see this as an appropriate function or compatible with their primary pedagogic responsibilities for a class. This is a viewpoint that may become more prevalent with recent policy developments, including local management of schools, the concentration on targets of attainment and a more competitive atmosphere in the education system. Health visitors have revealed themselves in this study as direct helpers and advisers to the Young family, a role which is easy to construe within their normal range of duties. However, they have also emerged as crucial links between children's normal milieus and the child protection system. The literature review showed that they have frequently been troubled by pressure to adopt a monitoring role or a more intense therapeutic contact than their workloads can accommodate but this study gave no explicit evidence of this concern.

Two thirds of respondents with relevant experience, whatever their profession, think that overall the local network coordinates work with abused children and their families reasonably well. However, only a fifth believe it functions very well at the assessment stage and many fewer rate cooperation in ongoing case management as highly. Over a quarter think continuing cooperation works rather or very badly. People spontaneously identified a wide range of factors that enhanced coordination but the most frequently mentioned tended to be tautologous; good communications and good relationships between practitioners were prominent but few people were specific as to how these should be established or sustained. Cued questions revealed widespread agreement that there are many obstacles to coordination, deriving from professional and logistical factors. Examples of the former are different workload priorities, goals and methods, and of the latter, predominantly staff time but also movements in the network and lack of administrative resources. Status is an evident criterion for the distribution of telephones and secretaries. It is inappropriate that health visitors, who emerge as crucial links between the outside world and the child protection system, and that social workers, who are designated case coordinators, have to complain most about adequate access to such essential tools of their trade.

Among the open-ended answers to questions about factors that facilitate or impede cooperation, interactions between practitioners were much more prominent than policies and procedures. Shared goals and mutual respect for each others' professional roles and skills were mentioned particularly often. Once again suggestive of their difficulties in establishing their place among others as professional peers, social workers and health visitors most frequently highlighted the need for mutual respect between workers. The difficulty that low status semi-professions have in developing a collegial relationship with those who are better endowed with training and prestige is a familiar issue. It is a theme of particular importance when the lead profession in the system of child protection is a junior partner in terms of status. It is difficult to visualise any remedy other than a major development in social work's research base and training and concomitant self-confidence. However, it is probably relevant and encouraging that respondents with experience of interdisciplinary training express fewer concerns about occupational rivalries and power struggles. The data have shown that there is much scope for expansion of such training.

Meanwhile, much remains unknown about the identification and selection of cases at intake and about the detailed outcomes of different interventions for different children in different situations. It also seems a modest but appropriate plea, in the light of evidence above about others' inconsistent or uncertain recommendations at stage three of the vignettes, for others to respect and support social workers' judgments in the management of children's careers through the child protection system. They are not only the key workers in the matter of coordination but it is their professional role and agency responsibility to deliver the continuing counselling, support and care that the children and their families need.

General conclusions

This research has confirmed that practitioners generally deem coordination or cooperation in child protection to be valuable and to be working reasonably well, despite many ambiguities and tensions. It remains difficult to define in general terms or to routinise through procedures; it consists of a multitude of individual decisions by street level bureaucrats about how they perceive particular facets of a child's life at particular moments in their own. Almost without exception, respondents appeared sensitive to the children's predicaments in the vignettes but had varying opinions about what should be done and who was the most appropriate contact. There were many evident individual and professional variations in rating the severity of the brief vignettes, which would affect decisions about referral for child abuse investigation. However, there was widespread consensus about severe cases and there was also a high level of agreement between the core professions on all the brief vignettes, which would suggest that once children are referred to them they are likely to rate them in compatible ways. Few people want children admitted to care and the more involved they are in child protection the less they want it. Social workers are more nearly unanimous in their preference for voluntary support to families than any other profession about any case management option.

Specific training in this field is extremely limited even for the core professions and half the sample have been untouched by any such training. It is generally appreciated by the participants and does appear to improve attitudes to cooperation. The few teachers who have attended are particularly likely to say such training has increased their knowledge about child abuse and the same might be expected to be true for the other infrequently involved profession of general practice. A greater involvement of doctors might mitigate some of the evident difficulties others have in relating to them. Teachers and general practitioners are rarely involved in child protection and a large number know little about the system. Whether they should know more and be drawn in more closely is an important point for their professions and policy-makers at large to consider. They are large workforces and upgrading their knowledge and understanding is a massive task.

Returning to the paths laid out in the introductory algorithm (Chapter One), this study has explored the paths (b-d–e-k) and (b-l–m/n–e-k). It confirms that coordination is not only a mandated policy but includes exchanges perceived as mutually beneficial and some which certainly fit into the 'power/resource dependency perspective' (Hallett and Birchall 1992, chapter 2). Most people deem cooperation important to care of the the children concerned. Most appreciate child protection conferences quite highly and think the local network functions reasonably well on the several dimensions that were examined. This general conclusion is important for two reasons: first, it is a corrective to the dominant perceptions of failure that have emerged from the succession of official inquiries into individual child abuse tragedies or apparent system failures such as Cleveland and Orkney; secondly, there is an extensive literature problematising the phenomenon of working together.

However, many inhibiting factors are also acknowledged, some of which could be remedied by modest investments in the system while others would require more effort and yet others are intrinsic to any human activity. There was evidence of the pertinence of all the factors (e-k) in the bottom row of the algorithm but it seems fairer to categorise them as causes of frequent friction rather than of major breakdown in the protection and care of children.

This is a preliminary study and much is essentially descriptive. In conjunction with the literature review and the more qualitative approach to real cases in Phase Three, it is hoped that the total research programme provides a well-founded and reasonably well-rounded view of a large and important but elusive topic. It cannot answer all the questions raised but it contributes a few steps to the progressive dance of theory, research design, data, refinement of theory, development of hypotheses for more focussed research, and so on. As Merton (1968) commended, one objective is the development of 'middle range theory' which is more abstract than a simple description but concrete enough to permit the generation of testable hypotheses, empirically grounded and focussed on practical problems. It is also, crucially, a response to a 'policy problem' as defined by current social values and is looking for 'clues to manipulation and action' (Greer 1978, p. 49). While it cannot hope to be definitive or exhaustive, it does offer concrete information and proposals for further improvement in the world of child protection.

The issue of achieving consensual definition of referral thresholds is evidently difficult in its own right but it is further complicated by questions about the value and the outcomes of putting families through the child protection machinery. The results are generally very encouraging, according to Pritchard (1992), but not every child and family is well-served by the system and it may be that less stigmatising modes of intervention would be equally effective for the majority. The assertion in *Working Together* that registration "should not be used to obtain resources which might otherwise not be available to the family" is a sad comment on the shortfall in the availability of appropriate help for many children. Registration does not create resources but it does, as the whole burden of guidance implies and SSI reports endorse (eg DH SSI 1990j), enhance the priority rating of a case. It remains to be seen how the definition of 'children in need' under the Children Act 1989 develops. There needs to be an equal commitment by practitioners and policy makers to interprofessional cooperation and a sufficient level of social work service in the context of general and as far as possible 'normalising' child care provisions.

Bibliography

ABRAHAMS, Nadine, CASEY, Kathleen, DARO, Deborah (1992) Teachers' knowledge, attitudes and beliefs about child abuse and its prevention, *Child Abuse and Neglect* 16, 2, 229–38.

ADCOCK, Margaret, and WHITE, R. (1991) *Significant harm*, London: Significant Publications.

ADMED, Shama, CHEETHAM, Juliet, and SMALL, John (1986) *Social work with black children and their families*. London: Batsford.

ALEXANDER, C. S. and BECKER H. J. (1978) The use of vignettes in survey research, *Public Opinion Quarterly* 42, 93–104.

ALVES, W. M. and ROSSI, P. H. (1978) Who should get what? Fairness judgments in the distribution of earnings, *American Journal of Sociology* 84, 3, 541–564.

Audit Commission (1986) *Making a reality of community care*. London: HMSO.

BABBIE, Earl (1989) *The practice of social research*, 5th edition Belmont, Calif: Wadsworth Inc.

BEBBINGTON, A. and MILES, J. (1989) The background of children who enter local authority care, *British Journal of Social Work* 19, 5, 349–68.

Beckford Report (1985) *A child in trust: the report of the Panel of Inquiry into the circumstances surrounding the death of Jasmine Beckford*, London Borough of Brent.

BEECHEY, Veronica, and WHITELEGG, Elizabeth (1986) *Women in Britain Today*. Milton Keynes: Open University Press.

BELSON, W. A. (1986) *Validity in survey research*, Aldershot: Gower.

BENNETT, H. G., COLLINS, S., FISHER, G. D., HUGHES, S. E., REINHART, J. B. (1982) SCAN: a method of community collaboration, *Child Abuse and Neglect* 6, 1, 81–5.

BERGER, R. M. and PATCHNER, M. A. (1988a) *Planning for research: a guide for the helping professions*, Newbury Park, Calif: Sage.

BERGER, R. M. and PATCHNER, M. A. (1988b) *Implementing the research plan*. Newbury Park, Calif: Sage.

BIRCHALL, Elizabeth (1989) The frequency of child abuse – what do we really know?, in O. Stevenson (ed). *Child abuse: professional practice and public policy*, Hemel Hempstead: Harvester Wheatsheaf.

BISSET, Ann and HUNTER, D. (1992) Child sexual abuse in general practice in north east Scotland, *Scottish Health Bulletin* 50, 3, 237–47.

BLAGG, and STUBBS, P. (1988) A child-centred practice? Multi-agency approaches to child sexual abuse, *Practice* 2, 1, 12–19.

BOTTOMLEY, A. K. (1979) *Criminology in focus*, London: Robertson.

BRAY, Tony (1991) Letter in *Social Work Today* 12th September.

BRECI, M. G. (1987) Police officers' values on intervention in family fights, *Police Studies*, 10, 4, 192–204.

BRILL, N. I. (1976) *Teamwork: working together in the human services*. Philadelphia: Lipincott.

British Paediatric Association (1966) The battered baby, *British Medical Journal* 1, 601–3.

BROWN, Louise and FULLER, R. (1991) *Joint police-social work investigation in child protection: a study of Central Region's joint initiative*. Social Work Research Group Paper 24. Stirling: Stirling University

Brunel Social Services Consortium (1988) *The professional management of child abuse* (unpublished draft report). Uxbridge: Brunel University.

BRYMAN, A. and CRAMER, D. (1990) *Quantitative data analysis for social scientists*. London: Routledge.

BULMER, M. (1977) (Ed) *Sociological research methods: an introduction*. London: Macmillan.

BULMER, M. (1978) (Ed) *Social policy research*. London: Macmillan.

BURGESS, R. G. (1982) (ed) *Field research: a sourcebook and manual*, London: Allen and Unwin.

BURGESS, R. G. (1982) Elements of sampling in field research, in (ed) R. G. Burgess (op. cit). 75–8.

BURGESS, R. G. (1982) The role of theory in field research, in (ed) R. G. Burgess (op. cit). 209–12.

BURNS, L. (1991) *Partnership with families: a study of 65 child protection case conferences in Gloucestershire to which the family were invited*. Unpublished conference paper.

BYNNER, J. and STRIBLEY, K. M. (1978) (eds) *Social research: principles and procedures*. London: Longman.

CARTWRIGHT, Ann (1967) *Patients and their doctors: a study of general practice*. London: Routledge and Kegan Paul.

CHANNER, Yvonne, and PARTON, N. (1990) Racism, cultural relativism and child protection, in Violence against Children Study Group (op. cit) 105–120.

CHAPMAN, Myra (1986) *Plain figures*, London: HMSO.

CHAPMAN, M. G. T. and WOODMANSEY, A. C. (1985) Policy document on child abuse written for the Society of Clinical Psychiatrists, *British Journal of Clinical and Social Psychiatry* 3, 2, Supplement.

CLARK, D. and SAMPHIER, M. (1984) Attitudes to custody, access and maintenance, *Adoption and Fostering* 8, 1, 56–61.

CLEGG, Frances (1982) *Simple statistics: a course book for the social sciences*. Cambridge: Cambridge UP.

Cleveland Report (1988) *Report of the Inquiry into child abuse in Cleveland 1987*, Cm 412. London: HMSO.

Colwell Report (1974) *Report of the Committee of Inquiry into the care and supervision provided in relation to Maria Colwell*, London: HMSO.

CREIGHTON, S. (1992) (informal communication).

CREIGHTON, S. and NOYES, P. (1989) *Child abuse trends in England and Wales 1983–1987*. London: NSPCC.

DALE, P., DAVIES, M., MORRISON, T. and WATERS, J. (1986) *Dangerous families: assessment and treatment of child abuse*, London: Tavistock Publications.

CRAIG, J. (1987) An urban-rural categorisation for wards and local authorities, *Population Trends* 47, 6–11. London: OPCS.

DEAN, J. P. and WHYTE, W. F. (1958) How do you know if the informant is telling the truth? reprinted in (eds) J. Bynner and K. M. Stribley (op. cit), 179–188.

Department of the Environment *Z Scores*.

Department of Health (1988) *Protecting children: a guide for social workers undertaking a comprehensive assessment*, London: HMSO.

Department of Health (1989) *Survey of Children and Young Persons on Child Protection Registers Year Ending 31 March 1988*.

Department of Health (1991a) *Working together under the Children Act 1989: a guide to arrangements for inter-agency cooperation for the protection of children from abuse*, London: HMSO.

Department of Health (1991b) *Child abuse: a study of inquiry reports 1980–1989*, London: HMSO.

Department of Health (1991c) *Children and young people on child protection registers, Year ending 31st March 1991: Provisional feedback*. London: DH.

Department of Health and Social Security and the Welsh Office (1988) *Working together: a guide to arrangements for inter-agency cooperation for the protection of children from abuse*, London: HMSO.

DH SSI (1989) *Report of inspection of child abuse services in Cumbria SSD*, Gateshead: DH.

DH SSI (1990a) *Working with abusing families: inspection of child protection services in Bedfordshire*, October 1990, DH SSI Thames/Anglia Region.

DH SSI (1990b) *Protecting the children: inspection of aspects of the child protection services in Buckinghamshire 1990*, DH SSI Thames/Anglia Region.

Dh SSI (1990c) *Report of an inspection of collaborative arrangements between child protection agencies in Cleveland*, DH SSI Northern Region.

DH SSI (1990d) *Inspection of the arrangements for the handling of sexual abuse cases in Derbyshire*, DH SSI London.

DH SSI (1990e) *Child protection in Kent*, London: DH SSI Southern Region.

DH SSI (1990f) *Child protection in London*, London: DH SSI London Region.

DH SSI (1990g) *Inspection of child protection servies* (Manchester SSD), Manchester: DH SSI North Western Region.

DH SSI (1990h) *Inspection of child protection services in Rochdale*, Manchester: DH SSI North Western Region.

DH SSI (1990i) *Report of inspection of child protection services in Staffordshire*, Birmingham: DH SSI West Midlands Region.

DH SSI (1990j) *Inspection of child protection practices and procedures: Wakefield Community and Social Services Department*, Leeds: DH SSI Yorkshire and Humberside Region.

DH SSI (1990k) *A guide to self-monitoring and self-inspection of child protection services*. Conference paper for ISPCAN, Hamburg.

DH SSI (1991) *An inspection of child protection cases in East Sussex*: London, DH SSI Southern Region.

DEUTSCHER, I. (1968) Asking questions cross-culturally: some questions of linguistic compatibility, in (eds) Becker, H. S. et al, *Institutions and the Person*, 318–41. Aldine Press: Chicago.

DEUTSCHER, I. (1973) *What we say/ what we do: Sentiments and acts*. Glenview, Ill: Scott, Foreman and Co.

DEUTSCHER, I. (1969/70) *Asking questions (and listening to answers): a review of some sociological precedents and problems*, reprinted in (ed) M. Bulmer (op. cit), 243–58.

DEVONS, E. and GLUCKMAN, M. (1982) Procedures for demarcating a field of study, in (ed) R. G. Burgess (op. cit), 19–22.

DEX, Shirley (1985) *The sexual division of work: conceptual revolutions in the social sciences*. Brighton: Wheatsheaf.

DINGWALL, R. (1980) *Problems of teamwork in primary care*, in Lonsdale et al (op. cit).

DINGWALL, R., EEKELAAR, J. and MURRAY, T. (1983) *The protection of children: state intervention and family life*, Oxford: Blackwell.

DIXON, Beverley R., BOWNA, G. D., ATKINSON, G. J. B. (1987) *A handbook of social science research*. Oxford: Oxford University Press.

DONNISON, D. (1978) *Research for public policy*, in Bulmer, M. (Ed). Social Policy Research. Macmillan.

DUELLI KLEIN, R. (1980) How to do what we want to do: thoughts about feminist methodology in (eds) G. Bowles and R. Duelli Klein *Theories of women's studies*, 48–64.

DUTT, R. (ed.) (undated) *Towards a black perspective in child protection*, London: Race Equality Unit.

ETZIONI, A. (1969) *The semi-professions and their organisation*, New York: Free Press.

FINCH, J. (1987) The vignette technique in survey research, *British Journal of Sociology* 21, 1, 105–114.

FOX, Susan, and DINGWALL, R. (1985) An exploratory study of variations in social workers' and health visitors' definitions of child mistreatment, *British Journal of Social Work* 15, 5, 467–477

FRUDE, N. (1987) *A guide to SPSS/PC+*. London: Macmillan Education.

GABE, J., CALNAN, M., BURY, M. (eds) (1991) *The sociology of the health service*. London: Routledge.

GEACH, H. and SZWED, E. (1983) *Providing civil justice for children*, London: Edward Arnold

GIL, D. G. (1975) Unravelling child abuse, *American Journal of Orthopsychiatry* 45, 346–54.

GIOVANNONI J. and BECERRA, R. (1979) *Defining child abuse*. New York: Free Press.

GRAHAM, P., DINGWALL, R., WOLKIND, S. (1985) Research issues in child abuse, *Social Science and Medicine* 21, 11, 1217–28.

GREER, S. (1961) On the selection of problems, reprinted in J. Bynner and K. M. Stribley, (1978) (eds) (op. cit)., 48–52.

GRIFFITHS, R. (1988) *Community care: agenda for action*. London: HMSO.

HALL, Jean Graham (1992) *Crimes against children*, Chichester: Barry Rose Law Publishers.

HALLETT, Christine, and STEVENSON, Olive (1980) *Aspects of interprofessional cooperation*. London: Allen and Unwin.

HALLETT, Christine (1989) (ed). *Women and social services departments*. Hemel Hempstead: Harvester Wheatsheaf.

HALLETT, Christine (1989) Child abuse inquiries and public policy, in (ed.) O. Stevenson (op. cit).

HALLETT, Christine, and BIRCHALL, Elizabeth (1992) *Coordination and child protection: a review of the literature*. Edinburgh: HMSO.

HARRIS, A. (1991) Editorial: General practitioners and child protection, *British Medical Journal* 302, 1354. (8th June).

HELM, Laura (1989) Informal communication.

HOINVILLE, G., JOWELL, R. and Associates (1977) *Survey research practice*. London: Heinemann Ed. Books.

House of Commons (1990–91) *HC570-1. Public expenditure on personal social services: child protection services*. London: HMSO.

JARMAN, B. (1983) Identification of underprivileged areas, *British Medical Journal* 286, 1705–9.

JARMAN, B. (1983) *Underprivileged areas: validation and distribution of scores*, British Medical Journal 289, 1587–92.

JASSO, G. and ROSSI, P. (1977) Distributive justice and earned income, *American Sociological Review* 42, 639–52.

JONES, D., PICKETT, J., OATES, Margaret, BARBER P. (1987) *Understanding child abuse*, 2nd edition. London: Macmillan Education.

KEMPE, C. H. and HELFER, R. E. (eds). (1972) *Helping the battered child and his family*, Philadelphia: Lippincott and Co.

KISH, L. (1959) Some statistical problems in research design, reprinted in Bynner, J. and Stribley, K. M. (eds) (1978) (op. cit) 64–78.

KITSUSE, J. I. and CICOUREL, A. V. (1963) A note on the use of official statistics, reprinted in Bynner, J. and Stribley, K. M. (eds) (1978) (op. cit) pp. 53–63.

Lancet (1991) Editorial: Child sexual abuse and the limits of responsibility, *Lancet* 337, 890. (13th April).

LAZARSFELD, P. (1958) Evidence and inference in social research, reprinted in M. Bulmer, (1977) (Ed) *Sociological research methods: an introduction*, 78–108, London: Macmillan.

LEA COX, C. and HALL, A. (1991) Attendance of general practitioners at child protection conferences, *British Medical Journal* 302, 1378–9. (8th June).

LIPSKY, M. (1980) *Street level bureaucracy*, New York: Russell Sage.

LONSDALE, S., WEBB, A. and BRIGGS, T. (eds) *Teamwork in the personal social services and health care*, New York: Syracuse UP.

LOUGHRAN, F. (1992) Informal communication.

MAHER, P. (1987) (ed) *Child abuse: the educational perspective.* Oxford: Blackwell.

MARNEFFE, C., ENGLERT, Y., SOUMENKOFF, G. HUBINONT, P. O. (1985) Can the action of the social worker lead to child abuse? *Child Abuse and Neglect* 9, 3, 353–7.

MERTON, R. K. (1968) *Social theory and social structure.* New York: Free Press.

MOSER, C. A. and KALTON, G. (1971) Question wording, reprinted in Bynner, J. and Stribley, K. M. (eds) (1978) (op. cit) pp. 140–155.

Municipal Yearbook 1989

NAGI, S. Z. (1977) *Child maltreatment in the United States: a challenge to social institutions,* New York: Columbia UP.

NALEPKA, C., O'Toole, R., and Turbett, J. P. (1981) Nurses' and physicians' recognition and reporting of child abuse, *Issues in comprehensive paediatric nursing,* 5, 33–44.

OPCS 1981 *Census*

OPCS (1987) *Key population and vital statistics: Local and Health Authority Areas England and Wales*

OPCS, Population Statistics Division (1986) Ethnic Minority Populations in Great Britain, *Population Trends* 46.

OPCS (1984) *Demographic Review*

OPPENHEIM, A. N. (1966) The quantification of questionnaire data, reprinted in Bynner, J., and Stribley, K. M. (1978) (eds) (op. cit) pp. 208–224.

PACKMAN, Jean, RANDALL, J., JACQUES, N. (1986) *Who needs care? Social work decisions about children,* Oxford : Blackwell.

PARTON, N. (1986) The Beckford Report: a critical appraisal, *British Journal of Social Work* 16, 5, 511–30.

PAWL, J. (1987) Infant mental health and child abuse and neglect: reflections from an infant mental health practitioner, *Zero to Three* 7, 4, 1–9.

PIGOT, Judge T. (1989) *Report of the Advisory Group on Video Evidence.* London: HMSO.

PLOWMAN, D. E. G. (1978) Public Opinion and the Polls, in Bulmer (op. cit).

POPPER, K. (1957) The unity of method, reprinted in J. Bynner and K. M. Stribley (eds) (1978) (op. cit), 17–24.

PRITCHARD, C. (1992) Didn't we do well? *Social Work Today* 23rd January, 16–17.

ROSENBERG, M. (1968) Extraneous variables, reprinted in J. Bynner and K. M. Stribley (eds) (1978) (op. cit), 263–277.

ROSENBERG, M. (1968) The meaning of relationships in social survey analysis, reprinted in (ed) M. Bulmer (1977) (op. cit). 93–108.

RUBER, M. (1988) *Child sexual abuse: a report on interagency cooperation from the perspective of Social Services Departments in England and Wales.* Heywood, Lancs: DH SSI.

SELLIN, T. and WOLFGANG, M. E. (1964) *The measurement of delinquency,* New York: Wiley.

SELVIN, H. C. and STUART, A. S. (1966) Data dredging procedures in survey analysis, reprinted in Bynner, J. and Stribley, K. M. (eds) (1978) (op. cit) pp. 278–284.

SHARKEY, P. (1989) Social networks and social service workers, *British Journal of Social Work* 19, 5, 387–405.

SHARPE, L. J. (1978) Government as clients for research, in Bulmer (op. cit).

SHAW, I. (1978) Consumer Opinion and Public Policy, in Bulmer (op. cit).

SHERIF, M. and SHERIF, Carolyn (1967) Attitude as the individual's own categories: the social judgment-involvement approach to attitude and attitude change, reprinted in (eds) Jahoda, M. and Warren, N. (1973) *Attitudes,* 2nd ed. 395–422. Harmondsworth: Penguin.

SIEBER, S. D. (1982) The integration of fieldwork and survey methods, in (ed) R. G. Burgess, (op. cit), 176–212.

SNYDER, Jane C. and NEWBERGER, E. H. (1986) Consensus and difference among hospital professionals in evaluating child maltreatment, *Violence and Victims* 1, 2, 125–139.

Social Services Yearbook 1989

Social Work Today (1992) News item about low use of Emergency Protection Orders, 6th February.

STEVENSON, Olive (ed) (1989) *Child abuse: professional practice and public policy,* Hemel Hempstead: Harvester Wheatsheaf.

THOBURN, June (1992) informal communication

THOMAS, T. (1986) *Police and social workers.* Aldershot: Gower.

THOMAS, T. (1986) Confidentiality: the loss of a concept? *Practice* 2, 4, 358–72.

TIBBITT, J. E. (1983) Health and personal social services in the UK: interorganisational behaviour and service development, in (ed) A. Williamson and G. Room *Welfare states in Britain,* London: Heinemann.

URZI, M. (1977) *Cooperative approaches to child protection: a community guide.* St Paul, Minnesota: State Department of Public Welfare.

Violence against Children Study Group (1990) *Taking child abuse seriously,* London: Unwin Hyman

WARBURTON, R. W. (1988) *Key Indicators of Local Authority Social Services*, London: Department of Health SSI

WEIGHTMAN, K. (1988) Managing from below, *Social Work Today* 29.9.88, 16–17.

WEST, P. (1982) *Reproducing naturally occurring stories: vignettes in survey research*, Glasgow: Medical Research Council Medical Sociology Unit.

WICKER, A. W. Attitudes vs actions: the relationship of verbal and overt responses to attitude objects, reprinted in (eds) Jahoda, M. and Warren, N. (1973) *Attitudes*, 2nd ed. 167–194. Harmondsworth: Penguin.

WOLOCK, I. and HOROWITZ, B. (1984) Child maltreatment as a social problem: the neglect of neglect. *American Journal of Orthopsychiatry* 54, 4.

ZELDITCH, M. (1962) Some methodological problems of field studies, reprinted in Bynner, J. and Stribley, K. M. (eds) (1978) (op. cit) pp. 123–136.

Appendix 1: Questionnaire

Identity No.   /   /

UNIVERSITY OF STIRLING

DEPARTMENT OF SOCIOLOGY AND SOCIAL POLICY

COORDINATION IN CHILD PROTECTION RESEARCH PROJECT

QUESTIONNAIRE

Research Director: Research Fellow:
Christine Hallett,   Elizabeth Birchall.
Reader in Social Policy,
University of Stirling,
Stirling,
FK9 4LA.

Secretary: Mrs P. Young,
0786-67742.

(Coded by Area & Profession).

Identity No: / / .

Advice to respondents on completion of the form:
In fixed choice questions, please tick the relevant box to indicate your response. In open questions, please answer briefly in the light of your normal practice, perceptions or experience.

1 Age: 20-24 ☐
25-29 ☐
30-34 ☐
35-44 ☐
45-54 ☐
55+ ☐

2 Sex: M ☐ F ☐

3 Do you have/have you had personal experience of bringing up children?

Yes ☐ No ☐

4 Country of birth:

UK ☐ Other ☐

5 Ethnic group: (Please describe your ethnic origins):

Bangladeshi ☐
Black - African ☐
Black - Caribbean ☐
Black - Other ☐
Indian ☐
Pakistani ☐
White ☐

Any other ethnic group (please describe)

[ ]

If descended from more than one ethnic or racial group, please tick the group to which you consider you belong.

6 What is your job title? Please indicate occupation and rank (if applicable):

[ ]

7   Please list your occupational training
     and qualifications, with dates:

[ ]

8.1   On completion of any basic training
      or qualification, what year did you
      start work in this profession?

[ ]

8.2   What year did you start work in your
      current rank?

[ ]

8.3   What year did you start work in this
      profession in this locality?

[ ]

9   **BRIEF VIGNETTES**

**The next section of the research schedule
is to ask you to respond to a batch of
brief vignettes. Please assume the child in
question is 5, unless otherwise specified.**

Many incidents have been classified as child
abuse or neglect. Some are considered very
serious acts, while others are not considered
serious. Each item in this list contains a
short passage describing a potential incident
of child abuse and/or neglect.

Please rate the incident on a scale of
increasing seriousness from 1 to 9, so that 9
means you believe the incident is very
serious and low numbers indicate incidents
which you believe are not so serious. You
are asked to make each judgment
independently of every other case in the list,
and you may rate any number of vignettes at
any level.

Rate each on a 9-point scale according to
the seriousness for the welfare of the child;
use 9 for the most serious acts and 1 for the
least serious acts. Base your decision on
your professional experience with children.
While there is not enough information on
the card to make a decision about the
appropriate professional action, your
opinions are still important. You may have
seen a variety of cases similar to this one,
but please make your rating on the basis of
the average case.

9.1   The parents constantly compare their child with the younger sibling, sometimes implying that the child is not really their own. The child continually fights with other children.

...

9.2   The parents always let their child run around the house and garden without any clothes on.

...

9.3   On one occasion the parent and the child engaged in sexual intercourse.

...

9.4   Although clean, the baby has a sore bottom and is difficult to feed. The toddler is poorly clad and difficult to control but healthy.

...

9.5   The parents immersed the child in a tub of hot water.

...

9.6   On one occasion the parent fondled the child's genital area.

...

9.7   The parents fail to prepare regular meals for their child. The child often has to fix his own supper. The child has an iron deficiency.

...

9.8   The parents ignore their child most of the time, seldom talking or listening to her.

...

9.9   The parents burned the child on the buttocks and the chest with a cigarette. The child has second degree burns.

...

9.10 The parents usually punish the child by spanking with a leather strap, leaving red marks on the child's skin.

...

9.11 The 8 year old girl has recently become distressed at school and is showing an interest in smaller boys' genitals.

...

9.12 The parents live with their child in a small rented house. No one ever cleans up.

...

9.13 A child has severe behaviour problems. The parents have allowed the child to undergo treatment but refuse to cooperate themselves.

...

9.14 The parents regularly left their child alone inside the house after dark. Often they did not return until midnight.

...

9.15 The parent and child repeatedly engaged in mutual masturbation.

...

9.16 Today the child was found wandering 2 streets away from home across a main road in a town.

...

9.17 The parents usually punish their child by spanking with the hand, leaving red marks on the child's skin.

...

9.18   The parents regularly fail to feed
        their child for at least 24 hours. The
        child was hospitalised for 6 weeks
        for being seriously malnourished.

                                ...

9.19   The parent repeatedly showed the
        child pornographic pictures. The
        child suffers recurring nightmares.

                                ...

9.20   The parents let their child sip out of
        their glasses when they are drinking
        whisky. The child has become
        intoxicated.

                                ...

9.21   The parents ignored their child's
        complaint of an earache and chronic
        ear drainage.

                                ...

9.22   The parents have kept their child
        locked in since birth. They feed and
        bathe the child and provide basic
        physical care.

                                ...

9.23   The parents hit the child in the face,
        striking with the fist.

                                ...

YOUR INVOLVEMENT IN CHILD ABUSE MATTERS

10.1   In your last 4 working weeks (please
        exclude your Christmas break and
        any other significant personal
        absences), please estimate how much
        of your working time was spent on
        child abuse matters. Please include
        any aspect of child abuse or child
        sexual abuse -investigation,
        treatment, administration or
        management:

        None   ☐
        Less than 0.5 days per month   ☐
        Less than 1 day per month   ☐
        1-2 days per month   ☐
        Less than 1 day per week   ☐
        Between 1-2 days per week   ☐
        More than 3 days per week   ☐
        Don't know   ☐

10.2   Was this time expenditure:

        Lower than normal?   ☐
        Typical?   ☐
        Higher than normal?   ☐
        Don't know   ☐

In view of the passage of time since the original mailings
of this questionnaire, please feel free to adapt questions
10.1, 13.1 and 14.1 to the more immediate past if that is
easier and more accurate. It would then be helpful if your
response would indicate the period you have used. Many
thanks.

10.3   If this period was not typical, please
        give the main reason.

        ┌─────────────────────────┐
        │   │
        │   │
        │   │
        │   │
        │   │
        │   │
        │   │
        └─────────────────────────┘

11   How do you think your normal time
        allocation to child protection work
        compares with your peers? (NB.
        Please do not compare yourself with
        any peers whose job definition
        excludes any child abuse work).

        Is yours:

        Less   ☐
        Same   ☐
        More   ☐
        Don't know   ☐

12   Is your immediate work unit one
        specialising in Child abuse work?

        Yes, exclusively   ☐
        Yes, largely   ☐
        No, it's just part of our
        general duties   ☐

13   Please state below how many child
        abuse cases you have been involved
        with.
        (NB. By involvement I mean any
        action or judgment however small,
        and I want you to include new
        referrals and ongoing cases,
        suspected or confirmed).

13.1   In your last 2 working months of
        1990 (please exclude your Christmas
        break and any other significant
        personal absences):

        0   ☐
        1-4   ☐
        5-9   ☐
        10-19   ☐
        20-39   ☐
        40+, ...*   ☐
        No firm idea,
        estimate....*
        Don't know   ☐
        * Please insert a figure if possible.

13.2   In the last year:

        0   ☐
        1-4   ☐
        5-9   ☐
        10-19   ☐
        20-39   ☐
        40+, ...*   ☐
        No firm idea,
        estimate....*
        Don't know   ☐
        * Please insert a figure if possible.

14   Please state how many Initial and
      Review Case Conferences, including
      "Case Core Group" meetings you
      have attended, in connection with
      child abuse cases:

14.1 In your last 2 working months of
      1990 (please exclude your Christmas
      break and any other significant
      personal absences):

      0   ☐
      1-4   ☐
      5-9   ☐
      10-19   ☐
      20-39   ☐
      40+, ...*   ☐
      No firm idea,   ☐
      estimate....*
      Don't know   ☐
      * Please insert a figure if possible. ☐

14.2 In the last year?

      0   ☐
      1-4   ☐
      5-9   ☐
      10-19   ☐
      20-39   ☐
      40+, ...*   ☐
      No firm idea,   ☐
      estimate....*
      Don't know   ☐
      * Please insert a figure if possible.

15.   If None, why is that?

      None have occurred in the area   ☐
      None involving my cases   ☐
      Not my job to go   ☐
      Never been invited   ☐
      Not important for/ to me to attend   ☐
      Important but I haven't the time   ☐
      I've sought them but they have not
      been convened   ☐
      They always occur at an impossible
      time   ☐
      I won't breach confidentiality   ☐
      Don't know   ☐

      Other (please specify)   ☐

      ┌─────────────────────────────┐
      │   │
      │   │
      │   │
      │   │
      └─────────────────────────────┘

16.   Is fitting these meetings into your
      work schedule generally:

      No problem   ☐
      Possible   ☐
      Difficult   ☐
      Extremely difficult   ☐

17.   Of the Case Conferences you attend,
      how often do you initiate a request
      for them?

      Almost always   ☐
      Often   ☐
      Sometimes   ☐
      Almost never   ☐

POST-QUALIFYING TRAINING

18.1   Have you had any formal training
       apart from supervised experience,
       specifically relating to abused
       children and/or Child Protection
       work, since your basic qualification ?

       Yes ☐   No ☐

       If No, please turn to question 21

18.2   If Yes, please estimate the total
       amount of any post-qualifying or in-
       service training, short courses and
       conferences you have attended,
       dedicated to child abuse/ Child
       Protection.

       None   ☐
       Less than 1 week   ☐
       1-2 weeks   ☐
       3-4weeks   ☐
       1-3 months   ☐
       More than 3 months   ☐
       Don't know   ☐

19.1   Was any of this training undertaken,
       in whole or in part, in
       interdisciplinary groups?

       No   ☐
       Yes, less than 1 week   ☐
       Yes, more than 1 week   ☐

       If None, please turn to question 21.

19.2   If Yes, with whom?   (Please tick
       all relevant groups)

       Social workers   ☐
       Health visitors   ☐
       Teachers   ☐
       Police   ☐
       General practitioners   ☐
       Paediatricians   ☐
       Lawyers   ☐
       Psychologists   ☐
       Psychiatrists   ☐
       Accident and emergency
       doctors   ☐
       School nurses   ☐
       School social workers/E.W.O's   ☐
       Other (please specify)   ☐

       [ ]

20.1   On the whole, how did you find such
       interdisciplinary training?

       Very helpful   ☐
       Helpful   ☐
       Unhelpful   ☐
       Very unhelpful   ☐

20.2   What are your reasons for that
       rating?

       [ ]

GENERAL POLICY AND PROCEDURAL QUESTIONS

(NB. If you have not formed an opinion, please feel free to respond "Don't know" in all appropriate places. It would then be helpful if you would indicate whether you feel that is due to your own insufficient experience or to the intrinsic difficulty of making judgments in the situation depicted).

21.   From your overall experience, do you consider case conferences generally helpful or unhelpful to the child concerned?

22.1   Do you think there should be a policy that parents should generally be invited to case conferences?

Yes, the whole conference   ☐
Yes, part of the conference   ☐
No   ☐
Don't know   ☐

22.2   Do you think children who are old enough to understand should generally be invited to case conferences?

Yes, the whole conference   ☐
Yes, part of the conference   ☐
No   ☐
Don't know   ☐

23   Please tell me if you can (in paraphrase) what are the criteria for holding an initial case conference?

24.1   Are criteria laid down for convening repeat case conferences?

Yes   ☐
No   ☐
Don't know   ☐

24.2   If so, please tell me if you can what
        they are (in paraphrase)?

25.　Which of these comments about Case Conferences best indicate your views? Please tick the appropriate boxes

	Strongly Agree	Agree	Disagree	Strongly disagree
1. Sharing info helps to clarify my diagnosis/assessment				
2. Sharing info helps to clarify others' diagnosis/assessment				
3. Sharing info enables me to plan my own intervention				
4. Sharing info enables me to mesh my interventions with others				
5. It lets me know who is responsible for the case				
6. It helps me to share anxiety and get a balanced feeling for the case				
7. It helps others to share anxiety and get a balanced feeling for the case				
8. I find the shared information and discussion generally educative to me				
9. Such sharing is generally educative to the participants				
10. Other positive values (please specify)				

25. (continued)	Strongly Agree	Agree	Disagree	Strongly Diasgree
11. They waste time				
12. They fudge individuals' responsibilities				
13. Crucial people are too often missing				
14. Too many people who don't know the case or haven't got the right skills are influencing the outcome				
15. People work up each others' anxiety unnecessarily				
16. Recommendations/ Decisions made at the CC can be overturned by any agency at any time				
17. Family's needs change from day to day. CCs can not keep intervention plans sensitively up to date				
18. They are too long for participants to concentrate				
19. Other negative values (please specify)				

26.1   Can you think of any improvements
        you consider important in the
        conduct of Case Conferences?

        Yes   ☐
        No   ☐
        Don't know   ☐

        If No or Don't know, please skip to
        question 27.

26.2   If Yes, what? (Please tick up to 5
        items, those you deem most
        important).

26.2.1 Timetabling of meetings   ☐
    2   Shorter meetings   ☐
    3   Longer meetings   ☐
    4   Prior written information   ☐
    5   Agendas on arrival   ☐
    6   Better attendances by
        crucial people   ☐
    7   Smaller meetings   ☐
    8   Larger meetings   ☐
    9   Chairing   ☐
    10 Content of discussion   ☐
    11 Minutes   ☐
    12 Having a Minutes Secretary   ☐
    13 Follow-up of recommendations   ☐
    14 Organisation of Review
        Conferences   ☐
    15 Accommodation   ☐
    16 Other (please specify)

    ┌─────────────────────────────────┐
    │   │
    │   │
    │   │
    │   │
    │   │
    └─────────────────────────────────┘

    17 Don't Know   ☐

WRITTEN COMMUNICATIONS

27   Messages are frequently passed
        between workers face-to-face or by
        phone. They can cover exchanges of
        information, requests, or referrals.
        They may or may not be recorded,
        either by an entry in the case notes
        or a letter or memo.

27.1   When, within your agency, you
        make any oral exchange regarding a
        child abuse/Child Protection case, do
        you write it down?

        Almost always   ☐
        Often   ☐
        Sometimes   ☐
        Almost never   ☐

27.2   Does the person you speak to
        confirm the exchange in writing?

        Almost always   ☐
        Often   ☐
        Sometimes   ☐
        Almost never   ☐

27.3   When you make any such oral
        exchange with an outside agency
        regarding a child abuse/Child
        Protection case, do you confirm it to
        them in writing?

        Almost always   ☐
        Often   ☐
        Sometimes   ☐
        Almost never   ☐

27.4   Does the external colleague confirm
        the exchange in writing?

        Almost always   ☐
        Often   ☐
        Sometimes   ☐
        Almost never   ☐

        Please continue on next page.

28.   A CASE VIGNETTE.

I would like you now to look at the sort of story you might come across in the course of
your professional work and then answer the questions in the light of your experience and
normal practice. If you hold a supervisory rank. or a combined practitioner/supervisor role,
please answer in terms of your own judgment about what you would think and do
yourself, or what you would delegate and expect a subordinate to do, as applicable.

There are no "right answers" against which your responses will be measured; child
protection is a problematic field, both in individuals' perceptions of information as being
possibly a case of abuse and also in their judgments of the best or feasible ways to handle
it. The purpose of this research programme is to identify and map the realities of those
varied perceptions and judgments.

It is important that you look at and answer the questions in the given order, as they are
designed to replicate the development of information and the sequence of small judgments
and decisions that practitioners actually follow in their everday work.

Assume the family falls within your personal catchment area or system or may already be
on your "list", but is <u>not</u> definitely and exclusively on the list of another professional in
the same discipline (i.e. if you are a GP, not on another GP's list; if you are a teacher, the
subject or another child of the family is in your class; if you are a social worker, the
whole family is not already allocated elsewhere, and so on).

Vignette A. Stage 1.

**In the course of your duties, you hear that a neighbour has said the 6 month old
baby next door has chilblains on her hands and is often crying. The mother is a 19
year old and has a toddler. She lives on Social Security and her fuel has been cut off.**

28.1 What are you now thinking in
response to that knowledge?

28.4 If you chose to take no action, what
was your reason(s)?

Story doesn't justify any
response.   ☐
I'm too busy to react in
present circumstances.   ☐
This message isn't my job; the
referrer ought to have gone
elsewhere (please specify)   ☐

Another agency is already
responsible (please specify)   ☐

28.2 Would you now take any action?

Yes ☐   No ☐

28.3 If Yes, what would you now do?

Other (please specify)   ☐

28.5   Agencies and individuals vary in the extent to which practitioners make decisions or take actions on their own initiative, without consulting others.

28.5.1   Would you need authorisation from a superior before following through (any of) your proposal(s) in question 28.2 or 3?

Yes   ☐   No   ☐   Don't know   ☐

28.5.2   Would you contact any colleague in another discipline or agency in connection with (any of) your proposal(s) in question 28.2 or 3?

Yes   ☐   No   ☐   Don't know   ☐

If No to both 28.5.1 and 28.5.2, please skip to 28.10.

28.6   If Yes to either 28.5.1 or 28.5.2, please say whom you would normally contact and tick for what purposes in the table below.

Job Title	To pass the case on only	To seek/ give info only	To seek advice/ direction	To discuss and decide jointly	To act jointly
1					
2					
3					
4					
5					

28.7   If you would be seeking guidance or
        direction, would it be:
        (Please tick any one or more).

        Professional/clinical ideas   ☐
        Procedural guidance   ☐
        Authorisation to act in a
        particular way   ☐

28.8.   Might you be giving guidance or
        direction to anyone?

        Yes   ☐
        No   ☐
        Don't know   ☐

        If No, please skip to question 28.10

28.9   If so, to whom might you be giving
        guidance or direction?

        Please tick as appropriate from your
        list in 28.6:

        1   2   3   4   5

        or give job titles:

28.10   Would you find out the
        child/family's current status on the
        Child Protection Register (either by
        your own direct approach or by
        asking someone else to enquire and
        tell you)?

        Yes   ☐
        No   ☐
        Don't know   ☐

        If you answered No or Don't know,
        please skip to question 28.12.

28.11   If Yes, why would that be?

        If you have answered this question,
        please skip to 28.13.

28.12   If No or Don't know, please tick
        your main reason:

        Don't know anything about the
        Register   ☐
        Don't know where to find it   ☐
        Can never get through on
        the phone   ☐
        Too busy   ☐
        Not my job, but N would
        (please specify)   ☐

        ┌─────────────────────────────┐
        │   │
        │   │
        └─────────────────────────────┘

        Story doesn't indicate I should
        (yet)   ☐
        I think it's out of date or
        inaccurate   ☐
        I consider it a breach of
        confidentiality   ☐
        I would already expect to know   ☐
        Other (please specify)   ☐

        ┌─────────────────────────────┐
        │   │
        │   │
        └─────────────────────────────┘

28.13   Would you seek a Case Conference
        at this stage?

        Yes   ☐
        No   ☐
        Don't know   ☐

        If Yes. please skip to question
        28.15.

28.14   If No or Don't know, please tick

        your main reason:

        Don't know anything
        about CCs   ☐
        Don't know how to organise
        them   ☐
        Can never get through on
        the phone   ☐
        Too busy   ☐
        Not my job, but my agency
        would   ☐
        Not my job, but I would expect
        .... (agency) to   ☐
        Story doesn't indicate I should
        (yet)   ☐
        No, they breach confidentiality   ☐
        Other (please specify)   ☐

        ┌─────────────────────────────┐
        │   │
        │   │
        └─────────────────────────────┘

        Don't know   ☐

28.15   Would you yourself attend if one
        were convened?

        Yes   ☐
        No   ☐
        Don't know   ☐

28.16 You may have responded to the previous questions in terms either of some or no contact with <u>other</u> disciplines or agencies. Whatever your responses have been, is the general pattern of your decisions and actions above typical of how you would respond to similar cases at this stage?

Yes ☐
No ☐
Don't know ☐

If Yes, please skip to question 28.18

28.17 If you replied No or Don't know to question 28.16, is there something that strikes you as not typical about this case? If so, please indicate what particular point(s).

If you would typically contact colleagues in another discipline or agency, please skip to question 28.19.

28.18 If it would be typical for you <u>not</u> to contact another agency at this point in cases similar to this, please give your reasons. (Then, skip to p 22 (Stage 2)

28.19 At this stage of a case, coordination with another discipline or agency may involve various activities. If you sometimes have such contacts with any colleague(s):

28.19.1 How often would you expect that contact to involve simply the exchange and discussion of information already to hand?

Almost always ☐
Often ☐
Sometimes ☐
Almost never ☐

28.19.2 How often would you expect to take some joint action or planning with them <u>beyond</u> exchange and discussion of initial information?

Almost always ☐
Often ☐
Sometimes ☐
Almost never ☐

28.20 If you would have continuing collaboration, even if only sometimes, who would that be with?

Their job title(s)/Their agency(s)

```

```

28.21 If so, even if only sometimes, what would you generally expect to be doing with them?

Giving case info ☐
Seeking case info ☐
Giving diagnosis/professional assessment/expert opinion ☐
Seeking diagnosis/professional assessment/expert opinion ☐
Jointly discussing early perceptions/conclusions ☐
Maintain liaison/update exchange of perceptions/concs ☐
Jointly plan separate interventions with feedback to each other ☐
Joint action - sharing assessment interviews ☐
Joint action - sharing face-to-face therapeutic activities ☐
Joint action - sharing formulation of reports ☐
Other ☐
Don't know ☐

29   **Vignette A. Stage 2.**

You now learn that the baby Sarah is below the third centile in weight and height. Margaret, the mother, says she is difficult to feed and is anxious about her. She is clean but has a sore bottom.

The toddler Jimmy is robust though not very warmly dressed. He is very active and rather rough with his toys and his mother.

Sarah has a bruise on her lower cheek.

29.1   What are you now thinking in
         response to that knowledge?

29.2   Would you now take any action?

         Yes ☐   No ☐

29.3   If Yes, what would you now do?

29.4   If you chose to take no action, what
         was your reason(s)?

         Story doesn't justify any response ☐
         I'm too busy to react in present
         circumstances.   ☐
         This message isn't my job; the
         referrer ought to have gone
         elsewhere (please specify)   ☐

         Another agency is already
         responsible (please specify)   ☐

         Other (please specify)   ☐

29.5 Agencies and individuals vary in the extent to which practitioners make decisions or take actions on their own initiative, without consulting others.

29.5.1 Would you need authorisation from a superior before following through (any of) your proposal(s) in question 29.2 or 3?

Yes
No
Don't know

29.5.2 Would you contact any colleague in another discipline or agency in connection with (any of) your proposal(s) in question 29.2 or 3?

Yes
No
Don't know

If No to both 29.5.1 and 29.5.2, please skip to 29.10:

29.6 If Yes to either 29.5.1 or 29.5.2, please say whom you would normally contact and tick for what purposes in the table below.

Job Title	To pass the case on only	To seek/ give info only	To seek advice/ direction	To discuss and decide jointly	To act jointly
1					
2					
3					
4					
5					

29.7 If you would be seeking guidance or
direction, would it be:
(Please tick any one or more).

Professional/clinical ideas   ☐
Procedural guidance   ☐
Authorisation to act in a particular
way   ☐

29.8. Might you be giving guidance or
direction to anyone?

Yes   ☐
No   ☐
Don't know   ☐

If No, please skip to question 29.10

29.9 If so, to whom might you be giving
guidance or direction? Please tick as
appropriate from your list in 29.6:

1   2   3   4   5

or give job titles:

```
┌─────────────────────────────────┐
│                                 │
│                                 │
│                                 │
│                                 │
└─────────────────────────────────┘
```

29.10 Would you find out the
child/family's current status on the
Child Protection Register (either by
your own direct approach or by
asking someone else to enquire and
tell you)?

Yes   ☐
No   ☐
Don't know   ☐

If you answered No or Don't know,
please skip to question 29.12.

29.11 If Yes, why would that be?

```
┌───────────────────────┐
│                       │
│                       │
│                       │
│                       │
│                       │
│                       │
│                       │
│                       │
└───────────────────────┘
```

If you have answered this question.
please skip to 29.13.

29.12 If No or Don't know, please tick
       your main reason:

       Don't know anything about the
       Register   ☐
       Don't know where to find it   ☐
       Can never get through on
       the phone   ☐
       Too busy   ☐
       Not my job, but N would
       (please specify)   ☐

       ┌─────────────────────────────┐
       │   │
       │   │
       │   │
       └─────────────────────────────┘

       Story doesn't indicate I should
       (yet)   ☐
       I think it's out of date or
       inaccurate   ☐
       I consider it a breach of
       confidentiality   ☐
       I would already expect to know   ☐
       Other (please specify)   ☐

       ┌─────────────────────────────┐
       │   │
       │   │
       │   │
       └─────────────────────────────┘

29.13 Would you seek a Case Conference
       at this stage?

       Yes   ☐
       No   ☐
       Don't know   ☐

       If Yes, please skip to question 29.15.

29.14 If No or Don't know, please tick
       your main reason:

       Don't know anything about CCs   ☐
       Don't know how to organise them   ☐
       Can never get through on
       the phone   ☐
       Too busy   ☐
       Not my job, but my agency would   ☐
       Not my job, but I would expect
       ....(agency) to   ☐
       Story doesn't indicate I should
       (yet)   ☐
       No, they breach confidentiality   ☐
       Other (please specify)   ☐

       ┌─────────────────────────────┐
       │   │
       │   │
       │   │
       └─────────────────────────────┘

       Don't know   ☐

29.15 Would you yourself attend if one
       were convened?

       Yes   ☐
       No   ☐
       Don't know   ☐

29.16 You may have responded to the previous questions in terms either of some or no contact with <u>other</u> disciplines or agencies. Whatever your responses have been, is the general pattern of your decisions and actions above typical of how you would respond to similar cases at this stage?

Yes ☐
No ☐
Don't know ☐

If Yes. please skip to question 29.18

29.17 If you replied No or Don't know to question 29.16, is there something that strikes you as not typical about this case? If so, please indicate what particular point(s).

```



```

If you would typically contact colleagues in another discipline or agency, please skip to question 29.19.

29.18 If it would be typical for you <u>not</u> to contact another agency at this point in cases similar to this, please give your reasons. (Then, skip to p 29 (Stage 3)

29.19 At this stage of a case, coordination with another discipline or agency may involve various activities. If you sometimes have such contacts with any colleague(s):

29.19.1 How often would you expect that contact to involve simply the exchange and discussion of information already to hand?

Almost always ☐
Often ☐
Sometimes ☐
Almost never ☐

29.19.2 How often would you expect to take some joint action or planning with them <u>beyond</u> exchange and discussion of initial information?

Almost always ☐
Often ☐
Sometimes ☐
Almost never ☐

29.20   If you would have continuing collaboration, even if only sometimes, who would that be with?

Their job title(s)/Their agency(s)

```
┌─────────────────────────────────────────────────────────────────┐
│                                                                   │
│                                                                   │
│                                                                   │
│                                                                   │
│                                                                   │
│                                                                   │
└─────────────────────────────────────────────────────────────────┘
```

29.21   If so, even if only sometimes, what would you generally expect to be doing with them?

Giving case info   ☐
Seeking case info   ☐
Giving diagnosis/professional assessment/expert opinion   ☐
Seeking diagnosis/professional assessment/expert opinion   ☐
Jointly discussing early perceptions/conclusions   ☐
Maintain liaison/update exchange of perceptions/concs   ☐
Jointly plan separate interventions with feedback to each other   ☐
Joint action - sharing assessment interviews   ☐
Joint action - sharing face-to-face therapeutic activities   ☐
Joint action - sharing formulation of reports   ☐
Other   ☐
Don't know   ☐

30.   **Vignette A. Stage 3.**

At Case Conference it emerges that Margaret has been depressed since
Sarah's birth. Sarah's father walked out on her just before and left a pile of
debts. He still comes back about once a week for the night and they sleep
together. Margaret would like him back even though he sometimes beats her
for not keeping the children quiet.

Margaret is not cooking or feeding herself very well. She gives Jimmy fish and
chips and apples, which he eats wandering about outside the house.

At times she says she gets very angry with the children's "whining" demands
and crying. Two days ago the Day Nursery noticed that Jimmy had red weals
on his calves and ?fingertip bruises on his upper arm. He has several bruises
around his lower legs and on his forehead. Margaret admits she wallops him
on the bottom and calves but denies she ever bruises him or hits his head.
Jimmy says she did hit his head when he wet his pants.

The baby's weight has fallen from 25th centile at birth to 3rd now. She has
had several minor chest infections and a recent diarrhoea.

Margaret had a child by another father. This child was adopted after strong
suspicions that he had broken her arm and ribs when exasperated with her
crying at night. She parted from this man when she was expecting Jimmy
because she did not want any further difficulties with Social Services.

The social worker and health visitor have been visiting weekly since the first
message 2 months ago. Margaret has been willing to talk to them, but finds it
difficult to follow their advice on the children's needs. She has not told either
of them much of this history, which has been collated from agency records.
She says she intends to attend a psychiatric Outpatient clinic soon.

30.1   Bearing in mind this information and the earlier stages of the vignette, a number of
the following might be attending the case conference. In your professional opinion,
whom would you want to be present to discuss this case? And whom, from your
experience in this locality, would you expect to be present?

AMENDMENT:

If you both want and expect an individual to be present, please
tick both columns on the following table. If you wish they would
attend but, in practice, do not expect them in your locality,
simply tick the first column. If you do not think their
attendance is important to discussion of this particular case but
it would be usual for them to be present in your locality, simply
tick the second column.

Please tick entries in either or both columns of the following table, as you deem appropriate:

Profession	Want	Expect
Accident & Emergency Consultant	. . . .	. . . .
Accident & Emergency Junior Doctor	. . . .	. . . .
Adult Psychiatrist	. . . .	. . . .
Child	. . . .	. . . .
Child Psychiatrist	. . . .	. . . .
Class Teachers	. . . .	. . . .
Clinical Med Officer Child Health	. . . .	. . . .
Community Psychiatric Nurse	. . . .	. . . .
Educational Welfare Officer/School SW	. . . .	. . . .
Educational Psychologist	. . . .	. . . .
Father	. . . .	. . . .
General Practitioner	. . . .	. . . .
Head Teachers	. . . .	. . . .
Health Visitor	. . . .	. . . .
Housing Dept Official	. . . .	. . . .
Local Authority Solicitor	. . . .	. . . .
Mother	. . . .	. . . .
NSPCC	. . . .	. . . .
Nursery Staff	. . . .	. . . .
Nurse manager Health Visiting	. . . .	. . . .
Paediatric Consultant	. . . .	. . . .
Paediatric Junior Doctor	. . . .	. . . .
Paediatric Ward Sister	. . . .	. . . .
Police Constable	. . . .	. . . .
Police Senior Officer	. . . .	. . . .
Probation Officer	. . . .	. . . .
Court Welfare Services Officer	. . . .	. . . .
School Nurse	. . . .	. . . .
Social Serv Line Manager	. . . .	. . . .
Principal grade/area manager	. . . .	. . . .
Senior Social Worker	. . . .	. . . .
Social Worker area team	. . . .	. . . .
Social Worker hospital	. . . .	. . . .
SSD Child Protection Services	. . . .	. . . .
Specialist adviser	. . . .	. . . .
Others: please specify	. . . .	. . . .
Having insufficient experience, don't know		

30.2 Do you think Sarah should be placed
      on the Child Protection Register?

      Yes   ☐
      No   ☐
      Don't know   ☐

30.3 Do you think Jimmy should?

      Yes   ☐
      No   ☐
      Don't know   ☐

30.4 Do you think Police investigation is
      right in this situation?

      Yes   ☐
      No   ☐
      Don't know   ☐

31   The following are a range of
      decisions regarding the children's
      future. Please select the option that
      you would support, if any:

31.1 Do you think the children can be
      sustained at home with their mother,
      being offered (voluntary) support
      from social and medical services?

      Yes   ☐
      No   ☐
      Don't know   ☐

31.2 Do you think the children can be
      sustained at home with their mother,
      by medical and social work
      interventions and home support under
      Supervision Orders?

      Yes   ☐
      No   ☐
      Don't know   ☐

31.3 Do you think mother should be
      encouraged to place either child
      voluntarily in care?

31.3.1 Sarah:

      Yes   ☐
      No   ☐
      Don't know   ☐

31.3.2 Jimmy:

      Yes   ☐
      No   ☐
      Don't know   ☐

31.4 Do you think an Interim Care Order
      should be sought:

31.4.1 For Sarah?

      Yes   ☐
      No   ☐
      Don't know   ☐

31.4.2 For Jimmy?

      Yes   ☐
      No   ☐
      Don't know   ☐

31.5 Do you think a full Care Order should be sought:

31.5.1 For Sarah?

      Yes   ☐
      No   ☐
      Don't know   ☐

31.5.2 For Jimmy?

      Yes   ☐
      No   ☐
      Don't know   ☐

32.1 Do you think an application for a full Care Order would succeed in court:

32.1.1 On Sarah?

      Yes   ☐
      No   ☐
      Don't know   ☐

32.1.3 On Jimmy?

      Yes   ☐
      No   ☐
      Don't know   ☐

33.1 In this case, do you think it would have been easy to achieve consensus in the case conference?

      Yes   ☐
      No   ☐
      Don't know   ☐

33.2 Do you think others would agree with the views you have put forward for the children's future?

      Yes   ☐
      No   ☐
      Don't know   ☐

33.3 If others did not agree with your point of view, what would you do?

PRACTICE AND PROCEDURES

(NB. If you have insufficient experience to have formed an opinion, please respond "Don't know" in all appropriate places).

34.   The following are said to be some of the causes when disagreements do arise in case conference. Would you please indicate how often you consider these to be important.

34.1   An individuals' occupational role?

Almost always ☐
Often ☐
Sometimes ☐
Almost never ☐

34.2   An individuals' personal beliefs and values?

Almost always ☐
Often ☐
Sometimes ☐
Almost never ☐

34.3   Individual differences of interpretation of the guidelines as to whether the case literally meets the relevant criteria?

Almost always ☐
Often ☐
Sometimes ☐
Almost never ☐

34.4   Differences of opinion about whether guidelines should be applied rigidly or flexibly?

Almost always ☐
Often ☐
Sometimes ☐
Almost never ☐

35   Professional opinions differ about how best to manage the initial stages of
        work with a family in which any form of child abuse has occurred:

        (a) Some argue the necessity of "accepting" and "supporting" a family in
        the early stages, without undermining them by making them face that they
        are personally responsible for their child's distressed condition.

        (b) Others argue that the parents' acknowledgement of responsibility for
        their child's distressed condition is essential before therapy can be
        successfully started.

35.1   Which view point do you generally support?
        Please tick (a) or (b).

        (a)   ☐   or   (b)   ☐

35.2   If you have mixed views, why is this?

┌───┐
│   │
│   │
│   │
│   │
│   │
└───┘

35.3   Factors people take into account in deciding about this point may be some
        of the following. Which, if any, seem relevant to your opinion on this
        point?

35.3.1 Do you see this issue as generally dependent on the category of case?

        Yes   ☐   Mixed views   ☐   No   ☐   Don't Know   ☐

35.3.2 If Yes or mixed views, when?

	Almost always	Often	Sometimes	Almost never
Physical Abuse				
Neglect				
Failure to Thrive				
Emotional Abuse				
Sexual Abuse				
Grave Concern				

35.4 Do you see the issue as dependent on the severity of the child's condition?

Yes ☐   No ☐   Don't know ☐

35.5 Do you see the issue as dependent on the caring professionals' assessment of the total family situation?

Yes ☐   No ☐   Don't know ☐

(Unless Yes to 35.5, skip to 36).

35.6   If Yes to 35.5, what opinion, if any,
        do you have about the sort of factors
        to be considered?

36.2   If not, where is the most accessible
        copy kept?

        Never seen them   ☐
        In the same building/same floor
        of a large building   ☐
        Elsewhere (please specify)   ☐

37   When did you last have occasion to
        refer to them?

        Within the last 24 hours   ☐
        Within the last week   ☐
        Within your last 4 working weeks   ☐
        Longer ago (please specify)   ☐

36.1   Do you have a personal copy of the
        local Child Protection Committee
        Guidelines?

        Yes   ☐
        No   ☐

        Never   ☐
        Don't know   ☐

38   Do you find the Guidelines generally
      helpful to you in handling child
      abuse matters?

      Regarding your own part:

      Yes   ☐
      No   ☐
      Don't know   ☐

      Regarding others' parts:

      Yes   ☐
      No   ☐
      Don't know   ☐

39.1 It seems probable that the Guidelines
      cannot always be followed precisely
      by everyone in the professional
      network in every suspected or actual
      case of child abuse, perhaps
      particularly in milder cases.

      Do you agree?

      Yes   ☐
      No   ☐
      Don't know   ☐

39.2 Can you (and, for supervisory ranks,
      all your subordinates) fully adhere to
      your part(s) in the Guidelines?

      Almost always   ☐
      Often   ☐
      Sometimes   ☐
      Almost never   ☐

39.3 How often do you think the
      Guidelines are fully adhered to by
      everyone else involved?

      Almost always   ☐
      Often   ☐
      Sometimes   ☐
      Almost never   ☐

39.4   Insofar as you agree that people do not always comply with the Guidelines, what are your opinions about the commonest reasons for yourself and for others?

Please tick all the factors you consider appropriate.

	Self	Others
Too busy to follow the Guidelines		
Not very relevant to good case management		
Not well-publicised and accessible		
Unrealistic		
Unclear		
Not well-taught		
Not well enforced		
Other (please specify)		
Don't know		

39.5   Insofar as you think everyone does not comply fully with the Guidelines, are the variations in your opinion generally on major or minor points?

Major   ☐
Moderately Important   ☐
Minor   ☐

40   In the following four questions regarding cooperation between the professions who may be involved in the management of child abuse cases, please tick the boxes you consider appropriate.

40.1   How easy/hard do you generally find it to collaborate with members of each profession?

	Very Easy	Fairly Easy	Rather Difficult	Very Diffi -cult	No Exper -ience	No Opin- ion
1 Social workers						
2 Health visitors						
3 Teachers						
4 Police						
5 General Practitioners						
6 Paediatricians						
7 Lawyers						
8 Psychologists						
9 Psychiatrists						
10 Accident and emergency (hospital) doctors						
11 School nurses						
12 School social workers/ EWO's						

40.2   How clear/unclear do you think the role of each is in child abuse cases?

	Very clear	Fair-ly clear	Rather unclear	Very Un-clear	No Exper-ience	No Opinion
1 Social workers						
2 Health visitors						
3 Teachers						
4 Police						
5 General Practitioners						
6 Paediatricians						
7 Lawyers						
8 Psychologists						
9 Psychiatrists						
10 Accident and emergency (hospital) doctors						
11 School nurses						
12 School social workers/ EWO's						

40.3   How important do you think the role of each is in child abuse cases?

	Essential	Impor-tant	Not very Import-ant	Not at all Impor-tant	No exper-ience	No opinion
1 Social workers						
2 Health visitors						
3 Teachers						
4 Police						
5 General Practitioners						
6 Paediatricians						
7 Lawyers						
8 Psychologists						
9 Psychiatrists						
10 Accident and emergency (hospital) doctors						
11 School nurses						
12 School social workers/ EWO's						

40.4 How well do you think each carries out their role in child abuse cases?

	Very well	Fairly well	Rather poorly	Very poorly	No Exper -ience	No Opinion
1 Social workers						
2 Health visitors						
3 Teachers						
4 Police						
5 General Practitioners						
6 Paediatricians						
7 Lawyers						
8 Psychologists						
9 Psychiatrists						
10 Accident and emergency (hospital) doctors						
11 School nurses						
12 School social workers/EWO's						

41.1   In your <u>area, how</u> well do you think initial case assessments are generally coordinated, following any allegation of child abuse?

      Very Well
      Rather Well
      Rather Badly
      Very Badly
      No Experience
      No Opinion

41.2   Insofar as you think coordination in assessment works well, what are your opinions about the reasons?

42   Insofar as you think coordination in assessment does not work well, what are your
      opinions about the reasons?

	Un-important	Rather Un-important	Rather Important	Impor-tant
1. Different Case Evaluations				
2. Different overall workload priorities for each occupation				
3.Conflicting values about goals of intervention				
4.Incompatible methods or time-scales of intervention				
5.Occupational rivalries (status, power, etc.)				
6. Concerns about confidentiality				
7. Insufficient knowledge about each others' roles and skills				
8. Other (please specify)				

43.1   In your area, how well do you think continuing interventions in ongoing cases are generally coordinated?

Very Well   ☐
Rather Well   ☐
Rather Badly   ☐
Very Badly   ☐
No Experience   ☐
No Opinion   ☐

43.2   Insofar as you think coordination works well in ongoing cases, what are your opinions about the reasons?

44. Insofar as you think this ongoing coordination does not work well, what are your
     opinions about the reasons? Please tick the appropriate boxes.

	Unimportant	Rather Unimportant	Rather Important	Important
1. Different Case Evaluations				
2. Different overall workload priorities for each occupation				
3. Conflicting values about goals of intervention				
4. Incompatible methods or timescales of intervention				
5. Occupational rivalries (status, power, etc.)				
6. Concerns about confidentiality				
7. Insufficient knowledge about each others' roles and skills				
8. Other (please specify)				

45.1 It is sometimes said that keeping in touch with everybody is extremely difficult for practical reasons. Do you agree?

Yes ☐   No ☐   Don't know ☐

If your answer is No, please skip to question 46.

45.2 If you do agree, how would you rate the following factors? Please tick the appropriate boxes.

	Unimpor-tant	Rather Un-important	Rather Important	Important
1. Your own (or your subordinates') time				
2. Other agencies' time				
3. Secretarial support				
4. Access to adequate phones				
5. Other admin factors (please specify)				
6. Movements of staff in the network				
7. Size of the total network				

46   I look forward to an opportunity to explore opinions further with some of you in a follow-up interview, but if there are particular observations you would like to make or questions which you feel have not been raised in the schedule, I would be very pleased for you to add them.

Thank you very much for giving your time to this important topic. If you would return the questionnaire by .... it would be very helpful. Although only a few of you will be asked to take part in a follow-up interview, I look forward soon to meeting some of you.

Elizabeth Birchall

Please return this questionnaire in the, S.A.E. provided, to me at:

V.AW

Appendix 2: Access Documents

Official Bodies and professional associations approached for general support:

Department of Education and Science, Her Majesty's Inspectorate

Department of Health Research Group and Social Services Inspectorate

Association of Directors of Social Services

Association of Chief Police Officers

Association of Police Surgeons

British Association of Social Workers

British Association for the Study and Prevention of Child Abuse and Neglect

British Paediatric Association

Health Visitors' Association

Law Society Local Government Group

National Association for Pastoral Care in Education

National Association of Head Teachers   (No response)

Police Federation

Royal College of General Practitioners

Society of County Secretaries

Superintendents' Association (Police)   (No response)

Local Area Child Protection Committees

The letter below was sent to the following agencies, with appropriate modifications of detail, requesting staff lists ansd access to subordinate staff:

Family Practitioner Committees and Regional Health Authorities,

Local Authority Social Services Departments,

Local Authority Legal Sections,

Local Education Authorities and individual school heads,

Local Health Authorities Health Visiting Services,

Chief Constables,

Paediatric Departments of hospitals in the catchment areas.

Dear

Coordination in Child Protection Research

This University is engaged in a major research programme, funded by the Department of Health, to investigate multidisciplinary and interagency coordination in child protection cases. We are now looking for access to the field staffs concerned and hope that you will be interested and will facilitate our access to your colleagues.

The research comprises 3 phases:

> a literature review covering the concept of coordination in health and welfare, and of interdisciplinary work in child protection;

> a study of perceptions of child abuse and of coordination held by a sample of the key professional groups (GPs, health visitors, local authority solicitors, paediatricians, police, social workers and teachers);

> an in-depth study of coordination policies and practices in a sample of cases.

Coordination has emerged as an imnportant and recurring problem in all the official inquiries into child abuse tragedies, and has also for many years been central to Government advice on professional management of the problem. It therefore seems very important to discover the actual experience of the professionals concerned, to locate in concrete terms whether and why coordination in case management is problematic, and to identify solutions and make the relevant policy recommendations.

The Research Director is Christine Hallett, MA, Reader in Social Policy, who has substantial experience in research into aspects of child protection services. The Research Fellow primarily responsible for the second phase is Elizabeth Birchall, MA, SSC, ASSC, CSWM, whose higher degree is in social services planning and who had long experience in social services area management before recently becoming a social researcher. The research team are therefore well-qualified to investigate the realities of the several prac-titioners' experience and needs, and to make a solid contribution to the development of policy and practice in this important and complex field.

We are now seeking access to agencies and professional groups in the (North of England), in connection with the study. We hope to start field work on Phase 2 of the study shortly, with a sample of approximately 30 professionals from each group drawn from the (area).

We have received support for this research project from the relevant professional associations (insert here only the body relevant to the addressee of this letter) including the British Paediatric Association, the British Association of Social Workers, the Association of Directors of Social Services, the Association of Police Surgeons, the Health Visitors' Association, the Royal College of General Practitioners.

If you would like further information or a meeting to discuss the project in greater depth, please phone Elizabeth Birchall. She would be very pleased to visit you or discuss the project over the phone. She can be located at most times at ...., or via our Secretary, ..., at the University in the mornings. We look forward to your favourable response.

Yours sincerely

Christine Hallett
Research Director

Letter to individual GPs, accompanying the questionnaire.

A similar letter went to individuals of other professions drawn in the sample, highlighting the support of their own professional association and their chief officer.

Dear

Coordination in Child Protection Research Project

This University is engaged in a major research programme, funded by the Department of Health, to investigate multidisciplinary and interagency coordination in child protection cases, fuller details of which are in the appendix to this letter. Approaches were made to relevant professional associations and the project has been widely welcomed. Support has been received from the Royal College of General Practitioners and the Association of Police Surgeons. Local support has been received from your Area Child Protection Committee and your Family Practitioner Committee and other relevant agencies in your area following our introductory letters dated January 1990, in connection with Phase 2 of our project. We therefore trust you may know by now about it in general terms and that your locality has been selected for fieldwork.

We are now seeking respondents from the field staffs concerned and anticipate that we will be seeking about 12 GPs, including some police surgeons, in each area. Your name has arisen by random sampling. We hope you will agree to participate and will find the subject personally interesting. The research explores professional staffs' experience of working together in child protection. You may appreciate that your individual contribution is important to a thorough understanding of a difficult topic of great current significance, and we would like to thank you in anticipation of your involvement.

Confidentiality is assured to respondents; neither individuals nor localities will be identified in any subsequent discussion or publication of the finding. All data will be collected and processed under code numbers, and at no stage will your name or place of work appear in the analyses.

This piece of the research comprises a questionnaire for completion by each respondent. It would be very useful to us both if you would complete and return the enclosed questionnaire quickly.

Yours sincerely

Elizabeth Birchall
Research Fellow

Appendix to introductory letters.

This is a major research programme funded by the Department of Health, to investigate multidisciplinary and interagency coordination in child protection cases. The research comprises 3 phases:

a literature review covering the concept of coordination in health and welfare, and of interdisciplinary work in child protection;

a study of perceptions of child abuse and of coordination held by a sample of the key professional groups (GPs, health visitors, local authority solicitors, paediatricians, police, social workers and teachers);

an in-depth study of coordination policies and practices in a sample of cases in 3 local areas.

Coordination has emerged as an important and recurring problem in all the official inquiries into child abuse tragedies, and has also for many years been central to Government advice on professional management of the problem. It therefore seems very important to discover the actual experience of the professionals concerned, to locate in concrete terms whether and why coordination in case management is problematic, and to identify solutions and make the relant policy recommendations.

The Research Director is Christine Hallett, MA, Reader in Social Policy at the University of Stirling. She has substantial experience in research into aspects of child protection services. The Research Fellow primarily responsible for the second phase is Elizabeth Birchall, MA, SSC, ASSC, CSWM, whose higher degree is in social services planning and who had long experience in social services area management before recently becoming a social researcher. The research team are therefore well-qualified to investigate the realities of the several practitioners' experience and needs, and to make a solid contribution to the development of policy and practice in this important and complex field.

The extensive literature review is now completed and we are now embarked on fieldwork in the (North of England). Phase 2 fieldwork encompasses approximately 240 staff, with random samples of 30–40 drawn from each professional group.

If you would like further information or a meeting to discuss the project in greater depth, please phone Elizabeth Birchall. She would be very pleased to visit you or discuss the project over the phone. She can be located at most times at ...., or via our Secretary .... at the University in the mornings.

Note: The postal survey was subsequently enlarged.

First follow up letter:

Dear

Coordination in Child Protection Research Project

I am writing to you again in connection with my letter to you in mid-February enclosing our research questionnaire and SAE. Although the original 'return by' date is now past, I would nevertheless be very grateful if you would look out the questionnaire again and complete it as soon as possible. If you would like to ring me on any point, please do so. At present I am available most of the time on .... but in the event of my being out, our Secretary ...., is available every morning. She would pass on a message to me and I would phone you back at a time convenient to yourself. If your response is actually on the way to me, please ignore this letter and accept my thanks. Should you have mislaid it, we can send you another one if you phone .... on the above number any morning.

In assisting us with this research project commissioned by the Department of Health you will be making a valued contribution to the understanding of an important area of professional practice, and the results will feed directly into the considerations of the central policy-makers. Whatever your experience and opinions relating to collaboration in child protection work, you can help us build up an informed picture of the real world in which a myriad individual professionals make their countless everyday decisions in regard to children who may be at risk of abuse.

Not only would I be very grateful for your answers to the specific questions; it would also be very helpful if you wish to make comments, critical or complimentary, on the questionnaire in general and on any particular questions.

I look forward to hearing from you, and would now ask for the questionnaire to be returned by Friday, 5th April 1991.

Yours sincerely

Elizabeth Birchall
Research Fellow

Second follow up letter:

Dear

Coordination in Child Protection Research Project

I am writing again in connection with my research mailed to you in (month) 1991. Although I do realise that responding to research questionnaires can be a difficult or irritating demand, I am sorry not to have received a response from you yet and am asking you to reconsider my request. Issues of child protection remain topics of great public interest and concern, but the attitudes and experiences of practitioners have not been systematically explored. This Department of Health-sponsored research project is therefore very significant. If you have mislaid the questionnaire, we will gladly send you a replacement if you would phone .... on ....

If work in connection with abused children or the child protection network is a significant part of your responsibilities and everyday practice, your experiences and opinions will make a vital contribution to a properly informed understanding of the issues.

Even if you feel you have little experience or involvement in child cases and cannot give positive answers or opinions on many of the questions I raise, you will be able and may be willing to answer parts of the questionnaire. I would stress that an incomplete response which can only give your biographical data and answers to factual questions, such as those about training, the number of cases met and your accesss to the official procedural Guidelines, in itself constitutes important information.

Your name arose by random sampling among seven professions identified as key members of the child protection network, and therefore your response will make an invaluable contribution to policy-makers' fuller understanding of the everyday context of child protection practice.

Yours sincerely

Elizabeth Birchall
Research Fellow

Statistical Appendices

The sampling fractions

By profession		By rank:	
SWs	24.4%	Principal	14.1%
HVs	35.4%	Supervisory	28.7%
Teachers★	2.3%	Maingrade	22.6%
Police	58.9%		
GPs	33.4%		
Paediatricians	41.2%		

★ Estimate, assuming that the random sample of schools reflects the staff numbers in all primary schools in the catchment areas.

By area:		By gender	
County	52.4%	Men	26.3%
City	45.8%	Women	20.0%
Metborough	37.7%		

In order to obtain adequate cell sizes from scarce populations, the specialist police and paediatric staff were heavily sampled from the beginning. The rate among health visitors had to be increased when their limited numbers became evident from staff lists. General practitioners were sampled relatively heavily in expectation that their poorer response rate to the pilot phase would continue into the main phase. The teaching profession is much the largest; therefore, despite again compensating for the rather poor response rate experienced in the pilot stage, the sampling fraction remains very small.

The varied fractions by rank reflect two factors: firstly, maingrade staff are numerous enough not to require heavy sampling; secondly, the lighter fraction of those classified as principals is because many such staff have broader functions than concern this project. In contrast, many of those designated supervisory are responsible for aspects of work or for maingrade staff relevant to the study.

The higher rate of sampling in County reflects the limited numbers of staff overall, whereas in City it reflects both the failure of one major agency to participate and the fact that major paediatric resources were extra-territorial.

The gender ratio is a product of the uneven gender distribution among the professions in combination with the above factors.

Table 3.3. **Rank distribution of participating agencies**

Area Rank	Principal		Senior		Maingrade		Total	
	N	%	N	%	N	%	N	%
County SSD:								
7 area teams	9	19.1	6	12.8	32	68.1	47	100.0
1 hospital team	2	33.3	1	16.7	3	50.0	6	100.0
City SSD:								
7 area teams	8	5.2	25	16.2	121	78.6	154	100.0
4 hospital teams			4	20.0	20	80.0	24	100.0
2 NSPCC teams			4	22.2	14	77.8	18	100.0
Metborough SSD:								
7 area teams	26	25.0			78	75.0	104	100.0
Sub-total	45	12.7	40	11.3	268	75.9	353	100.0
County HVs: 2 DHAs	3	3.0			96	97.0	99	100.0
City HVs: 2 DHAs	2	2.9	6	8.6	62	88.6	70	100.0
Metborough HVs: 2DHAs	2	2.9	10	14.7	56	82.4	68	100.0
Sub-total	7	3.0	16	6.8	214	90.3	237	100.0
Teachers*								
County: 31/101 schools	31	13.5	31	13.5	167	72.9	229	100.0
City: 37/175 schools	37	10.9	37	10.9	264	78.1	338	100.0
Metborough: 30/170 schools	30	10.1	30	10.1	238	79.9	298	100.0
Sub-total	98	11.3	98	11.3	669	77.3	865	100.0
County Police:	1	25.0	1	25.0	2	50.0	4	100.0
City Police:	1	6.7	3	20.0	11	73.3	15	100.0
Metborough Police:			1	14.3	6	85.7	7	100.0
Other Police:	1		5		24	80.0	30	100.0
Sub-total	3	5.4	10	17.9	43	76.8	56	100.0
GPs:								
County: 36 practices					107	100.0	107	100.0
City: 120 practices					288	100.0	288	100.0
Metborough: 81 practices					123	100.0	123	100.0
Sub-total					518	100.0	518	100.0
Paediatricians:								
County: 2 hospitals	6	37.5	2	12.5	8	50.0	16	100.0
City: 2 hospitals	8	42.1	3	15.8	8	42.1	19	100.0
Metborough: 2 hospitals	5	31.3	3	18.8	8	50.0	16	100.0
Other: 7 hospitals + CMOs	28	27.5	33	32.4	41	40.2	102	100.0
Sub-total	47	30.7	41	26.8	65	42.5	153	100.0
Grand total	200	9.2	205	9.4	1777	81.4	2182	100.0

* These figures relate only to the schools directly sampled. The subordinate structures of the other schools are unknown. The figures are not, therefore, directly comparable with those in Table 3.4.

Table 3.4. **Gender distribution of participating agencies**

Gender / Area	Male N	Male %	Female N	Female %	Not known N	Not known %	Total N	Total %
County SSD:								
7 area teams	17	36.0	28	59.6	2	4.3	47	100.0
1 hospital team			6	100.0			6	100.0
City SSD:								
7 area teams	48	31.2	101	65.6	5	3.2	154	100.0
4 hospital teams			4	16.7	20	83.3	24	100.0
2 NSPCC teams			5	27.8	13	72.2	18	100.0
Metborough SSD:								
7 area teams	48	46.2	55	52.9	1	1.0	104	100.0
Sub-total	113	32.0	199	56.4	41	11.6	353	100.0
County HVs: 2 DHAs			99	100.0			99	100.0
City HVs: 2 DHAs	1	1.4	69	98.6			70	100.0
Metborough HVs: 2DHAs	1	1.5	67	98.5			68	100.0
Sub-total	2	0.8	235	99.2			237	100.0
Teachers*								
County: 31/101 schools	86	31.3	160	58.2	29	10.5	275	100.0
City: 37/175 schools	135	29.6	316	69.3	5	1.1	456	100.0
Metborough: 30/170 schools	128	30.3	291	68.8	4	0.9	423	100.0
Sub-total	349	30.2	767	66.5	38	3.3	1154	100.0
County Police:	2	50.0	2	50.0			4	100.0
City Police:	6	40.0	9	60.0			15	100.0
Metborough Police:	2	28.6	5	71.4			7	100.0
Other Police:	9	30.0	21	70.0			30	100.0
Sub-total	19	33.9	37	66.1			56	100.0
GPs:								
County: 36 practices	90	84.1	17	15.9			107	100.0
City: 120 practices	198	68.8	90	31.3			288	100.0
Metborough: 81 practices	106	86.2	14	11.4	3	2.4	123	100.0
Sub-total	394	76.1	121	23.4	3	0.6	518	100.0
Paediatricians:								
County: 2 hospitals	8	50.0	7	43.8	1	6.3	16	100.0
City: 2 hospitals	10	52.6	5	26.3	4	21.1	19	100.0
Metborough: 2 hospitals	6	37.5	5	31.3	5	31.3	16	100.0
Other: 7 hospitals + CMOs	59	57.8	35	34.3	8	7.8	102	100.0
Sub-total	82	53.6	53	34.6	18	11.8	153	100.0
Grand total	959	38.8	1412	57.1	100	4.0	2471	100.0

* These figures include all primary school heads in two education authorities and in one division of County but the subordinate staff in only the schools directly sampled. The figures are not therefore directly comparable with those in Table 3.3.

Table 3.5. **A comparison of the final sample and responses by area**

Respondents Area	Sample N	%	Responses N	%	Response Rate %
County	144	25.6	92	27.1	63.9
City	209	37.2	119	35.1	56.9
Metborough	158	28.1	94	27.7	59.5
Elsewhere	51	9.1	34	10.0	66.7
Total	562	100.0	339	100.0	60.3

Table 3.6. **A comparison of the final sample and responses by profession**

Respondents Profession	Sample N	%	Responses N	%	Response Rate %
Social Workers	86	15.3	62	18.3	72.1
Health Visitors	84	14.9	68	20.1	81.0
Teachers	123	21.9	81	23.9	65.9
Police	33	5.9	22	6.5	66.7
General Practitioners	173	30.8	66	19.5	38.2
Paediatricians	63	11.2	40	11.8	63.5
Total	562	100.0	339	100.0	60.3

Table 3.7. **A comparison of the final sample and responses by rank**

Respondents Profession	Sample N	%	Responses N	%	Response Rate %
Maingrade	425	75.9	235	69.3	55.3
Supervisory Grade	58	10.4	52	15.3	89.7
Principal Grade	77	13.8	51	15.0	66.2
Not Known (no data)	2	0.4	1	0.3	50.0
Total	562	100.0	339	100.0	60.3

Table 3.8. **A comparison of the final sample and responses by gender**

Respondents	Sample		Responses		Response Rate
Profession	N	%	N	%	%
Male	255	45.4	124	36.6	48.6
Female	300	54.1	215	63.4	71.1
Not known	7	1.2			
Total	562	100.0	339	100.0	60.3

Table 4.7. **Number of respondents in each profession as a percentage of the sample by area**

	Agency Location								Total	
	County		City		Metborough		Other			
Profession	N	%	N	%	N	%	N	%	N	%
Social Workers	19	30.6	25	40.3	18	29.0			62	100.0
Health Visitors	26	38.2	18	26.5	24	35.3			68	100.0
Teachers	23	28.4	28	34.6	30	37.0			81	100.0
Police	4	18.2	8	36.4	2	9.1	8	36.4	22	100.0
General Practitioners	17	25.8	35	53.0	14	25.0			66	100.0
Paediatricians	3.	7.5	5	12.5	6	15.0	26	65.0	40	100.0
Total	92	27.1	119	35.1	94	27.7	34	10.0	339	100.0

Table 4.8. **An interprofessional comparison of the gender distribution at different ranks**

Profession	Rank	Maingrade N	%	Supervisory N	%	Principal N	%	Total N	%
Social Workers	M	14	58.3	5	20.8	5	20.8	24	100.0
	F	26	70.3	7	18.9	4	10.8	37	100.0
Health Visitors	M	0	0.0	1	50.0	1	50.0	2	100.0
	F	51	77.3	14	21.2	1	1.5	66	100.0
Teachers	M	6	27.3	3	13.6	13	59.1	22	100.0
	F	43	72.9	8	13.6	8	13.6	59	100.0
Police	M	4	66.7	1	16.7	1	16.7	6	100.0
	F	14	87.5	2	12.5	0	0.0	16	100.0
General Practitioners	M	43	100.0	0	0.0	0	0.0	43	100.0
	F	23	100.0	0	0.0	0	0.0	23	100.0
Paediatricians	M	3	11.1	9	33.3	15	55.6	27	100.0
	F	8	61.5	2	15.4	3	23.1	13	100.0
Total	M	70	56.5	19	15.3	35	28.2	124	100.0
	F	165	77.1	33	15.4	16	7.5	214	100.0

Table 5.6. **An interprofessional comparison of respondents' experience of post-qualifying training in child protection**

Respondent Amount	SW N	%	HV N	%	Teacher N	%	Police N	%	GP N	%	Paed'n N	%	Total N	%
None	7	11.7	6	9.0	51	63.0	5	22.7	51	79.7	18	46.2	138	41.4
Up to 1 week	3	5.0	30	44.8	24	29.6	0	0.0	9	14.1	11	28.2	77	23.1
1–2 weeks	16	26.7	18	26.9	5	6.2	7	31.8	2	3.1	3	7.7	51	15.3
Over 2 wks-1 mth	16	26.7	8	11.9	0	0.0	6	27.2	0	0.0	2	5.1	32	9.6
Over 1 mth–3 mths	7	11.7	3	4.5	1	1.2	4	18.2	1	1.6	1	2.6	17	5.1
Over 3 months	11	18.2	2	2.9	0	0.0	0	0.0	1	1.6	4	10.3	18	5.4
Total	60	18.0	67	20.1	81	24.3	22	6.6	64	19.2	39	11.7	333	100.0

Table 5.7. **A comparison of respondents' experience of post-qualifying training in child protection, by profession and rank**

Profession & Rank	Amount	None N	None %	Under 1 week N	Under 1 week %	1–2 weeks N	1–2 weeks %	Over 2 weeks N	Over 2 weeks %	Total N	Total %
SW	Maingrade	6	15.8	3	7.9	10	26.3	19	50.0	38	16.5
	Supervisory	1	8.3	0	0.0	2	16.7	9	75.0	12	23.1
	Principal	0	0.0	0	0.0	3	33.3	6	66.7	9	17.6
HV	Maingrade	6	12.0	23	46.0	14	28.0	7	14.0	50	21.7
	Supervisory	0	0.0	6	40.0	3	20.0	6	40.0	15	28.8
	Principal	0	0.0	1	50.0	1	50.0	0	0.0	2	3.9
Teacher	Maingrade	39	79.6	0	0.0	7	38.9	8	44.8	18	7.8
	Supervisory	4	36.4	5	45.5	2	18.2	0	0.0	11	21.2
	Principal	8	38.1	10	47.6	2	9.5	1	4.8	21	41.2
Police	Maingrade	3	16.7	0	0.0	7	38.9	8	44.4	18	7.8
	Supervisory	1	33.3	0	0.0	0	–	2	66.7	3	5.8
	Principal	1	100.0	0	0.0	0	0.0	0	0.0	1	2.0
GP	Maingrade	51	78.5	9	13.8	2	3.1	2	3.1	64	28.3
	Supervisory	–	–	–	–	–	–	–	–	–	–
	Principal	–	–	–	–	–	–	–	–	–	–
Paed'n	Maingrade	8	80.0	1	10.0	1	10.0	0	0.0	10	4.3
	Supervisory	6	54.5	5	45.5	0	0.0	0	0.0	11	21.2
	Principal	4	22.2	5	27.8	2	11.1	7	38.9	18	35.3
Total	Maingrade	113	49.1	45	19.6	35	15.2	36	15.7	229	100.0
	Supervisory	12	23.1	16	30.8	7	13.5	17	32.7	52	100.0
	Principal	13	25.5	16	31.4	8	15.7	14	27.5	51	100.0

Note: The rank of one respondent was unknown and there is therefore a discrepancy of 1 in the totals of the above two tables.

Table 5.8. **An interprofessional comparison of respondents' experience of interdisciplinary post-qualifying training in child protection**

Respondent Amount	SW N	SW %	HV N	HV %	Teacher N	Teacher %	Police N	Police %	GP N	GP %	Paed'n N	Paed'n %	Total N	Total %
None	10	16.4	10	14.9	60	74.1	7	31.8	56	87.5	21	53.8	164	49.1
Less that 1 week	28	45.9	45	67.2	20	24.7	8	36.4	7	10.9	15	38.5	123	36.8
More that 1 week	23	37.7	12	17.9	1	1.2	7	31.8	1	1.6	3	7.7	47	14.1
Total	61	18.3	67	20.1	81	24.3	22	6.6	64	19.2	39	11.7	334	100.0

$p = <.0001$, CC .54462.

Table 5.9. **A interprofessional comparison of respondents' experience of interdisciplinary post-qualifying training in child protection, by profession and rank**

Profession & Rank	Amount	None N	%	Under 1 week N	%	More than 1 week N	%	Total N	%
SW	Maingrade	8	20.5	19	48.7	12	30.8	39	17.0
	Supervisory	1	8.3	5	41.7	6	50.0	12	13.1
	Principal	1	11.1	3	33.3	5	55.6	9	17.6
HV	Maingrade	10	20.0	32	64.0	8	16.0	50	21.7
	Supervisory	0	0.0	12	80.0	3	20.0	15	28.8
	Principal	0	0.0	1	50.0	1	50.0	2	3.9
Teacher	Maingrade	42	85.7	7	14.3	0	0.0	49	21.3
	Supervisory	6	54.5	4	36.4	1	9.1	11	21.2
	Principal	12	57.1	9	42.9	0	0.0	21	41.2
Police	Maingrade	5	27.8	6	33.3	7	38.9	18	7.8
	Supervisory	1	33.3	2	66.7	0	0.0	3	5.8
	Principal	1	100.0	–	–	–	–	–	–
GP	Maingrade	56	87.5	7	10.9	1	1.6	64	27.8
	Supervisory	–	–	–	–	–	–	–	–
	Principal	–	–	–	–	–	–	–	–
Paediatrician	Maingrade	8	80.0	2	20.0	0	0.0	10	4.3
	Supervisory	6	54.5	5	45.5	0	0.0	11	21.2
	Principal	4	38.9	8	44.4	3	16.7	18	35.3
Total	Maingrade	129	56.1	73	31.7	28	12.2	230	100.0
	Supervisory	14	26.9	28	53.8	10	19.2	52	100.0
	Principal	21	41.2	21	41.2	9	17.6	51	100.0

Note: The rank of one respondent was unknown and there is therefore a discrepancy of 1 in the totals of the above two tables.

Table 5.10. **An interprofessional comparison of orientation to the start of intervention in child protection: professional acceptance or parental responsibility first?**

Approach	Profession	SW N	%	HV N	%	Teacher N	%	Police N	%	GP N	%	Paed'n N	%	Total N	%
Acceptance first		5	8.1	27	39.7	29	35.8	7	31.8	20	30.3	15	37.5	103	30.4
Responsibility		45	72.6	30	44.1	28	34.6	13	59.1	31	47.0	15	37.5	162	47.8
Both		10	16.1	8	11.8	9	11.1	1	4.5	3	4.5	4	10.0	35	10.3
Don't know		0	0.0	1	1.5	11	13.6	1	4.5	5	7.6	3	7.5	21	6.2
No Reply		2	3.2	2	2.9	4	4.9	0	0.0	7	10.6	3	7.5	18	5.3
Total		62	18.3	68	20.1	81	23.9	22	6.5	66	19.5	40	11.8	339	100.0

Table 6.12. **Recording behaviour regarding internal and external communications in child protection cases, expressed as percentage of respondents**

Frequency	Internal		External		Combined	
	Self recorded (n=306)	Other confirmed (N=295)	Self recorded (N=295)	Other confirmed (N=289)	Self recorded (N=601)	Other confirmed (N=584)
Almost always	60.1%	9.8%	28.8%	12.8%	44.8%	11.3%
Often	16.3%	6.4%	12.5%	12.5%	14.5%	9.5%
Sometimes	18.0%	39.0%	32.9%	38.1%	25.3%	38.5%
Almost never	5.6%	44.7%	25.8%	36.7%	15.5%	40.7%
	100%	100%	100%	100%	100%	100%

Table 6.13. **An interprofessional comparison of respondents' recording behaviour and expectations of others, averaging internal and external communications, in child protection cases**

		Self recorded %	Other confirmed %
SW (N=61/62)	Almost always	43.9	5.7
	Often	18.7	10.6
	Sometimes	30.1	49.2
	Almost never	7.3	32.0
HV (N=67/68)	Almost always	65.7	7.4
	Often	7.5	5.9
	Sometimes	15.7	29.4
	Almost never	11.2	54.4
Teacher (N=54/56)	Almost always	46.7	29.5
	Often	13.1	7.1
	Sometimes	20.6	26.8
	Almost never	19.6	31.3
Police (N=22/22)	Almost always	25.0	6.8
	Often	9.1	2.3
	Sometimes	31.8	38.6
	Almost never	29.5	52.3
GP (N=60/58)	Almost always	33.3	6.0
	Often	16.7	15.5
	Sometimes	32.5	37.9
	Almost never	17.5	40.5
Paediatrician (N = 37/36)	Almost always	34.7	8.3
	Often	21.3	6.9
	Sometimes	25.3	54.2
	Almost never	16.2	27.8

Table 6.14.   **A comparison of respondents' rates of ownership of the Area Child Protection Committee's procedural guidelines, by profession and rank**

	Maingrade N	Maingrade %	Supervisory N	Supervisory %	Principal N	Principal %	Total N	Total %
Social Worker	38	95.0	12	100.0	9	100.0	59	96.7
Health Visitor	38	74.5	15	100.0	2	100.0	55	80.9
Teacher	7	15.6	6	54.5	16	100.0	29	38.2
Police	12	66.7	3	100.0	1	100.0	14	72.7
General Practitioner	27	46.6					27	46.6
Paediatrician	4	40.0	6	54.5	18	100.0	28	71.8
Total	126	58.9	42	19.6	46	21.5	214	100.0

Table 6.15. An interprofessional comparison of respondents' most recent use of the Area Child Protection Committee's procedural guidelines

When	SW N	SW %	HV N	HV %	Teacher N	Teacher %	Police N	Police %	GP N	GP %	Paed'n N	Paed'n %	Total N	Total %
Last 24 hours	15	24.2	6	9.1	1	1.3	4	18.2	1	1.5	0	0.0	27	8.2
Within the last week	19	30.6	10	15.2	3	3.9	1	4.5	1	1.5	3	7.5	37	11.2
Within the last 4 weeks	13	21.0	19	28.8	9	11.8	9	40.9	3	4.6	4	10.0	57	17.2
1–3 months ago	5	8.1	8	12.1	2	2.6	2	9.1	4	6.2	8	20.0	29	8.8
4–6 months ago	6	9.7	2	3.0	1	1.3	1	4.5	3	4.6	2	5.0	15	4.5
6 months–1 year ago	1	1.6	3	4.5	4	5.3	1	4.5	15	32.1	2	5.0	26	7.9
Over 1 year ago	1	1.6	3	4.5	4	5.3	0	0.0	5	7.7	1	2.5	14	4.2
D/K or unspecified	1	1.6	12	18.2	8	10.5	2	9.1	11	16.9	10	25.0	44	13.3
Never	1	1.6	3	4.5	44	57.9	2	9.1	22	33.8	10	25.0	82	24.8
Total	62	18.7	66	19.9	76	23.0	22	6.6	65	19.6	40	12.1	331	100.0

Table 6.16a. **A comparison of social workers' most recent use of the Area Child Protection Committee's procedural guidelines, by rank**

When	Rank Maingrade N	%	Supervisory N	%	Principal N	%	Total N	%
Last 24 hours	4	10.0	5	41.7	5	55.6	14	23.0
Within the last week	15	37.5	3	25.0	1	11.1	19	31.1
Within the last 4 weeks	7	17.5	3	25.0	3	33.3	13	21.3
1–3 months ago	5	12.5	0	0.0	0	0.0	5	8.2
4–6 months ago	5	12.5	1	8.3	0	0.0	6	9.8
6 months–1 year ago	1	2.5	0	0.0	0	0.0	1	1.6
Over 1 year ago	1	2.5	0	0.0	0	0.0	1	1.6
D/K or unspecified	1	2.5	0	0.0	0	0.0	1	1.6
Never	1	2.5	0	0.0	0	0.0	1	1.6
Total	40	65.6	12	19.7	9	14.8	61	100.0

Table 6.16b. **A comparison of teachers' most recent use of the Area Child Protection Committee's procedural guidelines, by rank**

When	Rank Maingrade N	%	Supervisory N	%	Principal N	%	Total N	%
Last 24 hours	1	2.2	0	0.0	0	0.0	1	1.3
Within the last week	0	0.0	1	9.1	2	10.0	3	3.9
Within the last 4 weeks	2	4.4	2	18.2	5	25.0	9	11.8
1–3 months ago	1	2.2	1	9.1	0	0.0	2	2.6
4–6 months ago	0	0.0	0	0.0	1	5.0	1	1.3
6 months–1 year ago	1	2.2	1	9.1	2	10.0	4	5.3
Over 1 year ago	2.	4.4	1	9.1	1	5.0	4	5.3
D/K or unspecified	2	4.4	1	9.1	5	25.0	8	10.5
Never	36	80.0	4	36.4	4	20.0	44	57.9
Total	45	59.2	11	14.5	20	26.3	76	100.0

Table 6.16c.   **A comparison of paediatric doctors' most recent use of the Area Child Protection Committee's procedural guidelines, by rank**

When	Rank	Maingrade		Supervisory		Principal		Total	
		N	%	N	%	N	%	N	%
Never		0	0.0	1	9.1	2	11.1	3	7.5
Within the last week		0	0.0	1	9.1	3	16.7	4	10.0
Within the last 4 weeks		1	9.1	3	27.3	4	22.2	8	20.0
1–3 months ago		0	0.0	2	18.2	0	0.0	2	5.0
4–6 months ago		1	9.1	0	0.0	1	5.6	2	5.0
6 months–1 year ago		0	0.0	0	0.0	1	5.6	1	2.5
Over 1 year ago		3	27.3	1	9.1	6	33.3	10	25.0
D/K or unspecified		6	54.5	3	27.3	1	5.6	10	25.0
Total		11	27.5	11	27.5	18	45.0	40	100.0

Table 7.13. **Interprofessional comparison of respondents' attitudes to involvement in child protection conferences of parents or children of an age to understand**

Attitude	SW		HV		Teacher		Police		GP		Paed'n		Total	
Profession	N	%	N	%	N	%	N	%	N	%	N	%	N	%
Child:														
Whole conference	8	13.3	4	5.9	4	5.1	1	4.5	4	6.1	2	5.1	23	6.9
Part conference	39	65.0	44	36.1	31	39.7	7	31.8	40	60.6	16	41.0	177	53.2
No	10	16.7	12	17.6	21	26.9	13	59.1	12	12.2	15	38.5	83	24.9
Don't know	3	5.0	8	11.8	22	28.2	1	4.5	10	15.2	6	15.4	50	15.0
Total	60	18.0	68	20.4	78	23.4	22	6.6	66	19.8	39	11.7	333	100.0
Parent:														
Whole conference	20	33.3	5	7.4	9	11.4	1	4.5	12	18.5	1	2.6	48	14.4
Part conference	37	61.7	56	82.4	47	59.5	10	45.5	45	69.2	24	61.5	219	65.8
No	1	1.7	4	5.9	9	11.4	11	50.0	2	3.1	12	30.8	39	11.7
Don't know	2	3.3	3	4.4	14	17.7	0	0.0	6	9.2	2	5.1	27	8.1
Total	60	18.0	68	20.4	49	23.7	22	6.6	65	19.5	39	11.7	333	100.0

Table 9.23. **Respondents' initial thoughts on reading stage 2 of the vignettes**

Thoughts	Respondents (N=324)		Responses (N=629)
	N	%	%
Concern – child abuse?	124	38.3	19.7
Concern – other/unspecified	86	26.5	13.6
Assumption/probably child abuse	72	22.2	11.4
Could be malicious or baseless	57	17.6	9.1
Situation needs CP investigation	43	13.3	6.8
Situation needs unspecified follow-up	40	12.3	6.4
Mother needs support or help	38	11.7	6.0
Situation need inter-agency approach	37	11.4	5.9
Either parent abusive?	31	9.6	4.9
Child – assess/observe/examine/interview	29	9.0	4.6
Child need support or help	19	5.9	3.0
Not my (agency's) responsibility	7	2.2	1.1
Protect the child	6	1.9	1.0
Concern – other siblings	5	1.5	0.8
Exclude father	2	0.6	0.3
Interest in genitalia – probably insignificant	1	0.3	0.2
I ought to have spotted this	1	0.3	0.0
I ought to have been told	0	0.0	0.3
Interest in genitalia – ? sexual abuse	0	0.0	0.0
Multi/subcultural sensitivity	0	0.0	0.0
? offence	0	0.0	0.0
No concern	0	0.0	0.0
Other	29	9.0	4.6

Notes: Respondents were allowed multiple responses and therefore the first column sums to more than 100%.

Table 9.24. **Respondents' initial action proposals on reading stage 2 of the vignettes**

Action Proposals	Respondents (N=325)		Responses (N=581)
	N	%	%
Exchange evaluation/planning with other agencies	108	33.2	18.6
CP investigation; specialist medical; Interview familiy	92	28.3	15.8
Refer/leave issue to other agency/discipline	84	25.8	14.5
Actively initiate help	42	12.9	7.2
Report matter to superior/specialist within agency	31	9.5	5.3
Consult superior/specialist within agency	30	9.2	5.2
Inform other agency/discipline	29	8.9	5.0
Gather information from other agencies and/or CP Register	29	8.9	5.0
Joint visit with other agency	28	8.6	4.8
Seek child protection conference	21	6.5	3.6
Check story with child/PHCT* examination	18	5.5	3.1
Advocate/arrange (non-CP) services	16	4.9	2.8
Note information/observe/talk to peers	8	2.5	1.4
Ask another agency to assess and report back	7	2.2	1.2
Check own agency records/knowledge of case	6	1.8	1.0
Seek report from subordinate	6	1.8	1.8
? PSO, Care proceedings, CP Registration	3	0.9	0.5
Write parents/child to seek help	3	0.9	0.5
Talk to family or child opportunistically	2	0.6	0.3
Write inviting parent to office, clinic, etc.	2	0.6	0.3
Give background information to other discipline/ agency	2	0.6	0.3
Other	5	1.5	0.9
Nothing	7	2.2	1.2

Notes: 1. Abbreviations used in the table: PSO is a place of safety order; PHCT is the primary health care team including general practitioners, community nurses and health visitors.

2. Respondents were allowed multiple responses and therefore the first column sums to more than 100%.

Table 9.25. **Numbers of proposed contacts with each profession as a proportion of all communications with significant target professions, averaged across stages one and two of the vignettes**

Contacts with	N	%
Social Worker	163.5	28.8
Health visitor	142.5	25.1
Teacher	88.0	15.5
General practitioner	59.0	10.4
School nurse	35.5	6.3
Paediatrician	33.5	5.9
Police	32.0	5.6
Education welfare officer	14.0	2.5
Total	568.0	100.0

Table 9.26. **Purposes of immediate contacts with different professions at Stage 1 of the vignettes**

Target profession	Pass on case N	Pass on case %	Seek/give info N	Seek/give info %	Seek advice/ direction N	Seek advice/ direction %	Discuss/ decide jointly N	Discuss/ decide jointly %	Act jointly N	Act jointly %	Total N	Total %
Social Worker	24	36.9	19	13.3	12	18.5	59	29.4	27	21.7	141	23.6
Health Visitor	15	23.1	38	26.6	10	15.4	52	25.9	29	23.4	144	24.1
Teacher	4	6.2	36	25.2	15	23.1	34	16.9	20	16.1	109	18.2
School Nurse	2	3.1	13	9.1	6	9.2	15	7.5	10	8.1	46	7.7
General Practitioner	1	1.5	17	11.9	4	6.1	18	9.0	5	4.0	45	7.5
Educational Welfare Officer	0	0.0	5	3.5	4	6.1	4	2.0	5	4.0	18	3.0
Police	2	3.1	6	4.2	2	3.1	3	1.5	3	2.4	16	2.7
Paediatrician	3	4.6	0	0.0	4	6.1	3	1.5	6	4.8	16	2.7
Clinical Medical Officer	2	3.1	2	1.4	1	1.5	6	3.0	3	2.4	14	2.3
Other	12	18.5	7	4.9	7	10.8	7	3.5	16	12.9	48	8.2
Total	65	100.0	143	100.0	65	100.0	201	100.0	124	100.0	597	100.0

Table 9.27. **Purposes of immediate contacts with different professions at Stage 2 of the vignettes**

Target profession	Pass on case N	Pass on case %	Seek/give info N	Seek/give info %	Seek advice/ direction N	Seek advice/ direction %	Discuss/ decide jointly N	Discuss/ decide jointly %	Act jointly N	Act jointly %	Total N	Total %
Social Worker	29	42.0	16	12.9	18	19.8	67	32.8	56	31.8	186	28.0
Health Visitor	10	14.5	26	21.0	19	20.9	51	25.0	35	19.9	141	21.2
General Practitioner	2	2.9	28	22.6	11	12.1	24	11.8	8	4.5	73	11.0
Teacher	4	5.8	22	17.7	11	12.1	17	8.3	13	7.4	67	10.0
Paediatrician	10	14.5	1	0.8	15	16.5	8	3.9	17	9.7	51	7.7
Police	4	5.8	8	6.5	1	1.1	9	4.4	26	14.8	48	7.2
School Nurse	1	1.4	11	8.9	1	1.1	8	3.9	4	2.3	25	3.8
Educational Welfare Officer	1	1.4	1	0.8	3	3.3	3	1.5	2	1.1	25	3.8
Clinical Medical Officer	2	2.9	3	2.4	4	4.4	7	3.4	7	4.0	8	1.2
Other	6	8.7	8	4.9	8	8.8	10	4.9	8	4.5	40	6.0
Grand Total	69	100.0	124	100.0	91	100.0	204	100.0	176	100.0	664	100.0

Table 9.28. **Summary of all proposals for interdisciplinary contact between the respondent professions and significant target professions, averaged across stages one and two of the vignettes (weighted to equalise unequal size of professional groups)**

Contact proposed with	By	SW %	HV %	Teacher %	Police %	GP %	Paed'n %	Row Total %
Social Worker		4.0	6.1	2.3	9.4	4.6	6.2	32.7
Health Visitor		5.3	4.5	1.6	1.8	6.7	4.0	23.9
Teacher		2.9	2.4	4.9	1.8	0.4	1.4	13.9
General Practitioner		2.1	4.9	0.1	0.7	0.4	1.7	9.9
School Nurse		0.6	2.8	1.1	0.3	0.2	0.4	5.3
Paediatrician		1.0	0.2	0.0	0.3	2.2	2.2	6.1
Police		3.0	0.3	0.3	1.3	0.3	1.0	6.2
Education welfare officer		0.5	0.1	1.1	0.3	0.1	0.0	2.0
Total		19.4	21.3	11.5	15.7	15.3	16.8	100.0

Table 9.29. **Interprofessional contacts at stage one: the three vignettes compared**

Contact With	About	Family of UR* (N=85) N	%	Black family (N=85) N	%	Jane (N=163–7) N	%
Social worker		39	45.3	43	51.2	59	36.2
Health visitor		44	50.6	47	55.3	53	32.2
Teacher		20	22.9	9	10.6	90	54.9
General practitioner		7	8.0	16	19.0	22	13.3
School nurse		2	2.3	2	2.4	39	23.5
Education welfare officer		3	3.5	5	5.9	10	6.0
Paediatrician		2	2.3	3	3.5	11	6.6

* Family of unspecified race.

Table 9.30. **Interprofessional contacts at stage one: the three vignettes compared**

Contact With	About	Family of UR* (N=85) N	%	Black family (N=85) N	%	Jane (N=157–69) N	%
Social worker		39	45.3	49	57.6	98	61.6
Health visitor		44	55.8	45	52.9	48	29.6
Teacher		6	6.9	7	8.2	54	34.0
Police		4	4.6	1	1.2	41	26.4
General practitioner		21	24.1	24	28.2	28	17.2
Paediatrician		21	24.1	12	14.1	18	11.3
School nurse		1	1.1	2	2.4	22	13.5
Education welfare officer		1	1.1	3	3.5	6	3.7

* Family of unspecified race.

Table 11.13. **Non-Substantive Responses regarding ease of cooperation with other professions in the management of child protection cases**

Profession	Response Relevant Respondent Population	Maingrade		Supervisory		Principal		Total Non-Substantive Responses as % of relevant population	
		N	%	N	%	N	%	N	%
Social Workers	277	26	9.4	8	2.9	16	5.8	50	18.1
Health Visitors	271	22	8.1	5	1.8	15	5.5	44	15.4
Teachers	258	18	7.0	6	2.3	13	5.1	37	14.4
Police	317	49	15.5	13	4.1	23	7.2	85	26.8
General Practitioners	273	30	11.0	5	1.8	13	4.8	48	17.6
Paediatricians	299	53	17.7	8	2.7	14	4.6	75	25.0
Lawyers	339	119	35.1	23	6.8	22	6.5	164	48.4
Psychologists	339	68	20.1	17	6.8	23	6.8	108	33.7
Psychiatrists	339	102	30.1	19	5.6	30	8.9	151	44.6
Accident & Emergency Doctors	339	83	24.5	15	4.4	22	6.5	120	35.4
School Nurses	339	45	13.3	12	3.5	14	4.1	71	20.9
Education Welfare Officers	339	65	19.2	14	4.1	16	4.7	95	28.0

Notes: In the first six rows, respondents from the same profession are excluded.

Table 11.14.   **Summary of respondents' perceptions of the clarity of their own roles in child protection cases.**

Rating Of:	Very Clear N	%	Fairly Clear N	%	Rather Unclear N	%	Very Unclear N	%	Total N	%
Social Worker	48	78.7	13	21.3					61	100.0
Police	16	80.0	4	20.0					20	100.0
Paediatrician*	24	66.7	9	25.0	2	5.6	1	2.7	36	100.0
Health Visitor	38	57.6	24	36.4	4	6.1			66	100.0
Teacher*	20	32.3	24	38.7	16	25.8	2	3.2	62	100.0
General Practitioner*	16	28.6	28	50.0	10	17.9	2	3.6	56	100.0

* Excluding 1, 17 and 3 respectively with no opinion or experience of their own role.

Table 11.15.   **Summary of respondents' perceptions of the importance of their own role in child protection cases.**

Rating Of:	Essential N	%	Important N	%	Not very Important N	%	Not at all Important N	%	Total N	%
Social Worker	53	86.9	8	13.1					61	100.0
Police	14	70.0	6	30.0					20	100.0
Paediatrician*	22	55.0	16	40.0					38	100.0
Health Visitor	34	50.7	32	47.8	1	1.5			67	100.0
Teacher*	30	45.5	32	48.5	4	6.1			66	100.0
General Practitioner*	23	41.1	30	53.6	3	5.4			56	100.0

* Excluding 1, 3 and 11 respectively with no opinion or experience.

Table 11.16. Frequency of substantive opinions regarding ease of cooperation with, role clarity, importance and performance of other professions in the child protection network

Respondent Factor	1st quartile	Range %	2nd quartile	Range %	3rd quartile	Range %	4th quartile	Range %	Full Range %
Ease of Cooperation									
All	HV; T; SW; GP; AE; SN	84.5–79.1	Pd; P; EWO	74.9–72.0	Psyo	67.6	Psyi; Law	55.5–51.6	84.5–51.6
SW	P; HV, T, GP, Pd	93.4–96.8	Law; EWO	90.3–87.1	–		Psyo; AE; SN; Psyi	80.6–75.8	98.4–75.8
HV	SN; SW; T; Pd; GP; EWO	98.5–85.3	P	75.0	AE; Psyo	70.6–67.6	Psyi; Law	52.9–45.6	98.5–45.6
T	SN; P; EWO; Psyo; HV	82.7–66.7	SW; GP	61.7–54.3	–		AE; Pd; Psyi; Law	29.6–13.6	82.7–13.6
P	GP; SW, HV, T, Pd, AE	100–95.4	EWO, Law	90.8	–		SN, Psyo; Psyi	81.8–77.3	100–77.3
GP	HV; SW; Pd; T	87.9–78.8	AE; Psyo, P	69.7–60.6	SN	54.5	EWO; Law; Psyi	43.9–33.3	87.9–33.3
Pd	GP; HV; SW; T; P	95.0–82.5	AE; SN	75.0–72.5	EWO	62.5	Psyi; Psyo; Law	52.5–45.0	95.0–45.0
Clarity:									
All	T; SW; HV	87.6–83.4	P; GP; SN; Pd	82.6–79.0	AE; Psyo; EWO	74.0–72.0	Psyi; Law	68.2–65.8	87.6–65.8
SW	Hv; Pd; T, P, GP	98.4–95.2	Law	93.6	SN; Psyo, EWO, AE	90.3–87.1	Psyi	82.3	98.4–82.3
HV	SW; SN; P, GP, Pd	100–94.1	EWO	95.3	–		Law, Psyo, Psyi	76.5–70.6	100–70.6
T	SN; EWO; HV, SW	69.1–63.0	P, Psyo; GP	59.3–53.1	Pd	55.6	Psyi; AE, Law	43.2–25.8	69.1–25.8
P	SW	100	Pd, HV, T, GP	95.4	EWO, Psyo, Psyi, AE	90.8	SN	86.4	100–86.4
GP	HV, SW, Pd; P	84.8–78.8	AE; T, Psyo, Psyi	72.7–69.7	SN	59.1	EWO; Law	43.9–42.4	84.8–42.4
Pd	SW, HV; T; P, GP	92.5–87.5	AE	82.5	Psyi; SN	75.0–72.5	EWO; Psyo; Law	67.5–65.0	92.5–65.0

Importance:

All	T; SW; HV; GP	91.5–87.5	P; SN	74.9–72.9	EWO; Psyo	77.9–76.4	AE; Law; Pd; Psyi	75.8–70.2	91.5–70.2
SW	T; HV, GP, Pd, P, Law	98.4–95.2	–		SN	91.9	EWO; AE; Psyo; Psyi	88.7–80.6	98.4–80.6
HV	SW; P; GP, Pd; SN	98.5–94.1	T; AE, EWO	98.7–85.3	Law	77.9	Psyo; Psyi	76.5–70.6	98.5–70.6
T	SW; EWO; SN; HV	79.0–75.3	GP; P; Pd	70.4–66.7	Psyo	58.0	Psyi; Law; AE	65.6–49.4	79.0–49.4
P	SW, Pd, HV, T, EWO	100	SN, Psyo	95.4	Psyi, AE	91.8	Law	86.4	100–86.4
GP	SW; HV; Pd; T; P	86.4–78.8	AE; Psyo	77.3–71.2	SN; Psyi	69.7–68.2	Law; EWO	59.1–56.1	86.4–56.1
Pd	SW, HV, T; GP	95.0–92.5	AE, P	87.5	Psyi	77.5	Psyo; SN; Law, EWO	75.0–70.0	95.0–70.0

Performance:

All	T; SW; HV; GP	78.7–71.4	P; SN; AE	69.4–63.5	EWO; Pd	60.5–59.5	Psyo, Law; Psyi	52.2–45.4	78.7–45.4
SW	P; Pd, HV, T; GP	98.4–91.9	Law	87.1	AE; EWO; SN	80.6–77.4	Psyo; Psyi	69.4–66.1	98.4–66.1
HV	SW, GP; Pd, SN; T, P	92.6–89.7	EWO; AE	79.4–77.9	Law	60.3	Psyo; Psyi	54.5–47.1	92.6–47.1
T	SN; EWO; SW; HV	56.8–46.9	P, Psyo; GP	58.3–57.3	Pd; AE	29.6–28.4	Psyi; Law	22.2–17.3	56.8–17.3
P	Pd; SW; T	91.8–86.4	HV, AE, Law	81.8	GP; SN	77.3	EWO, Psyi; Psyo	72.7–68.2	91.8–68.2
GP	Pd; HV	90.8–78.8	SW; P; AE;	74.4–60.6	T	66.1	Psyo, Psyi; Law; SN; EWO	43.9–28.8	90.8–28.8
Pd	SW, HV	82.5	GP, AE; T	70.0–67.5	–		SN; Law, EWO; Psyo; Psyi	57.5–50.0	82.5–50.0

Notes:
1. No responses ranged from 4.1–8.3% on ease of cooperation; 4.5–4.6% on role clarity; 4.3–8.3% on role importance; 4.6–6.9% on role performance.
2. Semi-colons punctuate the professional groups where different response rates occur. Commas indicate groups where response rates were the same.
3. SW = social workers; HV = health visitors; T = teachers; P = police; GP = general practitioners; Pd = paediatricians; Law = LA solicitors; Psyo = psychologists; Psyi = psychiatrists; AE = accident and emergency doctors; SN = school nurses; EWO = education welfare officers.

Forthcoming complementary studies include:

Parental Perspectives in Cases of Suspected Child Abuse
Hedy Cleaver and Pam Freeman (The Dartington Team)
HMSO 1995. ISBN 0 11 321786 2

Child Protection Practice: Private Risks and Public Remedies
Elaine Farmer and Morag Owen (The University of Bristol Team)
HMSO 1995. ISBN 0 11 321787 0

The Prevalence of Child Sexual Abuse in Britain
Deborah Ghate and Liz Spencer (Social and Community Planning
Research)
HMSO 1995. ISBN 0 11 321783 8

**Development After Physical Abuse in Early Childhood: A Follow-
Up Study of Children on Protection Registers**
Jane Gibbons, Bernard Gallagher, Caroline Bell and David Gordon
(University of East Anglia)
HMSO 1995. ISBN 0 11 321790 0

Operating the Child Protection System
Caroline Bell, Sue Conroy and Jane Gibbons (University of East Anglia)
HMSO 1995. ISBN 0 11 321785 4

Inter-agency Coordination and Child Protection
Christine Hallett (The University of Stirling)
HMSO 1995. ISBN 0 11 321789 7

**Paternalism or Partnership? Family Involvement in the Child
Protection Process**
June Thoburn, Ann Lewis and David Shemmings (University of East
Anglia)
HMSO 1995. ISBN 0 11 321788 9

Printed in the United Kingdom for HMSO
Dd299968 3/95 C7 G559 10170